MW01013409

Bob Dylan

Prophet Without God

JEFFREY EDWARD GREEN

OXFORD
UNIVERSITY PRESS

OXFORD
UNIVERSITY PRESS

Oxford University Press is a department of the University of Oxford. It furthers
the University's objective of excellence in research, scholarship, and education
by publishing worldwide. Oxford is a registered trade mark of Oxford University
Press in the UK and certain other countries.

Published in the United States of America by Oxford University Press
198 Madison Avenue, New York, NY 10016, United States of America.

Library of Congress Cataloging-in-Publication Data
Names: Green, Jeffrey E. (Jeffrey Edward) author.
Title: Bob Dylan : prophet without God / Jeffrey Edward Green.
Description: New York, NY : Oxford University Press, 2024. |
Includes bibliographical references and index.
Identifiers: LCCN 2023043763 (print) | LCCN 2023043764 (ebook) |
ISBN 9780197651742 (hardback) | ISBN 9780197651766 (epub)
Subjects: LCSH: Dylan, Bob, 1941—Criticism and interpretation. |
Dylan, Bob, 1941—Philosophy. | Dylan, Bob, 1941—Religion. | Popular
music—History and criticism. | Popular music—Religious aspects. |
Popular music—Moral and ethical aspects. | Music and philosophy.
Classification: LCC ML420.D98 G73 2024 (print) | LCC ML420.D98 (ebook) |
DDC 782.42164092—dc23/eng/20231002
LC record available at https://lccn.loc.gov/2023043763
LC ebook record available at https://lccn.loc.gov/2023043764

DOI: 10.1093/oso/9780197651742.001.0001

Printed by Sheridan Books, Inc., United States of America

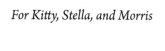

For Kitty, Stella, and Morris

CONTENTS

PREFACE

This book aims to demonstrate that Bob Dylan is not just a prophet but a prophet of a very special type: namely, not a prophet of salvation who transmits a singular fount of ethical direction (whether freedom, justice, or divinity) or for whom all three foundations coalesce into a no less singular source of normative direction, but rather what I call a *prophet of diremption*—or, metaphorically, *a prophet without God*—that is, someone who does indeed speak in support of a free selfhood, the claims of social justice, and adherence to God, but who continually insists, tragically, on the divergences and conflicts between these ideals and whose prophetic discourse is thus in a constant process of rearticulation rather than recurrence and stability.

What emerges in Dylan's telling from the diremption besetting these sources of normativity—freedom, justice, and God—is not mere confusion and indeterminacy, even if it is true that Dylan prophesizes our sense of not having figured out how to live by clarifying the clashes undermining our attainment of that ultimate wisdom. The most remarkable feature of Dylan's prophetic contribution is that the specific conflicts between the grounds of normativity are themselves imbued with ethical meaning.

Consider, for instance, the relationship between individual freedom and social justice, which I examine in Part I. Against the ideology of liberal democracy, which imagines both individual freedom and social justice being mutually realized in a well-ordered liberal-democratic state—and against the idealistic view of activists, civic leaders, journalists, and most philosophers that freedom and justice are mutually reinforcing social goals—Dylan sings as someone for whom social justice comes at the expense of individual freedom, as someone who, virtually without precedent (Ralph Waldo Emerson and Henry David Thoreau are the only historical analogues of whom I am aware), helps to inspire and lead a social justice movement (the civil rights movement of the 1960s) yet at the same time also comes to publicly acknowledge his lack of full commitment to that movement because of an overriding preference for the free use of his individuality. For we who are bourgeois, this conflict between self and other ought to be all too familiar, but it is a feature of bourgeois existence to resist confronting it at all costs. Dylan explodes this blockage, this lack of bourgeois self-awareness. He does not solve the problem of which way to go—justice or freedom—but he insists upon the dilemma of being pulled in two different directions, and when he does practice individual self-reliance he does so without the triumphalism and complacency that typically have accompanied the ideal, even and especially in Emerson's and Thoreau's foundational articulations of it. If for Emerson and Thoreau self-reliance is inseparable from "God-reliance" and faith in the providential achievement of social justice, Dylan models, by contrast, how to practice self-reliance in a world of permanent injustice and suffering, without appeal to unverifiable, metaphysical sources of comfort such as divinity and providence. When Dylan practices individual self-reliance, it is without the self-satisfaction of believing he is also adequately fulfilling his social responsibility or abiding by an individualism that everyone is equally free to practice if they wish. Self-reliance is indeed a value, but it is not the only one; while we ought to understand the genuine attraction of the ideal, we also ought to understand the moral costs. In helping us do so, Dylan performs prophetic leadership that operates not through the moral exemplarity frequently associated with prophetic figures, but through his testimony to his lack of full moral goodness—a paradox that is one key modality of what I mean by describing Dylan as a prophet without God.

Likewise, consider the conflict between individual freedom and divinity, which I analyze in Part II. Dylan is unusual because he gives voice to sharply divergent standpoints regarding the proper relationship between being a free-thinking individual and being religious. Although never, it seems, an atheist, from the 1960s to the late 1970s Dylan expressed profound skepticism that religion could provide any kind of meaningful ethical guidance and, as a countercultural icon, he seemed to many during this period to embody the value of being a self-directed individual over and against external sources of authority, including and especially religious ones. Yet, in a transformation as sharp and as controversial as his going electric and renouncing dependable social justice activism in the mid-1960s, Dylan underwent a public conversion to Christianity in the late 1970s, allegedly finding Jesus in a hotel room in Tucson on November 18, 1978, and for the next three years not only produced and performed Christian music explicating, defending, and celebrating his newfound faith but, to the shock of his audiences, interspersed virulent gospel speeches throughout his concerts. If the 1979–1981 period is the segment of Dylan's prophetic legacy in which he most closely resembles traditional prophets of the biblical type, it is also short-lived within the broader context of his now sixty-plus years on the public stage. Indeed, following his 1981 album *Shot of Love*, he entered a long and still ongoing postconversion period characterized by greatly diminished religious fervor, occasional though striking contemplation of the possible illusoriness of his religious commitments, and the return to non-religious topics in his music and public statements. Taken collectively, these three distinct attitudes toward religion—anti-religious skepticism, fervent evangelical embrace of Christianity, and the subdued and sometimes self-doubting religiosity of postconversion—make it hard to label Dylan according to common religious categories. Yet, when considered as divergent effusions of a single freethinking mind, they make Dylan perhaps the greatest representative of a *postsecular* mentality that understands both religion and non-religion as standpoints of equal integrity, which each of us might adopt at any time. In recent years, philosophers of postsecularism, such as Jürgen Habermas and Charles Taylor, have defended the need for a postsecular ethics according to which religionists and non-religionists learn to engage with each other with newfound respect and understanding. But their very status as philosophers, employing the language of secular reason, has, among other factors, made them more effective in confronting one half of the postsecular mission (the call for religionists to embrace certain political and scientific frameworks that make no appeal to religious values), leaving the other half—the call for the non-religious to manifest genuine respect for and engagement with the religious—far less developed or accomplished. It is precisely in regard to this latter dynamic that Dylan functions most distinctly as a prophet of the postsecular. Both Dylan's stature as a countercultural hero respected by secularists and the specific ways his religious music continually addresses itself to the standpoint of non-religion means that Dylan, almost uniquely in popular culture, has demonstrated for non-religious people the integrity, dignity, and plausibility of religiosity. If the function of traditional religious prophecy is to inspire audiences to religion, Dylan's role as a religious prophet, by contrast, should be appreciated for its challenge to secularists to overcome not their atheism per se, but their sense that such atheism is natural, rational, or otherwise superior to religiosity. As with the conflict between individuality and justice, Dylan does not solve the conflict between individuality and divinity—he seems, at different moments, to have found traditional religious belief as anathema to his individual freedom; as essential to, properly overriding of, or a manifestation of his freedom; or as having an uncertain value in light of an ongoing mix of religious adherence and religious doubt—but his meditation on these puzzles, communicated with undeniable prophetic fire, has made him a powerful deliverer of a postsecular message. In this role Dylan has been a prophet without God in the sense of being a prophet uniquely able to communicate religious topics to those who are godless. He thus has operated as a bridge between theism and atheism, faith and doubt, religiosity and non-religiosity, representing both sides of the deep cleavages besetting so much of contemporary culture.

Finally, consider the conflict between God and justice, which is the subject of Part III. If the usual prophetic standpoint is to affirm either the ultimate redemption of this world through a divinely assisted social justice or, alternatively, the radical separation of the sublunary and divine realms with the consequent expectation of divine justice in a world to come, Dylan often posits a human realm that is not only mired in violence, oppression, and injustice, but also not compensated by any kind of pronounced eschatological expectation. That is, Dylan invites us to see the world as fallen, without meaningful or likely exit. In this he is close to the position of political realists—figures such as Thucydides, Machiavelli, Max Weber, Hans Morgenthau, Henry Kissinger, and others—who make the irreducibility of politics to justice their central animating axiom and likewise generally rule out any divinely assisted escape from the world as we know it. Dylan, as a reader, is familiar with this tradition of political realism. And in key respects he is part of it. But Dylan's realism is, if anything, more real or in any case crucially different because for him the point of reflecting on the fallenness of the political world is not political mastery (the key concern of canonical political realists, who always address themselves to the situation of political *leaders*) but modeling how ordinary people can awaken to the nightmare of political reality and, in abandoning more familiar aspirational hopes, nonetheless "strengthen the things that remain." In other words, if pessimism most typically is rejected by leading philosophies and contemporary culture more generally, or communicated only as an esoteric truth for the few who rule, Dylan is different for so seriously contemplating a pessimistic view of the world and elucidating its ethical meaning on the ordinary civic level.

In each of these meditations on diremption, we see an instance of Dylan's unusual role as, not a prophet of salvation, but rather a prophet without God: a prophet who presents himself as not fulfilling the demands of social justice and thus is *not good*; a prophet who speaks most instructively not to the religious but to those without religion, without God, and with the purpose not of converting them to religion but of inculcating respect for it; and, finally, a prophet who confronts what it means to live in a world forsaken by God, in which either there is no arc to the moral universe or it bends toward injustice. These are both unusual concerns and unusual renderings of the prophetic consciousness.

For those who already treat Dylan as a seer and a sage—who find in his words meditations "on the art of living, written in a style of gemlike lucidity, radiant with humor and grace and large heartedness and deep wisdom: one of the wonders of the world"[1]—my effort in this book to describe, with specificity and seriousness, what is novel and significant in Dylan's prophetic impact will be greeted, at the very least initially, in a spirit of receptivity. But what meaning can the book have for those who find the idea of Dylan as a modern-day prophet preposterous,

---

[1] Stephen Mitchell, ed., *The Tao Te Ching* (New York: Harper Perennial, 1988), vii.

either because they cannot fathom treating Dylan in prophetic terms or, more broadly, because they find the whole notion of prophecy beyond the pale of serious philosophical analysis? The pages that follow aim to attend to such skeptical readers. In the introductory chapter I clarify the sociological, formalistic, and substantive features of the Dylan phenomenon that make the prophetic label credible. The bulk of the book then emphasizes not just Dylan's prophetic status, but the *ideas* that Dylan prophetically communicates: their originality, their significance within our culture, and their departure from the philosophical traditions to which they relate. My hope is that readers, however they ultimately come down on the prophet question, will come away with greater appreciation for the uniqueness and depth of Dylan's contribution to contemporary thought.

If I am successful in persuading or at least accommodating a skeptical reader, it is no doubt because I have known something like this skepticism myself. Criticism can work from two directions—in the modernist style of making a complex text more understandable, or in the postmodernist style of demonstrating the subtlety and complexity of an object wrongly thought to be of limited significance—and in approaching Dylan in this book I have moved from both standpoints. But it also has been from these two directions that I have doubted, at times, the propriety of the project, wondering at some moments if I was a worthy miner of Dylan's depths and, at others, if there was enough in the mine to justify my extraction. Such doubts sometimes have been fed by external criticism, such as that of a professor at Washington University in St. Louis, where I presented a paper on Dylan in 2017, who said of my work: "It reminds me why I never voluntarily listen to Bob Dylan." An unkind remark, to be sure, and one that perhaps can be refuted by the great degree to which we listen to Dylan not just voluntarily but *involuntarily*, due to the prevalence of his songs within contemporary culture and, as I hope to explain, the striking degree to which they speak perceptively to the ethical conflicts so many of us are likely to recognize in the twenty-first century.

Of course, what makes the matter vexing is that it is not just professional colleagues who have led me to doubt, but Dylan himself. In the eight years I have wrestled with Dylan, I sometimes have wondered what he might think of the project. Too often I have imagined him dismissive of this entire enterprise. This is no idle speculation but grounded in numerous disparaging reflections Dylan has made about those who would understand him. Consider:

> These so-called connoisseurs of Bob Dylan music. . . . I don't feel they know a thing, or have any inkling of who I am and what I'm about. I know they think they do, and yet it's ludicrous, it's humorous, and sad. That such people have spent too much of their time thinking about who? Me? Get a life, please. It's not something any one person should

do about another. You're not serving your own life well. You're wasting your life.[2]

What does Dylan mean and how can the book you hold before you defend itself against the intimation that perhaps it would be better if it did not exist?

One thing Dylan seems to mean, both here and in other reflections, is to devalue the work of professional interpreters both in itself and in comparison to the work of those who make the things that others are led to interpret. Despite his egalitarian spirit, at times Dylan seems to revel in the superiority of his vocation—a vocation he once described as "a folk musician who gazed into the gray mist with tear-blinded eyes and made up songs that floated in a luminous haze"—especially vis-à-vis the parasitic efforts of others to make sense of him.[3] It is not just that when Dylan asks the question—"An' you, just what do you do anyway?" ("She's Your Lover Now")—it is hard not to be humbled by the comparison. Beyond this, Dylan specifically has challenged the vocational integrity of professors, intellectuals, journalists, and other professional commentators. His criticisms here are legion. Perhaps most notable is his mockery of Mister Jones in "Ballad of a Thin Man":

> Ah, you've been with the professors
> And they've all liked your looks
> With great lawyers you have
> Discussed lepers and crooks
> You've been through all of
> F. Scott Fitzgerald's books
> You're very well-read
> It's well-known
> But something is happening here
> And you don't know what it is
> Do you, Mister Jones?

In "The Times They Are A-Changin'" Dylan patronizes "writers and critics":

> Come writers and critics
> Who prophesize with your pen
> And keep your eyes wide
> The chance won't come again

---

[2] Alan Jackson, "Dylan on Song," *Times Magazine*, September 8, 2001, 18–19.
[3] Bob Dylan, *Chronicles: Volume One* (New York: Simon & Schuster, 2004), 116.

And don't speak too soon
For the wheel's still in spin
And there's no tellin' who that it's namin'

This invitation is done from above, with Dylan telling commentators the conditions of their own discovery and analysis. It is also a dubious invitation since it instructs the writers and critics not to speak too soon and suggests that their attempts at profundity are likely to fail. That singing is superior to writing—that those who prophesize with their actual voice out in public are superior to those who prophesize only with their pen—is an idea lurking not very deep beneath the surface of Dylan's summons.

Even more aggressive are instances in which Dylan inveighs against the pointlessness of certain areas of study, such as his valediction to "memorizing politics of ancient history" ("My Back Pages") or, more brutally, from "Tombstone Blues":

Now I wish I could write you a melody so plain
That could hold you, dear lady, from going insane
That could ease you and cool you and cease the pain
Of your useless and pointless knowledge

Or consider Dylan's languid condescension in "Love Minus Zero/No Limit":

In the dime stores and bus stations
People talk of situations
Read books, repeat quotations
Draw conclusions on the wall
Some speak of the future
My love she speaks softly
She knows there's no success like failure
And that failure's no success at all

The juxtaposition of an elevated female love interest to insipid intellectualism is a repeated trope for Dylan. Consider this from "One More Cup of Coffee (Valley Below)":

Your sister sees the future
Like your mama and yourself
You've never learned to read or write
There's no books upon your shelf

As a trenchant opponent of intellectualism—as someone who, by contrast, communicates his ideas from the heart and encased in sonorous, poetic beauty— Dylan in effect challenges his non-poetic, non-singing interpreters to enjoy his music but be quiet about it and not try to attach themselves to his greatness. Of course, Dylan *has* been amenable to scholarship about him in crucial ways, so the challenge is less personal than ideational: calling into question what benefit interpretation could ever accomplish.

By way of response, I should emphasize that this book is not any kind of commentary but a philosophical one, aspiring to scholarly rigor and aiming to place Dylan into conversation with a broader tradition of ethical, political, and theological thought. There is something admittedly parasitic and limited about philosophy's grey on grey, especially vis-à-vis the resplendent brilliance of Dylan's blonde on blonde, but the effort to philosophize about Dylan's prophetic poetry ought not be ruled out even if it is in fact lower. Insofar as no author can exhaust the meaning of his or her ideas, there is an enduring place for interpretation. Indeed, as Dylan himself sometimes has acknowledged, he does not have a monopoly on his songs' meanings, occasionally going so far as to admit he does not even know what some of them mean at all. In the 1960s, for instance, he reportedly told Joan Baez:

> A bunch of years from now, all these assholes are going to be writing about all this shit I write, and I don't know where the fuck it comes from and I don't know what the fuck it's about, and they're going to write about what it's about.[4]

Here Dylan is close to Plato's view that poets do not know what their poems mean, even if Dylan does not deploy the idea, as Plato does, as part of a defense of philosophy's superiority to poetry. For Plato, the very dignity of philosophy lies in its capacity to make straightforward truth claims and thus enable its practitioners, unlike poets, to know what they mean to say. Dylan, like perhaps most people, does not share Plato's view and privileges poetry over the study of it. Still, as much as Dylan's comments are an especially cutting instance of his hostility to his interpreters, they are also, in Dylan's very confession of not knowing the meaning of his own words, an acknowledgment of the legitimate place for interpretation.

But what kind of interpretation? One approach, which I mostly avoid, is to claim to interpret the ultimate meaning of individual songs by translating their

---

[4] This is Joan Baez's account of what Dylan said, as related in her interview in *American Masters*, season 19, episode 7, "No Direction Home: Bob Dylan," directed by Martin Scorsese, aired September 27, 2005, on PBS, https://www.imdb.com/title/tt0367555/?ref_=adv_li_tt.

poetry into prose. But a different approach, which I have adopted, has been to make Dylan all the more meaningful by placing his ideas in a broader philosophical context. This has meant situating some of Dylan's key and recurring concerns—his felt conflict between freedom and justice, his religious conversion and its aftermath, and his pessimism—within wider and longer-standing traditions of thought, with the result that the originality, depth, and edge of his pronouncements can be more clearly perceived and appreciated. I do not deny that there is a modesty to such an endeavor. Indeed, there is something humbling about writing about someone else, especially a living person. But humbleness should not disqualify a work. Even if far more scholars fantasize about being rock musicians than vice versa—though, interestingly, Dylan himself recently has mused, "If I had to do it all over again, I'd be a schoolteacher—probably teach Roman history or theology"[5]—we cannot allow this to denigrate the integrity of scholarship. One can say with Czeslaw Milosz: "You who think of us: they lived only in delusion / Know that we, the People of the Book, will never die."[6]

But what if nothing is there? This is another kind of attack Dylan makes against his interpreters: not the lowness of criticism vis-à-vis poetry and song but the possibility that he has not given us enough to warrant close attention. Recall Dylan's objection to his interpreters: "That such people have spent too much of their time thinking about who? Me? Get a life, please." One modality of this concern is raised by the fact that some of Dylan's lyrics admittedly have a "sloven" quality, though the circumstance that a few of Dylan's words are like this is hardly a reason to reject the attempt to analyze any of them.[7] A more serious challenge is the idea that what Dylan actually stands for is constant transformation, and thus he has no stable underlying standpoint to represent besides ceaseless and searching reinvention. This perspective is memorialized in the title of Todd Haynes's great film on Dylan, *I'm Not There* (which itself is the name of one of Dylan's songs), and Dylan himself at times has encouraged it. Dylan routinely has said that interpreters project their own interests onto him, finding what they want to find in his words:

> Everything people say about you or me, they are saying about themselves. They're telling about themselves. Ever notice that? In my case, there's a whole world of scholars, professors and Dylanologists, and

---

[5] Robert Love, "Bob Dylan Uncut," *AARP: The Magazine*, February/March 2015, 32.

[6] Czeslaw Milosz, *Selected and Last Poems: 1931–2004* (New York: HarperCollins, 2006), 150.

[7] For examples of Dylan's sloppiness, see Michael Gray, *Song and Dance Man III: The Art of Bob Dylan* (London: Continuum, 2002), 130, 465–66.

everything I do affects them in some way. And, you know, in some ways,
I've given them life. They'd be nowhere without me.[8]

But it seems wrong to say that interpreters of Dylan find only what they themselves are looking for and never a more genuine perception of the man and
his work. Even if there are limitless possible accurate interpretations of Dylan,
this does not mean that all interpretations are accurate. And even if any accurate interpretation is itself limited—capturing only a sliver of what Dylan
represents—this does not make it false. Dylan is not, after all, a brook or a fire
in a hearth—objects that ignite intellectual reflection in those who gaze at them
but possess no cognitive content in themselves—as there is indeed potent cognitive content in Dylan, which is to say there are recurring ethical, political, and
theological concerns that abide within Dylan's oeuvre. In addressing these, I do
not claim to have addressed the entirety of Dylan's vast work, as much has not
been included. But in addressing what it has focused on—Dylan's withdrawal
from dependable social activism, his conversion, his pessimism—this book
cannot be said to have concerned itself with something that is not there.

Further, my approach has tried, more than many others, to respect and accept
the mysterious and ultimate inaccessibility of the man, as my purpose has not
been to assign familiar ideological labels to him—or to suggest that he provides
some singular or stable ethical message—but to understand Dylan as wrestling
with ethical conflicts that arise between the three sources of authority most typically at stake in the prophetic tradition: individual freedom, justice, and divinity.
In presenting Dylan as a prophet of diremption, not a prophet of salvation, I not
only emphasize how he differs from more typical expressions of the prophetic
conscience, but also make clear that he gives us no overarching answer—no "one
thing that is needful"—by which we might orient our lives. In this regard at least,
the book has respected the "I'm not there" idea, though the difference is that
the book attends to numerous ethical consequences that follow from Dylan's
tragic testimony of ethical conflict: his practice of a self-reliance without the
self-satisfaction that traditionally has accompanied the ideal, the demand for
postsecular respect for religiosity and non-religiosity as coequal possibilities for
any human being, and the call for a realer realism that gets beyond the elitism of
more familiar realists within the history of political thought.

Closely connected to the "I'm not there" refutation of Dylan scholarship is
the insistence that Dylan is not equivalent to the perspectives and personalities
from which he sings. Dylan himself has reminded us of this difference. He not

[8] Mikal Gilmore, "Bob Dylan Unleashed," *Rolling Stone*, September 27, 2012 https://www.rolli
ngstone.com/music/music-news/bob-dylan-unleashed-189723/.

only has suggested that Bob Dylan is a persona he wears—"I'm only Bob Dylan when I have to be"—but also, on the basis of his unique relationship to this persona, has cautioned against over-interpretation: "If I wasn't Bob Dylan, I'd probably think that Bob Dylan has a lot of answers myself."[9] In response to this challenge, it should be said that I do not think the book suffers if it turns out that it has analyzed only the persona of Bob Dylan and not the man behind the persona. The persona is itself sufficiently brilliant, perceptive, and distinct, regardless of whether it is authentically owned or only performed. Nonetheless, it needs to be stressed that the main ideas and concerns I have attributed to Dylan seem very likely to be those of the man himself. Is there any debate that Dylan withdrew from the social justice movements he had helped to inspire, thereby raising—and himself reflecting on—the question of the relationship between individuality and social justice? Does any biographer doubt the truth of Dylan's religious conversion in the late 1970s? Is there any evidence that Dylan's pessimism about the political world is not authentically held? These topics seem to have "been there." They constitute the abiding ethical, political, and religious issues that Dylan—and so many of us—wonder and worry about.

As Dylan has said, "Passion is a young man's game, older people gotta be wise."[10] Whether his words of wisdom are intentional or beyond his control, whether they reflect his own thoughts or those of someone he is pretending to be, whether they are consistently great or only unevenly so, the wager of this book is that they have made Bob Dylan an extraordinary contributor not just to popular music, but to our apprehension of the contemporary world and its challenges.

It is remarkable that Dylan's potency extends to his dismissal and would-be regulation of those who would aim to understand him. *Be awed by me, but don't think you can ever understand me*, he seems to say. But awe is the mother of philosophy. That which fascinates beckons us to understand. Whether my effort to do so has been for naught I leave not to Dylan but to you, the reader.

[9] "Dylan Press Conference, 1986, Brett Whiteley Studio, Sydney," posted by FilmStretch Australia, video, 18:21, May 23, 2013, https://youtu.be/pDq1jD9nqm4; Jonathan Cott, ed., "Interview with Ron Rosenbaum, *Playboy*, March 1978," in *Bob Dylan: The Essential Interviews* (New York: Simon & Schuster, 2017), 247. Also relevant is Dylan's claim "I don't think of myself as Bob Dylan." Liner notes to *Biograph* (1985) for "Up to Me," 37.
[10] Love, "Bob Dylan Uncut," 34–36.

Introduction

What Kind of Prophet is Bob Dylan?

When and if Bob Dylan dies, it will be a major event for our culture. We will have lost not just one of our greatest living artists but a prophet who, through both the form and substance of his work, has bestowed a prophetic message uniquely suited to a time, such as ours, deeply suspicious of the very possibility of prophecy. As the prospect of that sad day grows starker, it is worthwhile to understand what will have been, if not lost (since Dylan's words and music will last for posterity), at least closed and concluded. This work is hardly alone in such an endeavor as there are literally thousands of books, articles, and essays—not to mention films, poems, and songs—that have tried to make sense of the man and his work. But rather than be deterred by the plethora of other studies of Dylan, this book treats them—and, more generally, the sheer magnitude and intensity of the popular and critical reception that always has been part of the Dylan phenomenon from its inception more than sixty years ago—as its point of depar ture. If the most dominant approach to Dylan has been from biographical or aesthetic perspectives, this book treats Dylan in light of the fact that he not only has lived, written, sung, spoken, filmed, and performed, but done so in tandem with a mass audience that, more so than in the case of any other modern artist, has understood his life's work as having an oracular significance. Accordingly, the primary category from which this work approaches Dylan is *prophet*.

What Is a Prophet?

A prophet is someone others listen to and follow because of a perceived capacity for profound insight on matters of fundamental importance. We do not heed prophets because of their training, their accreditation as experts by other experts, their knowledge, or their technical skill. While a prophetic person might

Bob Dylan. Jeffrey Edward Green, Oxford University Press. © Oxford University Press 2024.
DOI: 10.1093/oso/9780197651742.003.0001

possess any of these qualities, what distinguishes a prophet is the perception of a wisdom exceeding what can be obtained from scientific experiment, mastery of a profession, or mere learnedness. This is not just because the prophet possesses an extrarational authority, but also because the topics the prophet illuminates, though vital, are themselves beyond the reach of conventional organs of learning. This feature is most obviously on display with regard to the traditional and paradigmatic topic of prophetic communication, the human relationship to the divine—though the matter is not limited to this subject, since not all prophets speak in behalf of divinity, as some appeal to the demands of justice or the responsibility individuals have to themselves as free beings.[1] In any case, prophetic messages, especially within the confines of disenchanted modernity, are beyond the boundaries of what ordinarily is considered scientifically communicable. Social scientists can provide facts on any given society or culture, but the prophet goes beyond this to tell us something about *the way of the world*, the total and general ethical situation these facts have engendered for human beings at a particular moment, if not more permanently. And if doctors, advertisers, friends, family, therapists, and teachers provide a steady flow of information regarding targeted aspects of a person's proclivities, habits, flaws, and dispositions, the prophet here, too, is different in communicating a similarly *total* message, attending not to how to maneuver this or that particular difficulty but instead to such fundamental concerns as the values that define a person's overarching conception of a good life, the person's relationship to justice, and also possibly the nature of the person's relationship to God.

Moral and political philosophy, it is true, sometimes also strive for such totalizing teachings and the ethical consequences that follow from them. But a prophet is not a philosopher, both because philosophers do not require a following to exist at all and because the vehicle of prophetic expression is not logic or argument or abstract considerations of right, but evocative statements of warning, dreams and visions, exhortation, indignation, and personal confession that shake listeners out of unthinking complacency to consider who they are, what they have done and are doing, and the personal meaning of their obligations. Today, it is not just sociological and formalistic differences that separate the prophet from the philosopher but substantive ones as well. Contemporary

---

[1] In singling out these three sources of normativity informing the prophetic conscience, I am not just taking heed of the fact that—as a matter of human history—justice, freedom, and God have been the main foundations of prophetic discourse. Viewed from an analytic perspective, they also share three interrelated foundations: the obligations I have to myself (which ground freedom); the obligations I have to others with whom I share a political community (which ground justice); and the obligations that I have, in the manner of revelation, to what is external to humanity and to secular reason, to the extent that it exists (which ground my relationship to divinity).

philosophy has become increasingly chastened by a postmetaphysical skepticism insistent that the traditional objects of classical philosophy, the so-called highest things (*ta megista*)—objects such as human nature, ethical instruction for how individuals might achieve happiness and fulfillment, and, for some skeptics, morality and justice themselves—are not knowable through reason. The prophet not only addresses the highest things differently but actually preserves attention to them as they are increasingly abandoned by the sobriety, cautiousness, and modesty of philosophy in its contemporary form. The immense silence in contemporary philosophy regarding edifying discourse on the highest things is the backdrop that enables new forms of prophecy to be more clearly discerned.

At the same time, it would be wrong to reduce the prophet to a holder of answers that followers simply accept. The distinctive sociological feature of prophecy—the maintenance of a *following*—does not require that all followers endorse what the prophet has to say. The Hebrew prophets were attended to as much by those who contested or remained unconverted by what the prophets proclaimed as they were by enthusiastic followers. But even those suspicious and cautious often stood transfixed by the inspiration, profundity, mystery, and strangeness of the prophetic consciousness in their midst. Moreover, if the traditional and paradigmatic function of the prophet is to bring about commitment to the cause the prophet serves, it is also the case, of special relevance in contemporary times, that the prophetic consciousness always has operated in a secondary way, inspiring in listeners their own personal clarification regarding questions of fundamental and vital concern: Who am I (i.e., what god do I serve, even if it is not the god of the prophet)? What is the world like (i.e., what should I expect to find, ethically and morally speaking, from others and the social bodies we collectively form)? What is my concept of justice and my relationship to its dictates?

If other sources of human direction—the desire for wealth and social status, the fear of punishment, the quest for fun and adventure, and the fascination with the ongoing revolution in technology—are largely silent, since they operate through a language that is either non-existent or reduced to the simplest and most ordinary forms of expression, a further distinguishing mark of the prophetic consciousness is its transmission through *words*, whose brilliance, poignancy, fecundity, uncanniness, arrestingness, and beauty are not merely poetic but at times rival the greatest poetry. In truth, the division between poetry and prophecy is difficult to demarcate—something I elaborate below—since the concrete experience of prophetic direction is a linguistic and oratorical one and, further, the capacity of prophets to win a following and be taken seriously flows directly from the unusual eloquence, freshness, and directness of their speech. A common and mistaken view of prophecy is to reduce it to the prediction of the future—which actually is not the main function of the greatest biblical prophets or the inheritors of the prophetic legacy today—as in fact the prophet's most genuine achievement is not divination but instruction stemming from inspired speech.

The last thing to emphasize about prophets, taken in a general sense, is their quasi-democratic aspect. Prophets are only what they are, sociologically speaking, insofar as they have a significant popular audience. This does not mean that the prophet simply represents the preferences and opinions of followers, since a follower need not agree with (only listen to) the prophet and, furthermore, the prophet's function is to generate reflection and inspiration that either were not there in the first place or existed only in a tacit, subconscious way. Still, the prophet's intrinsic connection to a broader populace is perhaps the best argument for not extending postmetaphysical skepticism (which has reduced the possible objects of philosophical and social-scientific learning) to prophecy itself. That the prophet speaks extrarationally is not a basis for the rational rejection of prophecy, especially within a democratic society in which concern for what is popular is paramount. Prophets are windows into those who recognize them. Heeding the prophet is also a kind of heeding of the People. The questions, then, to be asked of any prophet are not simply what did the prophet say, what kind of authority did the prophet claim, and whether or not such messages and authority are credible. There is an alternate, complementary angle of analysis that also asks: What does it say about a community or a culture at a given moment in time that it elevates this particular person, rationally or not, to the status of a prophet? If we want to know more about everyday members of contemporary democratic societies beyond what can be gleaned from the narrow, often constructed-from-above categories of party identification, religious affiliation, class position, and race and gender identity—if we want, beyond these categories, to arrive at some sense of the spiritual disposition that animates popular cultures—we need to seek out and recognize the persistence of the prophetic consciousnesses by which broad segments of the populace are inspired. This aim is especially needed in the contemporary context in which the prevalence of value-free social science, postmetaphysical philosophy, the destabilization of organized religion, and bourgeois neoliberal market utopianism might leave the false impression that the modal citizen of a secular, capitalist, liberal-democratic state is spiritually dead. The persistence of the prophetic consciousness even in such conditions is an opportunity for social science and philosophy to listen to and learn from the People and not just educate them. Taking seriously Bob Dylan's status as a contemporary prophet, albeit one who importantly reworks the meaning of prophecy and adopts the unusual posture of a "prophet without God," is an effort at such heedful listening.

In treating Dylan as a contemporary prophet I seek to overcome two very different interpretative obstacles that commonly arise within Dylan scholarship and analysis of Dylan more generally. On the one hand, the prophet label frequently is used approvingly by scholars and critics but without sufficient elaboration of what this designation actually means. On the other hand, many—often (but not always) including Dylan himself—have objected to the label as inaccurate on numerous grounds, invoking, for instance, the alleged distinction between being a musical artist and being a prophet. My central purpose here in this introduction is to argue that Dylan's prophetic status inheres in three different dynamics—sociological, formalistic, and substantive—and, in elaborating these, I aim both to more precisely define Dylan's prophetic status and to refute various forms of critique of this labeling.

The Sociological Grounds of Dylan's Prophetic Status

Sociologically speaking, the prophet is the quintessential case of charismatic authority, which is an authority that stems from an individual's capacity to win and maintain a following based on the unique *personal* qualities of the individual. As Max Weber describes it in his seminal account of the idea, charismatic authority arises when a mass of followers takes heed of a person not because that person possesses scientific learning, wealth, placement within a bureaucratic apparatus, or inherited title or status, but rather because the person is thought to be uniquely gifted, special, magical, or, in the ultimate sense of charisma, touched by or in communication with divinity. Accordingly, the Hebrew prophets, whom Weber studied as a paradigmatic example of charisma, operated as independent agents, outside of formal political and priestly hierarchies, and exercised an authority stemming entirely from their capacity to instill a belief in their own person in their followers. Weber understands charisma as one of the permanent dynamics in human relations, existing in numerous contexts, sometimes in combination with other types of authority as well, and thus capable of operating in both pure and more adulterated forms. This caveat is important in analyzing Dylan. Clearly, Dylan is not fully equivalent to a Hebrew prophet, as he does not (usually at least) communicate to his followers as a straightforward messenger from God. But if we uphold this strict standard of what a prophet is, we blind ourselves to the enduring traces of the prophetic legacy in our midst and also to the way that legacy has been reworked to function within the specific cultural, epistemological, and ethical conditions of our time. Dylan may not be a prophet in the Hebrew mold, but he stands alongside other, better-recognized recent prophetic figures, such as Mahatma Gandhi and Martin Luther King Jr., in bearing powerful traces of the prophetic consciousness and the charismatic authority on which it is based.

Dylan's charisma has been demonstrated throughout the entirety of his sixty-plus years on the public stage. That he has amassed a large public audience, significant segments of which follow him above all for who he is and not simply what he produces (i.e., follow him not because they enjoy his music, but rather enjoy his music because they follow him), is too obvious to need much substantiation.[2] Of course, there is a diversity of perspectives within any public audience. But the charismatic elements of this following are clearly detectable.

Most strikingly, many followers self-consciously follow Dylan as a prophet. David Remnick, editor of the *New Yorker*, observes that Dylan is someone who "ever since he's twenty years old, people think he's a deity."[3] Ellis Cashmore likewise describes the "deistic eminence" with which Dylan's fans have endowed him.[4] In his autobiography, *Chronicles*, Dylan himself acknowledges the extensive degree to which he has been treated as a prophet throughout his lifetime.[5] Throughout the last six-plus decades, countless individuals have flocked to Dylan, not just attending his performances but making pilgrimages to his home, confessing that their lives have been powerfully altered by his words and music, hounding him with an intensity and longevity that few other pop-cultural icons have experienced, and in one infamous case looking through his garbage for further clues about the man and his message.[6] Even more noteworthy is how prominent individuals, who know Dylan personally, have articulated the same belief in Dylan's prophetic status. Consider the following:

- Bob Johnston (producer of numerous Dylan albums from the 1960s and early 1970s): "I believe in giving credit where credit's due. I don't think Dylan has a lot to do with it. I think God instead of touching him on the shoulder he

[2] But it is worth endorsing Gilmour's observation: "Audiences frequently *receive* Bob Dylan and his work . . . assuming it possesses gravitas. When they speak about him and his work, this magnification frequently includes religion-laden terms." Michael J. Gilmour, *The Gospel According to Bob Dylan: The Old, Old Story of Modern Times* (Louisville, KY: Westminster John Knox Press, 2011), 21.

[3] Alec Baldwin, "David Remnick on Liebling, Dylan, and Glasnost," July 20, 2015, in *Here's the Thing*, produced by WNYC Studios, podcast, MP3 audio, 48:34, https://www.wnycstudios.org/podcasts/heresthething/episodes/htt-david-remnick.

[4] Ellis Cashmore, *Celebrity Culture* (New York: Routledge, 2006), 78; also see Gilmour, *Gospel According to Bob Dylan*, 53.

[5] Bob Dylan, *Chronicles: Volume One* (New York: Simon & Schuster, 2004), 116–17, 124.

[6] For evidence, both anecdotal and more systemized, of the large number of Dylan followers profoundly impacted by Dylan, and how this impact exceeds conventional norms of mere fandom, see David Gaines, *In Dylan Town: A Fan's Life* (Iowa City: University of Iowa Press, 2015); and David Kinney, *The Dylanologists: Adventures in the Land of Bob* (New York: Simon & Schuster, 2014). For Dylan's account of being hounded by followers, including by throngs at his house on MacDougal Street in New York City in the early 1970s, see Andrew McCarron, *Light Come Shining: The Transformations of Bob Dylan* (New York: Oxford University Press, 2017), 73.

kicked him in the ass. Really. And that's where all that came from. He can't help what he's doing. I mean he's got the Holy Spirit about him. You can look at him and tell that."[7] And also: "I truly believe that in a couple of hundred years they'll find out he was a prophet. I think he's the only prophet we've had since Jesus."[8]

- Ken Kesey: "I saw very clearly that Dylan was doing something with our consciousness, the extent of which will only be known hundreds of years from now. Dylan's not only a poet, he's as well a prophet, a prophet like happens once every five hundred years or so."[9] And also: "I've just figured out who this weird little fuck is. . . . Same guy who wrote the Book of Revelation."[10]
- Allen Ginsberg: "I guess he felt prophet show good example, / bring himself down in the world."[11]
- Jackson Browne: "He opened my eyes to the view / And I was among those who called him a prophet / And I asked him what was true."[12]
- Sam Shepard: "Two concerts sold out. . . . College types going to see the prophet."[13]
- Barry Feinstein (photographer, referring to 1966 audiences in the United Kingdom): "He was the god, he was their god of the times."[14]
- Regina McCrary (singer on numerous Dylan albums and tours): "Bob Dylan walked with God back then [during his gospel period]. And he walks with God now."[15]
- Al Kasha: "There's a kind of anointing about him. There's a kind of presence that you know someone you've met is special in your life and tells you the

[7] Interview in *American Masters*, season 19, episode 7, "No Direction Home: Bob Dylan," directed by Martin Scorsese, aired September 27, 2005, on PBS, https://www.imdb.com/title/tt0367555/?ref_=adv_li_tt.

[8] Quoted in Gilmour, *Gospel According to Bob Dylan*, 25.

[9] Quoted in Elizabeth Thomson and David Gutman, eds., *The Dylan Companion* (London: Macmillan, 1990), 143.

[10] Quoted in Gilmour, *Gospel According to Bob Dylan*, 25.

[11] Allen Ginsberg, "Blue Gossip," in *The Captain's Tower: Seventy Poets Celebrate Bob Dylan at Seventy*, edited by Phil Bowen, Damian Furniss, and David Woolley (Bridgen, Wales: Seren, 2011), 50.

[12] Jackson Browne, vocalist and writer, "Looking into You," recorded 1971, track 8 on *Jackson Browne*, Asylum, released January 1972.

[13] Quoted in Gilmour, *Gospel According to Bob Dylan*, 25.

[14] Quoted in Gilmour, 25.

[15] Quoted in Tim Ghianni, "'Don't Make Her Cry': McCrary's Life with Dylan," *Nashville Ledger*, December 8–14, 2017, A23.

truth. . . . I've always felt that Bob is an anointed child. I've always felt that from the time I met him. He is a special, special person."[16]

Another feature of Dylan's prophetic status relates to the almost unimaginable degree to which he has been studied and analyzed. As David Braun, Dylan's lawyer, states it: "In my twenty-two years' experience of representing famous personages no other personality has attracted such attention, nor created such a demand for information about his personal affairs."[17] A 2016 article in the *Washington Post* reports that there are over one thousand books on Dylan in English alone.[18] While only a minority of this literature highlights Dylan's prophetic role in contemporary culture—and even less of it attempts to delineate this prophetic function in any detail—at some point, as Hegel reminds us, quantity becomes quality. The enormous attention Dylan has received from interpreters, even if its most usual approach has been from the standpoint of biography, music history, or aesthetic analysis, itself embodies a collective fascination indicative of Dylan's charismatic, prophetic status. And further, there is, after all, also a literature that analyzes Dylan's religious and prophetic elements to which this study contributes (and from which it also *departs* in its particular conceptualization of Dylan as a prophet without God), and scholars in this genre not only have helped document features of Dylan's charismatic-prophetic authority but sometimes also have personally testified to Dylan's prophetic role in their own lives.[19] Michael Gilmour, for instance, a leading analyst of Dylan's religiosity, introduces one of his studies with the confession: "I find divinity

---

[16] Interview in the documentary *Inside Bob Dylan's Jesus Years: Busy Being Born . . . Again*, directed by Joel Gilbert, Highway 61 Entertainment, 2008, https://www.imdb.com/title/tt2165867/?ref_= tt_mv_close.

[17] Quoted in McCarron, *Light Come Shining*, 24–25.

[18] Valerie Strauss, "Teaching Dylan: 'His Work as a Whole Is as Staggering as That of Homer or Shakespeare,'" *Washington Post*, October 14, 2016, https://www.washingtonpost.com/news/ answer-sheet/wp/2016/10/14/teaching-dylan-his-work-as-a-whole-is-as-staggering-as-that-of-homer-or-shakespeare/?utm_term=.918ff8d4b7a5.

[19] Commentaries on Dylan emphasizing his religious or prophetic dimension include: Michael J. Gilmour, *Tangled Up in the Bible: Dylan and Scripture* (New York: Continuum, 2004); Gilmour, *Gospel According to Bob Dylan*; Scott M. Marshall, *Bob Dylan: A Spiritual Life* (New York: BP Books, 2017); Marshall, *Restless Pilgrim: The Spiritual Journey of Bob Dylan* (Winter Park, FL: Relevant Books, 2002); Stephen Webb, *Dylan Redeemed: From Highway 61 to Saved* (New York: Continuum, 2006); Clinton Heylin, *Trouble in Mind: Bob Dylan's Gospel Years* (New York: Lesser Gods, 2017); Stephen Pickering, *Bob Dylan Approximately: A Portrait of the Jewish Poet* (Philadelphia: McKay, 1975); Phil Mason, *A Voice from On High: The Prophetic Oracles of Bob Dylan* (self-pub., 2018); Seth Rogovoy, *Bob Dylan: Prophet, Mystic, Poet* (New York: Scribner, 2009); Jeff Taylor and Chad Israelson, *The Political World of Bob Dylan: Freedom and Justice, Power and Sin* (London: Palgrave Macmillan, 2015).

shining through his songs into my everyday life," adding, "I prayed it/played it often."[20] Gilmour in effect lends truth to his own observation that Dylan's "ardent fans often employ hyperbolic language soaked in religious concepts when discussing the man and his work (most commonly 'prophet')."[21] Of course, the prophet label is not "hyperbolic" if that is how Dylan in fact is perceived. In any case, Andrew McCarron is hardly exaggerating when he writes that "Dylan's celebrity more closely resembles the life of a living Hindu saint than a rock star."[22]

To be sure, Dylan's status as a prophet is not universally accepted, and many find the label absurd. In some sense, this contestation is part of the prophetic legacy itself, as a recurring, if not definitional, feature of bearing the prophetic consciousness is to be rejected by opponents as a false prophet. But in Dylan's case, the opposition has been less that he is a false prophet than that the whole category of prophecy does not make sense when applied to him. Specifically, one can distinguish three main reasons many have been skeptical of interpreting Dylan's mass following in prophetic terms. First, many students of Dylan do not deny that he possesses genuine charisma but insist that the prophet label misdescribes him, overlooking what he ostensibly seems (and usually claims) to be: a musician. A second criticism of the prophetic label closely follows from the first: that it is not at all surprising that Dylan, as a musician, has such an enthusiastic fan base, as this is what we have come to expect from celebrities within popular culture, and within the music industry in particular (as even concerts of groups like the Backstreet Boys have been characterized as a kind of "worship"[23]); so, the fact that Dylan has excited such a following hardly makes him unique but only places him within a category shared by numerous other leading pop-cultural artists of our time. And third, understanding Dylan as a musician leads to another related criticism of the prophetic label: namely, that Dylan is a musical *entertainer*, someone who performs for money and has become extraordinarily rich doing so, and thus, due to the business component of his enterprise, lacks the moral status of prophets, who traditionally have spoken in public free of charge. Keith Richards of the Rolling Stones, expressing this view, has called Dylan a "prophet of profit."[24]

The force of these objections stems not only from the apparent accuracy of the musician label but also from the fact that Dylan himself often makes just

---

[20] Gilmour, *Gospel According to Bob Dylan*, xiv.

[21] Gilmour, 22.

[22] McCarron, *Light Come Shining*, 193.

[23] See the review of a Backstreet Boys concert from *Express Writer* (August 16, 1998).

[24] Quoted in Gilmour, *Gospel According to Bob Dylan*, 80.

this kind of plea: that he be understood not as a prophet, but as a musical artist. Consider his reflection from his autobiography:

> It seems like the world has always needed . . . someone to lead the charge against the Roman Empire. . . . I really was never any more than I was—a folk musician who gazed into the gray mist with tear-blinded eyes. . . . Now it had blown up in my face. . . . I wasn't a preacher performing miracles.[25]

Likewise, Dylan muses:

> Eventually different anachronisms were thrust upon me—anachronisms of lesser dilemma—though they might seem bigger. Legend, Icon, Enigma (Buddha in European Clothes was my favorite)—stuff like that, but that was all right. These titles were placid and harmless, threadbare, easy to get around with them. Prophet, Messiah, Savior—those are tough ones.[26]

In a *60 Minutes* interview from 2004, Dylan similarly states:

> It was like being in an Edgar Allan Poe story. And you're just not that person everybody thinks you are, though they call you that all the time: "You're the prophet. You're the savior." I never wanted to be a prophet or savior. Elvis maybe. I could easily see myself becoming him. But prophet? No.[27]

It is not uncommon for commentators to heed Dylan in this regard and insist that he not be understood in prophetic terms.[28] Nonetheless, the objection that Dylan is not a prophet but only a musician is unpersuasive on numerous grounds.

---

[25] Dylan, *Chronicles*, 116.

[26] Dylan, 124.

[27] Also relevant to Dylan's denial of the prophetic status is his comment from a 1963 interview: "Music, my writing, is something special, not sacred." Jonathan Cott, ed., "Radio Interview with Studs Terkel, WFMT (Chicago), May 1963," in *Bob Dylan: The Essential Interviews* (New York: Simon & Schuster, 2017), 13.

[28] As examples, consider: Dylan's "grandiose reputation as . . . prophet rests . . . largely on . . . his penchant for surreal imagery" (Michael Coyle and Debra Rae Cohen, "Blonde on Blonde," in *The Cambridge Companion to Bob Dylan*, ed. Kevin J. H. Dettmar (New York: Cambridge University Press, 2009), 145–46); and "Dylan is not so much a prophet, then, gazing forward into the future, as he is a smirking antiquary" (Kevin L. Stoehr, "You Who Philosophize Dylan: The Quarrel Between Philosophy and Poetry in the Songs of Bob Dylan," in *Bob Dylan and Philosophy*, ed. Peter Vernezze and Carl Porter (Chicago: Open Court, 2005), 190).

For one thing, despite protestations to the contrary, Dylan himself *has* invited the prophetic label at various times throughout his life. This was most obviously the case during his so-called gospel period of 1979–81, in which Dylan routinely preached to audiences between songs and publicly testified to having been saved by Christ. In one of his impromptu sermons from this period, Dylan reflected on his long history of being perceived as a prophet in a manner that seemed finally to endorse the designation:

> Years ago they … said I was a prophet. I used to say, "No I'm not a prophet." They say, "Yes you are, you're a prophet." I said, "No it's not me." They used to say, "You sure are a prophet." They used to convince me I was a prophet. Now I come out and say Jesus Christ is the answer. They say, "Bob Dylan's no prophet." They just can't handle it.[29]

During the gospel period, Dylan routinely presented himself as transmitting the word of God. In an interview in 1979, for instance, he declared, "I follow God, so if my followers are following me, indirectly they're gonna be following God too, because I don't sing any song which hasn't been given to me by the Lord to sing."[30] And likewise: "The basic thing, I feel, is to get in touch with Christ yourself. He will lead you. Any preacher who is a real preacher will tell you that: 'Don't follow me, follow Christ.'"[31] Even his eventual turning away from evangelical sermonizing and performing only religious music was presented in prophetic terms. Reflecting back on the 1979–81 period and the question of whether or not he had any regrets, Dylan commented: "I don't particularly regret telling people how to get their souls saved. I don't particularly regret any of that. Whoever was supposed to pick it up, picked it up. But maybe the time for me to say that has come and gone. Now it's time for me to do something else. . . . Jesus himself only preached for three years."[32] Moreover, as this comment suggests, even beyond the gospel period Dylan has invited comparisons to Jesus, whether through certain song lyrics that suggest the idea, his physical appearance at certain moments of his life, or various offhand comments along

---

[29] Bob Dylan, performance on January 25, 1980, in Omaha, Nebraska. Quoted in Andrea Cossu, *It Ain't Me Babe: Bob Dylan and the Performance of Authenticity* (London: Routledge, 2016), 108–9.

[30] Cott, "Radio interview with Bruce Heiman, KMEX (Tucson, Arizona), December 7, 1979," in *Essential Interviews*, 289.

[31] Cott, "Interview with Robert Hilburn, *Los Angeles Times*, November 23, 1980," in *Essential Interviews*, 297.

[32] Interview with Robert Hilburn, "Bob Dylan at 42: Rolling Down Highway 61 Again," *Los Angeles Times*, October 30, 1983, quoted in Taylor and Israelson, *Political World of Bob Dylan*, 137.

the way.[33] The character Jack Fate, whom Dylan plays in the 2003 movie *Masked and Anonymous*, which he co-wrote, is likewise a Jesus-like prophetic figure.[34]

Dylan's gesturing toward his prophetic status is not limited to his relationship to Christianity or to the 1979–81 period in which his Christian commitments were paramount within his music. Dylan sometimes has suggested a self-understanding of his vocation in terms of being specially called by God or other supernatural forces.[35] And while it is true that explicit affirmations of his prophetic role are quite uncommon, much more frequent are instances in Dylan's music in which he impersonates the Hebrew prophets by repeating, sometimes verbatim, words of the Bible.[36] Even Dylan's ostensible protestations against being understood as a prophet sometimes only further suggest this identity. Nowhere is this more apparent than in Dylan's apparent denial of his prophetic status in his 1962 song "Long Time Gone," which paradoxically employs a direct quote from the prophet Amos to make the point:

> But I know I ain't no prophet
> An' I ain't no prophet's son

The biblical passage—Amos 7:14—reads: "Then Amos answered and said to Amaziah, 'I was no prophet, nor a prophet's son, but I was a herdsman and a dresser of sycamore fig.'"

Indeed, in downplaying his prophetic role, Dylan in some sense is only repeating the customary posture of the Hebrew prophets, of whom Abraham

---

[33] Three examples of songs in which Dylan invites the Jesus comparison are: "Bob Dylan's 115th Dream," "Shelter from the Storm," and "Maybe Someday." See Gilmour, *Gospel According to Bob Dylan*, 58. With regard to Dylan's personal appearance, consider the fact that the televangelist Pat Robertson unwittingly made use of a Dylan photo because it looked to him like Jesus. Likewise, the Dylan commentator Michael Gray wrote of Dylan's 1976 television special "Hard Rain" that Dylan looked "extraordinarily Christ-like" and "uncannily like Jesus Christ." Gilmour, 22–23.

[34] Jack Fate is told by the character Tom Friend, "You're supposed to have all the answers." Gilmour, 25.

[35] As Dylan put it in 1975: "I didn't consciously pursue the Bob Dylan myth. It was given to me by God. Inspiration is what we're looking for. You just have to be receptive to it." Quoted in Gilmour, 29. Similarly, consider how he describes his coming into his vocation: "Destiny was about to manifest itself. I felt like it was looking right at me and nobody else." Dylan, *Chronicles*, 291.

[36] There are so many biblical quotes and allusions in Dylan's music that entire books have been written on the subject. See Bert Cartwright, *The Bible in the Lyrics of Bob Dylan*, rev. ed. (Fort Worth, TX: Wanted Man, 1992); Gilmour, *Tangled Up in the Bible*. Dylan's allusions to the prophet label include the song "I Feel a Change Comin' On," in which he sings "I got the blood of the land in my voice"—a reference, as Gilmour explains, to Ezekiel 7:23 ("The land is full of bloody crimes") and Psalm 106:38 ("The land was polluted with blood"), among other biblical sources. In the song "This Wheel's On Fire," Dylan likewise impersonates the prophet Ezekiel in his challenging of God. In "Someone's Got a Hold of My Heart," Dylan sings, "I can still hear the voice in the wilderness," referencing Isaiah 40:3.

Heschel observes, "None of the prophets seems enamored with being a prophet nor proud of his attainment."[37] And the figure of the reluctant prophet is in fact quite familiar within the biblical tradition, as reflected by Moses, Gideon, Jonah, and Jeremiah, among others.

In any case, it is not ultimately for a prophet to decide the matter of his or her prophetic status, since, sociologically speaking, it is the charismatic *relationship* between followers and the person being followed that is definitive. There can be no doubt, as studies of Dylan enthusiasts demonstrate, that followers of Dylan routinely understand him as more than an artist, their devotion to him as more than mere fandom, and their engagement with him as generating wisdom and life direction rather than mere aesthetic enjoyment.[38] Dylan's incredibly influential protest songs of the early 1960s galvanized a mass audience to awaken to the militarism, racism, corruption, and unjust poverty of their societies, thus placing Dylan's art within a long-standing tradition of secular jeremiads. Many activists credited Dylan with being absolutely instrumental in inspiring the civil rights movement of the 1960s.[39] In the time since the 1960s, countless individuals have upheld Dylan as a moral leader. To give but one prominent example, in 1974 Jimmy Carter celebrated Dylan as one of two sources (the other being Reinhold Niebuhr) who gave him an "understanding about what's right and wrong in this society" and quoted Dylan's song "It's Alright, Ma (I'm Only Bleeding)" in his acceptance

[37] Abraham Heschel, *The Prophets* (New York: HarperCollins, 1962), 20.

[38] See Gaines, *In Dylan Town*; Kinney, *The Dylanologists*.

[39] Joan Baez makes this claim in her interview in *American Masters*, "No Direction Home: Bob Dylan." Also, in her song "To Bobby," Baez retrospectively reflected on what she perceived to be Dylan's earlier leadership of social justice movements, pleading:

> You left us marching on the road
> And said how heavy was the load
> The years were young, the struggle barely at its start
> Won't you listen to the lambs, Bobby?
> They're crying for you
> Won't you listen to the lambs, Bobby?
> They're dying . . .
> No one could say it like you said it
> We'd only try and just forget it
> You stood alone upon the mountain till it was sinking
> In a frenzy we tried to reach you,
> With looks and letters we would beseech you
> Never knowing what, where or how you were thinking

From Anthony Scaduto, "Won't You Listen to the Lambs, Bob Dylan," *New York Times*, November 28, 1971. The recorded version of the song, from Baez's 1972 album, *Come from the Shadows*, has somewhat different lyrics.

speech upon being nominated for president at the 1976 Democratic National Convention.[40] More broadly, ethnographic studies of Dylan followers emphasize the quasi-religious aspect of the following he induces, finding extremely high numbers of Dylan fans who report that Dylan's music has influenced their lives to a significant extent. Perhaps fans of other musical groups would voice similar sentiments, but these studies also find that compared to these other groups Dylan fans report being uneasy with or even ashamed of the label "fan," an uneasiness that speaks, I think, to the moral seriousness that informs both Dylan's writing of his music and its reception by his followers.[41] For many Dylan followers, there is always something that gets beyond mere music, mere art, mere entertainment. Even those who have resisted Dylan's impact in popular culture, such as Cardinal Ratzinger (later Pope Benedict XVI), have invoked the prophet label in describing him.[42]

It is also misguided to insist too strongly on the division between musician and prophet in all cases, especially given the significant impact of religion on the historical development of rock and roll (and by extension those genres closely connected to rock, such as folk, blues, and, of course, gospel). As numerous studies have shown, there is a profound interconnection between rock and Christian religiosity.[43] Some of the very earliest usages of the term "rock

[40] Jimmy Carter, "Georgia Law Day Address," University of Georgia School of Law School, May 4, 1974, Athens, GA, https://www.americanrhetoric.com/speeches/jimmycarterlawday1974.htm; Carter, "Address Accepting the Presidential Nomination at the Democratic National Convention," July 15, 1976, New York, NY, https://www.presidency.ucsb.edu/documents/our-nations-past-and-future-address-accepting-the-presidential-nomination-the-democratic.

[41] Gaines, In Dylan Town, 17. To be sure, the unease of Dylan fans with the "fan" label also has been interpreted in a different light: as a tacit concern over the potential inappropriateness of such a high level of devotion.

[42] In 1997, Ratzinger opposed Dylan appearing at a concert for Pope John Paul II, questioning "whether it was right to bring in these kinds of 'prophets'" and insisting on how different the pope's message was from "the stars, Bob Dylan and others whose names I don't remember" who performed for the pope. Joseph Ratzinger, John Paul II: My Beloved Predecessor (Boston: Pauline Books and Media, 2007), 20. Pope John Paul was different, having no such qualms and even quoting Dylan's "Blowin' in the Wind" at the event "to roars from his young audience." John L. Allen Jr., "Foreword," in Ratzinger, John Paul II, xi. Pope John Paul told the audience of three hundred thousand assembled Catholics that the answer was indeed "in the wind," but not in the wind that blew things away—instead, "in the wind of the spirit" that would lead them to Christ. Philip Pullella, "Pope [Benedict] Opposed Bob Dylan Singing to John Paul in 1997," Reuters, March 8, 2007, https://www.reuters.com/article/us-pope-dylan/pope-opposed-bob-dylan-singing-to-john-paul-in-1997-idUSL08626 23620070308.

[43] Randall J. Stephens, The Devil's Music: How Christians Inspired, Condemned, and Embraced Rock 'n' Roll (Cambridge, MA: Harvard University Press, 2018); David Hajdu, "How Christianity Created Rock 'n' Roll," Public Books, June 21, 2018, https://www.publicbooks.org/how-christianity-created-rock-n-roll/. Also see Jonathan Cohen, "Rock as Religion," Intermountain West Journal of Religion 7, no. 1 (2016).

and roll," including the first recorded instance of the phrase in the song "The Camp Meeting Jubilee" (circa 1900), had a distinctly religious meaning.[44] Early developers of the rock genre self-consciously adapted the sounds, words, and sensibilities of gospel to a blues, soul, and ultimately rock idiom.[45] The physical choreography of the rock concert experience—the congregation of individuals in a single, receptive place, with the expectation of ecstatic inspiration—itself recalls the experience of church.

Beyond this, it is not just that there is a Christian prehistory to rock, but so many leading rock figures understand their music, and have had their music be understood, as a religious enterprise, whether of the traditional variety or in newly created forms. Consider these important examples:[46]

- Jimi Hendrix: "Rock music is more than music, it's like church"; "I used to go to Sunday School but the only thing I believe in now is music"; "The music is a spiritual thing of its own"; "We're making the music into electric church music, a new kind of bible you can carry in your hearts."
- Bruce Springsteen for a long time would open his concerts with: "Welcome to the first church of the rock, brothers and sisters." Springsteen also said of Elvis: "Elvis is my religion. But for him, I'd be selling encyclopedias right now."
- Robbie Krieger (guitarist for the Doors), referred to himself and his band members as "revivalists [who] wanted our audience to undergo a religious experience."
- Before his death, Muddy Waters acknowledged that the blues was his religion.
- Craig Chaquico (guitarist of Jefferson Airplane): "Rock concerts are the churches of today. Music puts them on a spiritual plane. All music is God."

---

[44] The song, which was recorded in numerous versions including by the Edison Male Quartet and the Columbia Quartette at the beginning of the twentieth century, includes the lyrics: "Keep on rockin' an' rolling in your arms / Rockin' an' rolling in your arms / Rockin' an' rolling in your arms / In the arms of Moses."

[45] To give but one important example of this phenomenon, consider what David Hajdu notes: "African American musicians of the mid-century such as Ray Charles explicitly brought sacred and secular music together by turning gospel songs into R&B numbers. Charles changed a word here and there, pushed the beat, and shifted the emotionality from reverential adoration to unfettered sensual euphoria. Charles took 'Talkin Bout Jesus' and produced 'Talkin Bout You'; he used 'This Little Light of Mine' to make 'This Little Girl of Mine'; and he adapted 'It Must Be Jesus' into 'I've Got a Woman' (working with cowriter Renald Richard). Charles took a jackhammer to the wall dividing the two worlds. . . . Sam Cooke, Lou Rawls, Mavis Staples, and other African American artists followed Charles's suit, calling the music that linked spirit and body *soul*." Hajdu, "How Christianity Created Rock 'n' Roll."

[46] Unless otherwise stated, these examples come from David Cloud, *Rock Music vs. The God of the Bible* (Port Huron, MI: Way of Life Literature, 2000), https://www.wayoflife.org/reports/rock_mu sic_as_religion.html.

- Paul Stanley (guitarist for KISS), describes his function as "a holy roller preacher" during concerts, adding: "I'm testifying and getting everybody riled up for the power of almighty rock 'n' roll."
- Judas Priest, in explaining the meaning of their album *Defenders of the Faith*, clarified, "We're defending the faith of heavy metal music," adding: "Heavy metal isn't just music to us. It's a philosophy and a way of life."
- Michael Jackson: "On many an occasion when I am dancing, I have felt touched by something sacred. In those moments, I felt my spirit soar, and become one with everything that exists."
- George Harrison: "Through the music you reach the spiritual. Music is very involved with the spiritual, as we know from the Hare Krishna mantra."
- Brian Jones of the Rolling Stones: "Music is my religion."
- In his song "You Can't Kill Rock & Roll," Ozzy Osbourne sings, "Rock 'n' roll is my religion and my law / Won't ever change."
- John Denver: "As a self-appointed messiah, I view music as far more than just entertainment."
- Brian Eno reports that for him the discovery of rock and roll was "a spiritual experience" and it formed the religious part of his life.
- Jerry Garcia: "On a certain level [the music is] a religion to me." Garcia's bandmate from the Grateful Dead, Phil Lesh, similarly stated: "We used to say that every place we played was a church."
- Sting: "The pure essence of music is very spiritual"; "My religion would be music, and I had just received my first sacrament [upon hearing the Beatles for the first time at age eleven]."
- Remembering Bob Marley's concerts, Judy Mowatt, one of his backup singers, recalls: "It was a crusade; it was a mission. We were like sentinels, like lights. On tour the shows were like church, Bob delivering the sermon. There were mixed emotions in the audience: you see people literally crying, people in a frenzy, on a spiritual high. . . . These concerts were powerful and highly spiritual. There was a power that pulled you there. It was a clean feeling. . . . For months and maybe years it stays with you."
- Bono: "I stopped going to churches and got myself into a different kind of religion. Don't laugh, that's what being in a rock 'n' roll band is, no pseudo-religion either."[47]

---

[47] Quoted in Gilmour, *Gospel According to Bob Dylan*, 47.

Dylan himself has voiced this kind of thinking, acknowledging on numerous occasions his own sacralization of music as well as his own tendency, at certain pronounced moments and periods, to treat other musicians in prophetic terms.[48]

There is debate about how seriously to take the spiritual significance of rock music and other musical forms within pop culture. On the one hand, numerous recent academic studies have made the case that, within secular modernity, religious energies are increasingly deployed in the ecstatic heeding of musical groups. On the basis of examination of the communities connected to the Grateful Dead, electronic dance music, heavy metal, and hip-hop, Robin Sylvan, for example, concludes: "I have come to understand just how profound and significant a religious phenomenon is taking place in these musical subcultures. . . . Traditional institutional religion has become increasingly irrelevant to many people [and] the sector of popular culture has become the new arena for their religious expression."[49] Don Saliers likewise argues, "We may find stronger prophetic texts and musical lines outside the churches than inside," advising that contemporary observers need to overcome traditional understandings of the sacred-profane divide and instead "attend to what can be called the 'sacrality' or even the 'sacramentality' of music wherever and whenever we are moved out of ourselves and our habitual, common-sense world."[50] On the other hand, some critics have questioned the spiritual significance of rock, insisting on the merely watered-down, pale, and indiscriminate aspects of the religiosity that persists within it.[51]

---

[48] On Dylan's sacralization of music, see section II.7. With regard to Dylan's treatment of other musicians in prophetic terms, I examine numerous examples of this in section II.5. But, in advance of that, consider what Dylan says of Frank Sinatra: "I could hear everything in his voice—death, God and the universe, everything" (quoted in Gilmour, *Gospel According to Bob Dylan*, 38); and, likewise, Dylan's claim that for him listening to Woody Guthrie's songs is "like getting new hope out of old religion" (Gilmour, 38).

[49] Robin Sylvan, *Traces of the Spirit: The Religious Dimensions of Popular Music* (New York: NYU Press, 2002), 78, 215; also see Gilmour, *Gospel According to Bob Dylan*, 7, 40–41, 43. As Gilmour observes: "Scholars are increasingly cognizant that popular culture not only includes religious content but in some sense functions as a rough equivalent to religious experience, providing audiences with a venue to explore and a shared vocabulary to articulate their own spirituality" (41).

[50] Don E. Saliers, *Music and Theology* (Nashville: Abingdon Press, 2007), ix, 60.

[51] Charles Taylor, for example, understands rock concerts as "festive" (in which "moments of fusion in common action/feeling . . . both wrench us out of the everyday . . . and seem to put us in touch with something exceptional beyond ourselves") but also as "plainly 'non-religious'"—or, as he also suggests, as religious in only a "functional" sense but not a "substantive" one. Rock concerts represent for Taylor a phenomenon in which "the (putatively) transcendent can erupt into our lives," though in a manner that still takes place within "immanent understandings of order." See Taylor, *A Secular Age* (Cambridge, MA: Belknap Press of Harvard University Press, 2007), 482–83, 517–18, 780–81. Bryan Turner similarly understands rock concerts as emblematic of an increasingly commodified "low intensity religion," which he defines as "forms of religiosity [that] are low on commitment, individualistic, and highly subjective. As such, these religious styles are distinctly post-institutional, and it is doubtful that they will have a lasting impact on social structure or culture." Turner, "Post-Secular

Such critics might not be wrong to insist on the enduring difference between the rigorous intellectual content of traditional organized religion and the less cognitive spirituality infused in so much of popular culture, but to deny wholesale the philosophical import of the latter on the basis of the alleged superiority of the former would be both anti-democratic[52] and blind to the reality that in at least certain cases, most notably Dylan's, popular culture has provided spiritual ideas and instruction no less rich, original, or arresting than more traditional sources. Indeed, one of Dylan's distinguishing prophetic features is that he channels what for many other artists is only an obscure and diffuse spirituality into more concentrated, concrete, and distinctive forms. From the very beginning of his time on the public stage, Dylan has been clear about his intention to communicate weighty matters through his songs and to strive for a moral and intellectual seriousness not typically found in pop music. As he once observed, "I'm not just singing to be singing. There's a much deeper reason for it than that."[53] Or, as he also put it in a somewhat rare moment of immodesty, "I don't think I'm gonna be really understood until maybe 100 years from now. What I've done, what I'm doing, nobody else does or has done."[54]

Another key sociological feature of Dylan's prophetic status—which also differentiates him from virtually all of his fellow rock musicians who themselves have prophetic elements—is that his credentials as a prophet have been intensely discussed, criticized, and debated throughout his more than six decades on the public stage. There always have been outsized controversies surrounding Dylan, including criticisms seeking to expose the supposed falsity of his prophetic pretensions and, in opposite fashion, criticisms highlighting his alleged

---

Society: Consumerism and the Democratization of Religion," in *The Post-Secular in Question: Religion in Contemporary Society*, ed. Philip Gorski, David Kyuman Kim, John Torpey, and Jonathan VanAntwerpen (New York: NYU Press, 2012), 138.

[52] Consider Kelton Cobb's statement that pop culture "has become, for most, the primary instrument for forging personal identity and probing the cosmos for meaning." Cobb, *The Blackwell Guide to Theology and Popular Culture* (Hoboken, NJ: Wiley-Blackwell, 2005), 291–92.

[53] Quoted in Al Aronowitz, "A Family Album," in *The Age of Rock: Sounds of the American Cultural Revolution*, ed. Jonathan Eisen (New York: Vintage, 1969), 194. See also similar comments from Dylan's Nobel Prize acceptance speech in which he explains that what separated him from most other pop musicians was that he possessed "principles and sensibilities and an informed view of the world," which he had learned in large measure from his education in literature from his school days and which "gave [me] a way of looking at life, an understanding of human nature, and a standard to measure things by. I took all that with me when I started composing lyrics. And the themes from those books worked their way into many of my songs, either knowingly or unintentionally. I wanted to write songs unlike anything anybody ever heard, and these themes were fundamental." Bob Dylan, *The Nobel Lecture* (New York: Simon & Schuster, 2017), 5–6.

[54] Jim Ellison, ed., "Jesus, Who's Got Time to Keep Up with the Times?" (interview with Mick Brown in the *Sunday Times*, July 1, 1984), in *Younger Than That Now: The Collected Interviews with Bob Dylan* (New York: Thunder's Mouth Press, 2004), 187.

irresponsibility in failing to maintain his authentic prophetic role. Examples of the first kind include the 1963 revelation that Dylan was not in fact a Guthrie-like rambler who, having long lost contact with his parents, arrived in New York City after years of Western adventure, but instead Robert Zimmerman from Minnesota, who had grown up in a comfortable, middle-class, Jewish house-hold; allegations of plagiarism; aggressive criticism of the alleged vacuity of his prose-poetry collection *Tarantula* (1966), his movie *Renaldo and Clara* (1978), and his albums from the mid-1980s; and more recent objections to his being awarded the 2016 Nobel Prize in Literature as well as his insouciant conduct upon receiving the award. Examples of the second kind include his going electric in 1965 and thus defying the expectations of a conventional, socially respon-sible folk singer; his related move away from blatantly political songs of social protest in the mid-1960s, which for many on the Left represented Dylan's ir-responsible disclaiming of his genuine prophetic leadership in the ongoing civil rights movement;[55] his mysterious motorcycle accident in 1966, which began an eight-year break from touring; the intense controversy surrounding his conversion to evangelical Christianity of the late 1970s, with some finding in his Christian music and public preaching a genuine prophetic calling and others stunned and disconcerted by what they considered his abandonment of the freethinking, skeptical, anti-authoritarian values he had so iconically embodied earlier in his life; and the mirror image of this controversy during his postconversion period beginning in the early 1980s, when he no longer ag-gressively communicated a Christian message. The point to emphasize is that Dylan continually has generated incredible debate about his prophetic status and that this distinguishes him from other rock musicians who have attracted a quasi-religious following. There is simply no equivalent kind of controversy and contestation surrounding other musical figures or pop-cultural luminaries more generally. At some level the intensity of debate about Dylan's prophetic credentials must be seen as further proof of them. Recall that the charismatic community essential for any sociologically meaningful prophetic relation consists not only of approving followers, but also of skeptics, critics, rivals, and combaters. Controversy over one's prophetic status is thus an indication of that status. After all, only those thought to be prophets are accused of being false ones. Dylan's song "False Prophet," from 2020, adds to the controversy with its

---

[55] Consider the so-called Dylan Liberation Front, founded by A. J. Weberman but including many others, devoted to bringing Dylan back into dependable leftist political activism and, more modestly, a slew of leading social justice activists—including Joan Baez, Irwin Silber, John Lennon, Pete Seeger, and numerous others—who sought to recover what they considered Dylan's vital posi-tion of leadership within the social justice movements of the 1960s. Recall Baez's pleas from the early 1970s: "Won't you listen to the lambs, Bobby? They're crying for you." See footnote 39.

recurring line "I ain't no false prophet," which can be read as an affirmation of his prophetic role or a disclaiming of it, but in either case helps keep alive his uncommonly intense association with prophecy within contemporary music.

To be sure, these criticisms and controversies will seem to be only a pale version of the debates in antiquity surrounding prophetic figures in the Judeo-Christian tradition, the political firestorms generated by well-recognized modern prophets of justice (such as Gandhi and King), or the severe conflicts produced by recent prophets claiming divine sanction but accused by others of being cult leaders (Jim Jones, David Koresh, Shoko Asahara, and Acharya Rajneesh, among others). But if we remain blind to the Dylan phenomenon because of its relative paleness, we not only miss out on a truly meaningful if subtle messenger but also fail to appreciate that it is this very paleness—a prophetic consciousness that does *not* entirely meet the traditional expectations of how a prophet behaves—that is part of Dylan's contribution to contemporary culture and the reimagination of the prophetic legacy.

In summary, the ostensibly superior accuracy of labeling Dylan a musician rather than a prophet is not compelling because he does label himself at important moments in prophetic terms, significant portions of Dylan's followers relate to him in this fashion as well, and the rock genre whose intellectual profundity Dylan helped to develop more than anyone else is so intertwined with both traditional religion and newer forms of spirituality that the label "leading rock musician," far from replacing the prophetic label, only recommends its appeal.

The Formalistic Aspects of Dylan's Prophetic Status

Appealing to Dylan's status as a leading figure within rock and roll to support his prophetic credentials leads directly to another objection I have introduced: given that there are many prominent rock musicians who have won a mass following from audiences who understand their devotion in quasi-religious terms, Dylan's prophetic status could be seen as genuine but not particularly interesting or special in itself. In other words, Dylan is one of a number of musicians who have inspired in their followers a religious-like devotion, including such others as Elvis, the Beatles, John Coltrane, Jimi Hendrix, David Bowie, Led Zeppelin, the Grateful Dead, Bob Marley, Michael Jackson, Madonna, Beyoncé, and Taylor Swift. In one sense, I accept this objection, to the extent that I agree that it would be fruitful, as already has been done in numerous cases, to pursue the prophetic dimensions of these individuals and groups as a window into the distinct spiritual conditions of contemporary society. Still, the problem with this objection, which would render Dylan one of many, is that Dylan—especially from a prophetic standpoint—is so singular and so profoundly influential within popular culture that it would be a serious misdiagnosis to treat him like all the rest, as if Shakespeare and Marlowe were of equivalent impact, or Isaiah and Habakkuk.

It might seem like the height of puerility to rank musicians—and I have little interest in doing that in a purely aesthetic sense, even if the sonic quality of Dylan's music has been an important source of his extraordinary appeal—but it is in fact a premise of my argument that Dylan is an unrivaled prophetic voice within popular music. This assertion must ultimately rest on the *substance* of Dylan's message, which the rest of this book is devoted to examining, but, in advance of that, it is also worth attending to various *formalistic* aspects that imbue Dylan's contribution with such heightened prophetic aspects.

Popular music usually includes at least three elements: the sound of the instruments, the voice of the singer, and the lyrics. Without denying the significance of the first of these, when it comes to prophecy, which is inherently verbal and oratorical, the second and especially third elements are most critical. Many of the other popular culture figures I have mentioned as being like Dylan in inspiring a religious-like following from their fans diverge from Dylan in having voices that—from a prophetic standpoint, at least—are relatively more muted, because they either largely do not write their own songs (Elvis) or do so in collaboration, thereby attenuating the singularity of their voice (Hunter/Garcia and Barlow/Weir in the case of the Grateful Dead; Page/Plant, often along with Bonham and Jones, in the case of Led Zeppelin), or have no words at all (Coltrane). Invoking the heightened singularity of Dylan's prophetic voice does not mean that Dylan's music or message has been uniform—as, perhaps more than any other singer, he has adopted a tremendous variety of musical genres, sounded his words in radically divergent ways, and communicated distinct if still complementary moral messages (indeed, this great variety is itself something that makes Dylan stand out from other rock stars)—only that, more than many other hugely popular musicians, this kaleidoscopic artistry has been communicated through the vessel of a single biographic persona.[56]

---

[56] In invoking Dylan's "single biographic persona," it might appear that I have foolishly violated one of the mainstays of responsible Dylan criticism, repeatedly emphasized by many of his most thoughtful interpreters: namely, to refuse to attribute a false singularity to the man. There are at least two reasons customarily put forward for this refusal. On the one hand, it is said that Dylan the artist ought to be seen not as singing from his own perspective, but rather as impersonating a variety of standpoints, not all of which are his own. This is something that Dylan himself has sometimes stressed. On the other hand, one of the allegedly central meanings of the Dylan phenomenon is the dissolution of a stable self, whether in the form of Dylan's constant reinvention or in the form of the mystery, multivocality, playfulness, and unknown meaning of his words. This focus on the dissolution of the Dylan persona is celebrated in Todd Haynes's film *I'm Not There* and encouraged by,

If the singularity of Dylan's prophetic voice sets him apart from artists whose prophetic voices are more dissipated or muted, it is the poetic depth and brilliance of that voice that sets him apart from other singer-songwriters of mass appeal who themselves communicate primarily as individuals. There are dozens of other singer-songwriters who have won sizeable followings from audiences relating to them in a quasi-religious and prophetic manner. But Dylan alone is widely hailed as the greatest songwriter in the English language, with his poetic achievement frequently compared to that of Homer or Shakespeare. Part of the reason Dylan stands out is that his fellow songwriters are among the most vociferous in acknowledging his stature.[57] Poetic singers who themselves have won religiously infused mass followings routinely hail Dylan, in Bruce Springsteen's words, as "the father of my country."[58] The Beatles, who rival Dylan in generating a religious-like mass following from musical poetry, saw him as a leader, with Paul McCartney saying, "He was our idol" and Ringo Starr similarly acknowledging, "Bob was our hero."[59] Jimi Hendrix, who himself excited such intense devotion, was obsessed with Dylan.[60] Neil Young considers Dylan "the greatest that ever lived in the singer/songwriter/poet vein."[61] Sam Cooke credited Dylan with changing popular singing to become more about the communication of truth and less about the prettiness of the

among other things, Dylan's confessed fascination and "identification" with Rimbaud's famous reflection "Je est un autre." However, I depart from these ways of thinking. My primary reasons for doing so are discussed in the Preface. Here I would add only that we engage with Dylan not just through his words but also through his voice, and this voice—despite its tremendous internal variety—adds a unity to his words. That is, we do not just read Dylan's words but also hear him sing and speak them to us through his singular bodily voice. Even if there is a variety of impersonations being communicated, the impersonator remains, in a very real and palpable sense, the same, and someone we can strive to know.

[57] In the words of T-Bone Burnett: "There is no way to accurately or adequately laud Bob Dylan. He is the Homer of our time." Van Morrison: "Dylan is the greatest living poet." According to Colin Larkin, an encyclopedist of popular music: "Bob Dylan is unquestionably the greatest musical poet of the twentieth century and certainly one of the most important figures in the entire history of popular music." All quoted in Gilmour, *Gospel According to Bob Dylan*, 24. George Harrison said of Dylan: "Five hundred years from now, looking back in history, I think he will still be the man. Bob, he just takes the cake." Quoted in Anthony DeCurtis, *In Other Words: Artists Talk about Life and Work* (Milwaukee: Hal Leonard, 2005), 69.

[58] Bruce Springsteen, *Born to Run* (New York: Simon & Shuster, 2016), 166.

[59] "The Beatles Talk about Bob Dylan," posted by Gaius Musonius, video, 2:08, December 10, 2011, https://www.youtube.com/watch?v=49b2hQuRQpU.

[60] Barney Hoskyns, "How Jimi Hendrix's Obsession with Bob Dylan Led Him to Woodstock," *Medium*, March 15, 2016, https://medium.com/cuepoint/how-jimi-hendrix-s-obsession-with-bob-dylan-led-him-to-woodstock-a2ce99dca0d6. Hoskyns quotes Hendrix: "Dylan really turned me on. Not the words or his guitar, but as a way to get myself together."

[61] Quoted in Gilmour, *Gospel According to Bob Dylan*, 24.

voice.[62] Sometimes the fascination is strained by the anxiety of influence. David Bowie, for instance, confessed to being "green with envy" about Dylan's far more prolific output, composing his 1971 "Song for Bob Dylan" that at once celebrates Dylan's words of "truthful vengeance" and Dylan's having "sat behind a million pair of eyes / And told them how they saw" yet also imagines that Bowie himself might fill a void created by Dylan's withdrawal from regular public performing at the time.[63] Likewise, the enormously popular, poetic, and also prophetic John Lennon repeatedly attempted to react to and resist Dylan—invoking Dylan's name as something to get beyond in his 1969 "Give Peace a Chance"; professing "I don't believe in Zimmerman" in his 1970 track "God"; and penning "Serve Yourself" in 1980 in response to Dylan's "Gotta Serve Somebody"—thus testifying to his sense of Dylan's towering importance, even as he aimed to critique and limit it.[64] Of course, Dylan has had his own powerful influences—such as Hank Williams, Woody Guthrie, Johnny Cash, Robert Johnson, and so many other figures from the blues, early rock, and gospel traditions, about whom he has written or spoken admiringly for decades[65]—but he also writes of overcoming hero worship of prior idols,[66] rarely treats his own contemporaries in prophetic terms (and when he does

[62] As Bono recounts: "When Sam Cooke played Dylan for the young Bobby Womack, Womack said he didn't understand it. Cooke explained that from now on, it's not going to be about how pretty the voice is. It's going to be about believing that the voice is telling the truth." Quoted in "100 Greatest Singers of All Time (2008)," *Rolling Stone*, December 3, 2010, https://www.rollingstone.com/music/music-lists/100-greatest-singers-of-all-time-147019/bob-dylan-29-226832/.

[63] "David Bowie Jealous of Bob Dylan!," posted by snapsnap, video, 1:24, August 4, 2011, https://www.youtube.com/watch?v=1S5zzDL8Eis. On Bowie understanding his "Song for Bob Dylan" as a declaration of his commitment to fill a "leadership void" created by Dylan's retreat from the music scene during the early 1970s, see Jack Whatley, "Three Times David Bowie Covered Bob Dylan Perfectly," *Far Out*, July 25, 2021, https://faroutmagazine.co.uk/three-times-david-bowie-covered-bob-dylan-perfectly/.

[64] See Scott Beauchamp and Alex Shephard, "Bob Dylan and John Lennon's Weird, One-Sided Relationship," *Atlantic*, September 24, 2012, https://www.theatlantic.com/entertainment/archive/2012/09/bob-dylan-and-john-lennons-weird-one-sided-relationship/262680/.

[65] See Dylan's half-hour speech upon receiving the 2015 Person of the Year award from MusiCares, which deals heavily with his prior influences, at "Read Bob Dylan's Complete, Riveting MusiCares Speech," *Rolling Stone*, February 9, 2015, https://www.rollingstone.com/music/music-news/read-bob-dylans-complete-riveting-musicares-speech-240728/.

[66] In "Poem to Joanie," Dylan recounts: "An' my first idol was Hank Williams / For he sang about the railroad lines / An the iron bars an' rattlin wheels / Left no doubt that they were real." But then he discusses overcoming all worship of human idols:

> In later times my idols fell
> For I learned that they were only men
> An' had reasons for their deeds
> 'f which weren't mine not mine at all

it is different[67]), and quite simply has exerted an unmatched and hugely asymmetrical impact on his fellow singer-songwriters. He is also the first musician to be inducted into the American Academy of Arts and Letters and the only (with the exception of the Indian poet Rabindranath Tagore) to be awarded the Nobel Prize in Literature, having also been awarded a Pulitzer Prize in 2008, ten Grammys, an Oscar, and a Presidential Medal of Freedom, among numerous other accolades.

As important as Dylan's superlative literary accomplishment is to my insistence that he be recognized as a unique cultural figure deserving close philosophical attention, this feature also forms the context for another kind of objection to my treatment of him in prophetic terms: namely, that Dylan's indisputably magisterial talent as a singer-songwriter means that he is best approached as a *poet* rather than as a prophet. As with the musician label, the poet label seems, at first, more accurate than prophet and also is a designation that Dylan himself is much more willing to embrace. Still, it would be a mistake to insist upon a sharp differentiation between poet and prophet, especially in Dylan's case. For one thing, the history of the prophetic tradition always has had a strong poetic element. In Greek and Latin, the languages in which the West's prophetic tradition came to be widely disseminated, the word for prophet could also mean poet: *prophetes* in Greek and *vates* in Latin. The Hebrew prophets, who represent the originary prophetic formulation in the West, were themselves poets of a certain kind. They engaged in song and employed various forms of literary devices such as alliteration and paronomasia, couplets with numerous forms of parallelism in their word units (synonymous, antithetic, synthetic, and climactic), rhythm, a stanzaic organization, metaphor, and other imagistic and imaginative tropes.[68] It is also relevant that the Hebrew prophets were performers who, in addition to the dramatic speech of the prophetic message itself, spoke on a public stage and

> An' no more on them could I depend
> But what I learned from each forgotten god
> Was that the battlefield was mine alone
> An' only I could cast me stone

Bob Dylan, "Poem to Joanie" (liner notes to *Joan Baez in Concert Part 2*, 1963). As published on the album the poem had no title, but subsequent publications refer to the title I use here.

[67] The few individuals whom Dylan credits with a kind of prophetic impact in his adult life are typically nameless or obscure, not famous musicians with worldwide followings. I pursue these in section II.5.

[68] See Barry L. Bandstra, *Reading the Old Testament: Introduction to the Hebrew Bible*, 4th ed. (Belmont, CA: Wadsworth Publishing, 2009), 377–81. As Kaplan puts it, "The Hebrew prophets are so closely related to poets that their compositions are filled with poetic productions of every variety, poetic in thought, in expression, in form, in diction, among which are some belonging to the best of which universal literature can boast." Jacob H. Kaplan, *Psychology of Prophecy: A Study of the Prophetic Mind as Manifested by the Hebrew Prophets* (Philadelphia: Julius H. Greenstone, 1908), 61.

sometimes engaged in a variety of other forms of public spectacle to win, maintain, and instruct audiences.[69] And beyond the specific practices of the prophets, the Judeo-Christian tradition repeatedly presents poetic song as intertwined with the reception of religious truth. David could treat the Torah as itself a set of songs: "Your statutes are my songs, no matter where I make my home."[70] The Zohar, a foundational work of Jewish mysticism, instructs that there are some spiritual doors that can be opened only through song, and it claims that the capacity to sing is itself a sign of the suitability for religious leadership.[71] As the Kabbalist Nachman of Breslov put it: "One who knows how to make songs . . . is the one who should pray at the head of the congregation."[72] And from its earliest beginnings, Christian worship has involved singing, as seen in the injunction from Ephesians 5:19: "Speak to one another with psalms, hymns, and spiritual songs. Sing and make music in your hearts to the Lord." Paul's epistles contain numerous references to hymns sung by early Christians.[73] And one of the earliest descriptions of the practices of the Christians, Pliny's letter to the Roman Emperor Trajan in 112 CE, emphasizes the important role played by the communal singing of hymns.[74]

From the other side, poetry often has been imbued with powerful prophetic elements, whether a visionary quality, reliance on the imperative mood, or instruction about the most profound matters of human existence on the basis of an authority that comes from nowhere but from the individual's own power of lucid expression and evocative imagery. For Homer, the poet is someone "who makes the gods speak."[75] Plato describes poets as "prophets of the Muses" and

[69] Terry Giles, "Prophets as Performers," *Bible Odyssey*, n.d., https://www.bibleodyssey.org/en/passages/related-articles/prophets-as-performers.

[70] Psalm 119:54.

[71] See, for example, *Midrash ha-Ne'lam*, Parashat Shemot, 2:18b, in *The Zohar, Volume 10*, trans. Nathan Wolski (Stanford, CA: Stanford University Press, 2016), 499–500; also see Pickering, *Bob Dylan Approximately*, 14.

[72] Quoted in Pickering, 56.

[73] Philippians 2:6–11; I Timothy 3:16; Ephesians 5:14; and Colossians 1:15–20. These references come from Diane Severance, "Sing and Make Melody to God," *Christianity.com*, May 3, 2010, https://www.christianity.com/church/church-history/timeline/1-300/sing-and-make-melody-to-god-11629579.html.

[74] Pliny comments that Christians "were in the habit of meeting on a certain fixed day before it was light, when they sang an anthem to Christ as God, and bound themselves by a solemn oath not to commit any wicked deed." Quoted in Severance, "Sing and Make Melody to God." Severance adds: "The early Christians often adopted Scriptures for songs—such as the song celebrating the crossing of the Red Sea (Exodus 15:1–18), the song of Moses (Deuteronomy 32:1–43), and Mary's song of praise (Luke 1:46–55). Nine such scriptural songs are Odes or Canticles important in Greek Orthodox worship to this day."

[75] Homer, *Odyssey*, 1.371; 9.4.

understands both poetry and prophecy as divinely inspired forms of mania.[76] The potential overlap between poetry and prophecy has been especially important to modern biblical scholarship, beginning perhaps with Robert Lowth's 1753 book, *Lectures on the Sacred Poetry of the Hebrews*, which may be the first work to explicitly attend to the poetic structure of the Old Testament and in any case helped inspire later generations of Romantic, Transcendentalist, and other modern literary figures to understand the biblical prophets primarily as poets who created the divinities later transformed by priests into rigid dogmas.[77] The practical impact of this scholarship has been not simply to appreciate the poetic aspects of biblical prophecy but to encourage modern poets to understand themselves as prophets of their own time—to see their vocation as "the prophet of the present age, the truth teller, the gospel maker, the primary witness for his [or her] time and place."[78] This self-understanding of the poet as a kind of prophet finds explicit articulation in many central nineteenth-century poets, including Blake, Shelley, Coleridge, Emerson (who described Martin Luther as "the prophet, the poet of his time and country"[79]), Thoreau, and Whitman, among others. Moreover, such thinking instills the poet with a special role to play within a modernist culture that understands itself as alienated from the theology and practices of organized religion, skeptical that reason or science by itself might provide ethical direction, and thus always at risk of spiritual deadness and disenchantment. Under such conditions, modern poetry has been celebrated as having a unique potency to rekindle an otherwise unavailable prophetic legacy, with human imagination conceived not just as a device for fancy, amusement, or ingenuity, but as an organ capable of transmitting authentic, religiously inflected, non-dogmatic truths. Along with other Romantics, Blake thus invokes "poetic genius" as a substitute for the insufficiencies of mere empiricism.[80] Shelley both makes the historical observation that "poets, according to the circumstances of the age and nation in which they appeared, were called, in the earlier epochs

---

[76] See Plato, *Phaedrus*, 262d.

[77] See George Shulman, *American Prophecy: Race and Redemption in American Political Culture* (Minneapolis: University of Minnesota Press, 2008), 2.

[78] Robert D. Richardson Jr., *Emerson: The Mind on Fire* (Berkeley: University of California Press, 1995), 12.

[79] Quoted in Richardson, 196; also see 246 for more on Emerson's conception of the confluence of poetry and prophecy.

[80] See William Blake, *There Is No Natural Religion* (1788), whose first principle is "That the Poetic Genius is the True Man, and that the Body or Outward Form of Man is derived from the Poetic Genius. Likewise that the Forms of all things are derived from their Genius, which by the Ancients was call'd an Angel and Spirit and Demon." Also relevant is the fifth principle: "The Religions of all Nations are derived from each Nation's different reception of the Poetic Genius, which is every where call'd the Spirit of Prophecy." In *Poetical Works of William Blake*, ed. John Sampson (Oxford: Oxford University Press, 1913), 427.

of the world, legislators or prophets" and appeals to the more general idea of poets as the "unacknowledged legislators of the world."[81] Whether the emphasis is on making prophecy more sober and believable to a skeptical consciousness by describing it as poetry or elevating the stature of the poet by insisting on the unique capacities of human imagination to inspire and instruct, the tradition of modern poetry—from the Romantics to the present—very often has been presented and received as channeling a spiritual profundity that previously in the West had been more completely monopolized by traditional religion. Perhaps the greatest expression of this notion comes from Wallace Stevens's "Final Soliloquy of the Interior Paramour," which asserts that "the world imagined is the highest good" and appeals to poetic imagination as a source of illumination ("Wrapped tightly round us, since we are poor, a warmth, / A light, a power, the miraculous influence") in an otherwise disenchanted world: "We say God and the imagination are one . . . / How high that highest candle lights the dark."[82]

Of course, some observers sensitive to the mutual imbrication of poetry and prophecy also have insisted on the enduring differences between them. The poet, according to this line of thinking, can be satisfied if the poem merely pleases an audience and is content to leave its meaning undetermined and up for interpretation, whereas the prophet wants much more clearly to instruct listeners and bring about a well-defined and urgently needed alteration in mindset and behavior. Further, if poetry can inspire and enliven without appeal to universal sources of value, prophecy invokes such sources—divinity, justice, freedom—as the animating purpose of prophetic communication. And finally, while poems can exist in the absence of recognition, it remains essential to any sociologically relevant conception of prophecy that the prophet receive a following.

These caveats are important reminders of why not all poetry will achieve the prophetic potential its modern celebrators have found in it, but they are not dispositive in the case of Dylan. With regard to the matter of generating a following, it is a striking feature of Dylan's poetic music that it has gained such an intense, large, and long-standing audience. While there are other musical artists who have amassed even larger audiences or sold more records (Elvis, Michael Jackson, Madonna, and Garth Brooks, among others[83]), and while there are recent poets

---

[81] Percy Bysshe Shelley, *A Defence of Poetry* (Portland, ME: T. B. Mosher, 1910), 11, 86. The philosopher and author William Godwin, Shelley's father-in-law, likely influenced Shelley in this regard, himself defining the poet as "the legislator of generations and the moral instructor of the world." Godwin, *The Life of Geoffrey Chaucer* (1803), 1.370, quoted in Janet Todd, *Death and the Maidens: Fanny Wollstonecraft and the Shelley Circle* (Berkeley, CA: Counterpoint, 2007), 116.

[82] Wallace Stevens, "Final Soliloquy of the Interior Paramour," in *The Collected Poems of Wallace Stevens* (New York: Vintage Books, 1982), 524.

[83] A recent list of the best-selling musicians of all time, based on their total certified album units sold in the United States according to the Recording Industry Association of America, placed Dylan

who have won just as much or more critical acclaim (Frost, Yeats, Pound, Eliot, Crane, Hughes, Moore, Stevens, Auden, Bishop), there is no one alive who comes anywhere close to Dylan in combining mass appeal with literary acclaim.[84] A cursory Google analytics search suggests that Dylan has achieved 1.34 times the name recognition of *all ten of the modernist poets just named combined*.[85] This may be partially due both to the musical vehicle in which Dylan's poetry is communicated and to the historical accident that it has taken place in an unprecedented technological moment enabling radically expanded possibilities for recording and dissemination, but the fact remains the same: no poet of Dylan's caliber ever has reached more people in his or her lifetime, whether in absolute or percentage terms. This circumstance is both remarkable in itself and one important factor for understanding, in Dylan's case at least, the prophet and poet labels as being unified. It is also a reminder of the democratic aspect of Dylan's art, which is transmitted in the vernacular of everyday speech, often including the idioms of poor and unschooled rural America, and thus almost entirely bereft of sesquipedalian or obscure words.

With regard to the difference that prophets seek clear instruction (whereas poets are content to leave their works open-ended) through appeal to some allegedly universal source of moral authority (to which poets are not necessarily beholden), again this difference applies in many cases, but not to Dylan, for whom, as the rest of this book will explain, questions of ethics, justice, and divine obligation remain paramount, though admittedly not omnipresent, concerns. But even on the formalistic level, Dylan's deep immersion in the biblical legacy of Judeo-Christianity makes it unpersuasive to see him as engaged in a poetry divorced from prophecy. Dylan's relation to this legacy is complex given that his gospel period is only one era within a much longer, indeed lifelong, engagement with the Bible. Multiple books have been written with the aim of identifying the tremendous number of biblical allusions and quotations that recur throughout Dylan's work, often with the aim of distinguishing different roles the Bible has played for Dylan over the many decades of his musical career. Bert Cartwright's study—which differentiates five such functions—is exceptionally perceptive.[86] I think R. Clifton Spargo and Anne Ream are correct when they comment: "Even

---

at number 47. See Travis Clark, "The 50 Best-Selling Music Artists of All Time," *Business Insider*, March 9, 2022, https://www.businessinsider.com/best-selling-music-artists-of-all-time-2016-9. Of course, record sales are but one metric of mass appeal.

[84] For instance, an informal Google search reveals that Dylan's recognition is equivalent to that of the fifteen other most recent Nobel laureates for literature *combined* (as of December 19, 2022).

[85] There are 47 million web pages for Dylan versus 35 million for the others combined (as of July 9, 2019).

[86] Cartwright, *The Bible in the Lyrics of Bob Dylan*; also see the comprehensive work by Gilmour, *Tangled Up in the Bible*.

without the rebirth of 1979, Jewish and Christian idioms persist in his work to such a degree that Dylan would have to be reckoned one of the most powerful interpreters of religious language and sensibility in all of American pop culture."[87] As Christopher Ricks, one of the most influential recent commentators on Dylan, has put it, "Dylan not only opens his Bible; he opens up its radiations and its revelations."[88] Dylan's poetry is thus prophetic not simply in the way modern poets have conceived of it (understanding human imagination itself as a prophetic vehicle that might take the place of a fragmented and no longer authoritative body of traditional religious teachings and concepts), but also for engaging with many of the traditional teachings and ideas of organized religion. Of course, mere biblical allusion, even if incredibly extensive, is by itself only enough to produce the form of prophetic speech, not specifically meaningful content, but this formalistic element nonetheless sets Dylan apart and, as I aim to show, is often complemented by a substantive reworking of crucial ideas from the biblical tradition.

Another formalistic feature of Dylan's prophetic status—and one further differentiating him from other leading modern poets—is that in experiencing Dylan we relate not only to his words but also to the voice that transmits them. With very few exceptions, Dylan followers strongly prefer songs sung by Dylan himself rather than covers of his songs. As a side note, it should be mentioned that, outside of the Beatles, Duke Ellington, and Bing Crosby, Dylan is the most covered artist of all time.[89] Here I do not mean to get caught up in analysis and debate about the merits of Dylan's utterly distinct singing voice, with its signature phrasings, remarkable diversity of sounds over the years, and exceedingly difficult-to-describe tonal qualities. To be sure, both those who love Dylan and those who do not often cite his voice as a reason why. The point I want to make, though, is that the widespread desire of his followers to hear Dylan himself transmitting his words is part of what contributes to the prophetic aspect of his poetry. This preference reminds us that, with Dylan, what is at stake is not only the message but the man—or, better, that the man is intrinsic to the message. This interweaving of the individuality of the speaker with the content of what is spoken is definitive of prophets, whose contribution cannot be limited to their words but also involves their personal delivery of them. Of course, prophets who no longer are living can only be accessed through their words—at

---

[87] R. Clifton Spargo and Anne K. Ream, "Bob Dylan and Religion," in *Cambridge Companion to Bob Dylan*, ed. Kevin J. H. Dettmar (Cambridge, UK: Cambridge University Press, 2009), 98; also see Gilmour, *Gospel According to Bob Dylan*, 41.

[88] Christopher Ricks, *Dylan's Visions of Sin* (New York: HarperCollins, 2004), 210–11.

[89] Sam Gupton, "The Most Covered Artists of All Time," *24/7 Wall St.*, December 8, 2021, https://247wallst.com/special-report/2021/12/08/most-covered-artists/11/.

least before the invention of audio-visual recording technology. But the most active, animated, raw, and vital form of prophecy is inseparable from concrete performance, and virtually all of the prophets who are still remembered long after their deaths appear to have had followings grounded in the actual utterances of their words rather than in their words alone. In truth, most prophets—and certainly Dylan—have fascinated followers from both directions, sometimes on the basis of magnificently lucid and arresting speech and other times on the basis of a purely personal authority that precedes whatever words are spoken. The more amazing words a person utters, the more likely we are to take heed of whatever he or she says next. In any case, whereas successful poetry does not require the public expression of the poet's spoken voice, successful prophecy almost always does. The fixation of Dylan onlookers on the particular sonority of his voice is not simply an aesthetic preference, but a reminder that the Dylan phenomenon cannot be reduced to the power of poetry, as it involves, just as much, the perceived potency of Dylan's individuality as communicated through his singular voice.

There are numerous other formalistic features of Dylan's music that lend it a strongly prophetic quality, including its use of archaic language that seems to come from another (or timeless) time;[90] the epigrammatic structure it frequently employs (which is closely connected to Dylan's use of the imperative mood); and Dylan's often contestatory relationship with his listeners, which stems in part from Dylan *not* wanting to have an overly friendly connection with them and not wanting them to sing along.[91]

In short, Dylan's prophetic status does not stem merely from his being *any* rock star who, as such, engages with the inchoate spirituality of the concert phenomenon and channels the vestigial religiosity rock music inherits from its Christian prehistory. Dylan—formalistically speaking—is special and goes beyond this because of the singularity of his prophetic voice, the intense poetic quality that even his fellow musicians recognize separates him from themselves, and the way in which this poetic quality is itself a prophetic vehicle for Dylan, due not simply to the tremendous following it has inspired but to its infusion with religious language, constant biblical allusion and direct citation, and the fire of ethical exhortation.

---

[90] This feature is pursued by Andrew Muir in his recent book, *The True Performing of It: Bob Dylan and William Shakespeare* (Providence, RI: Red Planet, 2018).

[91] In an interview from 2007, Dylan comments: "To me, the relationship between performer and audience is anything but a buddy-buddy thing, any more than me going in and admiring a Van Gogh painting and thinking me and him are on the same level." Jann S. Werner, "Bob Dylan Hits the Big Themes, from Religion to the Atomic Age," *Rolling Stone*, May 11, 2011 (transcribed from 2007 interview), https://www.rollingstone.com/feature/bob-dylan-hits-the-big-themes-from-religion-to-the-atomic-age-242544/amp/.

The Substantive Features of Dylan's Prophetic Status

There is still a lingering objection to my account of Dylan as a prophet. On the one hand, it might be claimed that while the sociological and formalistic aspects of Dylan's prophetic art are real, they are woefully indeterminate. Such a critique accepts that rock music in general and specific artists in particular are indeed capable of generating a vague spiritual sense among their audiences, but still insists that this tells us little about any kind of concrete message being communicated, as one might expect from a prophet. This nondescript form of spirituality—which perhaps is its usual modality in musical artists who excite religious-like devotion[92]—is reason to be suspicious of such artists as anything more than superficially prophetic. In the case of Dylan, this criticism would go: even if his poetry is profound and Bible-laden, and even if his following large, this does not by itself reveal anything about the specific *meaning* of his alleged prophetic status within contemporary culture. On the other hand, a very different if ultimately parallel critique holds that Dylan is not, after all, that distinct, even if he is a musical prophet, since there are numerous other prophets, musical or otherwise, in our midst. There are, for instance, numerous individuals and groups that communicate a musically infused religious message, such as the now large set of Christian rock artists, Cat Stevens and other explicitly Islamic rock musicians, and Rastafarian artists. Bob Marley, in particular, not only sings as a kind of Rastafarian prophet but also can be seen as a prophet of justice. And then there are non-musical prophets who continue to lead movements for social justice, religious devotion, and so on. In other words, this second form of the critique holds that, since there already are many prophets in contemporary times, there is reason to question any claim of Dylan's special noteworthiness. Both forms of critique ultimately depend on the same issue: that the *content* of Dylan's prophetic art is either missing or simply a weak, unoriginal version of something with which we already are familiar.

Against this line of criticism I will argue in the remainder of this book that Dylan does offer a distinct prophetic message—or set of messages—best summarized through conceptualizing his prophetic achievement as his being a *prophet without God.*

---

[92] Susan Fast's comment about Led Zeppelin—that they exude an "undefined (or at least underdefined and therefore interpretatively open) spirituality"—applies, I think, to most musical artists who have attracted a quasi-religious following. Fast, *In the Houses of the Holy: Led Zeppelin and the Power of Rock Music* (New York: Oxford University Press, 2001), 60.

The most basic meaning of labeling Dylan a prophet without God is to differentiate him from the usual conception of the prophet, namely *a prophet of salvation*, who transmits a singular, steady, and coherent message about what should
be done and how one ought to live. Typically, prophets of salvation have drawn
from three sources of normative authority: the call of God, the demands of justice, or the obligation to live as a free individual. Probably the most common
tendency of prophets of salvation is to appeal to these three normative grounds
simultaneously on the assumption that all three are harmonious in dictating the
same singular cause of action and way of life. It was typical among the Hebrew
prophets, for instance, to link adherence to God with the performance of justice
in the political realm as well as with the promise that devotion to God/justice
would redound to the flourishing, if not the freedom, of individual followers. In
a very different way, a similar harmoniousness informs the prophetic writings
of certain prophets of freedom, such as Emerson, who, even if he seems to emphasize self-reliance (the free use of one's individuality) as the most central ethical message, consistently equates self-reliance with what he calls God-reliance
(the alleged divinity within) and links both to the expectation of unprecedented
social justice in the New World. More recently, two immensely influential
prophets of justice from the twentieth century, Gandhi and King, themselves
suggest a harmony between the grounds of normative authority. For Gandhi,
the political and social movements he led not only reflected a concern for civil
rights, self-determination, and peace, but were inextricably linked to divine adherence and the promise of a freedom (*swaraj*) that included personal and not
just political elements.[93] Similarly, King led his followers in the name of social
justice causes (against racism, militarism, and poverty), yet did so explicitly
informed by a religious faith in divine providence and, as with Gandhi, by the
expectation that freedom would mean not just the emancipation of oppressed
groups but enhanced personal liberty for all members of society.[94] To be sure,
it is also possible for prophets of salvation to insist upon an unbridgeable divergence between the sources of normative authority, as happens when one
fount of normative direction is privileged *at the expense of* the other two. The
paradigm case of upholding adherence to God over and against adherence to

[93] In regard to divine adherence, consider that Gandhi's seven rules "essential for every Satyagrahi
in India" has as its first requirement that a Satyagrahi "must have a living faith in God." Mahatma
Gandhi, "Qualifications for Satyagraha," *Young India*, August 8, 1929.

[94] As King put it in his "I Have a Dream" speech: "The marvelous new militancy which has
engulfed the Negro community must not lead us to a distrust of all white people, for many of our
white brothers, as evidenced by their presence here today, have come to realize that their destiny is
tied up with our destiny. They have come to realize that their freedom is inextricably bound to our
freedom. We cannot walk alone." Martin Luther King Jr., *A Testament of Hope: The Essential Writings
and Speeches*, ed. James M. Washington (New York: HarperCollins, 1986 [1963]), 218.

justice and individuality is Abraham's heeding of the call of God to sacrifice his son Isaac, since this sacrifice violates any imaginable standard of justice and morality as well as any conception of Abraham's flourishing, let alone freedom, as an individual. In parallel fashion, it is possible to read Lincoln's Second Inaugural Address, delivered near the conclusion of the American Civil War, as upholding justice (the need to end slavery and more fully realize the ideals of free and equal citizenship) over and against the claims of divinity (which Lincoln subtly suggests might not exist or, if it does, might not have a side in the Civil War) and also at the expense of the individuals fated to fight and die in the struggle.[95] Likewise, Nietzsche's call for free spirits to commit themselves to individual self-creation—in a manner that necessarily transgresses conventional moral norms (operating beyond good and evil) and that accepts that God is dead— propounds an individualism aggressively decoupled from both justice and religious piety. Yet, despite this difference among prophets of salvation—those who understand all three sources of normative authority as working in harmony with each other versus those who emphasize one source at the expense of the others—all prophets of salvation come forward with a singular message: an ultimate answer regarding the nature of our obligations and, accordingly, the question of how to live.

[95] Lincoln refers to, yet at the same time differentiates his prophetic message from, a religious perspective according to which justice is a duty following from a more fundamental commitment to God. For one thing, Lincoln raises the problem of the ultimate inscrutability of God. Both sides of the war appealed to God, Lincoln admits, and perhaps the slaveholding South was not wrong in doing so, since "the Almighty has His own purposes." Ultimately, the injustice of slavery is something "we shall suppose" rather than a message from on high. Further, Lincoln also subtly raises the possibility that God does not exist or that God is not interested in justice. In referencing the possibility that slavery might be "an offense" that entered into the world through God's providence—an offense that God now requires to be extirpated—Lincoln asks, "Shall we discern therein any departure from those divine attributes which the believers in a living God always ascribe to Him?" Not only is this posed as a question (so that the answer might be that such a circumstance refutes the existence of God), but "the believers in a living God" are presented as external to Lincoln and are thus not presumed to represent Lincoln's own perspective or the perspective of all the hearers of his address. Moreover, Lincoln also differentiates his prophecy of justice from any simplistic notion that the pursuit of justice will immediately redound to the personal benefit of the individuals who seek it. On the contrary, as much as Lincoln hopes for peace and prosperity, his speech announces his willingness for the American people to suffer as long as is necessary to end slavery and undo its awful legacy, even if this were to mean hardship persisting "until all the wealth piled by the bondsman's two hundred and fifty years of unrequited toil shall be sunk, and until every drop of blood drawn with the lash shall be paid by another drawn with the sword." Lincoln, then, is an authentic prophet of justice in the pure sense, not because he makes no reference to God or individual selfhood, but because these are demoted within his prophetic message, whose foundation is the secular commitment to struggle for justice in this world.

Dylan, as a prophet of diremption rather than a prophet of salvation, is different. He takes seriously the threefold sources of normativity—singing powerfully about God, justice, and individual freedom—yet, for him, these sources do not coalesce but conflict. Still, in testifying to these conflicts, Dylan does something more than simply diagnose our diffidence and reflect back to us our own sense of not having figured out fundamental questions. He does something more than take up the prophetic mantle with less dogmatism, incautiousness, and spiritual pride—and more incessant searching, humility, and self-effacement—than is commonly the case. Dylan makes the very conflicts between the grounds of normative authority ethically meaningful. He does not provide ultimate moral and spiritual direction in the manner of a prophet of salvation, but the very conflicts he discloses that make this ultimate wisdom impossible or otherwise unavailable also allow him to make pointed, distinct, consequential interventions into ongoing political and ethical debates. In the pages that follow, I elucidate three overarching contributions in this regard.

In Part I, I examine the conflict between individual freedom and justice. Although Dylan was hailed in the 1960s as an inspirer of social justice movements and an icon of self-reliant individuality, his most distinct prophetic gesture in this period was to testify, at the very height of the civil rights movement, that for him these two ends—devotion to social justice and devotion to being a free individual—are in insoluble conflict, with one coming at the expense of the other. Dylan does not ultimately teach whether to choose individual freedom or social justice, but he does inspire those who themselves embody this conflict— the bourgeois—to achieve self-consciousness and to practice individual self-reliance without the self-satisfaction, triumphalism, and complacency that typically have accompanied it.

In Part II, I confront another conflict central to Dylan's status as a prophet of diremption, the conflict between individuality and divinity. Dylan can never settle upon an answer about whether it is consistent with the skeptical consciousness of a freethinking individual to seek and find religious faith. Whether Dylan's Christian conversion and public embrace of evangelical Christianity during the 1979–81 period was a repudiation of his prior individualism or instead proof that a freethinking individual could find God remains, in the final analysis, unclear. But this very unclarity—combined with the short-lived nature of Dylan's gospel period and the fact that even at its height Dylan contemplated the illusoriness of his newfound religiosity—means that he, far from unifying the claims of individual freedom and religious piety, demonstrates his inability to settle on a clear relationship between the two (as the question of whether they are ultimately harmonizable—and, if not, which side is to be privileged— remains unanswered in any kind of stable way). Yet, even if Dylan does not solve the problem of whether a freethinking individual should accept or reject the idea of God—even if he can only represent but not finally unify the two poles of contemporary culture wars surrounding religion—he can at least suggest that each of us has the capacity to go either way. He does not provide a stable message about what kind of religious faith to adopt or whether to adopt one, but an abiding ethical meaning of his spiritual meandering is that it gives prophetic voice to what so far has been a merely philosophical notion: the *postsecular* idea that both religion and non-religion are coequal alternatives, neither of which is natural, modern, or better than the other. Dylan's most distinct prophetic function is not to convert the non-religious to God, though this sometimes has been reported, but to discipline the non-religious in their very non-religiosity not to see atheism as superior. Dylan achieves this not through dispassionate argumentation in the manner of a philosopher but through personal testimony to his own abiding religious sense, which demonstrates that the respect of the non-religious for religiosity is properly grounded not in generosity or tolerance toward some radical *other* but rather in the ever-present possibility for religiosity all of us possess, even if only some actualize.

In Part III, I confront yet another conflict between the traditional sources of normative authority that gets channeled within Dylan's prophetic consciousness: the conflict between justice and God. Rather than affirm a divine providence that might undergird the ultimate attainment of justice in the sublunary world, Dylan—in contradistinction to dominant trends in philosophy and the broader culture—contemplates that the so-called arc of the moral universe either does not exist or bends toward injustice; predicts that the world forever will be mired in violence, oppression, and plutocracy; and thus asserts that only partial and local acts of repair are possible, not overarching progress. Dylan's pessimism is close to the tradition of political realism—exemplified by such figures as Thucydides, Machiavelli, Clausewitz, Weber, Morgenthau, and Kissinger—which itself sees the world as permanently fallen. Yet here, too, Dylan offers a distinct message. While familiar as a reader with numerous canonical political realists, he articulates a political realism that is distinct in being targeted toward ordinary people rather than elite statesmen.[96] Its message is not the traditional realist concern with how to achieve political mastery in a permanently fallen world, but rather a call to "wake up and strengthen the things that remain." Specifically, Dylan imbues his pessimism with distinctive prophetic meaning when it leads him to indict more conventional understandings of political responsibility for failing to focus on basic needs like the alleviation of hunger; when he implicitly attacks the spirit of grandiosity that has informed the tradition of political

[96] Dylan discusses his reading of Thucydides and Clausewitz, for instance, in *Chronicles*, 36–37, 41, 45.

realism; when he testifies to a sense of futility regarding many of the world's problems yet also to how resignation can be a strategy of resistance and something conducive to the focus on small-scale, local improvements; and when he reverses the traditional paradox of the realists (that evil can be done for the sake of good) to alert ordinary citizens to how their own seeming innocence can deafen them to the call to address the sea of suffering that surrounds anyone fortunate enough to have avoided it. If the very idea of strengthening the things that remain has a theological provenance (Revelation 3:2), Dylan adapts the notion so that it is chiefly a political idea, at once summarizing a pessimistic account of the world and, over and against more familiar realist and idealistic perspectives alike, suggesting a distinctive ethics for ordinary individuals who accept that the world never will be properly fixed or sufficiently managed.

In each of these three conflicts, Dylan does not provide a message of salvation. He does not teach how all might be able to live in conditions of freedom. He does not instruct about how to achieve the everlasting grace of God. He offers no solution about how to redeem the world. More generally, he does not single out a particular basis of normative authority—individual freedom, justice, or God—that should be followed at the expense of the other two, nor does he suggest that all three bases might be pursued simultaneously and harmoniously. To be sure, Dylan's prophetic message *is* centrally informed by these three normative foundations, oscillating between ever-evolving considerations and combinations of what they might entail. He does not abandon the foundations that have informed the prophetic consciousness but continually explores and probes them. Still, if a prophet of salvation gives you an answer, a prophet of diremption such as Dylan explains to you why you may be spiritually and ethically confused, why you have not mastered the art of how to live, why your search for instruction is ongoing rather than accomplished. But the same conflicts that prevent a message of salvation also provide the setting for an alternate, more modest, yet still sharp and distinctive set of ethical teachings: the call for those who practice self-reliance to do so stripped of self-satisfaction, the call to achieve a postsecular mindset, and the call to practice a political realism that might have primary meaning for the relatively powerless rather than the specially empowered.

Part I

A Rebel Rebelling against the Rebellion

There have been prophets of social justice and prophets of individual freedom, but what distinguishes Dylan is that he sings to both commitments and, even more, suggests that there is a tragic choice between them. However much the poetic majesty of Dylan's songs of political protest may have helped to inspire the social justice movements of the 1960s, and however much Dylan's words, actions, and image rightly have made him an icon of self-reliant individuality, he is at his most prophetically distinct when he testifies to the collision between these two commitments and derives from this collision, if not a clear message about which way to go, at least a teaching about how to turn one's back on justice should one's individuality lead one to do so: without the self-satisfaction, triumphalism, and other forms of complacency that typically have surrounded the ideology of self-reliance.

This tension between social justice and self-reliance is at its height when Dylan declares, in both public statements and remarkable songs from the mid-1960s, that he cannot be a reliable activist in the service of social justice causes—not because he disagrees with the goals of such movements but because they impose a sacrifice of his individuality, of his independence of mind and spirit, that he is unwilling to make. Consider what Dylan proclaims in 1964 about the ongoing civil rights movement that he himself had participated in so visibly and, in the eyes of many, had brilliantly anthemized in numerous songs from the early 1960s:

> I agree with everything that's happening but I'm not part of no Movement. If I was, I wouldn't be able to do anything else but be in

Bob Dylan. Jeffrey Edward Green, Oxford University Press. © Oxford University Press 2024.
DOI: 10.1093/oso/9780197651742.003.0002

"the Movement." I just can't have people sit around and make rules for me. I do a lot of things no Movement would allow.[1]

This is not the perspective of someone who thinks the world is just as it is or who debates the urgency of progressive movements from some vantage point— libertarian, market-utopian, anarchist—that might call into question the importance of taking immediate social responsibility for others. Nor is Dylan's "agreement" with the civil rights movement merely rhetorical, as in the years before 1964 he authored and sang approximately thirty songs indicting society for its racism, militarism, and unacceptable levels of poverty and inequality; played prominent roles in protest rallies (such as the July 1963 rally in Greenwood, Mississippi, following the assassination of Medgar Evers and the November 1963 March on Washington for Jobs and Freedom); refused to appear on a national television program when network executives requested that he not perform his song mocking anti-communist paranoia; and attended numerous meetings with activists from Students for a Democratic Society (SDS), the Student Nonviolent Coordinating Committee (SNCC), and other leftist organizations. Yet Dylan's eloquence in support of civil rights came to be matched by a no less stunning set of works (such as "My Back Pages," "Restless Farewell," "To Ramona," "Chimes of Freedom," "It's Alright, Ma (I'm Only Bleeding)," and "Maggie's Farm") as well as public statements (most notably his speech upon receiving the 1963 Tom Paine Award from the Emergency Civil Liberties Committee, or ECLC) that announce his refusal to be a dependable political agent. Here we find Dylan in the mode of protest against protest or, as his musical collaborator Robbie Robertson expertly described him, as a "rebel rebelling against the rebellion."[2]

It needs to be emphasized how unusual this posture is as an explicitly stated position. There are only two figures of whom I am aware who are truly comparable to Dylan in testifying to the tension between self-reliant individuality and social justice obligation—Emerson and Thoreau—and even here, as I will elucidate, Dylan departs from their understanding of this tension in crucial respects. Samuel Johnson's striking quip about the limits of politics, "How small of all that human hearts endure / That part which laws or kings can cause or cure," decenters the political but does not address the problem—crucial to Emerson, Thoreau, and Dylan—that an individual may be unwilling to fulfill otherwise valid civic and moral duties out of a competing concern with maintaining a

---

[1] Quoted in Jonathan Cott, ed., "'The Crackin', Shakin', Breakin' Sounds,' by Nat Hentoff, *New Yorker*, October 24, 1964," in *Bob Dylan: The Essential Interviews* (New York: Simon & Schuster, 2017), 28.

[2] Robbie Robertson, "Bob Dylan," *Rolling Stone*, December 3, 2010, https://www.rollingstone.com/music/music-lists/100-greatest-artists-147446/bob-dylan-10-31068/.

sense of self-reliant individual freedom.[3] Oscar Wilde perhaps gives a nod to this problem with the remark commonly attributed to him that "the trouble with socialism is that it takes too many evenings," but Wilde's much more frequent position, to the extent he treated politics at all, was to defend and support a libertarian-anarchist variant of socialism that, in a utopian spirit, he believed would solve major social problems and thus free individuals from the need to attend to the unjust suffering of others.[4] Dylan has no such futural anticipation of a time when, for him or those like him, duty to self and duty to others will be harmonized. He testifies, then, not to the resolution of competing ethical duties in a better-organized future world, but to the permanent moral chaos of the present, in which individuals such as himself will routinely turn their backs on causes they otherwise recognize as just out of a competing commitment to their own freedom. Our literary and political tradition is simply bereft of this kind of testimony. Recent trends in political philosophy may gesture in this direction but here, too, as I will explain, Dylan is importantly different.

Yet, paradoxically, what also makes Dylan's protest against protest—his rebellion against rebellion—significant is that, even if this posture rarely has been expressed, it is still one in which many of us are likely to recognize ourselves. Who feels they satisfactorily have performed their moral duties to others and been appropriately vigilant in the fight against injustice? This problematic might not apply to everyone. But we who are *bourgeois*, even if we do not realize it, are ourselves rebels rebelling against the rebellion: we embrace the principles of equality and freedom for all, and we support institutions that partially realize these principles to some meaningful degree, but, in preferring our comfort and privilege and personal time over and against *what our own sense of moral obligation* tells us we ought to do to more fully realize such principles, our commitment to individuality exposes the limits of our commitment to social justice. Dylan thus mirrors a stance many of us will recognize in ourselves, even if we have not proclaimed it, nor understood its precise logic and grounds, nor probed its ethical consequences with as much perspicacity and courage as Dylan. Here Dylan's self-awareness becomes our own.

In what follows, I elaborate these claims. Section I.1 examines the profound ethical ambiguity that characterizes Dylan's understanding of his withdrawal from dependable political activism in the mid-1960s. I then characterize Dylan's

---

[3] Samuel Johnson, lines added to Oliver Goldsmith's *The Traveller* (1764), l. 429.

[4] See Oscar Wilde's essay, "The Soul of Man under Socialism," in *The Soul of Man under Socialism and Selected Critical Prose*, ed. Linda Dowling (London: Penguin, 2001 [1891]), 127: "The chief advantage that would result from the establishment of Socialism is, undoubtedly, the fact that Socialism would relieve us from that sordid necessity of living for others which, in the present condition of things, presses so hardly upon almost everybody."

testimony in this regard as bourgeois (section I.2), arguing that this posture is significant because it illuminates a situation that is pervasive if usually unacknowledged (section I.3) and, furthermore, because the precise terms of Dylan's testimony diverge from the leading discourses by which contemporary political philosophy has attempted to make sense of the tension between self-focused and other-directed obligations (section I.4). The remainder of Part I addresses the ethical implications of Dylan's confessed inability to harmonize his dual commitments to social justice and the free use of his individuality. Even though Dylan does not teach which way to go, his very appreciation of the problem that, for him, these two ends irreconcilably conflict means that when he does practice self-reliant individuality he does so without the self-satisfaction characteristic of Emerson's and Thoreau's seminal articulations of the ideal (section I.5). Further, Dylan's bourgeois self-awareness includes not just an understanding of his political withdrawal, but also recognition of a specifically bourgeois form of political *action* that differs from more militant forms in its practitioners being only partially and haphazardly committed. Section I.6 analyzes what is perhaps Dylan's most visible moment of political engagement—his participation at the 1963 March on Washington—to show that his message, in distinction from other activists at the March, such as Martin Luther King Jr., continually gestures to the situation of bourgeois activists and cautions this group against indecent triumphalism and complacency. In sum, as I argue in section I.7, Dylan develops the folk tradition he inherited not just in an aesthetic way (injecting rock elements into it) but in an ethical manner as well: transposing the clear conscience of the radical leftism that was so closely identified with folk into a bourgeois consciousness self-aware about its lack of full moral goodness.

I.1. The Ethical Ambiguity of Dylan's Withdrawal from 1960s Political Activism

If it were only a matter of confessing a personal failure to live up to moral ideals we hold dear—or, conversely, if it were only a matter of denying the obligatoriness of moral demands requiring too much sacrifice of our individuality—Dylan's public disavowal of social justice work would be more familiar to our ears. But Dylan's public testimony to his refusal to any longer be a reliable political activist is not so easy to comprehend. It is challenging, both intellectually and ethically. This is because Dylan's most characteristic expressions of his political apostasy bring together two sentiments that are usually opposed: confidence and an awareness of not being morally justified. That is, in privileging his individuality over and against his obligations to social justice, Dylan typically combines lack of contrition with a lack of any insistence that he is fully in the right. We are without ready-made philosophical categories for conceptualizing this posture, though below I situate Dylan's stance vis-à-vis numerous discourses in contemporary philosophy. Dylan's main expressions of his withdrawal from dependable social activism are thus vexing, provocative, and demanding of interpretation.

Consider, as a starting point, Dylan's appearance at the ECLC annual dinner in December 1963. The ECLC had been formed in 1951 to mobilize support for civil liberties. Its lawyers and activists had worked to fight against McCarthyism, segregation, and other social ills. Dylan was there because he was being honored with the Tom Paine Award for the contributions he had made to social justice. That Dylan, only twenty-two at the time, would be given such a prestigious acknowledgment of his political work is a reminder of his profound role—through his music and broader activism—in the civil rights movement of the early 1960s. In 1963 alone, Dylan had refused to perform on *The Ed Sullivan Show* (which would have been his first national television appearance) when prevented from singing a song mocking anti-communist hysteria; participated in rallies following the death of Medgar Evers, about whom he wrote and performed a beautiful paean; and performed at the March on Washington. By all accounts, Dylan seemed to be someone whose poetry and music were infused with progressive social purpose and who, individually, could be relied upon as a fellow traveler by left-leaning social justice groups. Dylan's acceptance speech, however, was one of the earliest instances in which he upset these expectations. Made uncomfortable by the environment of the annual dinner, Dylan gave a speech that became a rant in which he mocked the audience—many of whom had devoted their professional careers to civil rights and the protection of civil liberties—for their age, their baldness, and their hypocrisy. He also introduced a metaphor to describe his change of perspective—*getting younger*—which would become central to his single most significant statement of political disavowal, "My Back Pages," recorded a few months later.[5] Beyond simply rebuking the ECLC, Dylan declared a newfound indifference to politics itself:

[5] Dylan begins his remarks: "I haven't got any guitar, I can talk though. I want to thank you for the Tom Paine Award in behalf of everybody that went down to Cuba. First of all because they're all young and it's took me a long time to get young and now I consider myself young. And I'm proud of it. I'm proud that I'm young. And I only wish that all you people who are sitting out here today or tonight weren't here and I could see all kinds of faces with hair on their head—and everything like that, everything leading to youngness, celebrating the anniversary when we overthrew the House Un-American Activities just yesterday—Because you people should be at the beach. You should be out there and you should be swimming and you should be just relaxing in the time you have to relax. [Laughter] It is not an old people's world. It is not an old people's world. It has nothing to do with old people. Old people when their hair grows out, *they* should go out. [Laughter] And I look down to see the people that are governing me and making my rules—and they haven't got any hair on their head—I get very uptight about it. [Laughter]." Corliss Lamont, "Transcript of Bob Dylan's Remarks at the Bill of Rights Dinner at the Americana Hotel on 12/13/63," https://www.corliss-lamont.org/dylan.htm.

> There's no black and white, left and right to me anymore; there's only up
> and down and down is very close to the ground. And I'm trying to go up
> without thinking about anything trivial such as politics.[6]

In this early testimony to his refusal to be a dependable political agent, it is impossible to read Dylan as being fully justified. Dylan may not have been wrong
to criticize the ECLC membership for congratulating themselves at a luxurious
dinner, all in the name of helping those in need, but practically speaking Dylan
offers no alternative to the important work of the ECLC besides his personal unwillingness to be affiliated. Dylan further undermined any claim to a position of
unambiguous moral superiority by likening himself to Lee Harvey Oswald, who
had shot President Kennedy only a month earlier:

> I'll stand up and to get uncompromisable about it, which I have to be
> to be honest, I just got to be, as I got to admit that the man who shot
> President Kennedy, Lee Oswald, I don't know exactly where—what he
> thought he was doing, but I got to admit honestly that I too—I saw
> some of myself in him. I don't think it would have gone—I don't think
> it could go that far. But I got to stand up and say I saw things that he
> felt, in me—not to go that far and shoot. [Boos and hisses] You can
> boo but booing's got nothing to do with it. It's a—I just a—I've got to
> tell you, man, it's Bill of Rights is free speech and I just want to admit
> that I accept this Tom Paine Award in behalf of James Forman of the
> Students Non-Violent Coordinating Committee and on behalf of the
> people who went to Cuba. [Boos and applause][7]

Even those who see Dylan's critique of leftist politics of the 1960s as entirely
commendable recognize that the ECLC rant was not itself fully justifiable.[8]
Dylan himself offered an apology of sorts the following month.[9]

The question is whether the ECLC dinner was, in its ethical ambiguity, an
aberration in Dylan's public testimony to his political withdrawal or instead
the basic blueprint of what would follow. Mike Marqusee, one of the most

---

[6] Lamont, "Transcript of Bob Dylan's Remarks."

[7] Lamont, "Transcript of Bob Dylan's Remarks."

[8] Marqusee, for instance, calls Dylan's remarks at the ECLC dinner "illogical, arrogant, and self-
indulgent." Mike Marqusee, *Wicked Messenger: Bob Dylan and the 1960s* (New York: Seven Stories
Press, 2005), 105.

[9] Corliss Lamont, "Message from Bob Dylan to the E.C.L.C.," https://www.corliss-lamont.org/
dylan.htm.

perceptive commentators on Dylan's politics, takes the former view, writing that in "My Back Pages," recorded a few months after the award dinner, Dylan "transmutes the rude incoherence of his ECLC rant into the organized density of art."[10] There is no denying the poetic majesty of the song. It is one of Dylan's masterpieces. But independent of its fineness as a work of art, there is, on the *ethical level*, something rude and incoherent that persists. That is, "My Back Pages" confidently explains Dylan's withdrawal from dependable social justice activism yet does so in terms that fall short of morally justifying that position. There is an ineliminable element of ethical ambiguity that persists.

"My Back Pages" is the most direct, philosophically rich, and thus most important of Dylan's songs of valediction to leftist political activism. The song is syntactically and ideationally complex, in many places more suggestive than definitive in its points, but it remains Dylan's most significant statement of his withdrawal from political responsibility. At the core of Dylan's account of his political apostasy is his insistence that there was something impure about his more direct and impassioned commitment to social justice. This is most clearly affirmed in the song's penultimate verse, in which he speaks to the possibility, if not reality, of becoming his own enemy in the very moment of his public protestations against injustice:

> In a soldier's stance, I aimed my hand
> At the mongrel dogs who teach
> Fearing not that I'd become my enemy
> In the instant that I preach
> My pathway led by confusion boats
> Mutiny from stern to bow
> Ah, but I was so much older then
> I'm younger than that now

What is the meaning of this paradoxical idea of becoming one's own enemy in the apparent furthering of social justice causes? Dylan offers at least three answers, but in each case there is an element of ambiguity, a sense in which Dylan's confident critique of the movement he would no longer reliably participate in falls short of releasing him from moral responsibility to continue to work for social justice.

One answer concerns Dylan's confession about his own ethics: that he was hardly blameless in his period of more intense social justice activism, that the

---

[10] Marqusee, 111.

purity of his aims not only was not complemented by the purity of his character but in some sense marred that character. Consider the opening verse:

> Crimson flames tied through my ears
> Rollin' high and mighty traps
> Pounced with fire on flaming roads
> Using ideas as my maps
> "We'll meet on edges, soon," said I
> Proud 'neath heated brow
> Ah, but I was so much older then
> I'm younger than that now

Dylan thus describes himself as threatened by arrogance—"high and mighty traps," "proud 'neath heated brow"—as he was engaged in political activism. And not just arrogance, but an incomplete overcoming of prejudice too:

> Half-wracked prejudice leaped forth
> "Rip down all hate," I screamed
> Lies that life is black and white
> Spoke from my skull. I dreamed
> Romantic facts of musketeers
> Foundationed deep, somehow
> Ah, but I was so much older then
> I'm younger than that now

What kind of prejudice is it? Is it the enduring presence of racial prejudice? Probably not. More likely it is a prejudicial attitude toward his political opponents, reflected in the paradoxes of screaming against hate—a paradox Dylan pursues elsewhere in "It's Alright, Ma": "While others say don't hate nothing at all / Except hatred."

In any case, the thing to emphasize about this first dynamic is that Dylan is not criticizing *all* social justice advocacy, only the kind that *he, and others like him,* was practicing. He does not say that all leftist activism must be characterized by arrogance and prejudice, only that his has been and no doubt that of many other leftists too. That Dylan could not overcome arrogance and prejudice in pursuit of social justice is more a mar on his own character than on the integrity of social justice movements themselves.

Second, as the verses I have quoted additionally suggest, what Dylan also finds problematic about his earlier, "older," more politically engaged self is not simply his personal conduct as a social justice activist but some elements of the causes he understood himself to be serving. There is, for instance, a calling into question of "using ideas as my maps" which perhaps suggests the falsity of pursuing abstractions (like justice itself, humanity itself, freedom and equality themselves) at the expense of working for the more modest and concrete, but perhaps more real and realizable, aims of helping specific communities in need. "My Back Pages" explicitly raises this issue of abstraction with the lines:

> Yes, my guard stood hard when abstract threats
> Too noble to neglect
> Deceived me into thinking
> I had something to protect

Dylan likewise puts forward that, in addition to their abstraction, some of the causes he served may have been faulty for being too utopian or otherwise illusory. Consider the lines, already quoted: "Lies that life is black and white / Spoke from my skull" as well as "I dreamed / Romantic facts of musketeers / Foundationed deep, somehow."

We do not know just what kind of theories of justice Dylan is challenging here for being too ideational, too abstract, too romantic. But whatever the details, the key point to stress is that Dylan's withdrawal from social justice activism is not thereby exonerated. It is not credible to think that all social justice causes must suffer from excessive abstraction or romanticism. Dylan himself bears witness to an alternate (i.e., more concrete, local, and modest) form of engagement, as it is precisely this form that typifies his sporadic forays into social justice activism following his break with the Left in the mid-1960s. In the ensuing decades, Dylan occasionally has taken political action, for instance by memorializing the Black Panther leader George Jackson, supporting refugees from the 1971 Bangladesh genocide, contesting the imprisonment of Rubin Carter, playing a leading role in Farm Aid, and offering support to numerous charitable organizations including Feeding America and the United Nations World Food Programme. But if this alternative remains a possibility, then Dylan's adoption of a position of non-activism in the mid-1960s cannot be justified as avoiding abstraction and romanticism, because there are clear ways to work in behalf of justice that steer clear of these pitfalls.

Third, and most significant, Dylan introduces the idea that *any kind* of political movement is impure because, for him at least, it comes at a sacrifice of his freedom as a self-reliant individual. This idea—which, if persuasive, would represent a more radical challenge to social justice activism—is suggested by "My Back Pages" insofar as the song seems to oppose allowing the weight of social responsibility to undermine the free employment of one's individuality. Perhaps the greatest expression of Dylan's suggestion of a conflict between social justice and individual freedom occurs in this verse:

> A self-ordained professor's tongue
> Too serious to fool
> Spouted out that liberty
> Is just equality in school
> "Equality," I spoke the word
> As if a wedding vow
> Ah, but I was so much older then
> I'm younger than that now

Dylan's use of the marriage metaphor is revealing. It is not just that he no longer claims to be committed to equality—reiterating the song's main idea of a break from dependable social justice activism—but that he calls into question the devotion to equality he once possessed. Likening his earlier commitment to equality to a wedding vow suggests that this commitment was, if not misguided (a misdirection of erotic energy away from its proper object, a person, toward an abstract idea), then at least self-sacrificial: a commitment to one end at the expense of other worthy and attractive ones.[11] This is a sacrifice he no longer is prepared to make. Accordingly, Dylan's critique of the relationship of liberty to equality—his suggestion that it is naïve to consider liberty as "just equality in school"—should be read not simply as doubt that a political movement seeking rights and liberties (the proximate focus of 1960s civil rights legislation) could develop into a project for a more extensive social equality, but, more foundationally, as a warning that there is a vexing tension between equality and liberty: that the pursuit of equality (at minimum, basic rights for all) comes at a cost of the liberty of those who already are free. In pursuing social justice, those who already enjoy freedom must sacrifice not just their disproportionate privilege but also

---

[11] And, given the wedding metaphor of "My Back Pages," we can perhaps read Dylan's refusal to be a dependable romantic partner in "It Ain't Me, Babe," recorded at the same time as "My Back Pages," also in political terms:

> Go melt back into the night, babe
> Everything inside is made of stone
> There's nothing in here moving
> An' anyway I'm not alone
> You say you're lookin' for someone
> Who'll pick you up each time you fall
> To gather flowers constantly
> An' to come each time you call
> A lover for your life an' nothing more
> But it ain't me, babe
> No, no, no, it ain't me, babe
> It ain't me you're lookin' for, babe

the time and energy needed to make worthy causes—desegregation; civil rights; the amelioration of poverty, malnutrition, and other emergencies—a reality.[12]

In any case, the point to underline is that here, too, there is undeniable ethical ambiguity in Dylan's position. Unless we read Dylan as rejecting the goal of equality—and there is simply no evidence for this whatsoever—his announcement that he no longer will be faithfully devoted to equality has to be read with a sense of moral unease. Dylan never suggests that the underlying ideal of liberty and equality for all is undesirable on its face, only that it requires more from him as an individual than he is prepared to offer.

This aspect of "My Back Pages"—this critique of social justice movements not because they are wrong (misguided in their aims), nor because their practitioners have been hypocritical or arrogant, but because they impose costs that the singer simply does not want to bear—becomes, as ethically ambiguous as it is, one of Dylan's most frequent criticisms against the leftist politics of the mid-1960s. Dylan, in a variety of contexts, expresses an unwillingness to serve as such—an unwillingness that, far from cloaking itself in moral justification, presents and accepts itself as being without full justification.

It is, of course, possible to claim that, due to the excessive demands of social justice obligations, an individual would be fully justified in not performing them, and in what follows I will differentiate Dylan vis-à-vis this view as well as other recent philosophical paradigms wrestling with the question of an individual's responsibility to rectify injustice and needless suffering. But by way of anticipation of that discussion, let me emphasize the basic point that Dylan manifestly does not appear to do this. Not just at the ECLC dinner or in "My Back Pages," but in virtually all of his testimonials to his refusal to be a dependable agent in the service of social change, Dylan's invocation of his individuality as a countervailing consideration to social justice is presented confidently but *without a sense of full moral justification.*

More precise definitions and categorizations of moral theories will follow in section I.4, but for now consider these instances where Dylan announces a refusal of social responsibility not because it is wrong or not owed, but because it conflicts with his preference as an individual to live and operate with the most minimal kind of external expectations and restraints.

---

[12] Marqusee reads Dylan's calling into question of liberty as "just equality in school" as referring to the limitations of *school desegregation* (i.e., that the policy is not enough in itself to achieve liberty), but this strikes me as overly historicizing what otherwise can be read as a more general and philosophically profound idea: namely, that liberty (e.g., a society in which basic civil liberties have been secured) does not by itself lead to equality (i.e., a more robustly just society) due in part to the unwillingness of those who already are well situated to work dependably to eradicate the injustices preventing the fuller realization of social equality. See Marqusee, *Wicked Messenger*, 112.

In "Positively 4th Street," Dylan proclaims:

> I know you're dissatisfied with your position and your place
> Don't you understand it's not my problem

One could read these lines as Dylan announcing the limit to what he rightfully owes to others, but the harshness of his expression suggests a different idea: not the outright denial of a moral responsibility to help, but the refusal to act upon it even if it were to exist.

Dylan later puts forward a similar sentiment in "Idiot Wind":

> I can't help it if I'm lucky

We can empathize with someone who thinks like this, but it is, of course, not true: there is always something one *could* do to rectify unfair privilege. Dylan is electing not to do that—and owning it confidently—but this does not make it morally justifiable.

Dylan's rejection of political and social responsibility is also conveyed in "It's Alright, Ma," perhaps his greatest expression of what a commitment to self-reliant individuality entails. Dylan sings:

> Although the masters make the rules
> For the wise men and the fools
> I got nothing, Ma, to live up to

Like Socrates, who professed that he was neither wise nor ignorant but a knower of his ignorance, Dylan presents himself as neither wise nor foolish. But rather than inspire a passionate commitment to the missing wisdom—rather than dedicate himself, like Socrates, to the pursuit of—Dylan here disclaims any responsibility to follow rules (especially the unjust ones accepted by fools) or to discover and implement an alternate system that would be more just. Again, we can sympathize with the radical individuality being described here, but Dylan patently describes it as being discontinuous with wisdom and social responsibility.

Another key instance in which Dylan objects to moral causes not because they are wrong but because they impose costs on the free use of his individuality is "Maggie's Farm," whose refrain is "I'm not gonna work on Maggie's farm no more" and which contains the crucial line:

> They say sing while you slave [in collective efforts] and
> I just get bored

To invoke boredom as a reason not to do something is at once entirely familiar and understandable and yet without moral justification: if a goal is morally obligatory, the fact that the work needed to realize it is not intellectually interesting, personally alluring, or otherwise exciting is not typically considered a reason that it should not be done. Dylan's refusal to sacrifice for the community is not *morally* persuasive, but rather an admission of how a primary focus on selfhood can come at the expense of fully executing moral responsibility.

Similarly, consider Dylan's objection to pity in "It's Alright, Ma." The objection is not to the appropriateness of the sentiment—to the reality of the suffering of others in need of attention and support—but to the problem that the sentiment (and perhaps the moralized politics that follows from it) de-individualizes, leading us to feel and act the same:

> Watch waterfalls of pity roar
> You feel to moan but unlike before
> You discover that you'd just be one more
> Person crying

There are, in short, simply too many instances of Dylan juxtaposing an obligation to social justice to an obligation to his own individuality not to recognize this tension as a key aspect of his political apostasy. As early as his 1962 song "Bob Dylan's Blues," he laments:

> Fixin' ev'rybody's troubles
> Ev'rybody's 'cept mine

Dylan's subsequent public statements about his withdrawal from dependable leftist activism continually point not to the wrongness of numerous social causes, but to their costliness with regard to individual freedom. Sometimes it is artistic freedom that seems most at stake, as when Dylan disclaimed his role as political spokesman in part so as to free himself from having to continue to make "finger-pointing songs," a genre he felt had become all too common.[13] In other cases, he was candid that he was simply not willing to sacrifice his life for social justice, believing that anyone truly committed to fundamental political and social change would have to risk death—given the array of powerful interests to be contended with—and that this was something he simply would not do:

---

[13] Quoted in Cott, "The Crackin', Shakin', Breakin' Sounds," in *Essential Interviews*, 17.

All I can say is politics is not my thing at all. I can't see myself on a platform talking about how to help people. Because I would get myself *killed* if I *really* tried to help anybody. I mean, if somebody *really* had something to say to help somebody out, just bluntly say the truth, well obviously they're gonna be done away with. They're gonna be *killed.*[14]

Dylan's recognition of the ethical ambiguity of his posture is especially pronounced in his "apology" letter to the ECLC, in which he chides the organization for failing to acknowledge his own complicity in ongoing social ills and, by extension, that of other leftists assembled at the dinner:

> yes if there's violence in the times then
> there must be violence in me[15]

Where does this leave us? I have now introduced Dylan's principal articulations of his refusal to be a dependable agent of social change. And I have emphasized how these articulations are morally ambiguous. Even when Dylan appeals to the free use of his individuality as a value in competition with social justice, he never claims to be justified in turning his back on the fight for justice. He only asserts his refusal to be a dependable agent in that fight, regardless of what the moral consequences turn out to be. What remains to be demonstrated is how Dylan's posture in this regard is not only highly unusual but *prophetic*—how it reflects a prophetic role Dylan commentators have not appreciated; how it is likely to touch a broad segment of us; how it has ethical consequences; how, in short, it is an important element of Dylan's status as a "prophet without God."

I.2. Dylan as Bourgeois Prophet

Dylan's testimony to his unwillingness to be dependably committed to social justice causes he otherwise supports is one of the starkest instances of his status as a prophet without God, and in a double sense. On the one hand, Dylan is a prophet without God because he does not communicate a message of salvation or some other unified teaching about "the one thing that is needful." In pursuing his own individual freedom over and against the claims of a social justice movement, Dylan does not say that everyone should do this, nor that one would be wrong to make the opposite choice. There is thus "no God," no comprehensive

---

[14] Quoted in Anthony Scaduto, *Bob Dylan: An Intimate Biography* (New York: Grosset & Dunlap, 1971), 177.

[15] Lamont, "Message from Bob Dylan."

worldview, no universal source of normative direction informing Dylan's message, but rather a world of ethical diremption and tragic choice. On the other hand, Dylan is also a prophet without God insofar as, in testifying to the tragic tradeoff between social justice and self-reliant individual freedom, he breaks from the traditional moral idealization surrounding prophets. Whereas we usually expect the prophet to play a role of unambiguous moral leadership—whether by virtue of communicating a divinely sanctioned message or exhibiting an exemplary life[16]—Dylan does something different when he presents himself as a self-reliant individual unwilling to fully discharge his moral duty. Dylan is thus also a prophet without God in the sense of being a prophet who is *not good*. It might seem that such a stance disqualifies one's status as a prophet, but this is to forget that one of the functions of prophecy is as a mirror, to elicit self-recognition about the nature of the values people possess and the "gods" they serve.[17] Dylan, as I will show, does this, eliciting identification more than idealization. If his testimony to his inability to combine individual freedom and social justice does indeed remain in some sense exemplary, it is not as a moral saint—who demonstrates the highest possible ethical standards—but as a bourgeois, a prosperous and secure person who could do more in the service of social justice but elects not to do so. Dylan is so honest and perspicacious about this stance that it has ethical consequences for those of us who are similarly situated but much less self-aware. Because the bourgeois subjectivity is both pervasive and poorly understood—because Dylan's brand of self-reliance has not been adequately conceptualized within the terms of contemporary philosophy nor even within the tradition of self-reliance stemming from Emerson and Thoreau that he inherits—his meditation on the tragic divergence, *for him and those like him*, between social justice and individual freedom has a genuine prophetic significance within contemporary culture.

In approaching Dylan in such a manner I am breaking from the two usual ways in which Dylan's explicit turning away from leftist politics of the mid-1960s has been understood. Although these two interpretations are opposed in their judgment of Dylan—with one condemning and the other applauding him—both share the assumption that his prophetic quality, if it exists, inheres in his communicating and exemplifying moral purity.

One interpretation understands Dylan as sacrificing prophetic leadership when he no longer speaks out against injustice. Philippe Margotin and Jean-Michel Guesdon take it as given, for example, that Dylan's "My Back Pages,"

---

[16] Weber refers to these two roles as the ethical prophet and the exemplary prophet. See Max Weber, *The Sociology of Religion*, trans. Ephraim Fischoff (Boston: Beacon Press, 1993), 55.

[17] George Shulman, *American Prophecy: Race and Redemption in American Political Culture* (Minneapolis: University of Minnesota Press, 2008), 29.

his valediction to political activism that I have just examined, represents "a definitive, necessary break with the people who had crowned him a prophet after
'Blowin' in the Wind' and 'Masters of War.' "[18] Many on the Left in the mid-1960s
who were alienated and disturbed by Dylan's move away from social justice activism often expressed something like this view, bemoaning what they took to
be Dylan's sacrifice of his special role as a moral leader. Even if many accepted
Dylan's transformation on a personal level—respecting his freedom to do as he
pleased—they understood his earlier contributions to the civil rights movement, articulating its logic and inspiring its mood, as so singular and so potent
as to be definitive of a genuine prophetic calling that they desperately hoped he
would regain. For such individuals, Dylan's going electric in 1965 was infused
with political significance since it, in itself, seemed to signify his withdrawal
from dependable commitment to social justice. Folk was both a musical style
and a political sensibility; in going electric, Dylan, in the eyes of many, appeared
to be abandoning both. This perspective is perhaps most memorably expressed
in the "Open Letter to Bob Dylan," penned in 1964 by Irwin Silber, the radical political activist and longtime editor of the folk revival magazine *Sing Out!*.
Silber noted Dylan's shift from external causes to internal exploration, rejecting
it as part of Dylan's unfortunate complicity with an unjust economic and social
system.[19] The most extreme version of this kind of thinking—which sees Dylan,
in his withdrawal from conventional politics, as irresponsibly sacrificing his authentic prophetic role—is A. J. Weberman, founder of the Dylan Liberation
Front, whose manifesto was "to help save Bob Dylan from himself" and, in doing
so, free Dylan from his alleged bourgeois qualities. Weberman distributed "Free
Bob Dylan" badges, castigated Dylan for "deserting the movement," accused him
of becoming a junkie, and took issue with him turning away from social justice

---

[18] Philippe Margotin and Jean-Michel Guesdon, *Bob Dylan: All the Songs—The Story Behind Every Track* (London: Black Dog, 2015), 125.

[19] Silber wrote: "You seem to be in a different kind of bag now, Bob—and I'm worried about it. I saw at Newport how you had somehow lost contact with people. It seemed to me that some of the paraphernalia of fame were getting in your way. You travel with an entourage now—with good buddies who are going to laugh when you need laughing and drink wine with you and insure your privacy—and never challenge you to face everyone else's reality again . . . Your songs seem to be all inner-directed now, inner probing, self-conscious—maybe even a little maudlin or a little cruel on occasion. And it's happening on stage, too. You seem to be relating to a handful of cronies behind the scenes now—rather than to the rest of us out front . . . We are all responsible for what's been happening to you—and to many other fine young artists. The American Success Machinery chews up geniuses at a rate of one a day and still hungers for more. Unable to produce real art on its own, the Establishment breaks creativity in protest against and nonconformity to the System. And then, through notoriety, fast money, and status, it makes it almost impossible for the artist to function and grow. It is a process that must be constantly guarded against and fought." Quoted in Craig McGregor, ed., *Bob Dylan: The Early Years, A Retrospective* (Boston: Da Capo Press, 1990), 67–68.

critique in pursuit of more self-exploratory themes and purposes.[20] Weberman, often denounced as a crank, is only the most intense version of a widespread sentiment shared by other activists, artists, and critics during this time. John Lennon wore a "Free Bob Dylan" badge. Jerry Rubin, the radical social activist and countercultural icon, was tied to Weberman—sometimes as an encourager of the Dylan Liberation Front and other times as a critic, but in both instances motivated by the goal of luring Dylan to return to social justice activism and getting him to "agree to tour the country with John and Yoko, raising money for political causes and rallying people to go to San Diego [the site originally selected for the 1972 Republican Convention]."[21] Dylan himself may have understood his political withdrawal as a disclaiming of prophetic leadership, insofar as he suggested that in no longer making the unmasking of injustice as central of a concern in his music he also was ceasing to be a "spokesman" or the so-called voice of his generation. In 1964, for example, he said of his newer, post-leftist work:

> There aren't any finger-pointing songs in here. . . . Now a lot of people are doing finger-pointing songs. You know—pointing to all the things that are wrong. Me, I don't want to write for people anymore. You know—be a spokesman.[22]

In a very different but still related way, this assumption that the prophetic Dylan is the Dylan directly engaged in familiar political causes is reflected by interpreters of his politics who simply forget about his withdrawal from social justice activism, whether by excluding analysis of those songs and statements that announce his unwillingness to be a dependable agent of political change or by emphasizing the traces of his activism that persist in haphazard form following his mid-1960s break from close affiliation with the Left.[23]

In any case, the problem with this first interpretation is that it forgets that Dylan does not simply break from dependable social activism but sings about it, reflecting on it with some of his most poetically stunning and philosophically challenging works. These songs—which include such pieces as "My Back Pages," "Maggie's Farm," "It's Alright, Ma," "Restless Farewell," "To Ramona," "Chimes of Freedom," and perhaps also "It Ain't Me Babe," "It's All Over Now, Baby Blue,"

---

[20] See Peter Doggett, *There's a Riot Going On: Revolutionaries, Rock Stars, and the Rise and Fall of the '60s* (Edinburgh: Canongate, 2007), 232, 388–89, 428, 461.

[21] Quoted in Doggett, 463–64.

[22] Quoted in Cott, "The Crackin', Shakin', Breakin' Sounds," in *Essential Interviews*, 17.

[23] See, for example, Michael L. Perlin, "Tangled Up in Law: The Jurisprudence of Bob Dylan," *Fordham Urban Law Journal* 38, no. 5 (2010): 1395–430.

and "Farewell Angelina"—make clear that Dylan is not guilty of simple negligence or solipsism, but abandons his political responsibility in a spirit of profound self-awareness. To reject Dylan's abandonment of social activism without
attention to this essential body of work seems to miss what makes him so special. After all, there are many who have spoken eloquently and acted honorably
in pursuit of social justice, but hardly anyone has ever explained, from a position of moral leadership in pursuit of justice, his abandonment of that position.
Hardly anyone has ever proclaimed his unwillingness to be a dependable agent
in the service of political goals (such as equality, anti-racism, anti-militarism,
anti-poverty) he otherwise supports. But Dylan does precisely this. His stance
in this regard, however vexing, is one of the main reasons he is so important.
That many on the Left felt not just abandoned but *disconcerted* by these songs is
a further sign that Dylan's political withdrawal represented a redirection, rather
than abdication, of his prophetic role.[24] Dylan, in other words, does not cease
being a spokesman, despite his ostensible intentions to do so, simply because he
no longer is committed to protesting injustice. There are other ways of being a
spokesman. In testifying to his unwillingness to fully support just causes, Dylan
may have thought he was stepping down from his role as "voice of his generation," but in a sense he was only intensifying that role, mirroring the broader
culture's insufficient commitment to its own animating political ideals, bringing
to its attention the conflict between individuality and justice, and exploring the
ethical implications that follow from this tragic circumstance.

Approaching Dylan in this fashion means that my treatment of him also
diverges from the other leading interpretation of Dylan's turn away from the
leftist politics of the mid-1960s, which, in direct opposition to the first interpretation, applauds Dylan's protest against protest, his rebellion against rebellion,
as morally exemplary. There are different renderings of this position—Dylan's
protest against protest is a welcome pushback against hypocrisy among many
leftists, it reflects the artist's need not to be subservient to any political causes,
it embodies Dylan's ceaseless quest for individual reinvention and change—but
they all share the perspective of not being troubled by Dylan's leftist apostasy
and, even more, find in it the persistence of a pure form of moral leadership. This
exonerating impulse reaches its maximum point when Dylan's protest against
protest is interpreted as *more radical* than an enduring commitment to ending
racism, militarism, poverty, and other forms of injustice. Consider in this regard
Marqusee, who reads Dylan's abandonment of civil rights activism not just as
having a prophetic aspect (as being more than a "private maneuver" for Dylan,

---

[24] Marqusee, for instance, reports: "No song on [*Another Side of Bob Dylan*] distressed Dylan's
friends in the movement more than 'My Back Pages'"—a reminder that Dylan was not simply
withdrawing from the Left but challenging some of its pieties. Marqusee, *Wicked Messenger*, 111.

communicating something that has "touched and continued to touch others"[25]), but as signaling what he calls "a deeper kind of radicalism."[26] On Marqusee's reading, Dylan, on the one hand, exposes weaknesses within the Left of the 1960s—its authoritarian tendency, its problematic relationship to gender, above all its not going far enough in challenging society—and, on the other, admirably extends the pursuit of social justice to include the quest for a freer exercise of the mind, thereby treating the exploration of consciousness as an urgent political concern.[27] As Marqusee summarizes his account of Dylan's withdrawal from the Left: "[Dylan's] argument with the movement is partly that its definition of the political doesn't go far enough, isn't radical enough, partly that it is in itself a prison, a restraint, and partly that it is pompous and lame and no fun at all."[28]

Marqusee is hardly alone in assuming that if Dylan's withdrawal from dependable leftist activism is to continue to have prophetic value, then it must be morally pure—that is, articulate a higher kind of life, a deeper kind of freedom, a more radical political aspiration. When activist performers like Phil Ochs and John Sinclair defended Dylan from attacks like Silber's "Open Letter," for instance, they argued in such terms, claiming that, in ostensibly turning his back on social justice movements, in fact "Dylan has begun to go beneath the surface."[29] Even Silber himself, when he reconsidered his public critique of Dylan five years later, in 1969, came to the new conclusion that far from abandoning social responsibility, Dylan's withdrawal from the Left in the mid-1960s was an act of political radicalism: the Left had not realized the severity of the problems facing America, but Dylan, in refusing to go along with it, correctly understood just how bankrupt American society had become. Now referring to Dylan as the "emotional essentialization of the SDS generation," Silber reflected that though he and others had thought in 1964 that Dylan had abandoned those committed to progressive change, in fact Dylan had abandoned not them "but an outmoded style of values which had become unequal to the task of reclaiming America." On Silber's reinterpretation, Dylan's apparent disclaiming of social justice was actually a radical political gesture: "His newer songs began to reflect the death

---

[25] Marqusee, 117.

[26] Marqusee, "The Politics of Bob Dylan," *Red Pepper*, November 1, 2003, https://www.redpepper.org.uk/the-politics-of-bob-dylan/.

[27] On the interrelation, but also competition, between two different objects of the revolutionary spirit of the 1960s—politics and consciousness—see Fred Turner, *The Democratic Surround: Multimedia and American Liberalism from World War II to the Psychedelic Sixties* (Chicago: University of Chicago Press, 2013).

[28] Marqusee, *Wicked Messenger*, 112.

[29] Quoted in Marqusee, 105.

of that naïveté which led us to believe that we could change this system without destroying it."[30]

It is typical of those who understand Dylan's mid-60s withdrawal from the Left in this fashion that even his seemingly most indulgent and irresponsible moments—such as his lambasting of ECLC leaders for being old and bald—become imbued with moral leadership, as if he had a more principled and pious commitment to social justice than the lawyers and activists of the ECLC who had fought against McCarthyism, segregation, and other violations of individual liberty. Thus, on Jeff Taylor and Chad Israelson's account of the ECLC dinner: "The liberal establishment crowd was too bourgeoisie, conventional, and old. The speech illustrated Dylan's lack of connection to the mainstream liberal movement and also the generational rift that existed."[31] Similarly, for Marqusee, Dylan's refusal to play nice with the ECLC was based on the recognition that "any investment in the social order disarmed its opponents."[32] According to Marqusee, American abuses of civil rights raised the issue of the bankruptcy of American democracy and of the conventional political channels and ideologies by which many had thought to improve it: "The incandescent purity of SNCC's struggle in the South had exposed the emptiness not only of traditional politics, but of the entire discourse of American democracy." As a result, Marqusee concludes: "In Dylan's case, the perception of the scale and depth of society's dishonesty issued in (or *justified*) a repudiation of all forms of political engagement."[33] Marqusee thus sees in Dylan's ostensible disclaiming of political responsibility a genuine political radicalism.

The problem with this second interpretation, though, is that Dylan's works and statements of political apostasy cannot be interpreted as fully justifiable in a moral sense. As the initial survey of Dylan's key expressions of this apostasy discussed above make clear, Dylan does not understand it that way, nor should we. Dylan's most serious challenge to the Left is not to question its causes, but to state—as a matter of his personal freedom—his unwillingness to be a dependable political agent on its behalf. To treat him as being fully justified in his political withdrawal—as evincing a "deeper kind of radicalism," as going "beneath the surface," as illuminating the authoritarianism of the Left and the bankruptcy of American society—thus seems to me entirely mistaken, not just as a matter of moral judgment but as a matter of discerning just wherein Dylan's prophetic

[30] Irwin Silber, *Kaleidoscope* 1, no. 3 (December 20, 1968–January 2, 1969), 17.

[31] Jeff Taylor and Chad Israelson, *The Political World of Bob Dylan: Freedom and Justice, Power and Sin* (London: Palgrave Macmillan, 2015), 60.

[32] Marqusee, *Wicked Messenger*, 280.

[33] Marqusee, 94, 131 (emphasis added).

edge lies. What is so special and distinct about Dylan's withdrawal from social justice activism—so provocative and puzzling—is his honest acknowledgment of his unwillingness to make the leap and commit himself dependably to noble and worthy goals. Dylan may be celebrating individual self-development and care of self, but he is doing so—as he himself admits—in *transgression* of the full demands of justice. There is a courage here, but it is not precisely moral courage. And there is profound ideational content here, but it is not a roadmap to a truer approximation of justice or a more exemplary kind of life. Instead, Dylan provides testimony to the tragic conflict between the pursuit of justice and the pursuit of individual self-reliance.

This tragic conflict is not a universal feature of ethical life; it is not a metaethical truth. One can imagine numerous figures for whom it does not resonate or apply. For example, it likely would not apply to militants who do make a full commitment to the fight against injustice—who make it their personal vocation to fulfill their sense of moral responsibility and thereby overcome the tension between self and other. Likewise, it would not apply to those who, on balance, are victims of injustice rather than its beneficiaries or who otherwise lack the physical capacity or other resources required to fulfill the dictates of their social conscience; such people, when they fail to work sufficiently in behalf of social justice, lack the moral transgressiveness of prosperous and well-situated individuals when they fail to do the same. Finally, those who do not have a sense of a demanding moral call that they are not heeding—who think that the world is just as it is or that they are already discharging their moral responsibility—are also unlikely to recognize, as a matter of personal experience, the ethical conflict that arises when one privileges one's individuality over and against one's sense of what social justice requires.

But if Dylan has prophetic importance in his very turning away from social justice, it is because there are many who do in fact reside in the space he occupies. For those I will label "bourgeois"—who are not primarily victims of injustice but rather relatively privileged and prosperous individuals within a world they themselves recognize as unjust, who are not militants persistently demanding in the pursuit of social change but only haphazardly committed, who support aspirational moral ideals (such as freedom and justice for all, or the reduction of easily preventable suffering) but frequently prefer their own comfort, security, and individual freedom vis-à-vis what their own moral conscience tells them such ideals require—the tragic tension about which Dylan sings, between self and other, freedom and morality, individuality and justice, ought to be all too familiar.

Still, the bourgeois identity, as common as it is, is rarely articulated or acknowledged. The term is not typically used as a self-appellation; if invoked, it is usually as a label derogatively imposed from without, from a position of presumed non-bourgeois moral superiority.[34] We seldom, if ever, see expressions like Max Weber's from more than a century ago—"I am a member of the bourgeois class, I feel myself to be such, and I have been brought up on its opinions and ideals"—and even he did not intend to indicate with this designation the failure to fulfill otherwise recognized social justice obligations.[35] For some critics, the bourgeois' silence about themselves is part of their very being: to be a bourgeois is to be in denial about it, since self-awareness would somehow demand change.[36] But regardless of whether this lack of self-awareness is a function of thoughtlessness or mendacity, regardless of whether it is a contingent or intrinsic problem facing the bourgeois subject, the fact remains that Dylan's public disclaiming of a full commitment to social justice is striking—not because his stance in itself is uncommon, but because it is so honestly, clearly, and explicitly articulated. Dylan is self-aware about his bourgeois status as a socioeconomic creature only partially and insufficiently committed to social justice due to an overriding focus on the comforts and freedoms of a prosperous private life. And because one of the functions of prophecy is to make people clearer about who they are—more cognizant of which "gods" they serve—Dylan performs a prophetic role in spreading this self-awareness to others.

What I am suggesting, then, is reading Dylan's protest against protest as neither simply condemnable nor simply applaudable, but instead as a reflection of the foundational ethical moment of bourgeois existence that usually goes unnoticed—the moment when the bourgeois reaches a saturation point with social justice and turns, in retreat, to a primary foundation in the self instead. Such a turn need not be permanent (and indeed Dylan's own life includes future re-entries into other-regarding, justice-focused concerns), but it is something all bourgeois leftists will continually find themselves doing. Dylan sings here of what we do but do not admit. For it is not just Dylan who turns his back on justice: we all do, insofar as we are bourgeois.

---

[34] In European non-English usages, such as French, German, and Scandinavian languages, the term can be more nuanced—referring in some instances, for example, to civil society—but the derogatory meaning is present there as well.

[35] Max Weber, "The Nation State and Economic Policy," in *Political Writings* (Cambridge, UK: Cambridge University Press, 1994), 23 (translation slightly altered). Deirdre McCloskey's recent three-volume study on the bourgeois (*The Bourgeois Virtues*; *Bourgeois Dignity*; and *Bourgeois Equality*) does provide a sympathetic reading, but too sympathetic, as she overlooks the central ethical phenomenon of bourgeois life: only *partially* working to realize otherwise recognized moral principles.

[36] See Gyžrgy Lukács, *History and Class Consciousness*, trans. Rodney Livingstone (Cambridge, MA: Harvard University Press, 1971), 66; Roland Barthes, *Mythologies*, trans. Annette Lavers (New York: Farrar, Straus and Giroux, 1972), 141.

If the first interpretation of Dylan's political apostasy accuses him of complicity with bourgeois society, and if the second interpretation praises him for a radicalism that challenges both bourgeois and mainstream leftist values, my point is to see Dylan as owning up to a bourgeois identity. After all, a rebel rebelling against the rebellion is also a perfect description of bourgeois culture, which is revolutionary vis-à-vis a feudal order denying legal equality and basic civil rights, but anti-revolutionary in not extending freedom and equality to social and economic life where imbalances in income and wealth, the arbitrary conditions of one's birth, the lack of fair equality of opportunity, and much else instantiate profound inequalities and unfreedoms. Dylan's confident but not justified refusal to be a reliable agent of social change is thus the very signature of the bourgeois being, who, in his progressive heart, is committed to social change (to freedom and equality for all) but nonetheless—because he prefers his own comfort to the eradication of injustice and suffering, including suffering for which he is complicit; because he will not fully disclaim personal privileges and benefits he knows to be unfair; because he values his personal time too much to sacrifice it too frequently to social causes—does not fulfill what his *own* conscience tells him his moral responsibility requires.

Dylan, in his withdrawal, is telling you that he is serving himself—that his self-reliance conflicts with his social responsibility—and inviting you, in light of this tension, to identify where you stand. Perhaps you have a fuller commitment to social responsibility or do not recognize a moral obligation you are inappropriately failing to fulfill. But if not, maybe you are like Dylan: choosing self-directed aims over and against social responsibility, *without full justification*. Perhaps you, too, are a bourgeois.

I.3. The Pervasiveness of Bourgeois Back-Turning

In interpreting Dylan's public disavowal of social activism, I have departed from the usual interpretation of it among Dylan scholars, who either condemn Dylan for political irresponsibility or applaud him for rightly critiquing limitations of the leftist politics of the mid-1960s, but in either case fail to recognize his prophetically significant ethical ambiguity. Both sides assume, in other words, that prophetic leadership is moral leadership and that Dylan, in withdrawing from 1960s political movements, either abandoned or maintained this traditional prophetic role. Against these narratives, I have explained why it makes sense to see Dylan as effectuating his prophetic role precisely in his testimony to no longer being a reliable moral agent.

Part of what makes Dylan's stance significant is how unusual it is. Not only does one rarely hear someone say, as he does, that he will not do all he should in pursuit of justice, but, as I will relate in the following sections, his grounds for doing so are outside of the leading discourses of contemporary philosophy and different, too, from fellow travelers like Emerson and Thoreau, who themselves are unusual for also sometimes proclaiming that they will practice self-reliance rather than participate in behalf of otherwise worthy social justice causes.

Yet, paradoxically, what also makes Dylan's protest against protest so significant is that, even if this posture has rarely been expressed, even if the precise grounds informing his version of it are themselves unusual, the underlying stance itself—turning one's back to otherwise recognized social justice obligations—is all too pervasive today, especially given the way modern technologies and globalization have altered the terrain of moral responsibility. Who does not feel that they also have turned their back on the quest for justice?

My aim is not to prove, through logical deduction, the truth of a large and often unmet moral obligation, but rather to appeal to the sense you already may have of such an unfulfilled commitment to social justice. That is, my aim is not to demonstrate that those who deny that they are failing to meet large and extensive social justice obligations are most likely wrong. Rather, it is to explain why those who already feel some dim sense of falling short likely feel this way and why this feeling is increasingly common in the present context.

At every point in human history, there no doubt have been individuals who have understood themselves as not discharging the moral responsibility they owed to others because of an overriding competing attention to their personal selves. Yet the likelihood of this situation has never been as great as it is today. One reason is the heightened moral expectations of the present moment. Part of this comes from the prevalence of democratic norms in the contemporary context. Because no democratic state adequately realizes its commitment to free and equal citizenship—there is no nation, for instance, in which the rich and well born do not have, on average, disproportionate political or educational opportunities—then anyone committed to the democratic value of fair equality of opportunity today is likely to feel a sense both that his or her particular nation-state is unjust and that something, however incremental, might be done to improve it.[37] The fact that so many countries face even bigger obstacles in the way of democracy, like authoritarianism and the denial of basic rights, only further suggests the incumbency of social action. A sense of heightened expectations also has arisen in light of the horrors of the twentieth century.

---

[37] Of course, people will define the requirements of a democratic society differently, but it is telling that even libertarian approaches often understand current arrangements as deeply flawed—for example, in their failure to realize fair equality of opportunity—and thus recognize the need for democratically inspired political reform. See, for example, John Tomasi, *Free Market Fairness* (Princeton, NJ: Princeton University Press, 2012).

The so-called Responsibility to Protect, for instance, is a global political commitment, unanimously endorsed by member states of the United Nations in 2005, to protect all populations from atrocities such as genocide, war crimes, ethnic cleansing, and crimes against humanity. The persistence of these evils in the world thus has carried with it a sense of unmet responsibility, which, even if it applies first and foremost to states rather than individuals, is something that private individuals and voluntary organizations—who can, after all, work to address such problems—are likely, upon reflection, to recognize as well.

Another major reason individuals today are increasingly prone to feel, however dimly and in the background, a large and unfulfilled social obligation to others stems from the world's unprecedented interconnectedness, enabled by revolutionary communication and transportation technologies, global trade, and problems (such as the threat of nuclear disaster or environmental degradation) that are planetary in scope. To appreciate this transformation, consider the case of utilitarianism, the moral theory often thought to require the widest extent of social responsibility because its principle of maximizing the welfare of the greatest number would seem to demand that a person work for the collective betterment of society and sacrifice one's personal interests so long as these would be compensated by net benefits for the rest of humanity. Yet Henry Sidgwick, perhaps the greatest utilitarian theorist in the nineteenth century, thought that for most people the sphere of other-regarding obligation would be quite small, both because he thought the state (rather than individual acts of beneficence) would usually be the proper vehicle for maximizing collective welfare and because, within the technological situation he occupied, there was little he thought could be done to help ameliorate distant suffering.[38] Today, however, that situation has changed radically. We become aware of distant suffering and injustice— wars, famine, poverty, ecological disaster, oppression—in real time. Likewise, our capacity to take direct action to remedy such situations—through giving aid and rallying support, for instance—has become dramatically heightened; it is not just that we can usually provide aid at any instant but that Sidgwick's appeal to the state (instead of the individual) as the most proper vehicle for realizing most forms of social betterment becomes less persuasive in a context of *international* or *global* moral responsibility, not to mention one in which (for reasons discussed) no state sufficiently realizes democratic norms of free and equal citizenship. And it is not simply our ability to know about and address distant suffering that has changed since Sidgwick's time. What also is different is the greater

---

[38] See Katarzyna de Lazari-Radek and Peter Singer, *The Point of View of the Universe: Sidgwick and Contemporary Ethics* (New York: Oxford University Press, 2016), 318–19, 324–25.

likelihood of feeling that we have *caused* distant suffering.[39] In a globalized world, an unfair working situation in a developing country—such as sweatshops—can credibly be understood as being enabled by shopping preferences in wealthier nations; similarly, environmental disasters, which disproportionately burden poorer countries, plausibly can be seen as being disproportionately caused by production and consumption patterns of richer countries on the other side of the earth.[40] In light of the globalized conditions by which injustice today can be discovered, addressed, and caused, it is not uncommon for political philosophers to posit a very wide conception of moral obligation. Iris Young, for instance, argues against limiting moral responsibility to those who directly perpetrate injustice through intentional mistreatment of others or gross negligence; instead, she advocates for what she calls a "social connection model" according to which "all those who contribute by their actions to structural processes with some unjust outcomes share responsibility for the injustice."[41]

Regardless of whether one agrees with Young's theory, it is important as part of a broader set of works in contemporary political philosophy that make the case that, due to the specific structure of the world today and the nature of its evils, prosperous, well-situated individuals have extensive moral obligations to combat poverty, malnutrition, disease, genocide, political injustice, and other severe forms of suffering on the global level. This claim has been made not only by contemporary utilitarians, who, for reasons I have mentioned, depart from Sidgwick and contemplate a much more extensive form of social responsibility.[42] It also has been made by advocates of what is often seen as the main competitor to utilitarianism, deontological approaches, that have argued (albeit on different grounds) for extensive moral responsibilities in light of the major problems besetting the world today. Elizabeth Ashford, for instance, has made the case that "in the current state of the world it may not be possible to defend less demanding obligations [than those defended by utilitarianism] to those in need within an impartial moral framework."[43] Regardless of whichever metaethical doctrine

---

[39] Of course, for some utilitarians the causal issue is irrelevant. But I mention the enlarged scope of causation as part of my broader point of explaining why a more extensively felt form of social justice obligation is, at present, likely.

[40] Consider, for example, that "the average American is responsible for 33 times more planet-warming carbon dioxide than the average Bangladeshi." Somini Sengupta and Julfikar Ali Manik, "A Quarter of Bangladesh Is Flooded. Millions Have Lost Everything," *New York Times*, July 31, 2020, A13, https://www.nytimes.com/2020/07/30/climate/bangladesh-floods.html.

[41] Iris Marion Young, *Responsibility for Justice* (New York: Oxford University Press, 2010), 96.

[42] See, for example, Peter Unger, *Living High & Letting Die: Our Illusion of Innocence* (New York: Oxford University Press, 1996); Peter Singer, *The Life You Can Save* (New York: Random House, 2010); Lazari-Radek and Singer, *The Point of View of the Universe*.

[43] Elizabeth Ashford, "The Demandingness of Scanlon's Contractualism," *Ethics* 113, no. 2 (2003): 274.

one follows, the severity of the crises confronting the world—combined with the unprecedented capacity to address these problems along with the high idealism of pervasive anti-authoritarian, liberal-democratic commitments—makes it increasingly plausible to contemplate extremely demanding moral obligations. As Shelly Kagan puts it in his seminal contribution: "Given the parameters of the actual world, there is no question that promoting the good would require a life of hardship, self-denial, and austerity."[44] My point is not that everyone agrees with Kagan that morality demands significant sacrifice—as there is widespread philosophical debate that I will presently address—only that Kagan, along with numerous other voices of our present moment, makes vivid how it is at least possible to understand our current time as containing unprecedentedly extensive moral obligation and thus that Dylan's self-conscious turning of his back on the demands of social justice ought to have a powerful resonance in contemporary culture.

What also seems new about the present context, compared to earlier periods of human history, is how amenable it is to being described as in a state of emergency—that is, shaped by numerous crises, each of which is susceptible to meaningful help from outside individuals.[45] To invoke the concept of emergency is not just to invoke a context of dire deprivation, in which persons' basic interests are at stake, but one in which others are in a position to provide direct and substantial assistance, often without too much personal cost to themselves.[46] The more it is true that the world itself is in a state of emergency, the more it will happen that prosperous individuals, living in conditions of relative comfort, will experience a widened sense of social responsibility.

Different people and different philosophies will define what is owed differently, but it is sufficient for my purposes to attend to the widespread experience of not adequately fulfilling these duties however precisely they are defined. The various reasons why it has become plausible to imagine an unprecedentedly extensive set of moral obligations all have the effect of making it more likely than ever before that individuals who recognize these obligations also will understand themselves as not adequately fulfilling them. Again, not everyone will acknowledge such an experience. If you are primarily a victim of injustice, if you are in fact fully committed to fulfilling extensive social justice commitments, or

---

[44] Shelly Kagan, *The Limits of Morality* (Oxford: Oxford University Press, 1989), 360.

[45] Ashford, for instance, has argued for understanding the world in a constant emergency situation: Elizabeth Ashford, "Utilitarianism, Integrity and Partiality," *Journal of Philosophy* 97 (2000): 428–30; also see Ashford, "The Demandingness of Scanlon's Contractualism," 273–74, 280–84.

[46] See Craig Calhoun, "The Idea of Emergency: Humanitarian Action and Global (Dis)order," in *Contemporary States of Emergency: The Politics of Military and Humanitarian Interventions*, ed. Didier Fassin and Mariella Pandolfi (New York: Zone Books, 2010), 29–58.

if you insist that the sphere of your moral responsibility is actually quite narrow, then it is far less likely that you will find your own moral reality reflected back at you when Dylan sings about his unwillingness to dependably work in behalf of causes he otherwise recognizes as just. But if you walk past beggars and feel uncomfortable about your own lack of assistance, if you are aware of actions you could make right now to save a life but still elect not to do so, if you worry as a democrat about the lack of sufficient democracy in your nation-state but do little in response, if your failure to directly combat ongoing genocides and other heinous atrocities leaves you with some sense of complicity, if you feel that there is something more, however modest, you ought to be doing to address emergencies that appear on the front page of newspapers every day, then perhaps you are living in the situation that Dylan sings about in the mid-1960s: knowingly turning your back on obligations you take to be plausible moral expectations upon you. If this situation is in fact something you recognize, then Dylan's strange posture is not so strange after all. His *acknowledgment* of it and the *ethical implications* he derives from it are highly unusual—and these I will presently elaborate—but not the posture itself.

I.4. The Distinctiveness of Dylan's Testimony vis-à-vis Leading Discourses of Political Philosophy

If turning one's back on injustice is not in itself that unusual—and in fact may be more pervasive today than at any time in history—Dylan is distinct not just for being explicit about this stance but for reflecting upon it in an unusual way. He suggests a tragic disharmony between the claims of social justice and the claims of his own individuality. This contrasts with the prevailing spirit of political philosophy, and contemporary political culture more generally, which has oriented itself around the promise of some kind of *harmony* between duty to self and duty to others—around, that is, the possibility of delineating an individual's precise moral obligations with the expectation that these obligations can and should be met, so that the question of how to reconcile individual freedom and social justice would be solved. But Dylan, in his testimony to his inability or refusal to make good on what is owed to others, is more a poser than a solver of moral dilemmas. He does not deliver new truths in the sense of a new conception of social justice or a new understanding of what individual freedom is and why it is valuable. Instead, rather than specify and perform what is owed, rather than bring the claims of morality and personal freedom into some stable relation, Dylan prophetically testifies to his unwillingness to abide by his own sense of what social justice requires and, thus, to the moral chaos of refusing to fully perform obligations not because they necessarily are wrong, but because they ask too much of a sacrifice of his individuality.

One can see the distinctiveness of Dylan's testimony to moral chaos— to the lack of harmony between his self-reliant individuality and his social conscience—by comparing his conceptualization of the dilemma to *seven* more familiar approaches within political philosophy, in ascending order of similarity to his. What these other seven perspectives share is a commitment to the ultimate harmonization of duty to self and duty to other, as opposed to Dylan's appreciation of the possibility that no such harmony is possible. In each case, the particularity of Dylan's stance is reflected in the fact that, as has been discussed, he brings together two seemingly opposed mentalities. On the one hand, he is confident when he turns his back on his social justice obligations; he does not wallow in guilt. On the other hand, though, he does not claim to be fully justified, either: he neither explains why he is within his rights to turn his back on social justice nor suggests, in Nietzschean fashion, that he is rejecting moral categories and living beyond good and evil. If anything, Dylan occupies an ambiguous space *between good and evil*, between guilt and justification, in which his individualism is affirmed yet not as a universal value. As a result of combining these two seemingly opposed mentalities, Dylan breaks from the usual philosophical interest in resolving the tension between duty to self and duty to others, between freedom and morality, between self-reliant individuality and socially responsible commitment to justice.

First, the position that is least similar to Dylan's but probably most common within political philosophy and the broader political culture is to reject the very premise that freedom and morality might lead in different directions and thus be in tension, to suggest in other words that both are either identical or fully maximizable without tradeoff in an ideal order. In political philosophy, whenever morality is equated with freedom (Kant) or radical individualism becomes definitive of justice (as in certain strands of libertarianism or anarchism[47]), one finds a refusal to see the dilemma between the two. Relatedly, the dilemma is most obviously negated within the most common trope of political philosophy: theories of justice defining the ideal arrangements of the best possible regime that, in their dominant liberal-democratic mode, specify the conditions that would need to obtain for all citizens to enjoy free and equal citizenship. While there is, of course, substantial diversity within political philosophy about

---

[47] Mikhail Bakunin, for instance, articulates an ideal arrangement that contemplates the resolution of any conflict between the claims of morality and the desire for individual freedom: "Freedom, morality, and the human dignity of the individual consists precisely in this: that he does good not because he is forced to do so, but because he freely conceives it, wants it, and loves it." *Bakunin on Anarchy*, ed. Sam Dolgoff (New York: Knopf, 1972), 240.

how to define social justice—including Rawlsian models that define it as what free and equal citizens would agree to in a fair decision-making situation (usually construed as either property-owning democracy or liberal socialism); so-called capabilities approaches that look to maximize human welfare and development; neo-republican models with their emphasis on non-domination; Marxist models with their promise of human emancipation via revolutionary reordering of the means of production; and various discourses on global justice—what all of these perspectives share is a focus on defining a *future* state in which social justice would obtain and thus in which the problem of reconciling the freedom of the advantaged and the unfreedom of the disadvantaged would be solved, usually because equal political freedom has been secured for all.

What these approaches leave out is the very context that inspires Dylan's sense of a dilemma: all the work needed—all the sacrifice of individuality he and others like him would have to make—in order to bring about a more just situation in a particular political context. Because this sacrifice is ultimately about not only resources and power (playing by the rules of a more just system) but also time and energy (working to implement a more just set of rules in the first place), one cannot simply appeal to social justice itself as a motivation to act in behalf of it. The mere articulation of an ideal of justice overlooks how such results will be achieved and thus avoids the question of how much those who already are relatively free should sacrifice their time, independence of mind and spirit, and other resources to bring about a more just arrangement. It is not just political philosophy that often denies the very premise of a potential tradeoff between morality and freedom, but also numerous platitudinous tendencies within the contemporary culture. The American Pledge of Allegiance—"I pledge allegiance to the flag of the United States of America, and to the Republic for which it stands, one Nation under God, indivisible, *with liberty and justice for all*"—is one such instance. The familiar phrase "nobody's free until everybody's free" is another.[48] If this phrase were true, social justice would be much easier to motivate. Martin Luther King was more accurate when he famously proclaimed that "injustice anywhere is a *threat* to justice everywhere"—that those who possess liberty should be personally concerned with the unfreedom of others because that unfreedom *could* portend their own—but his no-less-famous next line, "we are caught in an inescapable network of mutuality," is unfortunately an exaggeration if it is taken to deny the all-too-common occurrence whereby some can live their whole

---

[48] This line is often attributed to the civil rights leader Fannie Lou Hamer.

lives in relative freedom, prosperity, and comfort, while others remain subject to unjust and unnecessary suffering and deprivation.[49]

A second approach, only slightly more similar to Dylan's, is to recognize that social justice requires a great deal from individuals—especially those who are prosperous and well situated—and to assert therefore that individuals have a duty to fulfill its obligations. As we have seen, such a view is increasingly common in philosophy and has been defended from a variety of metaethical standpoints. To give but one additional example, Katarzyna de Lazari-Radek and Peter Singer claim "that a highly demanding morality is reasonable, given the world in which we are living ... the state of the world is such that it is hard not to think that those who can make a positive difference to it face demanding obligations to do so."[50] Dylan does not deny the potential truth of a highly demanding morality, but nonetheless publicly refuses to commit himself to realizing it, invoking his competing desire to practice a life of individual freedom. Lazari-Radek and Singer are, of course, aware of the problem that moral obligation will be experienced as being in tension with individuals' self-focused aims, as this is precisely what is indicated when they call the morality they defend "highly demanding." But, unlike with Dylan, there is no spirit of tragedy in their reflections—no positing of an ultimate disharmony or chaos in our ethical lives—since the point for them is simply for individuals to realize that, whatever they do in practice, it is "reasonable" to fulfill their moral obligation to the maximum possible extent. If individuals fail to do this, this is only a sign that they themselves—not normativity in general—are in ethical disarray. Dylan's position is different because, while he does not deny the highly demanding quality of moral obligation, he testifies to the urgency of a rival concern—his commitment, in the name of self-reliant individuality, to self-exploration, creativity, the right to be left alone, and the maintenance of excess free time so as to pursue, or not to pursue, the passing impulse of the hour—that makes him not "unreasonable" in being unwilling to perform what is owed to others, but rather bereft of a sense of the reasonable, without faith in the ultimate harmonizability of the competing strains of his ethical life.[51]

---

[49] Martin Luther King Jr., "Letter from Birmingham City Jail," in *A Testament of Hope: The Essential Writings and Speeches*, ed. James M. Washington (New York: HarperCollins, 1986 [1963]), 290 (emphasis added).

[50] Lazari-Radek and Singer, *The Point of View of the Universe*, 328.

[51] To be sure, drawing on Sidgwick's distinction between what is owed and what we ought to blame others for, Lazari-Radek and Singer aim for what has been termed "effective altruism," meaning they do not want to condemn moral shortcomings if doing so would only lessen a person's remaining commitment to justice. See, for example, Lazari-Radek and Singer, *The Point of View of the Universe*, 331–33. But if this vantage point is one that, at least potentially, might lead Lazari-Radek and Singer not to directly condemn Dylan's self-reliance, it does not change the utterly untragic aspect of their moral outlook.

Other approaches in contemporary philosophy would express sympathy for Dylan's position—but too much so. That is, there are philosophical perspectives that would want to establish that Dylan's inability to realize a highly demanding moral obligation is itself reasonable and thus in various ways justified. Yet even if such perspectives suggest something distinct from the first two I have discussed, they are still informed by the same spirit of harmonization—the same interest in defining what an individual owes, with the expectation that what is owed can and should be fulfilled—that is absent from Dylan.

Consider in this regard a third philosophical approach that diverges from Dylan's. This concerns the idea of supererogation, which aims to instill harmony between self and other by making a distinction between two duties: those that are moral and required (the obligations an individual *must* fulfill) and those that are moral but not required, or *supererogatory* (which have moral worth and rightly bestow moral praise on those who fulfill them, but, if not fulfilled, are not a violation of moral obligation). Interestingly, the very conceptualization of the notion of supererogation dates almost precisely to Dylan's emergence on the public stage, perhaps because the mid-twentieth century, for the technological and social reasons I have discussed, was one of the first moments in human history in which such a radically extensive sense of moral obligation plausibly could be contemplated by a broad segment of the global population.[52] Yet, not only is the concept of supererogation contested within contemporary political philosophy, but, more to the point, it cannot be invoked to describe Dylan's pronouncement of his refusal to be a dependable agent in the service of social justice causes he otherwise supports. Dylan never suggests that the social justice causes he disclaims are not morally required. His thought here is provocative and arresting precisely because he suggests such causes *are* required, yet ones he nonetheless will not dependably support. For example, in an unpublished 1965 audio interview for *Playboy* with Nat Hentoff, Dylan reiterates his general withdrawal from ongoing social justice movements but then adds of such political work that "it definitely has to be done," acknowledging that "people are starving" and "lots of people are in bad trouble."[53] Dylan does not object here to the obligatoriness of the social justice work he disclaims but only explains that he no longer will be an active contributor to that work. Framed in the specific context of the 1960s, he nowhere states that individuals have no obligation to fight against racism, militarism, oppression, severe deprivation, and other social ills, such that individuals who failed to do these things would be free from blame, complicity, or other forms of moral

[52] J. O. Urmson, "Saints and Heroes," in *Essays in Moral Philosophy*, ed. A. I. Melden (Seattle: University of Washington Press, 1958).

[53] "Bob Dylan | Nat Hentoff *Playboy* Interview," posted by Route TV, video, 2:01:55, March 14, 2017, https://www.youtube.com/watch?v=4_WOtx9be0I, minutes 12–13, 15–16.

condemnation. When he himself ceases to work dependably in behalf of these ends, he does not claim to be limiting himself only to what is morally required but actually suggests that he is not doing what is required.

Fourth, and for related reasons, Dylan cannot be seen as espousing what has come to be known in philosophy as the "demandingness objection," according to which otherwise plausible theories of moral obligation should be rejected when they impose burdens on individuals that are too heavy.[54] For exponents of this approach, which is increasingly common in contemporary philosophy, more moderate alternatives regarding social obligation are justified precisely so as to restore the harmony between an individual's duties to others and his or her capacity to pursue private, self-directed aims. Rather than contemplate the potential demandingness of the current structure of the world, those who invoke the demandingness objection shrink what is required by social justice so as to accommodate the self-directed aims of moral agents and thus, from the start, rule out the possibility of an inescapable disharmony between these two sets of ends. The demandingness objection most commonly has been voiced in response to act utilitarianism, a philosophy typically seen as one of the most exacting because it would seem to require that an individual always behave in a fashion that maximizes the greatest overall good. As Richard Brandt expresses the objection: "Act-utilitarianism makes extreme and oppressive demands on the individual, so much so that it can hardly be taken seriously; like the Sermon on the Mount, it is a morality only for saints."[55] Brandt cites M. G. Singer, who likewise protests that act utilitarianism leads to "moral fanaticism, to the idea that no action is indifferent or trivial, that every occasion is momentous."[56] There is controversy in contemporary philosophy surrounding the demandingness objection, with numerous commentators reiterating sentiments similar to those of Brandt and M. G. Singer,[57] while others reject the objection either on the basis

[54] Here I follow Brian Berkey's definition: "It is common for philosophers to reject otherwise plausible moral theories on the ground that they are objectionably demanding, and to endorse 'Moderate' alternatives.'" Berkey, "The Demandingness of Morality: Toward a Reflective Equilibrium," *Philosophical Studies* 173, no. 11 (2016): 3015–35.

[55] Richard B. Brandt, *A Theory of the Good and the Right* (Buffalo, NY: Prometheus, 1998), 276.

[56] Singer quoted in Lazari-Radek and Singer, *The Point of View of the Universe*, 322. For the endorsement of the demandingness objection, made from a utilitarian perspective, see Brad Hooker, *Ideal Code, Real World: A Rule-Consequentialist Theory of Morality* (New York: Oxford University Press, 2003), 149–58. Non-utilitarian expressions of the demandingness objection can be found in the work of Bernard Williams (whom I discuss in the main text) and Samuel Scheffler, among many others. See Lazari-Radek and Singer, *The Point of View of the Universe*, chapter 11.

[57] Liam Murphy comments that "others who have made the objection are too numerous to mention." Murphy, *Moral Demands in Nonideal Theory* (Oxford: Oxford University Press, 2000), 136. One additional specific example is Kurt Baier, *The Moral Point of View: A Rational Basis of Ethics* (Ithaca, NY: Cornell University Press, 1966).

of logic (why should the demandingness of a moral obligation be a reason not to abide by it?[58]) or, as well, on claims that our current world is such that privileged, well-off people simply have large and demanding obligations to ameliorate poverty, disease, malnutrition, and other gross and correctible evils in the world.[59] Perhaps the most common response is that of philosophers, otherwise sympathetic to utilitarian ethics, who try to rescue utilitarianism from the demandingness objection, often by claiming that utilitarianism in fact requires a more moderate degree of social responsibility than others have supposed.[60]

However one comes down on the demandingness objection, it is difficult to read Dylan's pronouncement of his withdrawal from social justice as falling within it. Dylan does not insist on the wrongness or falsity of the moral obligations he does not fulfill. He never suggests that a moral obligation can be false simply because it is excessive or that any conceptualization of social responsibility, in order to be credible, must leave ample space for self-directed pursuits. He does not propose some more moderate amount of social responsibility he would be prepared to dependably fulfill. Rather than seek a reconciliation between social responsibility and self-reliance so that both commitments could be adequately addressed, Dylan points instead, in a tragic spirit, to the possibility that there is an inescapable tradeoff between the two. The problem that social responsibility poses to self-reliance, as he articulates it, is not simply that it may ask for too much (i.e., an excessive amount of time and resources as espousers of the demandingness objection worry) but that it requires a flattening of individuality, a conformity of mind and spirit, at which he bristles. Recall that when Dylan declares his refusal to continue to be a reliable member of the civil rights movement of the 1960s, he places special emphasis on the conformity it would impose upon him.[61] Dylan's objection to the perceived conformism imposed by social justice work, combined with the absence of any claim about the propriety of a less demanding form of social justice obligation, is a sign that he is not invoking the demandingness objection and likewise is not implicitly supporting some alternate arrangement in which duty to others and self-reliance might be harmonized. If espousers of the demandingness objection make the objection to refute particular moral obligations as excessive and false, Dylan leaves uncontested the idea that our responsibility to social justice is heavy and large, though

[58] See David Sobel, *From Valuing to Value: A Defense of Subjectivism* (Oxford: Oxford University Press, 2017), chapter 12.

[59] See Lazari-Radek and Singer, *The Point of View of the Universe*, chapter 11.

[60] See Sobel, *From Valuing to Value*, 238.

[61] Recall Dylan's statement "I agree with everything that's happening but I'm not part of no Movement. If I was, I wouldn't be able to do anything else but be in 'the Movement.' I just can't have people sit around and make rules for me. I do a lot of things no Movement would allow." Quoted in Cott, "The Crackin', Shakin', Breakin' Sounds," in *Essential Interviews*, 28.

in his case confidently unfulfilled due to the competing concern of self-reliant individuality.

A fifth discourse that would seem to gesture in the direction of Dylan's with-drawal from social responsibility, but in fact is also importantly distinct, comes from philosophers who challenge the so-called overridingness of morality.[62] If the most common conception of morality is that it necessarily overrides all other concerns,[63] critics of this idea suggest that morality is but one dimension of ethical life, such that other considerations—including legality, etiquette, and an individual's prudential interest in his or her own affairs—can be invoked over and against moral demands. In the context of the extensive moral obligations arguably placed upon privileged individuals within the current structure of the world, a challenger to morality's overridingness might claim that individuals have ethical interests besides those of morality that understandably will lead them to turn their back on social justice work from time to time. That is, a chal-lenger to the overridingness of morality might resist the demands of social jus-tice by calling into question not whether those demands are in fact what morality requires, but rather the place of morality within ethical life. It is true that this perspective resembles Dylan's withdrawal from social justice in the mid-1960s in certain respects. Like Dylan, it appreciates a situation in which one is led away from social responsibility because of a commitment to other values, such as indi-viduality; and like him, it does not deny that fulfilling these other commitments comes at the expense of fulfilling moral obligations. However, these similarities are outweighed by key differences. Purveyors of the challenge to overridingness still aim to seek ethical harmony between concern for self and duties to others. This is most obviously the case when the challenge to overridingness is intended to encourage attention to extra-moral factors thought to be needed to motivate support for moral ends, on the idea that moral aims, such as securing the welfare of others and their fair treatment, are only *effectively* binding on us insofar as they emanate out of an education that, through extra-moral considerations, cultivates an elevation of moral concerns.[64] But the spirit of harmony is also at play among challengers to overridingness who decenter morality and thus enable the pur-suit of non-moral concerns to take place free from blame or even any ethical ambiguity whatsoever. Wolf, for instance, criticizes so-called moral saints for

---

[62] See, for example, Joshua Gert, "Moral Overridingness," in *International Encyclopedia of Ethics*, 9 vols., ed. Hugh LaFollette (Hoboken, NJ: Wiley-Blackwell, 2013).

[63] See, for example, Richard M. Hare, *Freedom and Reason* (Oxford: Oxford University Press, 1963); Hare, *Moral Thinking* (Oxford: Oxford University Press, 1981). Also see Sebastian Schleidgen, ed. *Should We Always Act Morally?: Essays on Overridingness* (Marburg, Germany: Tectum Verlag, 2012).

[64] See Philippa Foot, "Morality as a System of Hypothetical Imperatives," *Philosophical Review* 81, no. 3 (1972): 305–16.

manifesting certain undesirable qualities.[65] Slote praises what he calls "admirable immorality"—situations in which an individual violates moral norms in ways that he thinks we would all support.[66] Others suggest that we would not want to live in a world in which morality was fully realized.[67] Dylan, however, does none of this. He does not criticize moral saints but routinely celebrates them, and not just in his gospel period but throughout his life.[68] He does not suggest that his own violations of social justice requirements are admirable or especially deserving of praise. He nowhere suggests that the world would be worse if social justice were more universally realized. In short, whereas a function of the challenge to overridingness is to re-establish a harmony between self and other—by delineating the conditions under which individuals might justifiably, though not morally, turn their backs on morality—Dylan does not go this far: he does not claim that his self-reliant individuality properly trumps his obligations to social justice. True, his actions and his pithy remarks suggest that, for him, he will often privilege individuality over justice, but this is a testimony more than a justification. That Dylan does not decenter morality—that he does not claim that the value of self-reliant individuality justifiably outweighs moral considerations or definitively delineates a space where he might blamelessly pursue non-moral, self-directed aims—is reflected in many of the contexts in which he expresses his unwillingness to participate in social justice. Whereas the examples Slote invokes to show that morality does not always override other considerations appeal to the alleged *necessity* of transcending morality for some supremely valuable end (as in Churchill firebombing civilians to beat the Nazis; Gauguin abandoning his family to pursue his art; the need for a leader to dirty his or her hands to properly defend the polity), the necessity of Dylan's withdrawal from social justice is never so clear. It is not just that attention to one's individuality perhaps pales in comparison to winning World War II, but that Dylan consistently reminds us that to be committed to individuality is about not only elevated purposes (creativity, non-conformity, independence) but capricious and indulgent ones too. To consider just one example of this, when asked in San Francisco in 1965 if he would be attending a protest against the Vietnam War later in the evening, he

---

[65] Susan Wolf, "Moral Saints," *Journal of Philosophy* 79, no. 8 (1982): 419–39.

[66] Michael Slote, *Goods and Virtues* (Oxford: Clarendon Press, 1993), chapter 4. Some have questioned, effectively in my view, just how compelling Slote's argument is in this regard. See Marcia Baron, "On Admirable Immorality," *Ethics* 96, no. 3 (1986): 557–66.

[67] As Bernard Williams writes: "While we are sometimes guided by the notion that it would be the best of worlds in which morality were universally respected and all men were of a disposition to affirm it, we have in fact deep and persistent reasons to be grateful that this is not the world we have." Williams, *Moral Luck* (Cambridge, UK: Cambridge University Press, 1981), 23.

[68] Dylan, for example, includes the song "They Killed Him"—celebrating the martyrdoms of Jesus, Gandhi, and King—in his 1986 album *Knocked Out Loaded*.

replied, almost laughing: "No, I'll be busy tonight."[69] This insouciance, with its abrasiveness and whim, is a reminder that Dylan, in testifying to his refusal to be a dependable agent of social justice, is not claiming to establish agreed-upon limits to what is owed to others, but rather is privileging self-reliant individuality without assurance that such limits exist, without—in other words—a sense of being in the right.

A sixth perspective, closer yet to Dylan but still not quite his own, is the critique of morality made by Bernard Williams in the name of what he calls integrity: namely, the capacity to act as a distinct agent, to operate in light of projects and commitments that are one's own and provide a sense of meaning to one's life.[70] Deontological moral theories, for Williams, treat moral agents as identical (as "*qua* agent," "as a rational agent and no more"[71]) and in this sense disrespect their integrity. Utilitarianism, he thinks, goes even further in denying integrity by abstracting the separateness of agents and focusing instead on collective outcomes—however these are achieved.[72] There is much in Dylan that suggests that, for him as well, part of the problem with moral obligation is that it undermines his integrity, in Williams's sense of the word. In "It's Alright, Ma," recall that Dylan objects to the moral sentiment of pity because it breeds sameness; likewise, in "Maggie's Farm," he makes a similar objection: the problem with working in collective efforts is that they inhibit one's specific individuality from shining through. What also makes Williams's position somewhat close to Dylan's is that in invoking integrity Williams sometimes is careful to argue that integrity does not invalidate moral theories, but rather stands outside of morality as a concern that morality cannot satisfactorily recognize or appreciate. Williams suggests something like this when he writes, taking utilitarianism as an object of critique, that the problem is *not* that utilitarianism is necessarily wrong in what it requires ("if [as I suppose] the utilitarian is right in this case"[73])—that, in other words, the problem with utilitarianism is not that it simply fails to include the good of integrity within its calculus.[74] Rather, Williams takes issue

[69] See Sean Curnyn, "What Dylan Is Not," *Washington Examiner*, October 2, 2006, https://www.washingtonexaminer.com/weekly-standard/what-dylan-is-not.

[70] Williams, "A Critique of Utilitarianism," in *Utilitarianism: For and Against*, ed. J. J. C. Smart and Bernard Williams (Cambridge, UK: Cambridge University Press, 1973), 108–18.

[71] Williams, *Ethics and the Limits of Philosophy* (London: Fontana, 1985), 69.

[72] As Williams puts it: "If Kantianism abstracts in moral thought from the identity of persons, utilitarianism strikingly abstracts from their separateness." Williams, *Moral Luck* (Cambridge, UK: Cambridge University Press, 1981), 3.

[73] Williams, "A Critique of Utilitarianism," 117.

[74] I am indebted to the perceptive analysis of Sophie-Grace Chappell, "Bernard Williams," in *The Stanford Encyclopedia of Philosophy*, ed. Edward N. Zalta and Uri Nodelman (Stanford, CA: The Metaphysics Research Lab, Philosophy Department, Stanford University, 2023), https://plato.stanford.edu/archives/sum2023/entries/williams-bernard/.

with utilitarianism at a more fundamental level, claiming that the very process of making felicific calculations, weighing costs and benefits and pleasure and pains, is in itself contradictory to the practice of agency: "The reason why utilitarianism cannot understand integrity is that it cannot coherently describe the relations between a man's projects and his actions."[75] In juxtaposing to morality the competing value of integrity, Williams would seem to be articulating a posture similar to Dylan's when Dylan turns his back on social justice movements because he feels they demand from him a boring conformity and flattening of his individuality.

But, in fact, Williams and Dylan do not share the same position, since Williams, much more than Dylan, ultimately destabilizes the authority of moral systems that cannot accommodate integrity, whereas Dylan is more consistent in acknowledging that the obligations he disclaims are, after all, fully appropriate as moral requirements. That is, unlike Dylan, Williams often objects to moral theorization as such.[76] Williams not only is more metaethically confident than Dylan in presenting integrity as an absolute, universal value,[77] but also claims, unlike Dylan, that a moral theory that cannot accommodate integrity becomes "absurd," thereby effectively rejecting the authority of utilitarianism and other parallel moral systems after all:

> It is absurd to demand of . . . a man, when the sums come in from the utility network which the projects of others have in part determined, that he should just step aside from his own project and decision and acknowledge the decision which utilitarian calculation requires. It is to alienate him in a real sense from his actions and the source of his action in his own convictions. It is to make him into a channel between the input of everyone's projects, including his own, and an output of optimific decision; but this is to neglect the extent to which *his* projects and *his* decisions have to be seen as the actions and decisions which flow from

[75] Williams, "A Critique of Utilitarianism," 100.

[76] See, for example, Williams, *Ethics and the Limits of Philosophy*, 117. As Chappell summarizes: "[Williams] rejected the codification of ethics into moral theories that views such as Kantianism and (above all) utilitarianism see as essential to philosophical thinking about ethics, arguing that our ethical life is too untidy to be captured by any systematic moral theory . . . He believes that ethical thinking cannot be systematised without intolerable distortions and losses, because to systematise is, inevitably, to streamline our ethical thinking in a reductionist style" ("Bernard Williams").

[77] Williams suggests the universality of integrity when he writes: "If you want the world to contain generous, forceful, resolute, creative and actually happy people, you do not wish it to contain people who uniformly think in such a way that their actions will satisfy the requirements of utilitarianism." Williams, *Moral Luck*, 51.

the projects and attitudes with which he is most closely identified. It is thus, in the most literal sense, an attack on his integrity.[78]

In calling such utilitarianism absurd, Williams suggests that it—and the broader system of morality of which it aims to be a part—is defective. As much as Williams sometimes tries to keep alive a sense that the morality that contradicts integrity may be correct, this subtle point is difficult for him to maintain. If utilitarianism is absurd, then it seems to be wrong after all, and the agent who does not abide by it is exonerated. It is not by chance that Williams is often seen as a leading progenitor of the demandingness objection and the challenge to morality's overridingness, because as soon as integrity becomes a value that rightly challenges the scope or content of otherwise plausible moral demands, his position collapses into these others.[79] In any case, Williams is different from Dylan in being led to challenge more aggressively the authority of a morality incompatible with integrity. After all, Williams, unlike Dylan, can express criticism of the very concept of what he calls "the morality system," which he refers to as a "peculiar institution."[80] Williams's anthropology of morality—his examination, in a spirit of detachment, of how the idea of morality has functioned in human ethical life—has made him one of the most important moral philosophers of the last half century, but his skepticism toward the very notion of a compelling theory of moral obligation has led some to read Williams (rightly, I think) as undermining the practice of moral obligation.[81] This quality distinguishes him from Dylan, who typically does not indict the moral obligations he does not meet as absurd or otherwise inappropriate.

If we look past the ambiguities of Williams's account of integrity, we can find him articulating a seventh position, closer still to Dylan's (yet nonetheless importantly distinct from him too): the idea that there is an irredeemably *tragic* element in ethical life such that certain equally valid commitments—like individuality and social justice—unfortunately conflict, so that people cannot expect to realize all of the ends they hold dear but must choose and, in choosing,

---

[78] Williams, "A Critique of Utilitarianism," 116–17.

[79] For an account of how Williams's objection to moral theories for failing to respect "integrity" has been closely related to, and instrumental to the development of, the demandingness objection, see Berkey, "The Demandingness of Morality," 3016, n. 1. For its connection to, if not equivalence with, the challenge to morality's overridingnness, see Sandra Jane Fairbanks, "A Defense of Overridingness," in Schleidgen, *Should We Always Act Morally?*, 11.

[80] Williams, *Ethics and the Limits of Philosophy*, 193–218.

[81] For an overview of the critique of Williams as being insufficiently committed to morality and drawing insufficient ethical conclusions—made by figures such as Martha Nussbaum, among others—see Mark P. Jenkins, *Bernard Williams* (Montreal: McGill-Queen's University Press, 2006), 6, passim.

experience regret about what is not pursued. Even if Williams does not consistently frame the problematic relationship between "integrity" and "the morality
system" precisely in these tragic terms, he nonetheless stands out for challenging
the prevailing and pervasive assumption in contemporary moral philosophy that
there can be no conflict of duties.[82] Thus, regardless of his specific account of
integrity, Williams might be seen as someone who in fact provides the philosophical apparatus by which to cognize Dylan's own sense of conflict between
his commitment to individual self-reliance and his commitment to social justice.

Yet here, too, there are key discontinuities that further help specify what is
fresh and distinctly provocative in Dylan's position. Yes, Dylan affirms a tragic
tradeoff between individual self-reliance and social justice, but the tragedy he
contemplates is of a different character from the one considered by Williams.
For one thing, tragedy for Williams is defined in terms of a situation of mutually exclusive ends in which it is logically or empirically impossible to perform two opposed actions. To illustrate this circumstance, Williams appeals to
Greek myth and literature, above all to Antigone, who cannot simultaneously
fulfill her familial duty to bury her brother and her civic duty to obey the state's
prohibition against his burial; and, likewise, to Agamemnon, who must choose
between sacrificing his daughter Iphigenia and losing the Trojan War. In these
cases, there is nothing that the individual can do to avoid the tragic tradeoff.
With Dylan, however, the ethical tragedy he contemplates is not of this type.
It is, after all, *possible* to employ one's self-reliant individuality in the service of
full devotion to social justice causes—to, in effect, make social justice definitive of one's personal sense of vocation. Even if some celebrators of self-reliance
have exaggerated this tendency and mistakenly assumed that self-reliance always
will be devoted to the liberation of others, it is nonetheless true that there exist
individuals—such as moral heroes routinely celebrated—whose sense of individual purpose is identified with effecting as much positive social change as is
possible in the world. Thus, Dylan has the option to overcome the tragic tradeoff
he faces in a way that Antigone and Agamemnon cannot. Put differently, what
leads Dylan to turn away from social justice is not simply the most noble aspects
of individuality that Williams associates with being an agent with integrity—
non-conformity, self-development, independence, creativity, and the like—but,

---

[82] See Williams, "Conflicts of Values," in *Moral Luck*, 71–82; and "Ethical Consistency," in
Problems of the Self (Cambridge, UK: Cambridge University Press, 1973), 166–86. Williams not only
insists upon the possibility of ethical conflict but also makes the case—correctly, I think—that in general moral philosophy has tended to deny this possibility. Williams claims, in other words, that it is
a feature of the so-called morality system that moral obligations "cannot conflict, ultimately, really, or
at the end of the line." Williams, *Ethics and the Limits of Philosophy*, 176. On the general tendency of
moral and political philosophy to deny the conflict of duties, see Jeffrey Edward Green, *The Shadow
of Unfairness* (New York: Oxford University Press, 2016), 206, n. 22.

as we have seen, more modest and ethically less appealing considerations, such as a simple desire to be left alone, an interest in avoiding risk and protecting himself from danger, and a refusal to consistently act on an obligation borne from privilege. True, one could reframe the problematic and say that Dylan in fact does face a tradeoff that is inescapable, since there is no way *for him* to combine the specific form of self-reliant individuality he prizes (with its element of whim, refusal to join any movement as such, and craving for excess time and resources so as to have maximum discretion in choosing what to do each day) with a dependable commitment to social justice. But this would not change the fact that Dylan's tragedy is different from Williams's because, for Dylan, it is not individuality as such that is in contradiction with morality, but only a particular, contingent, revisable, and ethically ambiguous *bourgeois* conceptualization of individuality that he hypothetically could abandon for another conceptualization at any time. And even if we were to frame Dylan's tragedy in a way more similar to Williams's, as something insoluble, the point remains that it would be empirical, not metaphysical or metaethical: that is, it would be based on not only a certain conception of individuality but a particular socioeconomic situation by which to enjoy it. Put another way, Dylan's sense of a tradeoff between justice and selfhood is inseparable from his occupying a bourgeois socioeconomic situation; were he to occupy a different socioeconomic situation (such as victim of injustice), the tragic tradeoff would dissolve. For this reason, Dylan's circumstance is not tragic in an absolute sense—his experience of an inescapable conflict between self and other refers not to a universal feature of humanity but to a particular, bourgeois lifeform. By contrast, an absolute tragedy of the kind invoked by Williams means that *whatever* you do, you will feel regret. Thus, the bourgeois tragedy of which Dylan sings, in which regret is not apodictically necessary but lived and chosen (i.e., we as bourgeois *opt* to live a kind of life that experiences duty to self as requiring us to turn our back to what we owe to justice), is one in which regret is contingently written into one's subjective identity, not imposed from without. Dylan is individualistic about his individuality—it is not inherent in individuality to turn one's back against the fight for justice. If you invoke individuality as a reason not to pursue otherwise required social justice obligations, it is not individuality or integrity itself—but a particular definition of these values, a particular choice about how you want to use your individuality—that you are invoking.

Relatedly, when Williams suggests a tragic tradeoff between individuality and social justice—or, in his terms, between integrity and the moral system—he does so on the basis of an alleged *universal* human interest in being an agent. That is, the "integrity" that Williams finds to be at odds with "the morality system" is presented as something that all of us are likely to recognize, without differentiation, as a vital human concern. Williams does not pursue the issue of the socioeconomic factors whereby both the capacity for and appreciation of agency are experienced differently by differently situated individuals. There is little awareness in Williams's work, for instance, that the value of integrity in his sense of the word is something that may matter less to those in a situation of extreme deprivation, disease, systematic violence, or other types of existential threat. Dylan, however, is much readier to acknowledge that the value of individuality as he defines it—of doing what one wants, controlling how one spends one's time, maintaining the discretion to drop out of any social commitment to pursue creative or inner aims *or no aims whatsoever*—is something closely connected to possessing a modicum of wealth, power, and privilege. The tragic situation he faces is thus not one we all face by virtue of our humanity, but rather one that only some of us confront: namely, those who are prosperous and well situated—"free," as Dylan might describe it[83]—and who therefore are well equipped to pursue a life of self-directed agency, yet who also recognize that this value is challenged by the call of moral conscience, especially in light of the specific crises and emergencies of the present world.

Dylan's tragedy is as real and vexing as Williams's conception of it, but it is more ethically ambiguous and, in a sense, more disharmonious in how it approaches the relationship of duty to self and duty to others. Williams's insistence, against the grain of most moral philosophy, that there are insoluble conflicts of values preserves some element of harmony that is lacking in Dylan, since the fact of this conflict means for Williams that we are all confronted by the same inescapable problem and in a certain respect, therefore, are all off the hook. Dylan's version of tragedy provides no such exoneration because the ethical conflict he faces is as much a product of his lifestyle and choice as of the moral structure of the universe. Dylan's is thus an empirical tragedy rather than a metaphysical one. It discloses a bourgeois subjectivity that lives as if individual self-reliance and social justice were in tension, rather than making the more speculative claim that this tension is a permanent and necessary feature of humanity. Because Dylan owns this tension—accepts it as a particular rather than universal problem—he introduces his own subjectivity into the discourse on the relationship of morality and freedom. He announces a certain way of living in the world, not the truth of how all must necessarily live within it. If we were not like him, his stance would matter less. But for reasons I have discussed, a great many of us are.

Dylan stands out for so starkly and openly facing the *moral chaos* of bourgeois disharmony between duty to self and duty to others—between the claims of freedom and those of justice. I do not mean to suggest that Dylan is altogether

---

[83] See, in this regard, "It's Alright, Ma (I'm Only Bleeding)": "For them that must obey authority / That they do not respect in any degree / Who despise their jobs, their destinies / Speak jealously of them that are free."

distinct in confronting the possibility of this chaos, as there are philosophical perspectives, including elements of some of the seven perspectives I have just outlined, that veer in Dylan's direction. But more so than the philosophers, Dylan leads us to confront the ethical implications that follow from an inability to clarify—let alone accomplish—the proper relationship between self and other. Even philosophers who have gestured toward an admission of chaos have run away from it at the same time. Consider in this regard Sidgwick, maybe the greatest expositor of utilitarian ethics, who acknowledges that figuring out the relationship between other-directed moral obligation and rational egoism— a challenge he sometimes summarized as the problem of "the Dualism of the Practical Reason"—is "the profoundest problem in Ethics."[84] Sidgwick strikingly concludes the first edition of his *Methods of Ethics* by acknowledging both that he has not been able to provide sufficient empirical or logical argument to overcome this problem and that, without untestable metaphysical faith in divine providence or some other conception of a perfect moral order—without, that is, "a hypothesis unverifiable by experience reconciling the Individual with the Universal Reason, without a belief, in some form or other, that the moral order which we see imperfectly realized in this actual world is yet actually perfect"— "the Cosmos of Duty is thus really reduced to a Chaos: and the prolonged effort of the human intellect to frame a perfect ideal of rational conduct is seen to have been foredoomed to inevitable failure."[85] Yet, if this admission would seem to point to the truth of moral chaos, Sidgwick moves in the opposite direction, whether by continuing throughout his life to make numerous additional philosophical attempts to solve the problem (all the while never claiming victory)[86] or explaining the appropriateness of the extrarational faith he felt to be indispensable until the problem was solved. In a letter to Roden Noel from 1870, for example, Sidgwick at once testified to the conflict between self-directed and other-directed duties—"In the face of the conflict between Virtue & Happiness, my own voluntary life, and that of every other man constituted like me, i.e. I believe, of every normal man, is reduced to hopeless anarchy"—yet also claimed that he had avoided this "intolerable anarchy" via his faith in "the Postulate of Immortality," that is, the providential belief that duty to others somehow ultimately fulfills duty to self.[87] Thus, for Sidgwick, chaos is avoided, on the one

---

[84] Henry Sidgwick, *The Methods of Ethics*, 7th ed. (London: Macmillan, 1907), x; 386, n. 4.

[85] Henry Sidgwick, *The Methods of Ethics*, 1st ed. (London: Macmillan, 1874), 473.

[86] For an overview of these, see Jerome B. Schneewind, *Sidgwick's Ethics and Victorian Morality* (Oxford: Oxford University Press, 1977), 374–79.

[87] Quoted in Bart Schultz, *Henry Sidgwick: Eye of the Universe* (New York: Cambridge University Press, 2004), 441.

hand, by "patience and hope"[88] in the future progress of philosophy and, on the other, by his willingness to see "belief in a Divine Being" as "indispensable to a normal human mind" and also as not inconsistent with the vocation of the philosopher.[89]

To consider a more recent example of a philosopher who is unusual for gesturing toward chaos but also, in a manner characteristic of contemporary philosophy, gravitates away from just this problem, Thomas Nagel is distinct for so honestly acknowledging the contemporary difficulty of squaring an impartial moral attitude with a partial concern with one's individual projects, concerns, and pursuits. In terms reminiscent of Sidgwick, Nagel calls the tension between the personal and the impersonal "the central problem of political theory," and also observes that the "conflict between personal and impersonal standpoints is particularly conspicuous for those who are relatively fortunate."[90] Nagel emphasizes just how vexing the situation is: "[T]he problem of designing institutions that do justice to the equal importance of all persons, without making unacceptable demands on individuals, has not been solved. . . . [W]e really do not know how to live together."[91] Nagel even suggests a further problem—that, given the magnitude of the moral responsibilities facing the world ("the alleviation of misery, ignorance, powerlessness, and elevation of most of our fellow human beings to a minimally decent standard of existence"), it might happen that even if duties to others and duties to self could be understood and agreed upon, there are scenarios, likely in existence today, in which the disadvantaged might *rightly* claim more than the advantaged *rightly* felt that they owed.[92] And yet, Nagel does not really dwell in such diffidence or puzzlement. The bulk of his analysis explores the institutions and principles by which the tension between duty to self and duty to others might be lessened within the contemporary context so

[88] Henry Sidgwick, *Philosophy, Its Scope and Relations: An Introductory Course of Lectures* (London: Macmillan, 1902), 231.

[89] Henry Sidgwick, "A Dialogue on Time and Common Sense," *Mind* 3, no. 12 (1894): 446.

[90] Thomas Nagel, *Equality and Partiality* (New York: Oxford University Press, 1991), 18.

[91] Nagel, 5.

[92] Or, as Nagel puts it, "The classes of outcomes that it is unreasonable for each of them to reject may not intersect," elaborating: "I believe the world contains inequalities so great that they generate this moral situation. To be sure, there are significant sacrifices—much greater than commonly accepted—that it is unreasonable for the rich to refuse for the benefit of the poor; and there are other sacrifices so great that it would be unreasonable of the poor to impose them on the rich, even if they were able to do so. But between these two outer boundaries there is a gap, within which fall all those levels of sacrifice which the poor would have sufficient reason to impose if they could and which the rich have sufficient reason to resist if they can. This may seem to authorize pure selfishness, but that is too harsh a word for resistance to a radical drop in the standard of living of oneself and one's family." Nagel, 172, 173–74.

that the "urgent needs and serious deprivation" suffered by many might thereby be alleviated.[93]

While Dylan recognizes the same disharmony between self and other addressed by Sidgwick and Nagel, he is different in abiding in the face of the chaos this causes rather than fleeing from it. Unlike Sidgwick, Dylan in the mid-1960s does not fall back on a speculative faith in an unobserved cosmic moral order, nor does he posit, without evidence, that future learning might finally reconcile self-directed and other-directed commitments. Dylan instead affirms his egoism over and against the claim of moral obligation to others, without articulating any faith, let alone certainty, that he is justified. And unlike Nagel, Dylan does not feel he must run away from the observation that we lack knowledge about how to live with each other, but instead affirms and practices a self-reliance that does not cancel this moral diffidence. Rather, Dylan in effect asks: If we truly do not know how to live with each other—if duty to self and duty to others remain unclarified and unharmonizable—how should I act when I privilege my individuality over and against otherwise plausible moral claims to help others? It is this kind of ethics—an ethics not about clarifying duties but about operating in the moral chaos of asserting individuality without either guilt or full justification—that Dylan practices. Here perhaps more than in any other context, we can appreciate Dylan when he says, "I accept chaos. I am not sure whether it accepts me."[94]

In the remainder of Part I, I pursue two ethical implications of Dylan's acceptance of moral chaos in which self and other are not in harmony, in which he turns his back on social justice in the name of his individuality without any assurance of being in the right. The first implication is that Dylan updates the ideal of self-reliance vis-à-vis its earlier articulation in the thought of Emerson and Thoreau. Emerson and Thoreau imbue their self-reliant withdrawal from social justice causes with a self-satisfaction that is lacking in Dylan, who is much readier to acknowledge the moral costs of self-reliance. This acknowledgment does not invalidate self-reliance but alters its epistemological, ethical, and political features, providing a variant of self-reliance more suitable to contemporary conditions. The second implication pertains not to withdrawal but to activism—specifically, to what it means to be a progressive insufficiently committed, but committed nonetheless, to social justice. Attending in particular to Dylan's underappreciated role

[93] Nagel, 12. For instance, Nagel explicitly differentiates his approach from pessimism and instead asserts: "The recognition of a serious obstacle is always a necessary condition of progress, and I believe there is hope that in the future, political and social institutions may develop which continue our unsteady progress toward moral equality, without ignoring the stubborn realities of human nature" (3).

[94] Liner notes to *Bringing It All Back Home* (1965).

at the 1963 March on Washington, I show that Dylan addresses the standpoint of the "bourgeois progressive" who is only partially devoted to rectifying injustice. Rather than satirize or simply reject the bourgeois progressive, Dylan calls for bourgeois self-awareness and, with it, anti-triumphalism. Together, these two implications show what it might mean for someone to knowingly recognize one's bourgeois status and honestly live in the moral chaos of preferring one's own individuality over and against *one's own sense* of what social justice requires.

I.5. Self-Reliance Without Self-Satisfaction

The idea of self-reliance has special relevance for the study of democracy. It is, in the words of George Kateb, the "philosophy of democratic individuality" and "the soil and fruit and flower of modern democracy."[95] The democratic credentials of self-reliance are usually thought to reside in the fact that self-reliance is an ethical disposition that motivates support for democratic institutions as well as a way of life likely to flourish in democratic regimes and, for this reason, to attract people to democracy. Self-reliance is not to be equated with mere egoism or individualism as such, but rather refers to a specific form of individualism committed to human equality and a non-antagonistic relationship to society. It needs to be distinguished, as Kateb points out, from forms of individualism that promote hierarchical judgments (Nietzsche), total war against society in the name of one's uniqueness (Byron), the use of others as one's artistic medium (Napoleon), or the idealist denial of any reality beyond one's own mind.[96] Underlying the democratic character of self-reliance is the belief that its most central practices—freedom of thought, creative expression, sympathetic heeding of the environment (both human and natural), liberation from drudgery, and, above all, a dedication to identify and live in light of one's innermost thoughts and convictions—are conducive not just to healthy self-development but to beneficial consideration and care for those around us. As Emerson, still the most influential philosopher of self-reliance, puts it: "He only who is able to stand alone is qualified to be a citizen," adding that "society can never prosper, but must always be bankrupt, until every man does that which he was created to do."[97] Emerson may hyperbolize here, but his statement is a

[95] George Kateb, *Emerson and Self-Reliance* (Lanham, MD: Rowman & Littlefield, 2002), 197, 202.

[96] Kateb, 31.

[97] Ralph Waldo Emerson, "Speech at the Kansas Relief Meeting in Cambridge, September 10, 1856," in *The Complete Works of Ralph Waldo Emerson*, ed. Edward Waldo Emerson (New York: Houghton Mifflin, 1903–4), 255–63; Emerson, "Wealth," in *The Conduct of Life* (Boston: Ticknor and Fields, 1860), 29.

powerful reminder of self-reliance's theorization as a specifically democratic form of individualism.

However, the relevance of self-reliance to democracy is not just that it claims to define the ethical disposition of the democratic character, but that in doing so it pays uncommon attention to a problem that rarely gets addressed in democratic theory and political philosophy more generally: that of democratic citizens *not* doing all they might do to support democratic reforms whose urgency and propriety they otherwise agree with and support. As much as self-reliance marks a democratic form of individualism, it is not, after all, reducible to democracy itself. It can be practiced (at least by some) even when democratic conditions of free and equal citizenship do not sufficiently obtain. This means that within political situations where there is injustice and dire need of reform, which arguably is the condition of all states today, citizens committed to self-reliance have to face the tradeoff between time spent on self-cultivation and time directly devoted to achieving critically needed political change. To deny this tradeoff, as some interpreters of self-reliance have done, by assuming that self-reliant individuals always will work to achieve the self-reliance of others[98]—or to deny it in opposite fashion, as some critics of self-reliance have done, by arguing that because self-reliance can lead its practitioners to turn away from politics it is not democratic at all[99]—is to miss what is so compelling and instructive about the political lives of the great thinkers of self-reliance, who were simultaneously democrats fighting against injustice but also honest about their unwillingness to devote themselves to their political causes completely or even dependably.

The three figures I examine here—Emerson, Thoreau, and Dylan—are to my knowledge unique within the history of political thought in acknowledging, in the name of self-reliant individuality, an unwillingness to consistently work in behalf of otherwise endorsed democratic causes. I already have described how unusual Dylan's position is in this regard within the context of recent and contemporary politics, but in fact his stance is preceded in key respects by Emerson and Thoreau, both of whom Dylan knows as a reader.[100] Dylan's reflections on

[98] See, for example, Michael Strysick, "Emerson, Slavery, and the Evolution of the Principle of Self-Reliance," in *The Emerson Dilemma: Essays on Emerson and Social Reform*, ed. T. Gregory Garvey (Athens: University of Georgia Press, 2001), 141–42.

[99] See, for example, Denis Donoghue, *The American Classics: A Personal Essay* (New Haven, CT: Yale University Press, 2005), 42–43, 51; Yvor Winters, *Maule's Curse: Seven Studies in the History of American Obscurantism* (Norfolk, VA: New Directions, 1938), 135.

[100] On Dylan's placement of himself within the Emersonian tradition, see Mark Ford, "Trust Yourself: Emerson and Dylan," in *"Do You, Mr. Jones?" Bob Dylan with the Poets and Philosophers*, ed. Neil Corcoran (London: Chatto and Windus, 2003), 127–42; Jonathan Lethem, "The Genius and Modern Times of Bob Dylan," *Rolling Stone*, September 7, 2006. Dylan's song "I Contain Multitudes" (2020), with its reference to the famous lines of Walt Whitman, himself an Emersonian, further links Dylan to the nineteenth-century philosophy of self-reliance spearheaded by Emerson.

self-reliance should be seen as updating a prior tradition (albeit a very rare one), not inventing it wholesale.

To give an initial sense of Dylan's antecedents, who themselves acted as rebels rebelling against the rebellion, consider what Emerson proclaims in his 1840 lecture "Reforms," in which he addresses reformers actively engaged in behalf of such causes as temperance, abolition, and peace:

> Though I sympathize with your sentiment and abhor the crime you as-
> sail yet I shall persist in wearing this robe, all loose and unbecoming as
> it is, of inaction, this wise passiveness until my hour comes when I see
> how to act with truth as well as to refuse.[101]

Emerson does not renounce such causes, only a permanent devotion to them. The matter is especially poignant with respect to slavery, the political issue that most galvanized Emerson during his lifetime. In a journal entry from August 1, 1852, he writes:

> I waked at night, & bemoaned myself, because I had not thrown myself
> into this deplorable question of Slavery, which seems to want nothing
> so much as a few assured voices. But then, in hours of sanity, I recover
> myself, & say . . . I have quite other slaves to free than those negroes, to
> wit, imprisoned spirits, imprisoned thoughts, far back in the brain of
> man,—far retired in the heaven of invention, &, which, important to
> the republic of Man, have no watchman, or lover, or defender, but I.[102]

While Emerson is not disclaiming any role in the anti-slavery movement, he acknowledges that he is not as steadily committed as abolitionists like William Lloyd Garrison or Wendell Phillips. To be sure, by 1852, Emerson had spent al-most a decade giving addresses in support of emancipation, writing and publicly circulating letters against slavery, and refusing to speak at Northern organiza-tions that did not admit blacks as members (such as the New Bedford Lyceum in 1846)—and he would go on to continue to speak out against slavery, sometimes at personal risk, and take other actions like providing material support to John Brown. Moreover, the immediate context of Emerson's journal entry is perhaps the high point of his anti-slavery activism, as it occurs in the period in which he was virulently calling for resistance to the 1850 Fugitive Slave Act as well as

---

[101] Emerson, "Reforms," in *The Early Lectures of Ralph Waldo Emerson*, ed. Robert E. Spiller and Wallace E. Williams (Cambridge, MA: Harvard University Press, 1959–1972), 3:266.

[102] Emerson, *The Journals of Ralph Waldo Emerson*, ed. Ralph H. Orth and Alfred R. Ferguson (Cambridge, MA: Harvard University Press, 1977), 13:80.

eschewing his normal avoidance of partisan politics by actively campaigning for Free Soil congressional candidate John Palfrey in 1851 and soon after Republican Charles Sumner in 1854. But even in this period, Emerson is self-conscious that he could be doing much more to fight slavery and that the reason for his not doing so stems from a more fundamental duty to self-reliant individuality.

Emerson's self-consciousness of his lack of full engagement in behalf of causes he supports is given perhaps its most memorable articulation in his 1841 essay "Self-Reliance," in which he takes critical aim at "miscellaneous popular charities" and "the thousandfold Relief Societies," presumably not because he opposes the objectives of all such organizations but because he lacks what he calls a "spiritual affinity" to them—that is, an authentically felt personal connection to these otherwise noble endeavors. Thus, in the same essay, Emerson provocatively proclaims: "Do not tell me, as a good man did today, of my obligation to put all poor men in good situations. Are they my poor?"[103] These are not the words of an oligarch, market-utopian, or anti-statist. Nor are they the expression of someone in denial regarding the problems of the world or their susceptibility to improvement from human action. What lends these words force and also makes them so unusual is that they are expressed by a man supportive of the progressive causes of his day—a man who not only worked to combat slavery but also spoke out against Indian removal, supported women's suffrage, and donated to a wide variety of local and national charities—yet who still invokes his commitment to his individuality as something that overrides his obligation to participate in social justice movements.

With Thoreau, too, as much as he has a well-deserved reputation as an activist engaged in civil disobedience to oppose an American regime that he considered corrupted by slavery and unjust conflicts like the Mexican War, there is a parallel articulation of an unwillingness to devote himself entirely to politics, even in behalf of manifestly just political movements. Thoreau can thus say:

> I do not think it is quite sane for one to spend his whole life in talking or writing about this matter [slavery], unless he is continuously inspired, and I have not done so. A man may have other affairs to attend to.[104]

Likewise, Thoreau refused to join Vigilance Committees, even as he praised them as organizations devoted to protecting the vulnerable and administering justice.[105] To be sure, there is some complexity in Thoreau's posture, insofar as

---

[103] Emerson, "Self-Reliance," in *Essays and Lectures*, ed. Joel Porte (New York: Library of America, 1971), 263.

[104] Henry David Thoreau, "A Plea for Captain John Brown," in *Thoreau: Political Writings*, ed. Nancy Rosenblum (Cambridge, UK: Cambridge University Press, 2000), 153.

[105] See Rosenblum, *Thoreau: Political Writings*, xviii.

often his very withdrawal from political responsibility—his urging of his fellow citizens to forswear allegiance to the US government by desisting from voting, service in the militia, and the payment of certain taxes—is an intensely political act of civil disobedience. But not all of Thoreau's disengagement is of this character. Thoreau spoke ironically and critically of "benevolent societies" and "philanthropic enterprises," claiming: "As for Doing-good, that is one of the professions which are full. Moreover, I have tried it fairly, and, strange as it may seem, am satisfied that it does not agree with my constitution."[106] Thoreau thus departs from later iconic activists his own civil disobedience helped to inspire— figures like Gandhi and Martin Luther King—by continually emphasizing his own lack of full commitment to eradicating the very evils he sometimes also was resisting. Indeed, what is importantly unusual about Thoreau is that, like King, he could indict the conventional kind of political moderation—taking to task "the freest of my neighbors" who do not wish to resist the government be- cause "they dread the consequences to their property and families of disobe- dience to it"[107]—but, unlike King, recognize and himself embody an alternate kind of moderation having to do with an unwillingness, as a matter of his own self-reliance, to be dependably committed to political causes.

Thus, Dylan is not altogether alone in his unusual public stance of disclaiming support for otherwise endorsed social justice causes.

But why should the public acknowledgment from Emerson, Thoreau, and Dylan of their unwillingness to fully devote themselves to democratic causes they support, however unusual, be of interest to us? One reason is that they are explicit and self-conscious about a problematic situation that, despite being de- finitive of a great deal of ordinary political experience today, is little discussed in contemporary political theory.[108] Given this current lack of theoretical

---

[106] Thoreau, *Walden*, 52. With regard to philanthropic enterprises, Thoreau writes: "But all this is very selfish, I have heard some of my townsmen say. I confess that I have hitherto indulged very little in philanthropic enterprises. I have made some sacrifices to a sense of duty, and among others have sacrificed this pleasure also" (52). On Thoreau's ironic treatment of benevolent societies, see Rosenblum, *Thoreau: Political Writings*, xxvii.

[107] Thoreau, "Resistance to Civil Government," in *Thoreau: Political Writings*, 12.

[108] There is of course lively debate about how to define social justice and, by extension, the ex- tent of social responsibilities a relatively secure citizen owes to those who are vulnerable, needy, and oppressed. Libertarians, liberal democrats, and socialists, for instance, offer distinct accounts about these issues; and within each paradigm there is debate about how territorial borders further impact the meaning of social justice. However, no matter which philosophy a well-off and secure person in- tellectually adopts, there is still the question of how willing this person is to act on the basis of it. And it is this often-forgotten issue—not the tension between competing philosophies, but the tension be- tween one's individuality and the requirements of social justice, however how one chooses to define it—that is given such powerful voice by the great thinkers of self-reliance. When one considers that the project of realizing social justice is at present unachieved to such an extent that any philosophy of justice, including libertarianism, places demands on citizens to advocate significant social reforms,

reflection, Emerson, Thoreau, and Dylan perform a function for ordinary citizens today similar to the function Emerson says poets play for the young: "The young man reveres men of genius, because, to speak truly, they are more himself than he is."[109] But the relevance of Emerson, Thoreau, and Dylan is not simply that they are reflective of common experience (that they publicly and contemplatively acknowledge what so many of us only silently and tacitly do), but that, taken together, they are instructive for democratic ethics. This instructive element stems from the fact that there is a key difference relating to the issue of whether the self-reliance informing inaction is imbued with a *spirit of self-satisfaction*—that is, an ultimate ease about the moral status of their self-reliant withdrawal from social justice activism. Emerson and Thoreau, but not Dylan, manifest such self-satisfaction in three distinct ways: their belief in the ultimate political efficacy of their withdrawal (their paradoxical idea that periods of political non-engagement are conducive to the highest forms of political activity); their providentialism (their faith in an ultimately benign and purposive cosmic order, which thus lessens the impact of their periods of inaction); and their view that they are largely free from complicity vis-à-vis the evils they elect not to fight. Dylan lacks these three forms of self-satisfaction, and also the speculative metaphysics on which they often rest, and as a result his approach to the tension between self-reliant individuality and social responsibility is not just distinct, but, I argue, preferable on epistemological, ethical, and political grounds.

I elaborate these claims as follows: after briefly detailing the common bases for all three men's resistance to full-time political activism, I describe the three ways in which Dylan's form of self-reliance lacks the self-satisfaction of Emerson and Thoreau, concluding with a discussion of what I take to be the salutary implications for democracy of adopting Dylan's rather than Emerson's or Thoreau's form of self-reliant political inaction.

Emerson, Thoreau, and Dylan's Shared Idea of Self-Reliant Inaction

Seen broadly and from a distance, there is generic similarity in the way Emerson, Thoreau, and Dylan articulate their respective refusals to be fully committed to social justice causes they otherwise support. The problem with activism, all three think, is that it usually requires affixing oneself to some larger organization (such as an association, movement, or party), which not only imposes bureaucratic

---

the question explored by Emerson, Thoreau, and Dylan—how committed a relatively free individual ought to be to his or her political commitments—has a palpable salience.

[109] Emerson, "The Poet," in *The Complete Works of Ralph Waldo Emerson*, 3:5.

requirements irreducible to the political cause such activism serves but in its zealotry can promote the myopia of a single issue or, just as bad, the adoption of an overly narrow political identity. The self-reliance informing all three men's resistance to full-fledged organizational membership is not itself a single issue (but an infinite fount of creativity, expression, and development) nor a narrow political identity (since it resists any easy identification with conventional political categories and demands that engagement with politics be conducted in one's own personal and evolving idiom).[110] All three, therefore, share the concern that organized activism will lead them to become, in Emerson's words, "mere mouthpieces of a party,"[111] an "instrument" of reform organizations,[112] or "fractions of men" who have to compromise some aspect of their individuality in service to a larger political organization.[113]

A further problem with social justice movements, identified by all three men, is that the individuals who operate within them as professional activists, philanthropists, and reformers are often morally compromised—in the sense either of pursuing social justice for the sake of personal ambition or of using social justice as a substitute for inner emptiness (a lack of self-reliance)—and in such cases do not deserve to be too closely associated with or followed. In a well-known passage from "Self-Reliance," Emerson takes issue with "malice and vanity wear[ing] the coat of philanthropy," hypothesizing "an angry bigot assum[ing] [the] bountiful cause of Abolition" out of "uncharitable ambition."[114] As Thoreau makes clear, the problem is not limited to exceptionally disingenuous philanthropists but is an endemic risk of philanthropy itself: "Philanthropy is almost the only kind of virtue which is sufficiently appreciated by mankind. Nay, it is greatly overrated; and it is our selfishness which overrates it." What Thoreau indicts here is less the philanthropist's own selfishness (though he criticizes philanthropists for so often overestimating what it is they accomplish and for using philanthropy to conceal their own "private ail" at not having a clearer, more authentic sense of self-directed purpose) than the selfishness of

---

[110] When Emerson criticizes creeds as a "disease of the intellect" ("Self-Reliance," 263) he has in mind those who "talk as Americans, as Republicans . . . [so that] each cunningly hides under these wearisome commonplaces the character and flavor that can really make him interesting and valuable to us. Of course, he only half acts,—talks with his lips and not his heart." Emerson, "Notes to 'Courage,'" in Society and Solitude, in The Complete Works of Ralph Waldo Emerson, 7:431. There is no such half-action for self-reliant individualists; thus, the individualism that underlies self-reliance is not itself properly understood as a creed in the sense decried by Emerson.

[111] Emerson, The Journals of Ralph Waldo Emerson, 13:282.

[112] Emerson, "Reforms," 3:260.

[113] Ralph Waldo Emerson, "New England Reformers," in The Political Emerson, ed. David Robinson (Boston: Beacon Press, 2004), 79.

[114] Emerson, "Self-Reliance," 262.

recipients of philanthropy who, in gratitude for the charity they receive, bestow excessive praise on their benefactors: "Every one must feel the falsehood and cant of this."[115] With Dylan, the hypocrisy comes from the fact that activists working in behalf of even just causes often receive their livelihood from such pursuits and thus to a meaningful extent are bound to pursue them in the way of most job holders, yet unlike other job holders repress this fact. Referring to the attendees of the 1963 ECLC fundraising dinner at which he was given the Tom Paine Award, Dylan reports a kind of disgust:

> These people at that dinner were the same as everybody else. They're doing their time. They're chained to what they're doing. The only thing is, they're trying to put morals and great deeds on their chains, but basically they don't want to jeopardize their positions. They got their jobs to keep. There's nothing there for me, and there's nothing there for the kind of people I hang around with.[116]

A third generic similarity, based on the first two, is that Emerson, Thoreau, and Dylan share the view that individuals should themselves determine their commitment to social justice. One chooses one's own commitment when selecting which issue to pursue and when engaging only because one personally feels one must, rather than out of some externally imposed social pressure. Thoreau is especially clear on this point: "The only obligation which I have a right to assume, is to do at any time what I think right."[117] And Thoreau is emphatic that this duty does not lead in a universal direction, nor does it involve any necessary connection to combating social injustice at all.[118] Believing that "you must have a genius for charity as well as for anything else," the key for Thoreau is to devote oneself only to political causes about which one feels a genuine sense of calling.[119] Emerson expresses similar sentiments, insisting, for example, on the need for each individual to discover one's own "private solution" to the "riddle of the age."[120] Dylan, while less explicit, seems to voice the same idea when, for instance, in "To Ramona"—a song addressed to a woman (often thought to be based on Joan Baez, in the context of the 1960s civil rights movement in the

[115] Thoreau, *Walden*, 54–56.
[116] Quoted in Cott, "The Crackin', Shakin', Breakin' Sounds," in *Essential Interviews*, 29–30.
[117] Thoreau, "Resistance to Civil Government," 2.
[118] Thoreau, 7.
[119] Thoreau, *Walden*, 52.
[120] Emerson, "Fate," in *Conduct of Life*, 1; also see "Reforms," 3:266.

United States[121]), described as "torn / Between stayin' and returnin' / Back to the South"—there is no answer but only the advice "Just do what you think you should do."

The limitation of one's social activism to genuine acts of conscience does not mean that cooperation with others to achieve reform is necessarily ruled out, only that ideally such collective efforts should be achieved by a group of like-minded individuals, each personally committed to the cause, rather than by collective entities imposing obligations upon their members. Emerson supports "natural and momentary associations" in which individuals do not have to compromise with the strictures of organization because, in the effervescence of their inspiration, they are fully supportive of the ends for which they are cooperating; hence, he writes: "The union is only perfect, when all the uniters are isolated."[122] Emerson gives an example in his 1837 lecture "Society":

> A society of twenty thousand members is formed for the introduction of Christianity into India or the South Sea. This is not the same thing as if twenty thousand persons without formal cooperation had conceived a vehement desire for the instruction of those foreign parts. In that case, each had turned the whole attention of the Reason, the quite infinite force of one man, to the matter, and sought by what means he, in his place, could work with most avail on this point.[123]

Thoreau, too, contrasts the "exceedingly partial and superficial" form of cooperation typical of most reform movements with a "true cooperation" that is usually imperceptible ("being a harmony inaudible to men") because it is conducted by individuals motivated first and foremost by conscience rather than affiliation with a specific group.[124] And Dylan as well imagines and voices support for a highly personalized kind of social activism, one in which individuals directly take responsibility for a specific cause unmediated by a primary attachment to a political organization.[125]

On the basis of these three overarching ideas, Emerson, Thoreau, and Dylan express a common unwillingness to devote themselves fully to causes they otherwise support, and in so doing give voice to a problem that, however familiar

[121] Baez reports that Dylan referred to her as "Ramona" and that they debated the importance of serving in movement politics. Joan Baez, *And a Voice to Sing With: A Memoir* (New York: Summit, 1987), 72, 95.

[122] Emerson, "New England Reformers," 78, 79.

[123] Emerson, "Society," in *The Early Lectures of Ralph Waldo Emerson*, 2:106.

[124] Thoreau, *Walden*, 51.

[125] See Lamont, "Message from Bob Dylan." I elaborate the specifics of Dylan's view in this regard in the penultimate portion of section I.5.

in ordinary civic practice, remains largely unaddressed in the tradition of political thought. To be sure, it is well known in political theory that social justice movements are undone not just by opponents but by sympathizers unwilling to devote themselves. But the usual way to make sense of this latter phenomenon is to attribute to the undedicated sympathizers various undignified standpoints— such as hypocrisy or cowardice—that have no intrinsic connection to the values of a democratic society. For instance, Martin Luther King, when he confessed, "I have almost reached the regrettable conclusion that the Negro's great stumbling block in the stride toward freedom is not the White Citizen's Counciler or the Ku Klux Klanner, but the white moderate," interprets the moderate's relative inaction as stemming from an unjustifiably excessive attachment to social order.[126] King's critique is paralleled by the long tradition in republican political thought that affirms a tradeoff between freedom and security, denouncing those whose addiction to the latter undermines a society's ability to maintain the former.[127] By contrast, the tradition of self-reliance reminds us that it is possible to resist social justice movements on a basis no less freedom-focused than the call for such movements themselves. As Emerson, Thoreau, and Dylan testify, social justice movements are moderated not just by a preference for gradualist policies but also by inconsistent commitment to even radical objectives—and that, furthermore, the motivation for such moderation need not be over-attachment to order and security but a preference for the free use of one's individuality over and against the seemingly limitless demands of social justice within a context of gross and widespread injustice.

But just as important as the similarities between Emerson, Thoreau, and Dylan are the differences between them. The tradition of self-reliance offers not simply an appreciation for the fact that the free use of one's individuality represents a check upon the claims of social justice movements, but a meditation on the appropriate manner in which individuals who do drop out of social responsibility ought to do so. There is an instructive difference between the way in which self-reliance informs the refusal of Emerson and Thoreau to be fullfledged political activists and the way it shapes Dylan's otherwise parallel refusal

---

[126] King, in his "Letter from Birmingham City Jail," (295), thus criticizes the moderate "who is more devoted to 'order' than to justice; who prefers a negative peace which is the absence of tension to a positive peace which is the presence of justice; who constantly says 'I agree with you in the goal you seek, but I can't agree with your methods of direct action'; who paternalistically feels he can set the timetable for another man's freedom; who lives by the myth of time and who constantly advises the Negro to wait until a more convenient season.".

[127] See, for example, Alexis de Tocqueville, *Democracy in America* (1835–1840), II.2, chapters 10–14; Benjamin Franklin, *Memoires of the Life and Writings of Benjamin Franklin* (London: Henry Colburn, 1818), 270; and, Jean-Jacques Rousseau, *The Social Contract*, trans. Maurice Cranston (London: Penguin, 1968), I.4.

in this regard. Emerson and Thoreau evince a self-satisfaction about their relative inaction that Dylan does not share—a self-satisfaction that can be seen in at least three different respects I will presently examine. To be clear, the self-satisfaction I find in Emerson and Thoreau applies only to their conceptualization of their political withdrawal, not to their assessment of their intimate relationships, literary output, or general conduct of their personal lives (topics about which their journals and letters often express genuine regret and dissatisfaction). But this self-satisfaction, even if circumscribed, is important since, as I explain, it has negative epistemological, ethical, and political implications. Because Dylan lacks these three forms of self-satisfaction, he embodies a self-reliance that is starker, harsher, and more bare but ultimately more honest and constructive.

The Self-Satisfaction of Thinking Self-Reliant Withdrawal from Politics Is Still Politically Efficacious

Part of the self-satisfaction of Emerson and Thoreau lies in the fact that they understand the activities that lead them away from consistent involvement in social justice movements as still consonant with the ultimate objects of those movements. They do this in two distinct ways: conceiving of their time away from politics as nonetheless focused on "self-reform" and "self-emancipation" (and thus as related to, if not directly preparatory for, the purposes of formal political involvement in a democratic society) and, second, claiming that limiting their political involvement to moments of personal inspiration actually makes them more effective political actors than if they were more permanently but less passionately dedicated.

With regard to the first of these, both Emerson and Thoreau repeatedly use political metaphors to describe their time away from formal politics. Both liken the intellectual and spiritual pursuits that they practice outside of politics to the liberation of actual slaves. In a passage from *Walden* in which Thoreau is troubled by Northerners' attention to the "somewhat foreign form of servitude called Negro Slavery . . . [remaining blind to] so many keen and subtle masters that enslave both north and south," he not only invokes the competing concern of self-emancipation but likens it to the mission of overcoming chattel slavery: "Self-emancipation even in the West Indian provinces of the fancy and imagination—what Wilberforce is there to bring that about?"[128] This is not an isolated instance but a repeated trope for Thoreau, who conceives of his project of living at Walden Pond not simply as a self-liberation structurally similar to the liberation of actual slaves but as a process that could ultimately promote

[128] Thoreau, *Walden*, 4.

the emancipation of actual slaves. Two days after moving to Walden, Thoreau writes of his overarching ambition: "Self-emancipation in the West Indies of a man's thinking and imagining provinces, which should be more than his island territory. One emancipated heart and intellect—it would knock off the fetters from a million slaves."[129] Later, in 1856, Thoreau invokes similar rhetoric when he analogizes the importance of having a personal vocation to efforts to combat the expansion of slavery in the western territories:

> For only absorbing employment prevails, succeeds, takes up space, occupies territory, determines the future of individuals and states, drives Kansas out of your head, and actually and permanently occupies the only desirable and free Kansas against all border ruffians.[130]

Emerson speaks in parallel fashion, invoking the political metaphor of liberation to describe the activities that keep him away from full-fledged social activism. In a public address in 1854, for example, he could claim that his own liberation was what inhibited a greater concern with public questions: "I have my own spirits in prison,—spirits in deeper prisons, whom no man visits, if I do not."[131] The metaphor appears, too, in Emerson's unwillingness to follow other Transcendentalists in accepting the invitation of George and Sophia Ripley to live in the utopian community of Brook Farm: "I do not wish to remove from my present prison to a prison a little larger. I wish to break all prisons. I have not yet conquered my own house."[132] One can challenge Emerson and Thoreau here for invoking a metaphysical conception of inner freedom and a no less speculative notion of "self-reform" to describe the literary and other activities that drew them away from politics. But even if Emerson and Thoreau are correct to suggest that we remain unfree to the extent we are distracted and disconnected from our innermost convictions, and even if they also are right that individuals who can reform themselves and discover and practice their authentic purposes can become all the more politically impactful as a result, the additional objection that should be raised to this kind of reasoning is that it allows Emerson and Thoreau to uncritically, and no doubt inaccurately, suggest that all of their time away from politics

[129] Thoreau, *Journal*, ed. John C. Broderick (Princeton, NJ: Princeton University Press, 1981), 1:362–63.

[130] Thoreau, 2:156.

[131] Emerson, "Fugitive Slave Law Address," in *Emerson's Antislavery Writings*, ed. Len Gougeon and Joel Myerson (New Haven, CT: Yale University Press, 1995), 73.

[132] Emerson, "Concerning Brook Farm," in *Political Writings*, ed. Kenneth Sacks (Cambridge, UK: Cambridge University Press, 2004), 93.

is in the service of becoming free (of achieving an urgently needed liberation) rather than taking advantage of the freedom they already enjoy.

Dylan does not do this. Rather than glorify his time away from social justice movements as being in the service of his own liberation, Dylan, in the condition of his political withdrawal, instead acknowledges his simple preference, as an already free individual, to pursue other matters. In "Maggie's Farm," a song that recalls experiments like Brook Farm, he impersonates an individual's unwillingness to participate in cooperative efforts that arises not because he needs to secure his own liberation first, nor because such collective pursuits are necessarily misguided, but because service to them flattens his individuality and thus becomes wearisome:

> Well, I try my best
> To be just like I am
> But everybody wants you
> To be just like them
> They say sing while you slave and I just get bored
> I ain't gonna work on Maggie's farm no more[133]

Likewise, when Dylan juxtaposes himself in "It's Alright, Ma" to those who "speak jealously of them that are free," he presents himself as someone who already is free, who thus cannot rely on the idea of self-liberation to justify any continuing respite from social justice movements and who accordingly has to face his time away from politics for what it is: a sacrifice of political conscientiousness. The virtue of these and other instances of Dylan's otherwise harsh disavowal of social responsibility—recall, as additional examples, "I know you're dissatisfied with your position and your place / Don't you understand it's not my problem" ("Positively 4th Street") and "I can't help it if I'm lucky" ("Idiot Wind")—is that they do not dress up the turn away from politics in the false vestments of an enduring commitment to liberation and reform but rather acknowledge how the call of individuality can sometimes come at the expense of concerning oneself with the alleviation of suffering and unfreedom.

---

[133] Thoreau, it is true, comes close to Dylan when, in his account of his own refusal of the offer to live on Brook Farm, writes in his journal: "As for these communities, I think I had rather keep bachelor's hall in hell than go to board in heaven." But Thoreau ends up falling back on his usual logic of morally justifying his non-participation by suggesting he would become less virtuous in such collective communities: "Do you think your virtue will be boarded with you? It will never live on the interest of your money, depend upon it." Accordingly, his provocative hypothesis of preferring a single room in hell is immediately softened, if not altogether neutralized, by the contrasting image of his anticipating a single room in heaven: "In heaven I hope to bake my own bread and clean my own linen." Thoreau, *Journal*, 1:227.

The second way in which Emerson and Thoreau, but not Dylan, present their lack of full-fledged engagement with social justice movements as still somehow consonant with those movements relates to their belief that limiting their formal political activities to moments of genuine inspiration is not only consistent with the ethics of self-reliance but essential for making their periods of political action maximally forceful and consequential. That is to say, while all three men affirm the ethic of only serving causes about which one feels a personal, inspired attachment, only Emerson and Thoreau add the supplementary idea that action so practiced will be much more effective. For Emerson, when we act on the basis of personal conviction, our service to others is not only "indirect" (since we are in fact primarily serving our own individual conscience[134]), but for that reason much more impactful. The "natural and momentary associations" Emerson supports, which involve impassioned individuals temporarily coming together because they each separately share the same heightened sense of moral conviction, "doubles or multiplies" the individual's own force, whereas uninspired service to causes leads to the opposite result: "In the hour in which [the individual] mortgages himself to two or ten or twenty, he dwarfs himself below the stature of one."[135] Emerson thus refers to the "loss of truth and power that befalls one who leaves working for himself to work for another. Absolutely speaking, I can work [effectively] only for myself."[136] And he states the paradox: "Why have the minority no influence? Because they have not a real minority of one."[137] Thoreau shares this idea of the superiority of indirect service: "What good I do, in the common sense of that word, must be aside from my main path, and for the most part wholly unintended."[138] Whether Thoreau and especially Emerson thought this consistently is a matter of scholarly debate,[139] but the fact that both can even suggest the superior effectiveness of indirect service—that Emerson, for example, can celebrate self-reliant activism as marking a "new and unprecedented

---

[134] As Emerson puts it: "Gift is contrary to the law of the universe. Serving others is serving us. I must absolve me to myself. 'Mind thy affair,' says the spirit:—'coxcomb, would you meddle with the skies, or with other people?' Indirect service is left." Emerson, "Uses of Great Men," in *Essays and Lectures*, 617–18; also see Emerson, "Politics," in *The Early Lectures of Ralph Waldo Emerson*, 3:246–47.

[135] Emerson, "New England Reformers," 79.

[136] Emerson, "Politics," 3: 246–47.

[137] Emerson, "Fugitive Slave Law Address," 83.

[138] Thoreau, *Walden* 52, also reflects the idea of service when he writes: "Be sure that you give the poor the aid they most need, though it be your example which leaves them far behind" (Thoreau, 52).

[139] See, for example, T. Gregory Garvey, ed., *The Emerson Dilemma*; Alan M. Levine and Daniel S. Malachuk, eds., *A Political Companion to Ralph Waldo Emerson* (Lexington: University Press of Kentucky, 2011); and Jack Turner, "Thoreau and John Brown," in *A Political Companion to Henry David Thoreau*, ed. Jack Turner (Lexington: University Press of Kentucky, 2009), 155.

way" of fulfilling social obligations[140]—separates both men from Dylan, who makes no claim that in limiting his social activism to fulfilling his own privately determined sense of conscience he will be doing more good in the world than if he had remained affiliated with formal associations and political movements.[141]

In understanding their disengagement from social reform movements as a kind of self-reform, their lack of full commitment to securing others' liberation as being for the sake of self-liberation, and their sporadic activity as being more impactful than a more permanent but less authentically felt kind of service, Emerson and Thoreau afford themselves a self-satisfaction that Dylan does not share.

The Self-Satisfaction of Providentialism

A second source of Emerson and Thoreau's self-satisfaction—which is lacking in Dylan—is that as much as they remain deeply critical of their society, they uphold the world as an ultimately just order, with such justice inscribed in the inherent goodness of human rationality, in nature, and in the eventual moral progress of humanity. Emerson, for whom self-reliance is always inseparable from God-reliance, claims that "democracy/freedom has its roots in the sacred truth that every man hath in him divine reason."[142] This happy "truth" is the foundation, for Emerson, of both the inherent goodness of the human being and the providential faith in the ultimate victory of justice in the world. Whether this providentialism is expressed in unrestrained terms ("the inconsistency of slavery with the principles on which the world is built guarantees its downfall"[143]) or more modestly (the existence in nature of "a small excess of good, a small balance in brute facts always favorable to the side of reason"[144]), Emerson can look upon the world as an essentially beautiful and good place. And, crucially, this providentialism allows him to remain morally uplifted even in the periods when he declines to fully devote himself to political causes he deems just. Thus, in an 1852 journal entry explicitly acknowledging how his preference for individual self-cultivation has diminished his involvement in the anti-slavery movement, any sense of remorse is immediately counterbalanced by the solace-giving

---

[140] Emerson, "Self-Reliance," 273.

[141] Recall what Dylan says in a 1965 interview in the context of his withdrawal from ongoing social justice movements: that the work of such movements "definitely has to be done" since "people are starving" and "lots of people are in bad trouble." Dylan thus seems to understand the moral costs of his political withdrawal. "Bob Dylan | Nat Hentoff *Playboy* Interview."

[142] Emerson, *The Journals and Miscellaneous Notebooks of Ralph Waldo Emerson*, ed. William H. Gilman (Cambridge, MA: Harvard University Press, 1960–82), 4:357.

[143] Emerson, "Fugitive Slave Law Address," 87.

[144] Emerson, "The Young American," in *Essays and Lectures*, 217.

thought that "God must govern his own world, & knows his way out of this pit, without my desertion of my post which has none to guard it but me."[145]

Emerson's providentialism leads him to some of his most metaphysically speculative ideas. For example, his notion of *compensation*, which he especially affirmed in the earlier part of his life, is a complex, multifaceted concept but one that nonetheless allows him to posit two different self-satisfying providential dynamics, each of which neutralizes the impact of his political inaction: the equality of human lives (according to which an individual's advantages and deficiencies are offset by each other) and the full operation of justice in the here and now (i.e., the view that "a perfect equity adjusts its balance in all parts of life").[146] At other times, as in Emerson's later essays "Experience" and "Fate," he acknowledges a discrepancy between ideal and actual arrangements, but not without asserting that the ultimate triumph of justice is inscribed in the very fiber of the universe. In "Experience," for instance, Emerson admits that "the world I converse with in the city and in the farms, is not the world I think" but nonetheless still concludes:

> Never mind the ridicule, never mind the defeat; up again, old heart! . . . there is victory yet for all justice; and the true romance which the world exists to realize will be the transformation of genius into practical power.[147]

The process of gradual moral progress is itself something for Emerson to celebrate: "It is a joyful change to see human nature unshackling herself & asserting her divine origin."[148] To be sure, Emerson came to see providence as requiring intentional human action for its fruition—"I hope we have come to . . . a belief that there is a Divine Providence in the world which will not save us but through our own co-operation"[149]—but his idea of providence was sufficiently robust that he could still imagine divine, or other human, forces working to accomplish the moral causes from which he periodically withdrew.

Thoreau shares Emerson's sense that "the Universe is not bankrupt"[150] as well as the idea that this providential fact lessens the significance of whether any particular individual chooses to fight against injustice:

> Probably I should not consciously and deliberately forsake my particular calling to do [instead] the good which society demands of me, to

[145] Emerson, *The Journals of Ralph Waldo Emerson*, 13:80.
[146] Emerson, "Compensation," in *The Complete Works of Ralph Waldo Emerson*, 2:102.
[147] Emerson, "Experience," in *The Complete Works of Ralph Waldo Emerson*, 3:48–49.
[148] Emerson, *The Journals and Miscellaneous Notebooks of Ralph Waldo Emerson*, 1:18.
[149] Emerson, "Fugitive Slave Law Address," 89.
[150] Emerson, "Anniversary of West Indian Emancipation," in *Emerson's Antislavery Writings*, 36.

save the universe from annihilation; and I believe that a like but infi-
nitely greater steadfastness elsewhere is all that now preserves it.[151]

As critical as Thoreau could be of existing politics and states, an underlying
faith in the ultimate moral enlightenment of humankind recurs throughout his
writing. His essay "Walking," for example, concludes with the image:

> So we saunter toward the Holy Land, till one day the sun shall shine
> more brightly than ever he has done, shall perchance shine into our
> minds and hearts, and light up our whole lives with a great awakening
> light, as warm and serene and golden as on a bankside in autumn.[152]

Dylan lacks this providential view of the world and thus also lacks any sense that
the non-politically active human being ought to find reassurance on the basis
of membership in a fundamentally just cosmic order. While Dylan can occasionally countenance Emerson and Thoreau's Transcendental quasi-gnostic idea
of human participation with divinity, he much more frequently gives voice to
the more orthodox Judeo-Christian notion of an absolute ontological separation between human and God and, with it, a pessimism about the human being
as a flawed and fallen creature. In a 1983 song, "Blind Willie McTell," which
addresses the persistence of racism in America, he sings:

> Well, God is in His heaven
> And we all want what's his
> But power and greed and corruptible seed
> Seem to be all that there is

With respect to nature, while Dylan is no less aware of the awe natural spaces can
evoke—his "Lay Down Your Weary Tune" sings powerfully of their splendor,
for example—he does not follow Emerson and Thoreau in treating nature
as a mirror of the human being's own moral potential or as a symbol of what
Emerson calls "the moral cause of the world."[153] If anything, when Dylan treats
nature as a mirror, what it reflects back is the human being as a dangerous and
unreliable being.

Consider in this regard Dylan's 1963 "Poem to Joanie," which appears to riff
off of Whitman's "A Child Says, What Is the Grass?" in his "Song of Myself."

---

[151] Thoreau, *Walden*, 52.

[152] Thoreau, *Walking* (New York: Value Classic, 2016), 41.

[153] Emerson, "Character," in *The Spiritual Emerson*, ed. David M. Robinson (Boston: Beacon, 2003 [1866]), 243.

Whitman answers the child by treating the grass as the "flag of my disposition," a mirror of Whitman's own selfhood and, in keeping with the Emersonian tradition, what is reflected in this mirror is imbued with a quasi-divinity, pointing to the elevation and ennoblement of the self: "hopeful green stuff," "the handkerchief of the lord," "a scented gift and remembrancer designedly dropped," a "produced babe," "a uniform hieroglyphic." Even the darkest rendering is still affirmative: "the beautiful uncut hair of graves."[154] In Dylan's poem, a child, in contemplating the grass and through the grass himself, savagely rips grass out of the ground, remorsefully acknowledges yet also interrogates his guilt (asking "How can this bother me?"), and then likens himself to "a frightened fox" and "a demon child."[155] This is but one example of how Dylan departs from Emerson and Thoreau, the latter of whom, for instance, concludes and counterbalances his grim castigation of his fellow citizens for their insufficient outrage against slavery in "Slavery in Massachusetts" by finding promise of redemption in a white water lily: "What confirmation of our hopes is in the fragrance of this flower!"[156]

While Dylan does think that local improvements in specific social contexts can be made—at least his own episodic political efforts imply as much—he rejects providentialism, contemplating that the arc of the moral universe either does not exist or bends toward permanent injustice.[157] Even if Dylan is less forthcoming than Emerson and Thoreau in expounding this competing, more pessimistic vision, his reticence in this respect itself has theoretical implications insofar as it leads him to refrain from the metaphysical excesses of Emerson and Thoreau when they imagine a divine spark existing within each human being, when they find moral reassurance in natural beauty, and when they postulate a divine energy working for the ultimate good of the world. Dylan's conception of self-reliance, and of the problem of a self-reliant individual turning away from the fight against injustice, is simply not buttressed by these speculative, self-congratulating logics. The question at stake is not simply whether, in the abstract, people should be optimistic or pessimistic about the direction of the world, but for whom such dispositions are relatively more appropriate. Hope

[154] Walt Whitman, "Song of Myself," in *Leaves of Grass*, 2nd ed. (New York: Fowler & Wells, 1856), 16.

[155] Bob Dylan, "Poem to Joanie" (liner notes to *Joan Baez in Concert Part 2*, 1963). As published on the album the poem had no title, but subsequent publications refer to the title I use here.

[156] Thoreau, "Slavery in Massachusetts," in *Thoreau: Political Writings*, 135–36.

[157] Consider Joan Baez's statement about Dylan: "I asked him what made us different, and he said it was simple, that I thought I could change things, and he knew that no one could." Baez, *And a Voice to Sing With*, 95. Such a viewpoint does not lead Dylan to diminish social reformers, but, as I explain in the final portion of section I.5, actually contributes to his enduring respect for some of the social justice work he disclaims.

means one thing when it inspires a militant fight against injustice, but threatens callousness and complacency in a context of inaction.

The Self-Satisfaction of Considering Oneself Not Complicit with Injustice

A third aspect differentiating Dylan from Emerson and Thoreau on the issue of self-satisfaction has to do with whether self-reliant individuals are, in the period of their withdrawal from causes to which they are sympathetic, complicit with injustice. Emerson and Thoreau contemplate their non-complicity in a manner totally lacking for Dylan.

In the case of Thoreau, however much he insists that there is no duty to combat injustice, he nonetheless affirms, often in the same breath, a duty to extricate oneself from injustice and thus the possibility of achieving non-complicity with it:

> It is not a man's duty, as a matter of course, to devote himself to the erad-ication of any, even the most enormous wrong; he may still properly have other concerns to engage him; but it is his duty, at least, to wash his hands of it, and if he gives it no thought longer, not to give it practically his support.[158]

Much of Thoreau's activism is connected to just this extrication (e.g., forswearing allegiance to the state by not voting, not paying taxes, living off the land, calling the U.S. Constitution evil). While Emerson does not countenance such whole-sale withdrawal, he himself entertains a similar lack of personal complicity with injustice (especially regarding non-slavery issues) by constantly referring to distance, both spatial and spiritual, as a barrier to his own moral culpability. Part of what makes Emerson's opposition to the Fugitive Slave Act perhaps his most impassioned political cause is its proximity to his home in Concord, Massachusetts, as the law required that Emerson and his neighbors actively as-sist the capture and punishment of runaway slaves. By contrast, the causes about which Emerson wavers or refuses allegiance—such as an "obligation to put all poor men in good situations" or the "tenderness for black folk a thousand miles off"—are often characterized by a distance that seems to negate his sense of re-sponsibility: "I tell thee, thou foolish philanthropist, that I grudge the dollar, the dime, the cent, I give to such men as do not belong to me and to whom I do

---

[158] Thoreau, "Resistance to Civil Government," 7.

not belong."[159] Relatedly, at certain points in his life, Emerson also expresses the view that clear thinking about a political question—establishing, as an intellectual matter, its rectitude or injustice—marks the extent of one's moral obligation, since no person can be expected to actively contribute to more than a small number of concerns.[160]

As much as Dylan confidently refuses dutiful service to otherwise just causes, there is nothing in his poetry or public statements that suggests a similar disclaiming of complicity with suffering or injustice, whether near to home or anywhere in the world. Dylan does not say with Emerson "Are they my poor?" And he does not follow Thoreau's provocatively reductive morality: "Rescue the drowning and tie your shoe-strings. Take your time, and set about some free labor."[161] Perhaps the difference is historical. In the nineteenth century, as has been discussed, distant ills were, in three different ways, more distant than those today: they were often not known until long after their actual occurrence, they were less susceptible to being aided by would-be helpers from far away, and they were not obviously caused by actions from those remotely situated. Today, all three aspects have changed, as we can witness distant suffering in real time, transportation and communication technologies render immediate aid an almost ever-present possibility, and globalization makes it more plausible to see far-off suffering (such as environmental degradation) as being connected to actions closer to home. For these and related reasons, Peter Singer, among others, turning Thoreau's metaphor on its head, argues that our responsibility to eradicate global poverty—"to put all poor in good situations"—is equivalent to our responsibility to rescue a child drowning before our eyes.[162] Whether Dylan's unwillingness to deny his complicity stems from this type of thinking is unclear, but what is straightforward is that however much he would like to follow Emerson's threefold dictum—"Speak as you think, be what you are, pay your debts of all kinds"[163]—the last of these is something he never claims to do.[164]

---

[159] Emerson, "Self-Reliance," 262.

[160] Consider Emerson's comment in 1837 regarding slavery, following the visit of abolitionists Angelina and Sarah Grimke to Concord: "When we have settled the right and wrong of this question I think we have done all we can. A man can only extend his active attention to a certain finite amount of claims." Emerson, *The Journals and Miscellaneous Notebooks of Ralph Waldo Emerson*, 12:154.

[161] Thoreau, *Walden*, 56.

[162] Singer, *The Life You Can Save*.

[163] Emerson, "Illusions," in *Conduct of Life*, 81.

[164] If anything Dylan is aware of an abiding guilt. In his follow-up to the ECLC award, whose fundraising he disturbed, he admits he has "a moral debt" to the organization—"I have a hatred of debts and want to be even in the best way I can"—but he does not seem to have rectified the situation nor claimed to have. Quoted in Lamont, "Message from Bob Dylan."

Evidence of Dylan's divergent attitude toward his own complicity can be found not only in the way he conceives of his inaction, but in the manner in which he makes sense of his periods of political activity as well. Dylan shares with Emerson and Thoreau the view that self-reliant people ideally should engage in social justice as individuals, cooperating with others only when temporarily and contingently side by side with like-minded others and thus not beholden to larger, more permanent organizational machines. But Dylan departs from Emerson and Thoreau not only because, as I have discussed, he refuses himself the comforting thought that self-reliant activism of this kind is more effective than submission to the strictures of organization, but also because the coalition of self-reliant individuals he imagines has the purpose not simply of combating injustice but of reminding individuals that, even when they support just causes, their hands are unlikely to be clean. In his 1964 "apology" letter to the ECLC, following the uproar he caused at its award dinner, Dylan insists that the proper mindset of any engaged set of individuals is for each to resist the thought that society as a whole is to blame for various social ills and instead recognize a more direct personal culpability:

> I am sick
> so sick
> at hearin "we all share the blame" for every
> church bombing, gun battle, mine disaster,
> poverty explosion, an president killing that
> comes about.
> it is so easy t say "we" an bow our heads together
> I must say "I" alone an bow my head alone . . .
> yes if there's violence in the times then
> there must be violence in me . . .
> once this is straight between us, it's then an
> only then that we can say "we" an really mean
> it . . . an go on from there t do something about
> it[165]

Dylan's greater openness to his complicity with injustice is also shaped by his refusal to characterize those political causes he supports as somehow uniquely urgent and as thus compensating for all the other kinds of political and social responsibilities he does not take up. As much as Emerson inveighs against reformers who pursue a single issue and thus falsely imbue their single cause

---

[165] Quoted in Lamont, "Message from Bob Dylan."

with an undeserved totality of importance,[166] the fact is that his own engagement with anti-slavery often took this form. He describes the issue that most spurred him to political action, the Fugitive Slave Act, as the "most detestable law that was ever enacted by a civilized state"[167] and treats it as a singular benchmark of morality, claiming in 1851 that if resistance to this law "is not right, there is no right."[168] Perhaps if Dylan had lived in the time of American slavery he would have done the same, but the truth remains that Dylan does not allow himself the self-satisfaction of treating the causes he does endorse as morally superior to the ones he does not. In his song "Tangled Up in Blue," he depicts a situation in which a would-be reformer has to face a world where slavery (and, by extension, the unique sense of urgency and clarity of purpose this evil can evoke) does not exist:

> I lived with them on Montague Street
> In a basement down the stairs
> There was snow all winter and no heat
> Revolution was in the air
> Then one day all his slaves ran free
> Something inside of him died
> The only thing I could do was be me
> And get on that train and ride[169]

The possessive "*his* slaves" refers here not to a slaveholder but to an activist; thus, the liberation of these slaves itself indicates not emancipation per se but a circumstance in which the activist has lost some kind of orientation. Perhaps

---

[166] Emerson can thus challenge single-issue reformers: "Do not be so vain of your one objection. Do you think there is only one?" Emerson, "New England Reformers," 77.

[167] Emerson, *The Journals and Miscellaneous Notebooks of Ralph Waldo Emerson*, 11:352.

[168] Emerson, "Address to the Citizens of Concord," in *The Complete Works of Ralph Waldo Emerson*, 11:186–87.

[169] This version is from a 1984 live performance at Wembley Stadium in London, released on Dylan's album, *Real Live*, and quoted in Domhnall Mitchell, "The Sonnet in Bob Dylan's 'Tangled Up in Blue,'" *Explicator* 69, no. 1 (2011): 43. The original version, released on *Blood on the Tracks* (1975), has a somewhat different verse:

> I lived with them on Montague Street
> In a basement down the stairs
> There was music in the cafés at night
> And revolution in the air
> Then he started into dealing with slaves
> And something inside of him died
> She had to sell everything she owned
> And froze up inside

Dylan means to depict a situation in which political success—the achievement of liberation, justice, and so on—has drained the one-time activist of purpose. But given his obvious appreciation for the endurance of injustice in the world (including, sadly, the persistence of slavery in some quarters), what seems more likely is that Dylan here is describing a situation in which the political reformer (with whom he has "lived" and by extension has been[170]) has lost not any kind of political purpose, but the sense of a specific political purpose being universal (i.e., being singularly urgent and thus superior to all other moral objectives). Without the self-satisfaction of conceiving of the causes one does work for as being morally higher than those one does not, the self-reliant individual cannot so easily avoid a sense of complicity in this latter regard.

Refusing to disclaim complicity with ongoing injustice need not demoralize an enduring commitment to realizing what change is possible, but it does prevent self-reliant individuals, in the moments of their disengagement, from imagining that they somehow have extricated themselves from responsibility for the persistence of injustice. Part of Dylan's lack of self-satisfaction stems from this uneasy recognition.

The Propriety of Self-Reliance Without Self-Satisfaction

Not only are Emerson, Thoreau, and Dylan uncommonly explicit about a circumstance that no doubt applies to many present-day citizens—inaction with respect to otherwise endorsed social movements—but, in offering divergent understandings of this situation, they in effect historicize self-reliance, demonstrate that it has alternate variants, and thereby raise the question of which variant is most suitable today. Emerson and Thoreau, it must be admitted, articulate with unrivaled eloquence the claims of selfhood that lead them away from being dependable political agents, but Dylan's less self-satisfied form of self-reliance, even if it is terser, has clear epistemological, ethical, and political advantages.

Epistemologically, the self-satisfaction of Emerson and Thoreau regarding their periods of withdrawal is not simply a matter of psychological disposition but stems from their adherence to various metaphysical ideas—such as

---

[170] For Dylan, first-person and third-person narratives often fluctuate even if they refer to the same individual. With regard to the song quoted here, "Tangled Up in Blue," Dylan is explicit in his acknowledgment of this: "I was just trying to make it like a painting where you can see the different parts but then you also see the whole of it. With that particular song, that's what I was trying to do . . . with the concept of time, and the way the characters change from the first person to the third person, and you're never quite sure if the third person is talking or the first person is talking. But as you look at the whole thing it really doesn't matter." Liner notes to *Biograph* (1985) for "Tangled Up in Blue," 34.

the Transcendental notion that the self is always the potential vehicle of a universal luminosity, the related idea that mind and nature are ultimately mirror reflections of each other, the attestation to divine providence, and an interpretation of their literary work as a kind of internal liberation—that cannot easily survive contemporary postmetaphysical skepticism. In translating self-reliance from a Transcendentalist to a more existentialist register, Dylan has fewer presuppositions and thus models self-reliance in a manner likely to have appeal for a wider range of people.

This epistemological modesty has ethical consequences. In dispensing with the speculative features of Emerson's and Thoreau's philosophies of self-reliance, Dylan also treats self-reliant withdrawal from political action as a more serious ethical problem. Even if Emerson and Thoreau repeatedly examine and personally acknowledge their lack of full support for causes they deem to be just, the effect of their three forms of self-satisfaction that I have outlined is to de-problematize their inaction—that is, to diminish its status as a fraught moral dilemma. Dylan, by contrast, because he lacks self-satisfaction regarding his self-reliant withdrawal from social justice movements, suggests that in fact the matter is vexing and not entirely soluble. In other words, if Emerson and Thoreau can find in their self-reliance the harmonization of duty to self and duty to others, Dylan articulates and performs a self-reliance characterized by a dissonance between these two duties. When Dylan's individualism leads him away from active support of causes he knows to be just, he is much more ready to acknowledge that this withdrawal has moral costs.

This acknowledgment of moral costs need not do fatal damage to the appeal of self-reliance, as some like George Kateb have worried, but rather has the potential to clarify and update the ethical meaning of self-reliance within the conditions of the twenty-first century—in which moral responsibility for distant suffering, the technology to alleviate that suffering should there be political will to do so, and arguably the degree of absolute suffering are unprecedentedly extensive. Kateb, in the conclusion to his book *Emerson and Self-Reliance*, which celebrates self-reliance as an ethical ideal for a contemporary liberal-democratic society, is aware of these conditions but understands them as "the great obstacle to finding self-reliance a genuine ideal."[171] Kateb acknowledges that what seems to differentiate Emerson and Thoreau's time from our own is the much greater possibility that "atrocity [has become] the norm."[172] Whereas slavery could be seen as an exceptional and aberrant mar upon an otherwise "preponderantly benign" nineteenth-century world, the present is characterized by a dramatically

---

[171] Kateb, *Emerson and Self-Reliance*, 198.
[172] Kateb, 198.

heightened sense of disorder and injustice.[173] Specifically, Kateb refers to contemporary pathologies including "mass wars," "extermination camps," "millions and millions of human beings living in inhuman conditions," "the deliberate infliction of suffering on a large scale," and a "quantity of material misery that is scarcely imaginable."[174]

Such conditions are potentially devastating to self-reliance, Kateb thinks, because he believes that a prerequisite of self-reliance being an attractive ideal is what he calls "innocence": both in the form of a world that is mostly good and in the form of the clear conscience of individuals practicing the cultivation of individuality over and against the claims of organized reform movements. In the absence of innocence, Kateb fears that self-reliance becomes "only a guilty luxury," "culpably indifferent," and thus "impossible to defend."[175] As a result of this manner of thinking, Kateb—who *does*, after all, defend the ethic of self-reliance—is led to sidestep and diminish the very premise from which he begins: the existence of significant evil in the world that would appear to demand "enlistment in a mobilized and full-time cause" and thereby override the pursuit of self-reliance.[176] This sidestepping takes numerous forms, including the conjecture that maybe it is "only an unhelpful exaggeration . . . [to] say that the world's condition is largely evil"; the suggestion that intermittent suspension of self-reliance in the name of social justice work may ultimately be consonant with self-reliance since such suspension provides experiences from which to grow and learn about oneself (which ignores the problem as Kateb has framed it, namely the need for "mobilized and full-time" political engagement); the notion that insofar as we believe that humanity should continue to exist we should endorse self-reliant individualism as the flowering of humanity; and, finally, the idea that because self-reliance is the authentic ethic of democracy, we should affirm self-reliance in order to affirm democracy itself.[177] These ideas may persuasively explain Kateb's enduring attraction to the ideal of self-reliance, but they fail to respond to the very issue he has introduced: how to reconcile self-reliance with the condition that atrocity has become the norm in the world.

Rather than restore self-reliance to a condition of innocence, the virtue of Dylan's contribution is that it models what self-reliance becomes when such innocence has been lost. It is simply not true that individuals need to feel innocent in order to practice the values of self-reliance. The ideal is sufficiently attractive that it continues to motivate adherence even in the ethically fraught

[173] Kateb, 199.
[174] Kateb, 198.
[175] Kateb, 200.
[176] Kateb, 200.
[177] Kateb, 200–2.

circumstances of the twenty-first century. Kateb himself admits that even today "most people, including myself, live life as they please."[178] Kateb's mistake is to insist on finding resources by which to "give myself a reprieve" for his continual support of self-reliance.[179] The real problem is not that individuals will lose their taste for the free use of their individuality—for nonconformity, creativity, self-expression, and duty to one's innermost convictions—in the absence of such a reprieve, but that the experience of such individuality cannot be experienced as a universal or otherwise perfect value when practiced within a context understood to be characterized by gross, pervasive, at least partially correctible suffering and injustice. Dylan testifies both to the enduring appeal of self-reliance in the face of such conditions (he is hardly a less effective ambassador for self-reliant individualism than Emerson and Thoreau, despite his attunement to the non-innocence of it) and yet also to how the practice of self-reliance becomes altered. Properly understood, self-reliance is an ethic of liberal-democratic society, but not the only one. There is a competing liberal-democratic ethic of working to improve the lot of people whose unjust suffering and oppression precludes them from a life of self-reliance. Dylan's refusal to deny that his periods of political withdrawal are complicit with the persistence of injustice does not lead him to accept a state of total guilt, but it does mean that he recognizes an inescapable tradeoff within a democracy, at least for bourgeois individuals such as himself, between practicing the self-reliant individuality it makes possible for some and actively struggling to enable the self-reliant individuality currently denied to others. This tradeoff does not altogether destroy self-reliance as an ideal, but it does require that self-reliance not be treated as pure or perfectible. Kateb thinks that self-reliance cannot stand in the face of an almost infinite debt to the broader community, when in truth the problem is that we, as bourgeois, are the bearers of two duties—to self and to others—that cannot be fully harmonized. But their not being fully harmonizable does not negate the importance of either.

The political upshot of Dylan's lack of self-satisfaction in his self-reliance is that he is much more aware than Emerson and Thoreau of how his self-reliance is a product of privilege unavailable to others and that this awareness makes him more respectful of both the urgency of the social reform he disclaims and the individuals devoting themselves to it. Emerson and Thoreau, by contrast, evince a more persistent and pronounced tendency to diminish the work of the reform movements in which they elect not to participate. This diminishment—which is not, of course, the same as outright rejection—can be seen most clearly in their repeated challenge to what they see as *mere moral goodness* (defined as selfless

[178] Kateb, 201.
[179] Kateb, 201.

devotion to helping others). When Emerson states, "Your goodness must have some edge to it,—else it is none"[180]—and when Thoreau similarly exhorts his readers, "Aim above morality. Be not simply good—be good for something"[181]— they do not merely enunciate the view (shared by Dylan) that they wish to limit their own social action to situations in which it is interwoven with a personal sense of conscience and vocation, but imply (unlike Dylan) that a more sacrificial and selfless kind of political engagement is spiritually and ethically lesser. Whereas Thoreau, for instance, can take pride in his restriction of activism to causes in which he has a personal investment—quipping, in respect to his disengagement, "I never heard of a philanthropic meeting in which it was sincerely proposed to do any good to me, or the like of me"[182]—Dylan recognizes there is indeed a vital place for selflessness. It is not that Thoreau rejects selflessness altogether, but that he depreciates it in a twofold way, imagining that its proper function is limited to face-to-face emergencies and claiming that efforts to respond to such emergencies—because they stem from a supposedly automatic, obvious, not even specifically human instinct, in which the performance of one's distinct individuality plays no role—are inferior to more self-directed (i.e., vocational and personally inspired) forms of ethical action. Both of these kinds of depreciation are expressed when Thoreau writes:

> A man is not a good man to me because he will feed me if I should be starving, or warm me if I should be freezing, or pull me out of a ditch if I should ever fall into one. I can find you a Newfoundland dog that will do as much.[183]

Dylan, who seems to understand that contemporary individuals are implicated in emergencies that are vast and global, does not treat the moral goodness of those who respond to them as being in any way lesser to other forms of action.

The relative diminishment by Emerson and Thoreau of the work of social reform is also reflected in their more frequent attack on politics itself, with Emerson confessing that for him public life often seems "odious and hurtful"[184] and Thoreau describing political functions as something "vital" yet also "trivial" and thus as "infra-human, a kind of vegetation . . . [which] should be unconsciously performed, like the corresponding functions of the physical body."[185]

---

[180] Emerson, "Self-Reliance," 252.

[181] Thoreau, *The Correspondence of Henry David Thoreau*, ed. Robert N. Hudspeth (Princeton, NJ: Princeton University Press, 2013), 362.

[182] Thoreau, *Walden*, 53.

[183] Thoreau, 53.

[184] Emerson, "Fugitive Slave Law Address," 73.

[185] Thoreau, "Life without Principle," in *Thoreau: Political Writings*, 120.

Dylan has his own parallel frustration with politics, especially in its conventional electoral and partisan form, but is more careful to exclude the work of well-meaning and effective social justice activists from the brunt of his critique.[186] Similarly, Emerson and Thoreau worry about the excessiveness of certain reform ambitions, with Emerson invoking the example of "a naked New Zealander" as being in no better or worse condition than a "well-clad, reading, writing, thinking American, with a watch, a pencil and a bill of exchange in his pocket"[187] and Thoreau reporting that every time he was persuaded by reformers to take a greater interest in the poor and aim to maintain "certain poor people in all respects as comfortably as I maintain myself," the intended recipients declined, as "one and all unhesitatingly preferred to remain poor."[188] Dylan is aware of the somewhat similar problem that any specific reform objective can crowd out attention to other reform goals that are just as significant—he laments, for example, that leading civil rights organizations of the 1960s did not address the plight of "junkies, all of them poor . . . they need freedom as much as anybody else, and what's anybody doing for them?"[189]—but he does not suggest that the causes that are focused upon are necessarily less urgent or valuable than the ones that are not.

What underlies the greater tendency of Emerson and Thoreau to diminish the work of social reformers is their view, entirely lacking in Dylan, that self-reform is often a superior substitute—or necessary prerequisite—for social and political reform. The lack of self-satisfaction in Dylan's self-reliance makes him utterly unable to share Emerson's claim that "society gains nothing whilst a man, not himself renovated, attempts to renovate things around him,"[190] nor Thoreau's parallel assertion: "The true reform can be undertaken any morning before unbarring our doors. It calls no convention. I can do two thirds the reform of the world myself."[191] Even if Dylan agrees with Emerson and Thoreau that reformers who lack a personal vocation may turn out to be hypocrites—concealing behind their apparent philanthropy mere spiritual emptiness or, worse, an all-too-familiar

---

[186] Part III highlights Dylan's critique of politics, which includes an account of the political world as inherently fallen (III.1), an opposition to false activism that does not achieve its goals (III.5), and an opposition, as well, to the excessive attention received by partisan and electoral politics that comes at the expense of an alternate, "emergency" conception of political responsibility (III.3). Yet, as Part III also shows—as have elements of the argument here in Part I—even when highly critical of politics, Dylan evinces respect and appreciation for those effectively committed to political and social reform within local contexts.

[187] Emerson, "Self-Reliance," 279.

[188] Thoreau, *Walden*, 52.

[189] Quoted in Cott, "The Crackin', Shakin', Breakin' Sounds," in *Essential Interviews*, 29.

[190] Emerson, "New England Reformers," 77.

[191] Thoreau, *Journal*, 1:247.

socioeconomic ambition—he cannot endorse Thoreau's extreme statement that "there is no odor so bad as that which arises from goodness tainted."[192] Dylan understands the work, even as he disclaims it, to be too valuable to diminish even its half-hearted agents. Whereas Emerson declares, "Accept the reforms but accept not the person of the reformer,"[193] Dylan understands that this proposed differentiation, and the diminishment of full-time reformers it implies, is neither possible nor desirable within the contemporary context. To be sure, in the case of at least Emerson there are moments when something like Dylan's less self-satisfied form of self-reliance—and its deference to the reformers who are not joined—seems to be shared, as when in declining to live on Brook Farm Emerson writes, "I have decided not to join it and yet very slowly and I may almost say penitentially"[194] or when he confesses: "When a zealot comes to me & represents the importance of this Temperance Reform my hands drop—I have no excuse—I honor him with shame at my own inaction."[195] But these are exceptions, not entirely free from irony, and dwarfed by opposing sentiments such as Emerson's suggestion that his writing might be a worthy compensation for the political action he forgoes.[196] Because Dylan is more aware of the contingency and good fortune by which he has achieved self-reliance, he is more respectful of the permanent need to resist injustice in its various forms.

Seen biographically, the value of Dylan's variant of self-reliance is harder to perceive, since Emerson and Thoreau contributed, if anything, more time and energy to the fight against injustice than Dylan. But viewed ideologically, the distinct perspective on self-reliance that Dylan represents—with its epistemological, ethical, and political departures from the Emersonian and Thoreauvian tradition—provides a more honest account of what a life of self-reliance actually entails, the moral costs of this life, and the proper attitude by which these costs should be borne. For those of us who turn our backs to injustice, Dylan provides a more worthy example of how to do so.

---

[192] Thoreau, *Walden*, 53.

[193] Emerson, "Reforms," 3:260.

[194] Emerson, "Letter to George Ripley, December 15, 1840," in *Selected Letters of Ralph Waldo Emerson*, ed. Joel Myerson (New York: Columbia University Press, 1997), 244.

[195] Emerson, *The Journals and Miscellaneous Notebooks of Ralph Waldo Emerson*, 5:437.

[196] As Emerson puts it: "I have been writing with some pains Essays on various matters as a sort of apology to my country for my apparent idleness." Emerson, *The Journals and Miscellaneous Notebooks of Ralph Waldo Emerson*, 7:404–405. Note here Emerson's refusal to fully acknowledge his political inaction, speaking of only his "apparent" idleness.

I.6. Dylan at the March on Washington

In attending to the distinctiveness of Dylan's prophetic stance regarding the disharmony between individual freedom and social justice, I so far have addressed the meaning of this stance from the perspective of political withdrawal. Yet, as Dylan's role at the 1963 March on Washington for Jobs and Freedom demonstrates, his status as a bourgeois prophet also functions within a context of political action.

In describing Dylan, in his role at the March, as bourgeois, I do not mean to say that he is a defender of capitalism over and against socialism or that he is a voice of reaction over and against social progressivism, but rather that his three songs performed at the March address much more the perspective of the bourgeois progressive (who is only partially committed to rectifying injustice and whose relative privilege stems in part from the persistence of injustice) than that of the militant progressive (who is fully committed to the fight against injustice) or the victim (who is primarily a sufferer of injustice and who may or may not also be a militant). Social justice movements in a liberal-democratic society, including and especially the American civil rights movement, depend on bringing together all three constituencies,[197] but this does not mean that the ethical responsibilities are identical for each. Of the three, the bourgeois progressive is clearly the most ambiguous figure, at once a benefactor and opposer of unfairness and oppression—and, likewise, at once taking some action to rectify social injustice but at the same time doing substantially less than could or ought to be done. Dylan's songs at the March address this figure and help bring it to self-consciousness.

My definition of the bourgeois progressive in terms of a partially complicit relationship to injustice is not meant to undermine a more traditional socioeconomic conception—which refers to someone who, though formally committed to free and equal citizenship, nonetheless lives off of capital while others must rely entirely on their labor; employs the labor of others but does not necessarily sell his or her own labor; and holds an economic privilege that is either not fully merited or unfairly allowed to generate extra-economic advantages (such as in political and educational opportunity)[198]—but rather is intended to address this socioeconomically conceived figure in the moments of his or her political activism. After all, critics of the bourgeois are too quick when they imagine that

---

[197] This point is made by Martin Luther King Jr. See his work *The Trumpet of Conscience*, in *Testament of Hope*, 640–47.

[198] On aspects of this socioeconomic definition of the bourgeois, see Henry Heller, *The Bourgeois Revolution in France, 1789–1815* (New York: Berghahn, 2011), 6.

the bourgeois, as such, have no interest in progressive politics.[199] It is truer to note, with Marx, that bourgeois society is simultaneously progressive in its anti-feudal impact yet also profoundly defective in its failure to bring about a more genuinely emancipatory condition of freedom and equality for all. The bourgeois progressive embodies this double movement at the characterological level, at once committed to eradicating injustice and yet at the same time, due to the non-militancy of this commitment and the position of comfort and privilege enjoyed within and from an insufficiently just liberal-democratic society, complicit with injustice as well. Neither primarily a victim of an unjust order, nor someone who is consistently demanding and persistent in seeking to rectify it, the bourgeois progressive favors emancipatory change but also values his or her own individual security, comfort, and advantage such that this commitment to change is watered-down and ambiguous.

One way to address the ambiguities of bourgeois progressivism is simply to reject the bourgeois progressive as hypocritical or bankrupt in the name of the morally superior perspective of the militant activist who is unambiguously committed to fighting against the economic injustice, racism, and militarism that persists within liberal democracies and of course elsewhere. Within the world of 1960s protest music, something like this approach is suggested in Phil Ochs's ironic 1966 song "Love me, I'm a Liberal." Dylan is a prophet of the bourgeoisie, and not simply its critic, because what he most calls for is not the negation of the bourgeois approach to social justice but honesty from the bourgeois about the nature of their social activism and the liberal-democratic societies they typically inhabit.[200]

In a context of gross and widespread injustice, mere honesty from the bourgeois might seem like too tepid of a goal, but for three different reasons bringing the bourgeois progressive to a state of self-awareness is in fact meaningful. First, insofar as we lack today Marx's confidence in the ultimate transcendence of bourgeois society—insofar as bourgeois culture, politics, and economics remain hegemonic in much of the world—then the bourgeois progressive, willing to make only partial efforts to achieve incremental social transformation, will continue to be, however imperfect, a vital contributor to social change and thus someone whose self-awareness matters. Second, the bourgeois are notoriously

---

[199] Thus I disagree with strictly critical analyses, such as Nicolas Berdyaev, *The Bourgeois Mind and Other Essays* (Freeport, NY: Books for Libraries Press, 1966 [1934]), 11–26.

[200] In this context, Dylan's castigation of Ochs takes on added relevance. Dylan told Ochs in 1964: "The stuff you're writing is bullshit, because politics is bullshit. It's all unreal. The only thing that's real is inside you. Your feelings. Just look at the world you're writing about and you'll see you're wasting your time. The world is, well . . . it's just absurd." Quoted in Scaduto, *Bob Dylan: An Intimate Biography*, 176.

mendacious, in denial not only about the divergence between mere juridical equality and a more genuine free and equal citizenship but also about their own status as bourgeois. If Lukács is correct that bourgeois denial and self-deception regarding their identity is a condition for the very functioning of bourgeois society, then honest self-awareness would itself be a step, however modest, toward more effective social change.[201] This leads to the third point: self-aware bourgeois progressives are better able to participate in social justice movements. Even if they fail to do all they might to eradicate injustice, they can at least attain a more minimal standard of decency—the decency of avoiding triumphal feelings of exultance too incongruous with the persistence of unjust suffering in the world; the decency of remaining profoundly dissatisfied in the face of the world and thus passively open to the changes being advocated by the totally committed; the decency of not imagining any collective social movement could absolve one's personal responsibility to ameliorate one's immediate surroundings; and, finally, the decency of admitting that, in failing to sufficiently execute this responsibility, one is not fully good. In other words, a self-aware bourgeois progressive is more likely to defer to the moral leadership of the more committed militant—to, in Dylan's words, "get out of the new [road] if you can't lend your hand" ("The Times They Are A-Changin'"). In short, bourgeois progressives who understand themselves as such do not let moments of relative success—when incremental improvement is achieved—turn into a triumphal complacency about themselves, about the liberal-democratic order, or about some alleged providential force working on the side of justice. Such triumphal ideas may be appropriate and even necessary for militant progressives and victims of injustice, but they become obnoxious, false, and counterproductive when voiced by bourgeois progressives.

Dylan's songs at the March on Washington cultivate this honesty and its concomitant benefits. They also signal the distinctiveness of Dylan's prophetic function. If most speakers at the March addressed the assembled marchers from a standpoint of militancy, Dylan's three songs—two performed by him, the other by the group Peter, Paul, and Mary—contain as their primary political purpose not the call to militancy and the total castigation of an unjust society, but the more modest (though still deeply relevant) function of inculcating honest self-awareness from bourgeois progressives about their own nature and that of the capitalist liberal-democratic regimes whose values they, more than anyone else, embody. Elsewhere, especially in the years immediately following the March, Dylan, as we have seen, sometimes challenges protest movements

[201] Lukács, *History and Class Consciousness*, 66.

and leftist politics themselves, announcing a kind of turning away from the political in the name of individual self-reliance. While Dylan's gesture of withdrawal
is itself marked by an uncommonly self-conscious and honest bourgeois posture, since it admits to its abandoning of a full-fledged social responsibility, what
is remarkable about Dylan's contribution to the March on Washington, the most
significant social justice event of his lifetime, is that it suggests what a politically
engaged bourgeois consciousness might look like when disciplined by an awareness of its limited commitment to justice and the parallel limitations besetting
the liberal-democratic regime.

Dylan, King, and the Question of Hopefulness

Mary Travers of the group Peter, Paul, and Mary, which performed two songs
at the March on Washington, later reflected that in looking out at the approximately 250,000 attendees, she had a sudden moment of recognition: "I started to
sing, and I had an epiphany, looking out at this quarter of a million people . . . and
I truly believed it was possible that human beings could join together to make
a positive social change." The song she was singing in that instant was Dylan's
"Blowin' in the Wind." Her fellow group member Paul Stookey similarly reported how singing the song at the March made vivid a sense of social and political achievement: "And then all of a sudden the lyrics are coming out, you
know, 'and how many years must people exist before they can be free,' and you're
thinking—Wow! This is it, this is the integration of everything we sing and feel
strongly at the moment."[202]

As such statements make clear, Travers and Stookey interpret the March in
a spirit of *triumphal hopefulness*. Such hopefulness has at least three elements.
On the level of political mechanisms, Travers's and Stookey's reactions reflect
both an abstract faith in the capacity of collective action to make a meaningful
difference and a concrete belief that the protest movement before their eyes was
bringing about "positive social change." On the personal level, their reflections
indicate that they consider themselves as fully part of this solidaristic effort to
achieve social justice. And with respect to the all-important question of whether
justice could ultimately be achieved in America, Travers and Stookey signal that
the March betokened for them the possibility of the full realization of social justice (or "the integration of everything we sing and feel strongly about"), if not
in 1963, then at least in a future moment even more perfected by progressive

[202] The comments of Travers and Stookey come from their interviews in the documentary *The
March*, directed by John Akomfrah (2013), which aired August 27, 2013, on PBS; see "Peter Paul &
Mary Talk about The March On Washington & Sing Songs 1963," posted by Sam Rosenburg, video,
5:52, August 30, 2013, https://www.youtube.com/watch?v=GUpG0Cev7qc.

collective action. Hence, their exultant feelings of "epiphany" and "Wow! This is it."

Such triumphal hopefulness fits easily with the usual way the March has been celebrated. Martin Luther King's great speech, which sits at the epicenter of most accounts of the March, itself provides a message that is hopeful in the same three ways suggested by Travers's and Stookey's interpretation of their own participation. Praising the "marvelous new militancy which has engulfed the Negro community" and the March itself as being "the greatest demonstration for freedom in the history of our nation," King's address credits the civil rights movement as bringing "my people" to a point where they "stand on the warm threshold which leads into the palace of justice." Although aware of a diversity of perspectives within the movement, King in his speech presents himself as a leader with a total commitment to social justice and addresses most directly listeners with a similarly unambiguous devotion ("you [who] have come here out of excessive trials and tribulation . . . the veterans of creative suffering"). And on the issue of the full realizability of justice, while not denying the severity of the obstacles ahead, King does not waver in his faith in the ultimate achievement of racial and economic justice for all Americans. Stating that "now is the time to make real the promises of democracy," King portrays America as a country that, though sick, can overcome injustice and fulfill its stated commitment to liberty and equality for all.[203]

Travers and Stookey, in singing "Blowin' in the Wind" at the March on Washington, felt themselves to be communicating the same hopeful message as King, but the words—Dylan's words—tell a different story. Indeed, what is remarkable about "Blowin' in the Wind," in addition to the two other songs Dylan himself sang at the March, is that it so clearly resists and criticizes a spirit of triumphal hopefulness. King's speech imagines a realizable future, in which we can say, as in the last lines of his address, "Free at last! Free at last! Thank God Almighty, we are Free at Last." Dylan's short song, by contrast, is full of questions (nine to be exact), not answers—all having to do with the central question of why it is that so many of us do not do the things we know to be just. And while a single, repeated answer is given to these questions, it is an answer that is no answer, the enigmatic answer that is "blowin' in the wind."

To frame the matter more precisely, "Blowin' in the Wind" leaves untouched only the first of the three elements of triumphal hopefulness expressed by Travers and Stookey in their reminiscences and expressed by King in his majestic speech: the idea that political action could effect meaningful social change and that, specifically, black people in America might overcome their oppression

---

[203] King, "I Have a Dream," in *Testament of Hope*, 217–19.

through a successful political movement.[204] Lyrics in the song—especially two of its questions—did, after all, harmonize with these core aspirations and were experienced as such by participants at the March:

> How many roads must a man walk down
> Before you call him a man?

And:

> Yes, 'n' how many years can some people exist
> Before they're allowed to be free?

But "Blowin' in the Wind" refuses to let the possibility of a specific political success (the achievement of civil rights for African Americans) become the basis for the other two elements of triumphal hopefulness: the good conscience of being self-consciously solidaristic with a just cause and the faith that the full realization of justice (free and equal citizenship for all) might itself be accomplished within a liberal democracy.

With regard to the first of these critical gestures, Dylan raises the uncomfortable question of just how much self-described activists and progressives fully desire the change they claim to seek. Dylan's song challenges his listeners to question how committed they are to the cause of justice:

> How many times must a man look up
> Before he can see the sky?
> Yes, 'n' how many ears must one man have
> Before he can hear people cry?

The polemical target of these lines, sung before amassed protestors, is not merely those who oppose justice and thus represent forces of reaction. These lines are all the more forceful when they identify and interrogate what I am calling "bourgeois progressives"—that is, those who support justice but do so inconstantly and imperfectly.

---

[204] To be sure, as Part III discusses, Dylan evinces a caustic pessimism about politics through virtually the entirety of his sixty-plus years on the public stage. Yet, as Part III also explains, Dylan's pessimism does not mean that local improvements—such as those represented by the American civil rights movement—are impossible but rather predicts that, on balance, the *world as a whole* is unlikely to progress morally and that the *full achievement* of relations of free and equal citizenship is unlikely to be accomplished or satisfactorily approximated anywhere.

King himself was all too aware that the movement he led brought together different constituencies and that, specifically, the militancy he advocated and represented had to cooperate, often unsuccessfully, with other, less steadfastly committed progressive communities, such as white moderates, liberal politicians, church leaders (both black and white), and some middle-class African Americans. King defined the militant in terms of totality of commitment—"to be militant merely means to be demanding and to be persistent"[205]—and he knew that not everyone sympathetic to the cause of social justice would qualify. But a feature of King's spirit of triumphal hopefulness is that his message serves to bridge the potential rift between militant and non-militant and, in general, avoids shaming non-militants for their failure to act and sacrifice sufficiently.[206] He does this, first of all, because his own totality of commitment—reflected not just in his concrete activism, but in the personal risks and sacrifices he endured (jailed twenty-nine times in his life, stabbed once, constantly harassed by death threats with his home bombed on three occasions, and ultimately assassinated)—inspired many others to become militants themselves.[207] He further erodes the boundary between militant and non-militant in conceiving of non-violent mass protest as a political vehicle that can bring together radical activists and more ambivalent young people who, though critical of America, were still, in his words, "struggling to adapt [themselves] to the prevailing values of our society."[208] And, perhaps most of all, King softens the divide between militant and non-militant through his frequent use of rhetoric that enables non-militant listeners to feel themselves as fully committed to the cause. His "I Have a Dream" speech at the March, for instance, even as it privileges the perspective of the militant, sometimes invites all of its listeners to imagine that they might be militants too. That is, King does not always distinguish the community of those physically assembled before the Lincoln Memorial ("we [who] stand today" in Lincoln's "symbolic shadow") from the community of those totally committed to social justice: "we [who] can never be satisfied" until, as the last lines of speech conclude, "we are free at last." In one passage in particular, King seems to invite all of his listeners to conceive of themselves as militants:

[205] King, "Conversation with Martin Luther King," in *Testament of Hope*, 661.

[206] To be sure, sometimes King wondered whether the white moderate was an even greater threat to the civil rights movement than outright racists, but this idea was overshadowed by a much more dominant focus on unifying the moderate and militant, which I discuss in the main text.

[207] See King, "*Playboy* Interview: Martin Luther King, Jr. (1965)," in *Testament of Hope*, 341. On his inspiration of others to be militants, consider King's account of meeting young black students, including "stylishly dressed young girls," who say, "Dr. King, I am ready to die if I must." King, "The Time for Freedom Has Come," in *Testament of Hope*, 161.

[208] King, *Trumpet of Conscience*, 642.

With this faith we will be able to hew out of the mountain of despair a stone of hope. With this faith we will be able to transform the jangling discords of our nation into a beautiful symphony of brotherhood. With this faith we will be able to work together, to pray together, to struggle together, to go to jail together, to stand up for freedom together, knowing that we will be free one day.[209]

In contrast, the probing questions of "Blowin' in the Wind" expose and emphasize the contrast between those who are militants and those who are not:

> Yes, 'n' how many times can a man turn his head
> Pretending he just doesn't see?

Dylan's song thus explores the limits of the progressive conscience, reminding us that the situation of many progressives—specifically bourgeois ones—is that they are not progressive all the time, that their moments of activism are complemented by other periods, probably much more numerous, of compromise and comfort. The bourgeois progressive represents not any kind of non-militancy (such as that of those who lack all interest in fighting injustice or of those who, not obviously beneficiaries within an unjust system, may lack the resources for such a fight) but rather refers to non-militants who, as relatively prosperous and comfortable members of an insufficiently just society, embody a non-militancy that is primarily a function of their haphazard and imperfect commitment to causes they otherwise know to be just.[210]

If we turn to the second aspect of Dylan's challenge to a spirit of triumphal hopefulness—his questions about whether justice, in the full sense, is even possible—we find another way in which his message addresses the bourgeois: not just exposing certain progressives as bourgeois (in their insufficient

---

[209] King, "I Have a Dream," 219.

[210] In emphasizing the material comfort and economic privilege definitive of the bourgeois, I do not mean to reduce the bourgeois identity to a strictly economic category, since the bourgeois' economic privilege might stem from extra-economic sources, such as race. Within the mid-twentieth-century American context of the March, for example, it was not uncommon to link the bourgeois also with a white racial privilege stemming from Jim Crow and legalized discrimination. As one musical example of this phenomenon, consider Lead Belly's 1937 song "Bourgeois Blues," which includes the lines, "Well, me and my wife we were standing upstairs / We heard the white man say 'I don't want no n****** up there' / Lord, in a bourgeois town / Uhm, bourgeois town." Regardless of the semantics of the word *bourgeois*, the point is to recognize that there are multiple sociological factors that might shape the identity of individuals who are at once holders of unfair advantages stemming from an unjust order and, at the same time, unwilling to fully do what their own conscience suggests they should do to help rectify the situation.

concern for justice), but exposing the liberal-democratic regime, so often seen as a morally perfect political ideal, as merely bourgeois (in its inescapable favoring of the economically privileged) and also as having an enduring connection to violence.

The song, for example, not only concerns implicit support for racial equality but also takes issue with violence. At least two of its questions speak to the quest for peace:

> Yes, 'n' how many times must the cannonballs fly
> Before they're forever banned?

And:

> Yes, 'n' how many deaths will it take till he knows
> That too many people have died?

But is peace—the cessation of interstate violence, killing, weaponry—a possibility? Perhaps, on the basis of the alleged declining incidence of war, one can look forward to the greater approximation of peace.[211] But unlike overcoming legalized racial discrimination within a particular society, peace seems much more doubtful as an achievable goal. And by extension, there are other commitments that likewise may be constitutively out of reach. For example, the long-standing liberal-democratic ambition that one's socioeconomic status have no bearing on one's political voice or educational opportunities is noble as an ideal to work toward, but nonetheless is not fully realizable so long as there are institutions like private property and the family, as I elsewhere have argued.[212] Dylan's song, with its recurrent appeal to an "answer" that cannot be implemented but remains in the wind, makes intimations of a justice that is not of this world, and in so doing raises the possibility that living under conditions of less-than-full justice is part of the human experience itself.

The question of whether it is appropriate to have hope in the ultimate realizability of justice can be evaluated from two different perspectives: whether it is true that justice someday can be achieved and whether, regardless of its truth, it is productive or otherwise beneficial to think that it can be achieved. King's hopefulness stemmed from both sources. He not only evinced an earnest faith in the full realization of justice, whose most memorable, but hardly sole, aspect was his often-expressed remark that the arc of the moral universe bends toward

---

[211] Steven Pinker, *The Better Angels of Our Nature: Why Violence Has Declined* (New York: Viking, 2009), 189–294.

[212] Green, *The Shadow of Unfairness*, 43–61.

justice.[213] King also suggested that this optimistic metaphysical view enabled the militancy he advocated and thus for this reason, too, independent of its truth, was justified.[214] Dylan's challenge to hopefulness itself operates within these two dimensions, with his songs at the March both questioning whether justice can ever be fully achieved and implicitly cautioning that, at least for bourgeois non-militants, too much hope in the future might generate an inappropriate complacency. King himself was not unaware of this latter problem, as he occasionally recognized that hopefulness in the ultimate perfection of society might undermine individual responsibility in the here and now,[215] but the fact is that this concern was dwarfed by his primary focus on inspiring and maintaining a spirit

[213] On King's idea that "the universe is on the side of justice," see his "Facing the Challenge of a New Age," 141, and "A Christmas Sermon on Peace," 257, both in Testament of Hope. However, King's faith in the ultimate realizability of justice was not limited to this cosmological notion but included both his faith in a "God [who] is interested in the freedom of the whole human race and in the creation of a society where all men can live together as brothers, where every man will respect the dignity and the worth of human personality" ("The American Dream," 215; also see "A Testament of Hope," 314, and Stride Toward Freedom, 438, all in Testament of Hope) as well as his faith that the scientific and technological revolutions of modernity might be complemented by a spiritual or moral revolution through which humanity might become a brotherhood (see "Facing the Challenge of a New Age," 144; "If the Negro Wins, Labor Wins," 203–4; and Where Do We Go From Here?, 621, all in Testament of Hope). On these bases, even as he remained deeply aware of obstacles, King could still maintain that "we have before us the glorious opportunity to inject a new dimension of love into the veins of our civilization" which would carry with it "an exuberant gladness of the new age" ("Facing the Challenge," 140). And he could anticipate the full realization of the liberal-democratic regime, in which America would be "born again" (Where Do We Go From Here?, 251), in which "we will be able to emerge from a bleak and desolate midnight of man's inhumanity to man into the bright and glittering daybreak of freedom and justice" ("The American Dream," 216), in which "we [will] be able to bring into full realization the dream of American democracy" ("The Rising Tide of Racial Consciousness," in Testament of Hope, 151), and in which "in luminous splendor, the Christian era will truly begin" ("A Testament of Hope," 328).

[214] The practical, rather than metaphysical, commitment to hope is perhaps most succinctly expressed in King's 1967 sermon, aired on Christmas Eve in Canada in 1967, in which he stated, "If there is to be peace on earth and good will toward men, we must finally believe in the ultimate morality of the universe, and believe that all reality hinges on moral foundations" ("A Christmas Sermon on Peace," 257). Also see "Nobel Prize Acceptance Speech," in Testament of Hope, 225–26; Where Do We Go From Here?, 583–84.

[215] See, for example, King, "Facing the Challenge," 141: "Before closing I must correct what might be a false impression. I am afraid that if I close at this point many will go away misinterpreting my whole message. I have talked about the new age which is fastly coming into being. I have talked about the fact that God is working in history to bring about this new age. There is a danger, therefore, that after hearing all of this you will go away with the impression that we can go home, sit down, and do nothing, waiting for the coming of the inevitable. You will somehow feel that this new age will roll in on the wheels of inevitability, so there is nothing to do but wait on it. If you get that impression you are the victims of an illusion wrapped in superficiality. We must speed up the coming of the inevitable."

of militancy for which such hopefulness was, in his view, as practically necessary as it was metaphysically true. But Dylan, who lacks this militancy, sings most poignantly to those not altogether persistent or demanding in the fight against injustice and who actually prosper in the face of injustice. To such people, it becomes important (in a way lacking for the militant) to acknowledge the remoteness, if not outright impossibility, of full justice as well as the ways in which even a much-reformed liberal-democratic society that had overcome legalized racial discrimination would continue to unfairly advantage the rich and well born and other privileged identities. The importance of such sober reflections lies not only in their claim to truth (as they seem at least as persuasive as King's metaphysical optimism) but also in their disciplining bourgeois progressives so that, even if they fail to do all they might to eradicate injustice, they can at least attain a more minimal standard of decency by not indulging in the undeserved self-celebration of triumphal hopefulness.

Travers and Stookey, in singing Dylan's words, felt themselves to be militants when in fact the song they sang should have reminded them that they were not militants but only bourgeois progressives. If one cringes upon hearing Travers and Stookey, ultimately more entertainers than social activists, reflect on their epiphanies while performing at the March on Washington, it is because one recoils at their triumphalism and how it signifies their misidentification of themselves and their role within an unjust society.

The Dilemmas of Bourgeois Triumph

As I have stressed, in defining the bourgeois progressive in terms of a non-militant, partially complicit relationship to injustice, my purpose is not to challenge a more familiar socioeconomic conception of the bourgeois (as the holder of economic privilege and unfair advantages within an insufficiently just democratic order) but rather to examine the form of political action most characteristic of those who occupy this socioeconomic position. Given this perspective, it is relevant to consider one of the sharpest criticisms of the bourgeois, socioeconomically conceived: the bourgeois' profound *illusion* about themselves (their belief that they are not bourgeois) and about their society (their belief that it instantiates free and equal citizenship). As Lukács puts it, "The veil drawn over the nature of bourgeois society is indispensable to the bourgeois itself."[216] Barthes goes even further, insisting on a constitutive inability of the bourgeois to name themselves as such: "The flight from the name 'bourgeois' is not therefore an illusory, accidental, secondary, natural or insignificant phenomenon: it is the

---

[216] Lukács, *History and Class Consciousness*, 66.

bourgeois ideology itself, the process through which the bourgeoisie transforms the reality of the world into an image of the world, History into Nature. And this image has a remarkable feature: it is upside down. The status of the bourgeois is particular, historical: man as represented by it is universal, eternal."[217] Such criticisms are relevant not only in their suggestion that simply being aware of oneself as a bourgeois would already be a consequential political act, but in their emphasis that such self-consciousness likely proceeds by overcoming comforting, self-congratulating illusions.

There no doubt are many illusions that might be unmasked within a bourgeois society, but in the context I examine here—the bourgeois in moments of dedication to social justice—the illusion most clearly involved concerns the bourgeois commitment to freedom. This illusion is hardly total. After all, bourgeois society so often came into being in the overthrow of feudal societies that did not recognize, even as bare principles, notions of freedom and equality. The antifeudal, liberal-democratic state, which is the bourgeois system of government par excellence, affords basic liberties to its citizens in a manner unprecedented in political history. The bourgeois always have the option to act in accordance with their official political philosophy and seek to further the reach and meaning of these liberties, opposing gross injustices like racial and gender discrimination, promoting liberal democracy in areas of the world where it does not exist, and working within their own liberal-democratic society to diminish the arbitrary impact of socioeconomic status on civic opportunities and life prospects.

But bourgeois freedom is never complete. And the possibility of conflating the real particular that is achieved with the imaginary universal that is not is thus always a risk for the bourgeois. Ending gross oppression is not the same as introducing a robust liberal-democratic order. Even a so-called well-ordered liberal-democratic state will not be able to fully realize the conditions of free and equal citizenship (e.g., social class will continue to impact politics and education).[218] And furthermore, there is a kind of freedom, inherently elite in character, that exceeds the principles of free and equal citizenship—not the freedom to compete for opportunities on fair terms, but the freedom from having to compete at all: the freedom from obligatory work. Dylan often speaks of this kind of freedom, which exists within but also beyond the institutions of bourgeois liberal democracy, as when he attends in "It's Alright, Ma" to a category of persons who may be legal citizens in a prosperous liberal democracy but suffer from envy in the knowledge that they are not fully free:

---

[217] Barthes, *Mythologies*, 141.
[218] See Green, *The Shadow of Unfairness*, 43–61, 84–91.

For them that must obey authority
That they do not respect in any degree
Who despise their jobs, their destinies
Speak jealously of them that are free
Do what they do just to be
Nothing more than something
They invest in[219]

To live without labor is the ultimate form of bourgeois comfort, even if it remains, for most bourgeois, just an aspiration or something they will only very partially experience. Nonetheless, that only a few will enjoy this freedom reminds us, along with the other factors, that there is no straightforward, equal, or complete accomplishment of freedom in even the best liberal-democratic societies.

The bourgeois progressive, then, when honest, seeks freedom but understands that not everyone can be equally free. Yet it is precisely in moments of triumphant transformation, when genuine political success has been achieved, that the subtlety of the authentic bourgeois standpoint becomes difficult to maintain. In such moments, the bourgeois who supports a just cause is prone to forget that he or she is, after all, a bourgeois, not a universal being. Much like Francis Fukuyama, who, on the eve of the West's defeat of communist regimes in Eastern Europe, falsely imagined liberal democracy as a near-perfect political system representing nothing less than the end of history, so are all bourgeois, in their successful support of just ends, at risk of going overboard and falling into a self-satisfaction that is as obnoxious as it is undeserved. The bourgeois thus struggles with the proper way to be triumphant. To deny bourgeois progressivism any expression of satisfaction in its victories would be unfair to its achievements. But to exaggerate these achievements is offensive not just in its bravado but also in its fundamental dishonesty about the profound limits to the kind of freedom that is possible within a bourgeois, liberal-democratic order. Such exaggerations—such excessive and inappropriate self-regard—are also counterproductive when they instill a new complacency that erodes further progressive commitments. In more recent times, Slavoj Žižek seems to have had his finger on this concern when, in addressing protestors in Zuccotti Park

---

[219] Here I follow the version as recorded on Dylan's 1965 album, *Bringing It All Back Home*, which differs somewhat from the version in the anthology *Bob Dylan: The Lyrics, 1961–2012* (New York: Simon and Schuster, 2016), 157. The anthology has the last lines of the verse as: "Cultivate their flowers to be / Nothing more than something they invest in." On Dylan's concept of freedom, also see his song "If You See Her, Say Hello," released in 1975, with its line: "I always have respected her for doin' what she did and gettin' free." On the other hand, consider "Ballad in Plain D," from 1964, with its question: "Are birds free from the chains of the skyway?"

in New York City at the Occupy Wall Street movement, his chief advice was, "Don't fall in love with yourselves. . . . Carnivals come cheap."[220]

One of the two songs Dylan himself performed at the March on Washington, "When the Ship Comes In," speaks insightfully to the issue of bourgeois triumph, for it concerns both triumph and its limits. This was a fitting theme for the occasion since the March was both an instrument in the pursuit of progress and a celebration of recent and anticipated successes in the civil rights movement. In a sense, the very gathering was itself an achievement since it manifested, in its peaceful magnitude, the growing potency of the commitment to progressive change in the United States. King's famous speech, after all, begins by referring to the March as nothing less than "what will go down in history as the greatest demonstration for freedom in the history of our nation."[221]

That the central theme of the song is triumph—success and prosperity—is indicated by the key idiomatic metaphor of a ship coming to harbor and, with it, the profitable realization of a commercial venture. One need not be on the ship that comes in. The merchant Antonio, in *The Merchant of Venice*, waits expectantly on shore for "my ships."[222] And in the nineteenth century, the land-bound wives of sailors at sea, women who had purchased goods on credit from local tradesmen, promised to repay what they owed when their "ships came in"—that is, when their husbands returned with money.

At the same time, Dylan also employs the metaphor in a secondary way, referring to the ship of state that has overcome unjust enemies (and "the chains of the sea") and, now landing on shore, has the potential to start anew. Indeed, for the American context in which Dylan was singing, such a ship was not merely metaphorical but quite literal, since the country was founded by European colonists who made the sea voyage over the Atlantic—sometimes with commercial interests foremost in mind, other times in pursuit of a new and better world, and perhaps usually with some mix of the two. One of the prophetic documents of the American experience—John Winthrop's "A Model of Christian Charity"—is supposed to have been preached aboard the *Arbella* as it made its way from England to Salem in 1630, effectively founding the Commonwealth of Massachusetts. After delineating the principles of justice according to which the new colony should be organized, Winthrop's sermon famously exhorts his fellow Puritans to treat their nascent society as a beacon to the world: "For we must consider that we shall be as a city upon a hill. The eyes of all people are

[220] Quoted in Aaron Gell, "Slavoj Žižek Speaks to Occupy Wall Street," *New York Observer*, October 9, 2011, https://observer.com/2011/10/slavoj-zizek-speaks-to-occupy-wall-street/.

[221] King, "I Have a Dream," 217.

[222] William Shakespeare, *The Merchant of Venice* (New York: Viking, 2006), 1.3.177.

upon us."[223] Dylan seems to repeat these words in the fifth verse of "When the Ship Comes In," which imagines the landing of the ship and the disembarkation:

> Then the sands will roll
> Out a carpet of gold
> For your weary toes to be a-touchin'
> And the ship's wise men
> Will remind you once again
> That the whole wide world is watchin'

There are, then, two logics in the song: triumph and justice. How are they to be related? The all-too-easy, self-congratulating linkage—which appeals to bourgeois progressives when they are complacent and unreflective about their bourgeois nature—is to think that the triumph is the construction of a just society. This was Winthrop's vision in his sermon, which outlines the way in which the new colony might abide by the "two rules whereby we are to walk one towards another: Justice and Mercy" and also abide by "the Law of Nature and the Law of Grace." Winthrop calls on his fellow colonists to embody the highest form of moral rectitude and follow the instruction of the Hebrew prophet Micah:

> Now the only way to avoid this shipwreck, and to provide for our posterity, is to follow the counsel of Micah, to do justly, to love mercy, to walk humbly with our God. For this end, we must be knit together, in this work, as one man. We must entertain each other in brotherly affection. We must be willing to abridge ourselves of our superfluities, for the supply of others' necessities. We must uphold a familiar commerce together in all meekness, gentleness, patience and liberality. We must delight in each other; make others' conditions our own; rejoice together, mourn together, labor and suffer together, always having before our eyes our commission and community in the work, as members of the same body.[224]

Clearly, the America that was founded did not live up to Winthrop's moral vision—and Winthrop also was wrong that the new country would need to abide by this vision in order to survive at all and "avoid shipwreck." Even as an ideal, though, his conception of justice is wanting, both in its theological aspect and in its too easy acceptance of inequality. The address begins: "God Almighty in His

---

[223] Edmund S. Morgan, ed., "A Model of Christian Charity by John Winthrop (1630)," in *Puritan Political Ideas, 1558–1794* (Indianapolis: Bobbs-Merrill, 1965), 90–91.
[224] Morgan, 91.

most holy and wise providence, hath so disposed of the condition of mankind, as in all times some must be rich, some poor, some high and eminent in power and dignity; others mean and in submission."[225] Winthrop could have attained something resembling bourgeois self-consciousness if he had acknowledged this circumstance as a reason not to expect the nascent political community to fully abide by the dictates of justice. Instead, he still thinks a just and pious republic is possible in spite of these profound socioeconomic divisions. The point, though, is not to indict Winthrop per se, but any bourgeois society, grounded on private property and the family, that fails to see how these institutions infect and inhibit the full realization of its professed principles.

The subtlety of Dylan's song is that it does not equate triumph and justice, but recognizes a triumph that is something less. The ecstasy of beating back enemies (of overcoming some condition of gross oppression) is not allowed to uncritically become the positive achievement of a full-fledged good society. If there is a kind of moral purity, it is reserved for the negative and finite experience of liberation, as distinguished from the ongoing and imperfect effort to achieve concrete free and equal citizenship in a specific political community:

> And the words that are used
> For to get the ship confused
> Will not be understood as they're spoken
> For the chains of the sea
> Will have busted in the night
> And will be buried at the bottom of the ocean
>
> A song will lift
> As the mainsail shifts
> And the boat drifts on to the shoreline
> And the sun will respect
> Every face on the deck
> The hour that the ship comes in

The greatest attainment of equal respect is afforded to the sailors still on board the ship, before it has landed and the new society begun. This is the equality of being partners in a specific effort at liberation, which as such is momentary and finite and not itself instantiated in a new constitutional structure. It is fitting, then, that Dylan describes the equality as coming from a non-human source (the sun), suggesting that when humans try themselves to be the source of each other's mutual recognition there will be problems and distortion. These two

---

[225] Morgan, 90.

verses immediately precede the one I already have cited, which, now in context, appears in an even more ambiguous hue:

> Then the sands will roll
> Out a carpet of gold
> For your weary toes to be a-touchin'
> And the ship's wise men
> Will remind you once again
> That the whole wide world is watchin'

As much as these lines speak to the responsibility of a people, in the condition of its post-liberation, to make good on its promises and be a beacon for the rest of the world, they also suggest that any particular constitutionalization of liberty into a governmental and socioeconomic structure will be something less equal than the ephemeral experience of liberation itself. Both the image of a "carpet of gold" and the figure of "wise men" imply the return of socioeconomic inequality (goods to compete over on the basis of a "merit" that may always have at least a somewhat dubious quality about it). This is the only verse where the pronoun *you* is used, with the hypothetical listener directly addressed, and it is significant that this "you" is not allowed to stand for everyone but is immediately distinguished from the "wise men" doing the reminding (and no doubt leading, ruling, etc.).

The one place where the collective *we* is used is the song's conclusion, which emphasizes not the new society that we will have built (for in fact this society will divide us from ourselves) but the old society that we collectively have come to oppose:

> Oh the foes will rise
> With the sleep still in their eyes
> And they'll jerk from their beds and think they're dreamin'
> But they'll pinch themselves and squeal
> And know that it's for real
> The hour when the ship comes in
>
> Then they'll raise their hands
> Sayin' we'll meet all your demands
> But we'll shout from the bow your days are numbered
> And like Pharaoh's tribe
> They'll be drownded in the tide
> And like Goliath, they'll be conquered

Whereas Winthrop draws on the biblical legacy to incite his listeners to follow a prophet of justice—Micah—and become a fully good people, Dylan's biblical references are to figures that achieve a monumental liberation but then go on to a life of ambiguity and transgression, whether the Israelites' continual forgetting of God and regression to idolatry in the years after their escape from bondage in Egypt or David's seduction of Bathsheba and killing of her husband Uriah in the period after his victory over Goliath.

That the triumph will be short-lasting is emphasized by the fact that the song does not celebrate the ship coming in *tout court*, but the *hour* that the ship comes in. This temporal constraint, which occurs in each of the four instances in which the song's title is sung, indicates a victory limited to the overcoming of enemies and to the promise of newness itself (when "the morning will be breaking"). Nowhere is this constraint more starkly and ominously presented than in the song's first verse:

> Oh the time will come up
> When the winds will stop
> And the breeze will cease to be breathin'
> Like the stillness in the wind'
> 'Fore the hurricane begins
> The hour when the ship comes in

If Winthrop's prophecy concerns how to avoid once and for all the shipwreck of political disorder and injustice, the victory Dylan foretells comes both after an oppressive past that has been escaped and before a future—when "the hurricane begins"—in which, presumably, other disorders will reappear (perhaps of the kind Winthrop himself identifies but does not problematize: "the condition of mankind [according to which] in all times some must be rich, some poor, some high and eminent in power and dignity; others mean and in submission"). The point is not to see the earlier injustice as fully equivalent with the later ones, but to recognize that progress from worse to better still leaves a lack—powerful elements of unfairness and suffering that limit the progressive achievement being accomplished and thus make any excessive triumphalization of it repugnant to an honest, genuinely self-conscious bourgeois perspective.

The Possibilities and Limits of Bourgeois Political Action

The other song Dylan performed at the March on Washington, "Only a Pawn in Their Game," was perhaps most topical for the occasion, since it was about the recent assassination of Medgar Evers, a civil rights activist and field secretary for the NAACP in Mississippi. On June 12, 1963, the morning after President Kennedy had made a television address in which he described civil rights as "a moral issue" and pledged support for new civil rights legislation (what would become the Civil Rights Act of 1964), Evers was gunned down by Byron De La Beckwith Jr., a member of the white supremacist White Citizens' Council and the Ku Klux Klan.

The surprising refrain of the song, which repeats four times, is that Beckwith "can't be blamed"—or similarly that "it ain't him to blame"—because he is only "a pawn in their game": a patsy manipulated by richer and more powerful beneficiaries of a broader social system that is economically and racially unjust. Crucial to Dylan's approach is that Beckwith is never named in the song. In redirecting moral outrage away from the killer himself and toward the institutional sources of racial hate, Dylan hardly absolves Beckwith but rather condemns him in a different way: as someone who, in spite of the seeming significance of his deed, does not even deserve to be remembered as an actor because his motivations are so clearly manufactured by larger power interests that are at odds with his own well-being. The crushing last verse concludes with Dylan prophesizing the anonymity Beckwith will suffer for being a mere tool of corrupt power:

> Today, Medgar Evers was buried from the bullet he caught
> They lowered him down as a king
> But when the shadowy sun sets on the one
> That fired the gun
> He'll see by his grave
> On the stone that remains
> Carved next to his name
> His epitaph plain:
> Only a pawn in their game

Dylan thus only further condemns Beckwith in claiming not to blame him. At the same time, the dominant message of "Only a Pawn in Their Game" is the extension of blame to forces and individuals whose complicity in the killing of Evers would be concealed by a wrongly microscopic focus on the single person shooting the gun. Dylan singles out Southern politicians:

> A South politician preaches to the poor white man
> "You got more than the blacks, don't complain
> You're better than them, you been born with white skin,"
>   they explain
> And the Negro's name
> Is used it is plain

> For the politician's gain
> As he rises to fame
> And the poor white remains
> On the caboose of the train
> But it ain't him to blame
> He's only a pawn in their game

A racist culture does serve some economic interests beyond those at the top, but the poor and impoverished—whose interests are not being served—are tricked and manipulated, through indoctrination into racial hatred, so that they cannot perceive the fact of their economic exploitation:

> The deputy sheriffs, the soldiers, the governors get paid
> And the marshals and cops get the same
> But the poor white man's used in the hands of them all like a tool
> He's taught in his school
> From the start by the rule
> That the laws are with him
> To protect his white skin
> To keep up his hate
> So he never thinks straight
> 'Bout the shape that he's in
> But it ain't him to blame
> He's only a pawn in their game

There are varying degrees of economic inequality in any society, of course. What makes "the poor white man" so susceptible to perpetuating a system of racial hatred at odds with an actual furthering of his economic and political interests is that he is not merely poor, but often impoverished: destitute and disadvantaged to such a degree that it damages his humanity and, in particular, his ability to think for himself. As Dylan sings:

> From the poverty shacks, he looks from the cracks to the tracks
> And the hoofbeats pound in his brain
> And he's taught how to walk in a pack
> Shoot in the back
> With his fist in a clinch
> To hang and to lynch
> To hide 'neath the hood

To kill with no pain
Like a dog on a chain
He ain't got no name
But it ain't him to blame
He's only a pawn in their game

As a descriptive matter, such reflections on the interpenetration of economic class and racism are, of course, familiar to historians who have long understood how racism strengthened interclass solidarity among American whites and, more recently, to contemporary scholars of intersectionality attuned to how systems of domination often make use of multiple categories (including race and class) to produce social hierarchies.[226]

But "Only a Pawn in Their Game" is not merely a description. It carries within it the unmistakable pathos of the desire for social change. After all, Dylan sang this song at the March on Washington for Jobs and Freedom, which he presumably supported—and he had sung it eight weeks earlier, on July 6, when he performed it at a civil rights gathering in Greenwood, Mississippi, just three weeks after Evers's assassination (and one hundred miles from Jackson, Mississippi, where Evers was killed).

On the one hand, the political message of the song seems clear. If racial hate is founded on economic injustice—poverty and the severe maldistribution of resources—then these economic problems must be solved if a society can hope to overcome bigotry in its social institutions. Such a message, however, was hardly particular to Dylan. King's speech at the March, even if it largely looks past the economic element of racial liberation, once refers to "the Negro [who] lives on a lonely island of poverty in the midst of a vast ocean of material prosperity"[227]; and, of course, poverty would become a primary focus for King in the last years of his life. Even more, other leaders of the March, and civil rights activists more generally, insisted that civil rights could not be achieved without economic justice.[228] At the conclusion of the March on Washington, Bayard Rustin, its deputy director, read aloud eight demands that had emerged from the March's proceedings and that he—along with nine other leaders—would deliver to President Kennedy. Rustin referred to them as "the demands of this revolution." Two of these demands pointed to economic justice and the dignity this would bring to the poor:

---

[226] See, for example, Ange-Marie Hancock, *Intersectionality: An Intellectual History* (New York: Oxford, 2016).

[227] King, "I Have a Dream," 217.

[228] See, for example, William P. Jones, "The Forgotten Radical History of the March on Washington," *Dissent* 60, no. 2 (2013): 74–79.

#6: We demand that every person in this nation, black or white, be given training and work with dignity to defeat unemployment and automation.

#7: We demand that there be an increase in the national minimum wage so that men may live in dignity.[229]

Slightly different versions of the March's demands only served to emphasize how much Rustin's sixth demand required. According to an alternate list of ten demands, the seventh, repeating the key criterion of dignity, called for "a massive federal program to train and place all unemployed workers—Negro and white—on meaningful and dignified jobs at decent wages."[230]

If implicitly supporting the kind of economic justice demanded by the protestors, Dylan's song makes its distinct—and distinctly bourgeois—contribution in challenging both the possibility of full-fledged economic justice and the robustness of his listeners' commitment to fight for it. Even as it attends to how racial hate feeds off of economic injustice, it describes economic injustice in terms that are not as readily solvable as Rustin and other like-minded protestors suggest. If poverty is not just material but relative, how can it be fully addressed? Whereas Rustin imagines a threshold level of material well-being past which all "men may live in dignity," Dylan's metaphor of the "poor white [who] remains on the caboose of the train" envisions social hierarchy—and the indignity and indignation generated by it—as inescapable.[231] Further, as the marchers realized, the economic policies they demanded were "massive"—amounting to nothing less than the ambition "to defeat unemployment." Has any society achieved such a goal? Even states with ample provisions for the unemployed can hardly be said to have placed all of their citizens in "meaningful and dignified jobs." If racial hate stems in part from an economic injustice that has never yet been—and might not ever be—satisfactorily addressed, then actual social change likely will be more modest and imperfect than what many at the March contemplated.

Of course, the problem is not just the world but the people in it. Not everyone—certainly not all progressives—wants to do the things that would need to happen in order to bring about even the non-revolutionary but still massive changes to the economic system, such that there would be greater economic equality, no destitution, and thus only relative (but not absolute) poverty. I have

---

[229] Quoted in Frederick Douglass Opie, *Southern Food and Civil Rights: Feeding the Revolution* (Mount Pleasant, SC: American Palate, 2017), 120.

[230] James W. Ivy, ed., "March on Washington," *The Crisis* 70, no. 8 (1963): 460.

[231] On the inevitable inability of any liberal democracy to fully respect the dignity of its citizens, and the indignation this generates, see Green, *The Shadow of Unfairness*, 1–7, 61–66.

labeled this incomplete, haphazard, partially complicit dedication to fighting injustice as a bourgeois, rather than militant, form of progressivism. If the customary rhetoric of the March served to elide the figure of the bourgeois—either by directing itself to militants or, what is almost the same thing, by allowing bourgeois protestors to imagine themselves as fully allied with militants—"Only a Pawn in Their Game" celebrates the militancy of Evers in such a fashion, as a "king" making the ultimate sacrifice of his life, that excludes any easy (and false) identification from the bourgeois listener. The separation of the bourgeois from the militant is encouraged by Dylan's metaphor of a *pawn in a game*, with its reference to the hierarchical differentiation of pieces in a game of chess—and Beckwith's self-understanding as a *knight* within the KKK only accentuates the chess metaphor. Consider the differentiated roles:

> *Pawns*: People like Beckwith who, in Dylan's view, are exploited by an unjust society yet themselves commit gross injustices to perpetuate the functioning of that society.
>
> *Knights*: Keeping with the terms employed by white supremacist organizations like the Ku Klux Klan, of which Beckwith was a member, Beckwith might have presented himself as a "knight."[232] Yet the force of Dylan's song is to tell Beckwith, you think you're a knight, but you're only a pawn.
>
> *Kings*: People like Medgar Evers who sacrifice themselves for justice. Describing Evers's burial, Dylan sings, "They lowered him down as a king." In so labeling Evers, Dylan emphasizes the extraordinary quality of militancy and, thus, its difference from more common forms of progressivism. That the king in chess is both the most important and yet most vulnerable piece is also in keeping with Evers's sacrificial heroism.
>
> *Them*: That is, the "they" whose game it is: those who callously perpetuate an unjust society.

The chess metaphor is useful because it suggests how Dylan's celebration of Evers's kingly militancy differentiates Evers not just from racist pawn-like figures such as Beckwith, but also from bourgeois progressives who do not rise to Evers's level. Consider two additional chess figures, implied by the metaphor even if formally absent from the song, that represent the bourgeois progressive:

> *Castles*: This is a fitting piece for the bourgeois, since the root meaning of bourgeois comes from the word *burg*, meaning fortress, tower, or castle. The castle is a piece of substantial but still secondary might. In the present

---

[232] The 2012 documentary about Beckwith and his son is called *The Last White Knight*.

context, it symbolizes a space of protection and well-being within a surrounding sea of suffering and injustice. As a model of progressive action, it
stands for bringing as many people caught in this sea onto islands of security (i.e., prosperity, non-oppression).

Pawns in our game: Beckwith is a pawn in their game, but this very characterization opens up the possibility of a different kind of pawn: someone who
works or contributes only modestly to combat injustice. This modesty can
take the form of being merely a foot soldier within a social justice organization, lacking leadership, but, considering the meaning of bourgeois progressivism, it also designates not doing all one could to fulfill one's own
sense of moral obligation within an unjust society.

Dylan thus describes the main players of the battle for social justice in America
in terms that differentiate the bourgeois from the militant. Most significantly, the
bourgeois is not a king, because, as bourgeois, he will not go all the way, will not
make the ultimate sacrifice, either in the sense of literally sacrificing his life for justice or, more figuratively, in the sense of sacrificing the time, energy, and resources,
in the manner of a militant, required to instill in him the sense that he is sufficiently
contributing to the fight against the racial and economic injustice in his midst.

The bourgeois self-consciousness of "Only a Pawn in Their Game" is rendered
all the more vivid when the song is compared to a seemingly similar piece Dylan
wrote the year before, in 1962, "The Death of Emmett Till," about the murder
of the fourteen-year-old African American teenager from Chicago who was
lynched in Mississippi in 1955 after allegedly flirting with a white woman there.
Dylan quickly dismissed this latter song as "bullshit."[233] The last two stanzas are
likely what Dylan found problematic—and in any case represent a perspective
of bourgeois progressivism that has fallen into self-congratulatory illusion and
self-deception:

> If you can't speak out against this kind of thing, a crime that's so unjust,
> Your eyes are filled with dead men's dirt, your mind is filled with dust
> Your arms and legs they must be in shackles and chains, and your blood
>   it must refuse to flow
> For you let this human race fall down so God-awful low!
>
> This song is just a reminder to remind your fellow man
> That this kind of thing still lives today in that ghost-robed Ku Klux Klan
> But if all of us folks that thinks alike, if we gave all we could give
> We could make this great land of ours a greater place to live

---

[233] Quoted in Marqusee, *Wicked Messenger*, 52.

Despite concerning the same topic of racial injustice as "Only a Pawn in Their Game," this song expresses an entirely different mindset, much more in keeping with the prevailing mentality of participants at the March on Washington in its failure to differentiate the bourgeois and militant forms of progressivism. Yes, what happened to Till is an awful crime. It need not happen. But Dylan locates himself here in an unambiguous place of righteous indignation. Most of all, he holds out the solution: "But if all of us folks that thinks alike, if we gave all we could give / We could make this great land of ours a greater place to live." However, giving all that one can is precisely what the bourgeois progressive does not do. Situated in comparison to "The Death of Emmett Till," the freshness of Dylan's angle of analysis in "Only a Pawn in Their Game" becomes all the more apparent. In addition to deftly criticizing Beckwith without mentioning him and indicting the broader unjust socioeconomic system Beckwith unwittingly serves, the song is no less shrewd in employing metaphors that locate bourgeois listeners as individuals who will not be dependably engaged in the pursuit of justice.

Historians report that when Dylan sang "Only a Pawn in Their Game" at the March, it was greeted with a "tepid response" and "scattered applause."[234] The usual interpretation of this reaction is that the audience did not fully understand the song: that Dylan's refrain that Beckwith "can't be blamed" confused them, as his broader critique of the society that produced Beckwith was too complex to digest on first listen. What such an interpretation leaves out is that those who did understand the song might themselves have been led to a muted response, not because they did not appreciate its message, but because this message—with its somber eulogy for Evers, its condemnation of the political economy of racism in America, and, as I am emphasizing here, its implicit differentiation between militants like Evers and bourgeois individuals who ultimately prefer themselves to others and are not fully engaged in the contestation of the "game" of injustice—could not but dampen their exultance.

As a coda to my analysis of Dylan's participation at the March, I turn to the most mysterious line in "Only a Pawn in Their Game," the second line of the opening verse:

> A bullet from the back of a bush took Medgar Evers' blood
> *A finger fired the trigger to his name*
> A handle hid out in the dark
> A hand set the spark
> Two eyes took the aim

---

[234] William P. Jones, *The March on Washington* (New York: Norton, 2014), 192.

> Behind a man's brain
> But he can't be blamed
> He's only a pawn in their game

The phrasing is strange, as normally one would say that the trigger fires a gun, not that a trigger is itself fired. Further, what would seem to be the meaning here—that Beckwith shot and killed Evers's name—makes no sense at all. In a song about who gets to have names, it does not follow that Evers—the person who (unlike Beckwith) is being named, remembered, and celebrated as a "king"—would have his own name destroyed. Thus, I disagree with what may be the usual interpretation of these lines.[235] Although the phrasing is syntactically awkward, a more fitting interpretation would be that Beckwith's finger (his killing of Evers) made Evers's name into a trigger (a militant martyr who would inspire hundreds of others to take action against racial injustice). That is, Beckwith's folly is not simply that he unwittingly served an oppressive social system of which he himself was a victim, but that he did not even succeed in this regard: his evil act had the unintended consequence of making Evers like a king and generating support to bring down Jim Crow.

But the bourgeois, too, is without a name, an ordinary—if prosperous and comfortable—member of society. Sometimes the bourgeois are "fired up" by the trigger of Evers, King, and other heroes of militancy who have sacrificed themselves for social justice, but other times they are uninspired and do not act. Frederick Douglass understood well that, to achieve justice in a bourgeois society, "it is not light that is needed, but fire."[236] But if the bourgeois were always aflame, they would no longer be bourgeois. The intermittent flicker is all that the bourgeois progressive can muster.

At the March on Washington, Martin Luther King was hailed as the "moral leader of our nation." But for those who are more bourgeois than revolutionary, more haphazard in their activism than steadfast, perhaps Dylan is no less deserving of the title. The reason to take seriously the bourgeois form of progressivism is not that it is better than the militant variant (for it is typically worse), but that most of the time it is the much more common approach to combating injustice, yet one that remains hidden by various tendencies—triumphal hopefulness, a conflation of liberation from oppression with the full-fledged achievement of free and equal citizenship, and a too-easy identification with the militant—that threaten an inappropriate complacency toward oneself and toward the nature of

---

[235] Daniel Karlin, for example, interprets the lines as: "[Evers's] killing is represented as an attack on his name." Karlin, "Bob Dylan's Names," in Corcoran, "Do You, Mr. Jones?", 34.

[236] Frederick Douglass, "The Meaning of July Fourth for the Negro," in *Selected Writings and Speeches*, ed. Philip S. Foner (Chicago: Lawrence Hill, 1999), 196.

a liberal-democratic society. Dylan combats the various forms of self-deception whereby the bourgeois might escape, in the very moments of political activism, an honest self-assessment.

Some criticized Dylan's participation at the March for drawing attention away from the real activists and leaders of the civil rights movement. The comedian Dick Gregory, who had endured arrests and beatings as a result of his activism in the South, objected, "What was a white boy like Bob Dylan there for? . . . To support the cause? Wonderful—support the cause. March. Stand behind us—but not in front of us."[237] While it is true that Dylan did take the stage, his message to privileged bourgeois onlookers ultimately was not that different from Gregory's.

I.7. Dylan's Bourgeois Appropriation of the Radical Folk Tradition

As a prophet of the bourgeoisie, Dylan is honest about how his self-preference overrides his social conscience. I have emphasized that this dynamic applies not only to Dylan's withdrawal from social justice activism. It also relates to the bourgeois nature of his activism itself. That is, Dylan's honesty extends beyond admitting that he is turning his back on social justice in the name of self-reliant individuality; it also includes, as his role at the March suggests, self-awareness about the limits of his social commitments in the very moments of his activism. To be sure, Dylan's performance at the March only intimates these limits, as his songs there serve more to recognize the position of the bourgeois progressive than to occupy it personally. It is thus important to consider how, even in the midst of Dylan's closest association with leftist politics prior to and immediately following the March, there were always signs that his engagement was different from—that is, more bourgeois than—more militant and radical forms of devotion to social justice.

Dylan came on the scene in the early 1960s as a folk singer, an inheritor of folk's long tradition of songs, sounds, and sensibilities, but in a brief time he developed that tradition not just in the *musical* way that so often has been addressed by commentators (blending folk with rock and roll) but also in a *political* way, providing, as it were, a bourgeois rejoinder to a folk movement intimately associated with the radical Left.

The folk tradition of 1930s, 1940s, and 1950s was closely tied to political radicalism: the ambition to transcend the status quo of liberal-democratic politics and produce a more egalitarian and communitarian society. Alan Lomax,

---

[237] Quoted in Marqusee, *Wicked Messenger*, 14–15.

the ethnomusicologist who assembled a series of highly influential recordings of early twentieth-century folk music and became instrumental to the mid-century American and British folk revivals, served as musical director for Henry Wallace's 1948 third-party presidential bid—a campaign that was actively supported by the Communist Party USA (CPUSA), whose endorsement Wallace refused to disavow.[238] Woody Guthrie, perhaps the most visible folk musician of this period, referred to himself as a "full blooded Marxican" and spoke out repeatedly against the rich. He upheld Jesus as a "socialist outlaw" and claimed that those who killed Jesus were "the bankers and the preachers, [who] nailed him to the cross." His 1940 *Dust Bowl Ballads* sang of the desperation and dislocation of individuals uprooted by capitalism. Guthrie was thus hailed on the Left as a folk poet. One of the most influential folk bands from this period, the Almanac Singers, which was founded by (along with Guthrie) Millard Lampell, Lee Hays, and Pete Seeger, was a Popular Front music group, many of whose members were either CPUSA members or sympathizers. During 1940–1943, the Almanac Singers wrote and sang songs in support of anti-war, anti-racist, pro-labor, and pro-union ideologies. Following World War II, another highly prominent folk organization, People's Songs, founded in 1945 by Lomax, Seeger, and Hays, among others, set out to "create, promote and distribute songs of labor and the American people," publishing its quarterly *Bulletin*, which, in its combination of folk music and radical leftist politics, would become the template for later folk magazines such as *Sing Out!* and *Broadside*.[239] The point is not simply that mid-century folk singers were closely connected to the socialist politics of the radical Left, but that they were persecuted for this connection during the Red Scare that followed World War II. Members of People's Songs, for example, were excluded from performing and distributing materials at Congress of Industrial Organizations (CIO) unions, and the group was forced to disband due in part to the financial struggles it faced in the wake of anti-communist persecution.[240] Lomax in effect lived in exile in Europe during this period. Likewise, the Weavers—an influential folk quartet formed in 1948 featuring Ronnie Gilbert, Hays, Fred Hellerman, and Seeger—was blacklisted and essentially forced to break up in the early 1950s. The FBI identified Seeger and Hays as communists, and they were compelled to appear before the House Un-American Activities Committee (HUAC) in 1955, with Hays pleading the Fifth and Seeger also refusing to testify but on First Amendment (free speech) grounds. As a result, Seeger was found guilty of contempt of Congress in 1957

[238] See Marqusee, 30.

[239] People's Songs Inc., *Bulletin of People's Songs*, 1.1 (February 1945): 1, https://singout.org/ps-archive/.

[240] Marqusee, *Wicked Messenger*, 30.

and placed under travel and other restrictions until his conviction ultimately was overturned in 1961. Not all folk musicians resisted the witch hunt, with many succumbing, providing confessions and naming names—which was but another form of persecution.[241] Folk music was thus centrally involved with mid-century anti-communist red-baiting. As Marqusee aptly puts it, "Folk music became politically tainted, a rich hunting ground for the inquisitors."[242]

Dylan is the knowing inheritor of this tradition. Yet, as much as he may have revered the musical talent, political courage, and ethical integrity of so many of the earlier generation of folk musicians, he also enacted his own bourgeois departure from that tradition. I have emphasized Dylan's role at the March on Washington as evidence of this. But beyond the March, even as Dylan engaged in many of the same political causes and politically charged musical events as the earlier generation of folk singers, he repeatedly provided signs that he was different. Perhaps the most succinct encapsulation of this difference relates to his 1962 "Song to Woody," in which Dylan's encomium to Guthrie includes self-awareness of the discontinuities between himself and the folk icon who had so inspired him:

> I'm a-leavin' tomorrow, but I could leave today
> Somewhere down the road someday
> The very last thing that I'd want to do
> Is to say I've been hittin' some hard travelin' too

In more subtle ways, as well, Dylan also marked his divergence from the folk tradition and its radical, leftist bent. The Almanac Singers had chosen their name, as co-founder Lee Hays explained, from their claim to be providing their listeners a kind of direction: "If you want to know what the weather is going to be, you have to look in your almanac." Dylan, however, seems to directly reject this idea and the ideology to which it is implicitly connected, when, in his 1965 "Subterranean Homesick Blues," he sings one of his most memorable lines:

> You don't need a weatherman
> To know which way the wind blows

---

[241] Josh White and Burl Ives, for instance, provided such testimony, with White going so far as to publish his as an essay entitled "I Was a Sucker for the Communists."

[242] Marqusee, *Wicked Messenger*, 31.

It is thus bizarre and almost inexplicable that the radical leftist group the Weathermen (later the Weather Underground) took its name from Dylan's song, distributing at a June 1969 SDS convention in Chicago a position paper entitled "You Don't Need a Weatherman to Know Which Way the Wind Blows" and splitting off from SDS later that year.[243]

Dylan juxtaposed his message to the earlier folk tradition represented by the Almanac Singers in other ways as well. One of the biggest hits of the Almanac Singers was "Which Side Are You On?," recorded in 1941 (though written in 1931 by activist Florence Reece). The song was a call for class-based political consciousness. One of the verses of Dylan's 1965 "Desolation Row," however, appears to push back against the Almanac Singers:

> Praise be to Nero's Neptune
> The Titanic sails at dawn
> And everybody's shouting
> "Which Side Are You On?"

Another key example of Dylan's sympathy with, but also bourgeois divergence from, the radical Left concerns his "Talkin' John Birch Society Paranoid Blues," a song ridiculing the anti-communist John Birch Society as fascistic lunatics. Dylan's lyrics for the song initially appeared in the first issue of *Broadside*, a topical song magazine launched by Seeger, Sis Cunningham, and other folk singers deeply connected to leftist politics. The song became part of a highly visible public controversy in May 1963 when Dylan walked out of rehearsals for *The Ed Sullivan Show*, where he was planning to perform the piece as part of his first national television appearance, after CBS network executives—worried that "Talkin' John Birch Society Paranoid Blues" might be too inflammatory, especially in associating the John Birch Society with the Nazis and thus risking legal liability for the network—asked him to play a different song.[244] Dylan refused to change his set and cancelled his performance, reportedly saying, "No, this is

---

[243] See Dan Berger, *Outlaws of America: The Weather Underground and the Politics of Solidarity* (Oakland, CA: AK Press, 2005), 95. For the position paper, see https://web.archive.org/web/200 60328145901/http://martinrealm.org/documents/radical/sixties1.html.

[244] In the song, Dylan mocks the John Birch Society as saying:

> Now we all agree with Hitler's views
> Although he killed six million Jews
> It don't matter too much that he was a Fascist
> At least you can't say he was a Communist!
> That's to say like if you got a cold you take a shot of malaria

what I want to do. If I can't play my song, I'd rather not appear on the show."[245] This episode initially added to Dylan's reputation as a hero of the Left, and it apparently was instrumental to his being given the Tom Paine Award by the ECLC later that year. But there are nonetheless elements of Dylan's behavior that point to a distinctly bourgeois rather than radical leftist position—that is, to a form of engagement in which the commitment to social justice is matched, and in a sense overridden, by a commitment to one's own personal success and well-being. It is not just that Dylan's precise stance in the song—being anti-anti-communist—is not the same thing as being in favor of socialism or other radical alternatives. More specifically, even if Dylan refused to replace the song at *The Ed Sullivan Show*, he did bow to legal pressure from CBS (which also owned the Columbia record label under which he recorded his music) not to include it on his 1963 album, *The Freewheelin' Bob Dylan*.[246] In typical bourgeois fashion, then, Dylan did not go all the way, but at some point compromised, choosing his own material self-interest over and against what was likely his own sense of what was morally right.

Dylan also enacted a bourgeois modulation of the Left in his aforementioned acceptance speech at the ECLC annual dinner on December 13, 1963, at which he received the organization's Tom Paine Award. The ECLC initially had been formed in 1951 to defend the civil liberties of citizens and immigrants threatened by anti-communist laws like the McCarran Act. It would go on to devote itself over the next many decades to the civil rights movement and other progressive causes. The Tom Paine Award was given each year to an individual who embodied and furthered the ECLC's values. I already have examined Dylan's caustic, provocative behavior at this event, but the point here is that in castigating committed leftists, civil libertarians, and social justice activists, Dylan took issue with what he found to be their inappropriate high regard for their own moral standing. Against this, Dylan presented himself as someone who is not fully good—who, in his own being, replicates the violence and injustice of the world around him—thus announcing and performing an ethically ambiguous bourgeois subjectivity that refuses to congratulate itself in awards or imagine itself as being unquestionably committed to social justice.[247]

What all of these vignettes share is that they present Dylan as an uneasy leftist, breaking with the traditional socialist leaning of the Left, its optimism in

---

[245] Michael A. Schuman, *Bob Dylan: Singer, Songwriter, and Musical Icon* (New York: Enslow Publishing, 2019), 45.

[246] See Scaduto, *Bob Dylan: An Intimate Biography*, 139–41.

[247] Recall Dylan's confession and key conclusion from his "apology" letter to the ECLC: "if there's violence in the times then / there must be violence in me." Quoted in Lamont, "Message from Bob Dylan."

the future, and its understanding of being unequivocally on the side of morality. Dylan's bourgeois reworking of the folk tradition leads him to abandon, and at times critique, the militancy, radicalism, and pure conscience with which that tradition has been associated.

Perhaps the most obvious way Dylan departed from the radical leftist bent of the folk tradition he inherited was the tremendous wealth he quickly came to enjoy. Already a millionaire by his early twenties, Dylan simply did not occupy the same socioeconomic position of a typical folk singer, let alone of the destitute so often addressed in folk music. Dylan's great wealth, which has steadily increased throughout his life, and the business acumen from which it partially stems not only make him bourgeois in the most basic sense of the term, but often have been invoked by critics questioning Dylan's prophetic status as well. The aforementioned A. J. Weberman, the eccentric who founded the Dylan Liberation Front that unsuccessfully aimed to return Dylan to his early 1960s social justice activism, told Dylan in 1971: "But you're just a capitalist."[248] Syd Barrett of Pink Floyd wrote a song in 1965, "The Ballad of Bob Dylan," that took aim at Dylan's early 1960s folk image, having the figure of Dylan exclaim: "Roam from town to town / Guess I get people down / But I don't care too much about that / 'Cause my gut and my wallet are fat."[249] Even Dylan's father, in 1963 no less, seemed intent on exposing the commercialism that lay behind Dylan's public profile as a poetic vagabond with prophetic gifts: "My son is a corporation and his public image is strictly an act."[250]

Dylan's capitalism and commercialism are important reminders of his bourgeois status and of his divergence from the practice of biblical prophets who spoke for free in the streets. But his moneymaking ought not be invoked to deny his prophetic quality altogether. If the argument of Part I has been correct, Dylan's capitalist features are not antithetical to his prophetic message, but part of it. Dylan channels the prophetic consciousness to testify to the diremption besetting the human ethical situation—at least in its bourgeois form—presenting himself as someone who chooses his individuality at the expense of what his

---

[248] "Dylan/Alan J. Weberman Phone Conversation: Jan '71," transcript, https://www.interfere nza.net/bcs/interw/weberman.htm; "AJ Weberman Tapes," posted by Jack Frost, audio, 49:31, July 13, 2017, https://www.youtube.com/watch?v=DBbw7Fo8UUQ.

[249] The song makes explicit reference to Dylan's alleged prophetic quality: "Well I sing about dreams / And I rhymes it with 'seems' / 'Cause it seems that my dream always means / That I can prophesy all kinds of things." And in undermining that quality, it emphasizes Dylan's commercialism with another set of lines as well: "Make a whole lotta dough / But I deserve it though / I've got soul and a good heart of gold / So I'll sing about war in the cold."

[250] Dylan's father, Abe Zimmerman, was quoted in a 1963 article in the *Duluth News Tribune*. See Michael Olson, "Bob Dylan's Roots Revisited," *MPR News* Statewide Blog, May 24, 2011, https://www.mprnews.org/story/2011/05/24/bob-dylans-roots-revisited.

own conscience tells him is owed to others. This stance is uncomfortable, and it breaks from the usual moral exemplarity surrounding prophetic figures, but it is honest about the self-preference definitive of bourgeois life in a capitalist society and instructive about how this life, so often mired in mendacity, might be led with greater self-awareness and decency.

Part II

Never Could Learn to Drink that Blood and Call It Wine

It is with regard to religiosity itself—specifically Dylan's so-called gospel period of 1979–1981—that Dylan's status as a prophet is both most straightforward and yet paradoxically hardest for many to believe. It is straightforward because, following a conversion experience in which he found Jesus in late 1978 or early 1979, Dylan shed his usual denial of his prophetic role and seemed to embrace it at last. He spent three years writing and performing religious music testifying to his newfound Christian life, and for some of this time (1979–1980) performed *exclusively* Christian music. He shockingly interspersed musical performances at his concerts with caustic gospel speeches, stunning and disconcerting large portions of those in attendance. And he made explicit statements in which he acknowledged both the history of his being perceived as a prophet and his sudden willingness to now accept something like that role. Recall what Dylan said to an audience in 1980:

> Years ago they . . . said I was a prophet. I used to say, "No I'm not a prophet." They say, "Yes you are, you're a prophet." I said, "No it's not me." They used to say, "You sure are a prophet." They used to convince me I was a prophet. Now I come out and say Jesus Christ is the answer. They say, "Bob Dylan's no prophet." They just can't handle it.[1]

---

[1] Bob Dylan, performance on January 25, 1980, in Omaha, Nebraska. Quoted in Andrea Cossu, *It Ain't Me Babe: Bob Dylan and the Performance of Authenticity* (London: Routledge, 2016), 108–9. Dylan similarly said at a concert in 1979: "I told you 'The Times They Are A-Changing.' And they did! I said the answer was 'Blowin' in the Wind,' and it was! And I'm saying to you now, Jesus is coming back, and he is! There is no other way to salvation" (108).

Bob Dylan. Jeffrey Edward Green, Oxford University Press. © Oxford University Press 2024.
DOI: 10.1093/oso/9780197651742.003.0003

And yet, as he himself suggests in this statement, from a certain perspective Dylan's most explicitly religious period could be seen as one in which his prophetic function was in abeyance rather than at its height. As a profession of Christian theology, Dylan's message is hardly distinct or original: he was just one of many voices supporting Jesus within a still largely Christian culture. Commercially, culturally, and critically, Dylan's music enjoyed less success in this period compared to many of his earlier albums and some of his later ones too. And perhaps most of all, while countless people have been moved by the music and lyrics of Dylan's Christian albums and some even converted, it seems clear that Dylan disturbed secular listeners more often than he inspired religious devotion to Christ. Compared to his 1960s prophetic legacy—in which unmatched poetic intensity (for a popular singer, at least) was joined to the ethical calls for social justice, individual self-reliance, and appreciation for the tragic conflict between the two—Dylan's Christian message could be seen as derivative and flat. If the purpose of Dylan's religious prophecy was to teach adherence to Jesus, it would seem that Dylan had a far more meager impact on the culture than in the 1960s, when, according to many, his music was instrumental to propelling a spirit of social activism throughout large segments of America and the world.[2] This is perhaps unsurprising: in 1979, Dylan was a countercultural icon who had come to fame over the past two decades challenging received pieties and propaganda of all forms. His subsequent embrace of Christianity seemed, to many, deeply incongruous with what they thought he stood for. While Dylan's other topics of prophetic communication—whether the fraught relationship between justice and selfhood discussed in Part I or Dylan's profound pessimism about the world, which Part III will examine—appear far more credible to the secular, skeptical, would-be hip who disproportionately make up Dylan's audience, Christianity was something that fewer were able to genuinely believe and take as authoritative from the mouth of Dylan.

But I will argue that we misjudge the meaning of Dylan's gospel period if we evaluate it only in terms of the propagation of the doctrines and practices of Christianity. We misjudge it, too, if we make the metric of prophetic success the conversion of the non-religious to religiosity. Rather than see the shock and disconcertion Dylan received from secular audiences as counter to his prophetic achievement, I propose that the secular audience is the core audience of Dylan's gospel period—or, more precisely, the constituency in relation to which

---

[2] As but one example, consider how Corliss Lamont, chairman of the Emergency Civil Liberties Committee (ECLC), put it in 1963, "Whether we approve or not, Bob Dylan has become the idol of the progressive youngsters of today, regardless of their political factions." Lamont, "Letter to Attendees of the [1963 ECLC] Dinner," December 19, 1963, https://www.corliss-lamont.org/dylan.htm.

his message finds its characteristic novelty and edge. The fact that Dylan's audience has always been not at all specifically Christian makes his Christian conversion and gospel period significant not for bringing listeners to Christ but for exemplifying for secular—and especially secular*ist* audiences—how religious faith is possible, how it can respect and reflect intellectual integrity, and thus how the non-religious themselves possess the *potential* to pursue religiosity at any time (independent of the question of whether or not they should).

Scholarly interest in Dylan's gospel period thus far has centered on traditional theological questions (e.g., the content of Dylan's beliefs, the relevant Judeo-Christian traditions that best characterize these beliefs, and the evolving nature of Dylan's use of biblical sources to express his newfound faith) and biographical questions (above all, the question of how Dylan came to make profession of his faith in Jesus/God definitive of his three albums, performances, and public statements during 1979–1981).[3] This literature provides a useful and illuminating resource for Dylan scholarship, but it risks ignoring what may be the most singular aspect of Dylan's conversion and its most meaningful implication within popular culture: namely, that Dylan demonstrates for *non-religious people* the integrity, dignity, and plausibility of religiosity. If the function of traditional religious prophecy is to inspire audiences to religion, Dylan's role as a religious prophet should be appreciated for what I call its *postsecular* aspect—that is, its challenge to secularists to overcome not their atheism per se but their sense that such atheism is natural, rational, or otherwise superior to religiosity.

There are numerous reasons why Dylan's public testimonies to his religiosity have this postsecular character. For one, he has tremendous credibility within *secular* society. As a countercultural hero of the 1960s, Dylan, prior to his conversion, seemed to embody a self-reliant skepticism toward all external sources of authority, including religious ones.[4] In his own terms, prior to his conversion

---

[3] For the former, see, for example, Stephen Webb, *Dylan Redeemed: From Highway 61 to Saved* (New York: Continuum, 2006); Scott M. Marshall, *Bob Dylan: A Spiritual Life* (New York: BP Books, 2017); Marshall, *Restless Pilgrim: The Spiritual Journey of Bob Dylan* (Winter Park, FL: Relevant Books, 2002); Michael J. Gilmour, *The Gospel According to Bob Dylan: The Old, Old Story for Modern Times* (Louisville, KY: Westminster John Knox Press, 2011); Gilmour, *Tangled Up in the Bible: Bob Dylan and Scripture* (New York: Continuum, 2004). For the latter, see, for example, Clinton Heylin, *Trouble in Mind: Bob Dylan's Gospel Years—What Really Happened* (New York: Lesser Gods, 2017).

[4] I do not mean to say that Dylan was an atheist prior to his public conversion in the late 1970s, only that whatever adherence to traditional religious doctrines he possessed was not emphasized in this period and that, furthermore, he made many statements that suggested deep skepticism toward organized religion. With regard to the latter dynamic, consider his 1964 letter to *Broadside* magazine, which contained these lines:

> thru all the gossip, lies, religions, cults
> myths, gods, history books, social books,

"the whole idea of Jesus was foreign to me."[5] Dylan's status as a freethinking poet of genius meant that his turn to religion could not easily be written off by secularists in the usual fashion—as merely a product of ignorance, idiocy, unthinking cultural inheritance, or weakness. For anti-religious Dylan enthusiasts, Dylan's gospel period challenged them to consider their own atheism in ways that ordinary religionists could not. Beyond this, there is the simple sociological fact that the most conspicuous social impact of Dylan's gospel period was not the conversion of onlookers to the same faith he professed (though there are certainly reports of this[6]), but virulent criticism and consternation from non-religious audiences disturbed by Dylan's proselytization. Dylan engaged secularists in a way very few devoutly religious people can.

Furthermore, Dylan himself directly contributes to the postsecular aspect of his cultural impact by refusing to perform a straightforward or consistent profession of faith; indeed, almost as remarkable as Dylan's public conversion to

> all books, politics, decrees, rules, laws,
> boundary lines, bibles, legends, and bathroom
> writings, there is no guidance at all except
> from ones own natural senses
> from being born
> an it can only be exchanged
> it cant be preached
> nor sold nor even understood

Quoted in Stephen Petrus and Ronald D. Cohen, *Folk City: New York and the American Folk Music Revival* (Oxford: Oxford University Press, 2015), 287. Consider, too, from the same year, Dylan's declaration in his poem "11 Outlined Epitaphs":

> I am ragin'ly against absolutely
> everything that wants t' force nature
> t' be unnatural (be it human or otherwise)
> an' I am violently for absolutely
> everything that will fight those
> forces (be them human or otherwise)

Bob Dylan, "11 Outlined Epitaphs" (liner notes to *The Times They Are A-Changin'*, 1964), in *Bob Dylan: Lyrics, 1962–1985* (New York: Alfred A. Knopf, 1985), 109. This hesitance toward the public embrace of a religious identity persisted through 1978, when Dylan claimed in an interview: "I feel a heartfelt God. I don't particularly think that God wants me thinking about Him all the time. I think that would be a tremendous burden on Him, you know. He's got enough people asking Him for favors. He's got enough people asking him to pull strings. I'll pull my own strings, you know." Jonathan Cott, ed., "Interview with Ron Rosenbaum, *Playboy*, March 1978," in *Bob Dylan: The Essential Interviews* (New York: Simon & Schuster, 2017), 248.

[5] Cott, "Interview with Robert Hilburn, *Los Angeles Times*, November 23, 1980," in *Essential Interviews*, 296.

[6] See, for example, Stephen Bullivant, "How Bob Dylan Led Me to Jesus," *Catholic Herald*, October 3, 2016, https://avemariaradio.net/bob-dylan-led-jesus/.

evangelical Christianity are his public statements of doubt about his religiosity. Many of these statements appear after the 1979–1981 gospel period.[7] But even some lines from songs from within this period could be interpreted as expressions of doubt.[8] In any case, what seems unquestionable is that following his third gospel album, *Shot of Love* from 1981, Dylan entered into a postconversion period that he still occupies. Although he never has renounced his religiosity, he has ceased to proclaim it with the frequency, fervor, or directness of his gospel period and, more than this, has provided powerful statements appearing to question his religious beliefs. Chief among these statements is the release of his 1983 album, *Infidels*, and in particular the song "Jokerman," in which the eponymous figure is suggested as a designation of both Jesus and Dylan himself. Dylan's uncertainty about his faith makes him the ultimate representative for a culture itself increasingly torn between religious fundamentalism and militant atheism, and perhaps in need of some rapprochement between those two poles. Individual doubts and contradictions become, on the level of his prophetic reception, evidence of Dylan's own wrestling with his faith—a wrestling that serves the postsecular role of disciplining both religious fundamentalists and militant atheists alike.

The fact that we often relate to Dylan through *recorded* music that spans more than six decades—so that a listener is simultaneously aware of both Dylan's explicitly religious and more doubtful or non-religious periods—only further enhances the postsecular quality of Dylan's message. When we hear Dylan articulate a religious or anti-religious message, we know that neither is his final or ultimate answer but that each has a certain integrity within his body of work.

In short, analyzing Dylan's religiosity from a postsecular lens crystallizes what makes it special and innovative. As a statement of Christian theology, Dylan's gospel period may be beautifully communicated through music and poetry, but it lacks originality and, as I have just emphasized, does not establish a consistently held, long-term public testimony. Viewed from a postsecular perspective, however, Dylan's religious music and message take on special meaning in their role of challenging the non-religious—and especially the anti-religious—to achieve greater self-reflexivity and open-mindedness.

In what follows I aim to demonstrate some of the key postsecular features of Dylan's contribution to religion. After discussing the concept of the postsecular and the need for prophetic (not just philosophical) voices to advocate postsecular ethics (sections II.1 and II.2), I turn to four specific ways in which Dylan cultivates in his non-religious listeners a greater appreciation for

---

[7] I discuss many of these in section II.7.

[8] As examples, consider: "Now that you're gone I got to wonder / If you ever were here at all" ("Making a Liar Out of Me"); "Sometimes I turn, there's someone there, other times it's only me" ("Every Grain of Sand").

the dignity, integrity, and plausibility of religion (sections II.3–II.6) and then provide some additional evidence of these effects in his audience (section II.7).

Throughout, I argue that Dylan is not only a postsecular prophet (someone who, in transgressing traditional boundaries between the secular and religious, destabilizes familiar expectations of what it means to be a prophet) but also a prophet of the postsecular. In this latter role, he offers a prophetic voice that serves less to convert the non-religious to religion than to inspire in them an abiding respect for traditional religious faith. If it is customary for the non-religious to see religiosity as a private choice—with no grounding in objective truth—the effect of Dylan's postsecular prophecy is to encourage secular individuals to see their own non-religion itself as a *choice* (an existential stance), not a *truth* supported by external reality, and thus as a standpoint that, properly conceived, contains the same contingency, potential instability, and possibility for transformation as religious belief itself.

I am aware that the framework of Part II could be dismissed on the basis of recent trends in the scholarship of religion that, on the one hand, deconstruct the very boundary separating the religious from the non-religious and, on the other, object to the purported tendency to presuppose a Western, Protestant, belief-centric conception of religion that marginalizes non-Western or non-Christian conceptions shaped less by beliefs than by all-encompassing cultural practices. However, I think such a rejection would be hasty. As vexing as the question of how to define religion may be (something I have discussed elsewhere[9]), a refusal to make use of the dichotomy between religiosity and non-religiosity would undermine our capacity to reflect on genuine experiences, questions, and problems. That is, unless we are prepared to assert that all of us are equally religious, or that each phase of our life is equally religious, or that religiosity ultimately has no meaning, we have good reason to distinguish religion from its opposite. Further, while there are certainly differences in the ways that religions prioritize practices vis-à-vis beliefs, the practice-belief dichotomy is overdrawn if it fails to appreciate that most, if not all, religions necessarily contain elements of both beliefs and practices. In any case, I use the term *belief* as a metonym for religiosity more generally, certainly not to refer to a particular, Protestant conception, even if it is true that Dylan's conversion brings him close to just that tradition of Christianity.

---

[9] See Heather J. Sharkey and Jeffrey Edward Green, "The Landscape of Religious Freedom," in *The Changing Terrain of Religious Freedom*, ed. Sharkey and Green (Philadelphia: Penn Press, 2021), 1–31.

II.1. The Idea of the Postsecular

The idea of the postsecular has been developed in numerous different ways—not all of them consistent with one another—but at the most general level it can be said that postsecularity refers to a kind of rapprochement between religiosity and secularity. This rapprochement can take a variety of sometimes competing forms. One can distinguish, for instance, between *ideational* and *institutional* renderings of the notion. Ideationally, the postsecular has been associated with efforts to bridge the analytical dichotomy between religion and non-religion and, in particular, to demonstrate that religion and secularism are not pure opposites, since each often draws its meaning from the constitution and regulation of the other. Relevant here are historical efforts to show, for instance, that within the medieval Church the concept of secularity was used to refer to non-monastic *clergy*, or recent critical claims exposing how, despite pretensions of a statecraft neutral toward religions, the so-called secular state in fact often has attempted to define what counts as a proper religion, fomented tensions between religious groups, exacerbated inequalities between majority and minority religions, and expanded governmental intrusion into the regulation of family life.[10] A more aspirational form of this ideational interest in destabilizing the familiar opposition between religion and non-religion can be found in recent philosophies that articulate a "third way" spiritual standpoint, irreducible to familiar religious or non-religious perspectives.[11] Institutionally, the notion of the postsecular has been invoked not to undermine the distinction between the religious and the non-religious as such, but rather to draw attention to a variety of practices that, in intertwining secular and religious standpoints, promise (in the eyes of some) positive social outcomes. Such positive outcomes have been conceived as enhanced governance: for example, the increased reliance of even avowedly secular states on faith-based organizations in order to better promote human welfare; the strategic use of military chaplains in wartime; and more generally, the recognition of the role that communities of faith can play within the public sphere regarding matters such as the environment, public health, gender equality, and the inspiration to understand and fight injustice.[12] Relatedly,

[10] See Talal Asad, *Formations of the Secular: Christianity, Islam, Modernity* (Palo Alto, CA: Stanford University Press, 2003); Saba Mahmood, *Religious Difference in a Secular Age: A Minority Report* (Princeton, NJ: Princeton University Press, 2015).

[11] See, for example, Simon Critchley, *The Faith of the Faithless* (New York: Verso, 2012); Anthony Kronman, *Confessions of a Born-Again Pagan* (New Haven, CT: Yale University Press, 2016); Ronald Dworkin, *Religion Without God* (Cambridge, MA: Harvard University Press, 2013); Richard Kearney, *Anatheism: Returning to God After God* (New York: Columbia University Press, 2009).

[12] See James Beckford, "Public Religions and the Postsecular: Critical Reflections," *Journal for the Scientific Study of Religion* 51, no. 1 (2012): 1–19.

institutional postsecularism also has been associated with the proliferation of religious standpoints that, when they accept the values of liberal democracy or embody new forms of spirituality that overcome traditional divisions (sacred versus profane, religious versus commercial), have the potential to re-enchant, without undermining, a public culture shaped by putatively secular values of individual choice, diversity, business, and modern science.[13] Debates about these institutional claims have been definitive of much postsecular discourse.

Underlying both the ideational and institutional formulations of postsecularism is a third rendering of the term that, though more minimal in its scope, is perhaps the most coherent, most precise, and least controversial— and, importantly, the rendering with the most straightforward and concrete *ethical implications* for citizens within contemporary democratic societies. On this interpretation, the postsecular draws its meaning from polemical negation of the so-called "secularization thesis," especially dominant in the middle of the twentieth century, which understands religiosity as a vestigial remnant of premodern society and thus as destined to fade in the face of the ever-intensifying collection of factors constituting modern industrial/postindustrial life: affluence and the expectation of perpetual increases in living standards, ongoing progress in science and technology, urbanization, the bureaucratic rationalization of state administration, and the hegemonic status of liberal-democratic institutions and norms. Here postsecularism stands as the idea that, contra the secularization thesis, modernity does not imply the dissipation of traditional organized religion (let alone newer or non-traditional forms of spirituality) and that, accordingly, "advanced," "Western," "developed," or otherwise "modern" societies—both now and in the future—should expect the permanent endurance of religion. There is debate about the nature of the sociological evidence refuting the secularization thesis, with some invoking an alleged resurgence of religiosity throughout the West and others, like Jürgen Habermas, claiming that while evidence in Europe still supports the negative relationship between modernization and religiosity, there are numerous other reasons to dispense with the thesis's prediction of the eventual disappearance of religion from the world.[14]

---

[13] See, for example, Robbie B. H. Goh, "Market Theory, Market Theology: The Business of the Church in the City," in *Space, Theory and Practice*, ed. Justin Beaumont and Christopher Baker (New York: Continuum), 60–68; John D. Caputo, *On Religion* (Oxford: Routledge, 2001); John A. McClure, *The Future of Christianity: Reflections on Violence and Democracy, Religion and Secularization* (Surrey, UK: Ashgate Publishing, 2001).

[14] For Habermas, even if the secularization thesis is not disproven, there are at least three reasons for adopting a postsecular perspective. First, even in Europe "religious communities continue to exist in a context of ongoing secularization," and, relatedly, the persistence of global conflicts infused by religion undermines the "secular*istic* belief that religion is *destined to disappear* and purges the secular understanding of the world of any triumphalism." Second, Habermas observes that "religious organizations are increasingly assuming the role of 'communities of interpretation' in the political life

But, in fact, the deepest meaning of this third and perhaps most fundamental rendering of the postsecular rapprochement between religiosity and secularity is not strictly sociological, but ethical. It refers not just to macroscopic trends in religious practices and beliefs but also to a specific and salutary *state of consciousness* that recognizes the equal dignity and value of both religious and non-religious mentalities as well as the need for contemporary societies to find ways for religious and non-religious citizens to engage with each other in a manner of mutual respect, learning, and productive collaboration. As Hans Joas puts it, the postsecular does not "express a sudden increase in religiosity, after its epochal decrease, but rather a change in mindset of those who, previously, felt justified in considering religions to be moribund."[15] While this state of consciousness can be descriptive (Habermas, for instance, appeals to its growth as one reason why the secularization thesis's prediction of the disappearance of religion should be jettisoned), it fundamentally involves the prescriptive idea that in a postsecular democratic society both religious and non-religious individuals need to overcome any sense of the relative superiority, naturalness, or propriety of their respective positions and find ways to relate to each other in a newfound spirit of genuine respect. This ethical rendering of the postsecular—as a call for greater harmony and mutual understanding between the religious and non-religious— has been at the forefront of the most influential philosophies of the postsecular (above all, those of Habermas and Charles Taylor) and is the primary point of contact for my own discussion.

Some might think that the ethical aim of postsecularism I have just described is too tepid or obvious a goal. Talal Asad, for instance, writes, "If anything is agreed upon, it is that a straightforward narrative of progress from the religious to the secular is no longer acceptable."[16] But it is wrong to conflate academic appreciation for the falsity of the secularization thesis with the *actual ethical*

of secular societies"; that is, in debates on issues like abortion, healthcare, and the environment, religious communities can and do "exercise influence on the formation of public opinion and political will by making relevant contributions on key issues, irrespective of whether their arguments are convincing or objectional." Third, ongoing processes of immigration, including refugees seeking asylum and guest worker programs, highlight the need for even predominantly secular societies to better address citizens' pluralism of religious orientation. Jürgen Habermas, "Religion in the Public Sphere of 'Post-Secular' Society," in *Postmetaphysical Thinking II* (Cambridge, UK: Polity, 2017), 213–14.

[15] Hans Joas, *Do We Need Religion? On the Experience of Self-Transcendence* (Boulder, CO: Paradigm Publishers, 2008), 106.

[16] Asad, *Formations of the Secular*, 1. Relatedly, Mariano Barbato and Friedrich Kratochwil comment, with regard to Habermas's theory of postsecularism, "What for Habermas in perspective of the domestic public appears as a revolutionary step, i.e., admitting religion to the public discourse, is, for international relations, a rather obvious presupposition." Barbato and Kratochwil, "Habermas' Notion of a Post-secular Society. A Perspective from International Relations," EUI Working Papers (MWP 2008/25), Florence, Italy: European University Institute (2008), 21.

achievement of ordinary citizens who, coming from divergent religious and non-religious perspectives, in fact exhibit mutual respect toward each other. Perhaps the most well-known obstacle to the achievement of this mutual respect is the persistence and even growth of certain so-called religious-fundamentalist perspectives that deny the findings of natural science, reject the rights and values of democracy, and in effect make any genuine rapprochement with secularity impossible. But one of the main ethical virtues of the idea of postsecularism is that it reminds us of the opposite problem—that is, of not merely secular but *secularist* citizens, defined as those who have not achieved postsecular consciousness because they continue to understand religiosity as irrational, unnatural, vestigial, or otherwise inferior to a non-religious perspective. If the fundamentalist challenge to postsecularism is starkly apparent and often boldly stated, the secularist challenge is usually subtler because it typically is joined to commitments such as humanism, skepticism, and liberal democracy that promote the formal right of religious communities to practice their beliefs. But notwithstanding the affirmation of this right, secularists still disrespect religiosity in a variety of ways that manifest contempt. The paradigmatic instance of this subtle secularist view remains Max Weber, who in one sense respects the integrity of religious belief (studying its variety with profound skill as a sociologist; defending the liberal *Rechtsstaat*, which affords religious liberty; and propounding a pluralistic, decisionist ethical theory that understands all individual determinations of what constitutes "time not misspent," including both religious and non-religious ones, as having equal plausibility and existential integrity), yet, at the same time, disrespects religiosity in two ways: insisting that it involves a "sacrifice of the intellect" and, even more, claiming that it is out of touch with what he calls the "fate of the times."[17] Thus, even if Weber respects religiosity from the perspective of legal rights and individual choice, he nonetheless presents it as a commitment that is backward, unmodern, contrary to science, and unwilling to face up to the alleged truth of the disenchantment of the world. Weber thereby unintentionally clarifies the ethical mission of postsecularism, which is not to convert the secular to religion but to instill in them an honest and reflective self-consciousness that ceases to erroneously justify secularism as more true than religion and that, relatedly, does not invoke any implausible and self-serving claims about the direction of history to cover up the fact that non-religiosity—like religiosity—is a choice, not a truth.[18]

---

[17] Max Weber, "Science as a Vocation," in *Vocation Lectures* (Indianapolis: Hackett, 2004), 24, 27, 29, 30.

[18] Of course, phenomenologically speaking, we often have the experience that religious communities choose us: that we are born into preexisting religious identities that shape our lifelong attitudes toward religion. I do not deny this phenomenology or the role of acculturation. In invoking

Weber's subtle secularist perspective finds echoes in contemporary culture. Even if the perspective is a minority one, it is still sizeable and disproportionately influential. As much as there has been attention to a rising category of individuals who describe themselves as spiritual but not religious, a significant portion of Western societies is characterized by people who identify as *neither spiritual nor religious*. In the United States, this group makes up 18 percent of the population and appears to be growing, while in fifteen European nations it averages an incredibly high 53 percent, including majorities of the population in Sweden (66 percent), Denmark (64 percent), Belgium (62 percent), Norway (62 percent), and the Netherlands (60 percent).[19] While this standpoint does not in itself designate a secularist degrading of religion, the fact remains that those who adopt it are likely to hold views that disparage religiosity. For example, the Pew Research Center, on the basis of extensive 2018 survey data, divided up the American populace into seven categories of religiosity. The least religious category, the Solidly Secular, which comprises 17 percent of the population and overwhelmingly defines itself as neither religious or spiritual,[20] tends to hold highly critical attitudes toward religiosity. Significant proportions of the Solidly Secular report "a mostly negative" view of churches and organized religion (52 percent), claim that religious institutions "do more harm than good" (43 percent) and have "too much influence in politics" (75 percent), deny that "religious beliefs help a lot of family relationships" (99 percent), believe that churches and religious organizations "weaken morality in society" (28 percent), and reject the idea that religion overall does more good than harm (71 percent). It should also be pointed out that the Solidly Secular hardly monopolize antireligious sentiment in the United States. The second least religious category, the Religious Resisters—who, unlike the Solidly Secular, tend to believe in some higher power or spiritual force (though not the God of the Bible) and comprise

---

the notion of choice, what I mean is that religion is a human decision—on *either* the cultural or personal level—and not a function of truth, honesty, reason, or the objective state of the universe.

[19] For US figures, see Michael Lipka and Claire Gecewicz, "More Americans Now Say They're Spiritual but Not Religious," Pew Research Center, September 6, 2017, https://www.pewresearch.org/fact-tank/2017/09/06/more-americans-now-say-theyre-spiritual-but-not-religious. With regard to Europe, see Pew Research Center, "Attitudes toward Spirituality and Religion," in *Being Christian in Western Europe*, May 29, 2018, 119, https://www.pewforum.org/2018/05/29/attitudes-toward-spirituality-and-religion/.

[20] Of the 17 percent of Americans who are "solidly secular," 97 percent say they are neither somewhat nor very religious, 78 percent say they are neither somewhat nor very spiritual, 99 percent say they don't believe in God as described in the Bible, less than 1 percent report deriving a great deal of meaning or fulfillment from their religious faith, and only 2 percent claim to find a great deal of meaning or fulfillment in spiritual practices such as meditation. Becka A. Alper, "From Solidly Secular to Sunday Stalwarts, A Look at Our New Religious Typology," August 29, 2018, Pew Research Center, https://www.pewresearch.org/fact-tank/2018/08/29/religious-typology-overview/.

an additional 12 percent of the American population—report an even higher level of negativity toward churches and organized religion (57 percent).[21] To be sure, as the very category of the Religious Resister suggests, there are many reasons to be skeptical of organized religion, not all of which indicate a hostility to religion or spirituality as such. But as the Religious Resisters also demonstrate, secularist tendencies (e.g., profound suspicion toward prevailing forms of religious practice and belief) are not necessarily limited to self-described atheists and agnostics but can be voiced from other quarters as well.

In Europe, in which being neither religious nor spiritual is three times more common than in the United States (53 percent vs. 18 percent), one likewise finds secularist contempt toward churches and organized religion, with 43 percent of those who are neither spiritual nor religious claiming that religion does more harm than good.[22] Perhaps most striking from Europe is data relating to the proportion of national populations that reports deep criticism of religiosity. Among fifteen Western European nations, the median percentage of the national population that agrees that "overall, religion causes more harm than good" is 33 percent, with some countries approaching a majority: Sweden (50 percent), Norway (48 percent), Denmark (47 percent), Belgium (44 percent), the Netherlands (42 percent), and Finland (41 percent). Among these countries, the median percentage of the national population that claims that "science makes religion unnecessary in my life" is 32 percent.[23] Relatedly, 67 percent of the religiously unaffiliated in Europe have a negative attitude toward religion.[24] To be sure, this data is only a snapshot, and there is no doubt a great deal of internal diversity underlying ostensibly common views about the net harm or perceived meaninglessness of traditional religious belief and practice. But when one considers the tremendous size and cultural and economic impact of Europe, this data suggests a profound secularist strain in Western culture.

Part of what gives this secularist strain force is that it is disproportionately expressed by those who are socioeconomically advantaged and otherwise privileged. In the United States, the Solidly Secular group (the 17 percent of the population that identifies mostly as neither spiritual nor religious and holds high levels of negativity toward organized religion) is, relative to the other six more religious categories, significantly richer (46 percent make more than $75,000 per year), more educated (45 percent have college degrees), white (79 percent),

---

[21] Pew Research Center, "Attitudes toward Organized Religion," in *The Religious Typology: A New Way to Categorize Americans by Religion*, August 29, 2018, 53–58, https://www.pewforum.org/2018/08/29/attitudes-toward-organized-religion-2/.

[22] Pew Research Center, *Being Christian in Western Europe*, 122, 131.

[23] Pew Research Center, 130.

[24] Pew Research Center, 133.

and male (65 percent). In a parallel fashion, the countries in Europe with the highest secularist elements (the Nordic countries) are not just among the world's wealthiest, most educated, least corrupt, and safest, but they also have perhaps the best funded and most extensive social welfare systems in the West. While secularists often invoke elements of this data to justify their stance—arguing that a perspective that is disproportionately shared by the educated and those least suffering from material deprivation is, due to these very qualities, all the more likely to be superior to its rivals[25]—the opposite dynamic seems relevant as well: because the critique of religiosity is more likely to be voiced by those advantaged by virtue of their race, gender, education, and wealth, anti-religion can be experienced not simply as one view among many in a vibrant public sphere but as an aspect of elite condescension that intensifies religionists' sense of being beleaguered.

For some religionists, this sense of beleaguerment is further magnified by the customary political and educational institutions of a secular liberal-democratic society, which, even if legitimate, clearly privilege secular reason over religiously inspired forms of discourse. Even Habermas, who, in the name of postsecularism, advocates the inclusion of religious speech and perspectives within the public realm, limits this inclusion to the informal public sphere, expecting the formal work of legislation and administration to be conducted exclusively in non-religious language.[26] Like Habermas, I find this restriction appropriate and not in itself discriminatory toward religion, but it reminds us that, culturally speaking, the bureaucratic field—which makes powerful and frequent inroads into contemporary daily life—is much more likely to generate a sense of the normalcy or default quality of non-religion than to remind citizens of the coequal integrity of religious and non-religious perspectives. Something similar occurs in liberal-democratic educational systems in which, even if citizens enjoy latitude to pursue religious schooling, secular reason still dominates, not just by virtue of the predominance of non-religious schools but in the profound tendency to equate the development of secular-rational capabilities (skepticism, historicism, materialism, the experimental method, evidence-driven findings, discourse that does not presuppose shared metaphysical conceptions) with education itself. It is also true that some of the most studied frameworks within higher education— Hobbesian liberalism, Marxism, Nietzschean existentialism, Freudianism, and Weberian sociology, among others—do not just adopt a familiar methodological atheism but can be read as being aggressively anti-religious in their message.

---

[25] See Hemant Mehta, "Pew Analysis: The 'Solidly Secular' Are Young, Rich, White, Educated, and Male," *Friendly Atheist*, August 29, 2018, https://friendlyatheist.patheos.com/2018/08/29/pew-analysis-the-solidly-secular-are-young-rich-white-educated-and-male/.

[26] Jürgen Habermas, *Between Naturalism and Religion* (Cambridge, UK: Polity, 2008), 2–3.

As with the political institutions of a secular liberal-democratic society, these educational tendencies seem to me entirely acceptable. But they nonetheless point to an asymmetry in a liberal democracy's effort to reach harmonious accord between the non-religious and the religious. Even if appropriate as a matter of institutional structure and general public welfare, this asymmetry represents a potential challenge to the postsecular goal of having both religious and non-religious citizens recognize each other as coequal partners deserving mutual respect. Specifically, it suggests why the non-religious, even when they do not hold explicitly anti-religious views, may be culturally unprepared to afford the religious genuine consideration and reciprocal regard.

And of course, a religionist's sense of beleaguerment is most explicitly provoked by the rise of so-called new or militant atheists who aggressively attack the intelligence and integrity of religious belief, whether by insisting upon religion's vestigiality and therefore predicting its inevitable disappearance in the face of modern science, technology, and reason; subjecting certain religious assertions and practices to ridicule for their apparent irrationality; denouncing the deleterious social and political consequences religion has had in the world; or, most mercilessly, suggesting a causal linkage between stupidity and vileness on the one hand, and certain forms of religiosity on the other.[27] Such perspectives, voiced by prominent figures like Richard Dawkins, Sam Harris, and Christopher Hitchens, have come to take on more visibility within contemporary public culture.[28] To be sure, there is nuance and internal variety among the militant atheists, and it is also true that their atheistic fundamentalism is matched by an even greater degree of intolerance from certain religious fundamentalists in the world today. Nonetheless, militant atheism is yet another indication of how the postsecular ethical project defended by Habermas, Taylor, and others—which calls for mutual respect and collaborative interaction between religious and non-religious citizens within the public sphere—remains unachieved.

[27] For enduring defenses of the secularization thesis, see Steve Bruce, *God Is Dead: Secularization in the West* (Oxford: Blackwell, 2002); Mark Chaves, "Secularization as Declining Religious Authority," *Social Forces* 72, no. 3 (1994): 749–74.

[28] As James Wood summarizes the perspective of the new atheists, "It is a settled assumption of this kind of atheism that there are no intelligent religious believers." Wood, "God in the Quad," *New Yorker*, August 31, 2009. In keeping with this summary, the influential American TV host Bill Maher, in the wake of the 2015 Paris attacks, asserted: "First of all, there are no great religions. They're all stupid and dangerous. And we should insult them, and we should be able to insult whatever we want. That is what free speech is like." THR Staff, "Bill Maher Weighs In On Paris Attack: 'There Are No Great Religions—They're All Stupid and Dangerous,'" *Hollywood Reporter*, January 9, 2015, https://www.hollywoodreporter.com/news/general-news/bill-maher-weighs-paris-attack-762247/.

II.2. The Need for Prophets of the Postsecular: Beyond Habermas and Taylor

How can postsecular ethics be achieved? Thus far, more attention has been paid to overcoming religious fundamentalism than to overcoming secularist intolerance of religion. This may make sense insofar as religious fundamentalism is the bigger problem, but there already are various forces at work, including those from within numerous religious traditions themselves, that encourage religionists of this type to overcome fundamentalism and adopt forms of religiosity that are consistent with the values of liberal democracy and respectful dialogue with the non-religious.[29] With regard to overcoming secularist intolerance of religion, however, advocacy for postsecularism has been less common and also constrained by the current philosophical form in which such advocacy has occurred. Indeed, the call for mutual respect and reciprocity between the religious and non-religious has been expressed most influentially by two contemporary philosophers: the aforementioned Jürgen Habermas and Charles Taylor. If their work has profoundly shaped the very discourse on postsecularism—and taken seriously the problem of secularist intolerance—it also has been limited in two key respects. On the one hand, there is the generic problem that Habermas and Taylor, as contemporary philosophers, write in the language of secular reason and, accordingly, adopt the standpoint of an impersonal observer. This is to be expected, of course, but it also is problematic. The effort to shake secularists out of smug and excessive self-confidence regarding secular reason—and to encourage them to recognize the integrity and potential political value to the public sphere of certain kinds of religious speech—can go only so far if this effort is itself conducted in the language of secular reason. The detached impersonality of philosophic discourse—which excludes emotionality, testimony, confession, and statements of self-evidence—is constrained in how well it can establish the integrity of expressions of faith, religious conscience, and wrestling with the divine that have no other persuasiveness than the intensely personal sincerity with which they are believed, practiced, and communicated. On the other hand, beyond these generic limitations, it is also the case that there are specific features of both Habermas's and Taylor's theories

---

[29] These forces include the impact of the secular state and secular reason (contact with which is inescapable for many); numerous religious traditions and movements that themselves advocate for the acceptance of modern science and the vital importance of a political culture shaped by rights, the norm of equal human dignity, diversity, and a public sphere that does not discriminate on the basis of religion; and influential liberal theories of justice that explain why citizens cannot expect to live in a theocracy or share the same religious commitments when they engage with each other in the public realm.

that remain disproportionately concerned with the threat posed by religionists to the achievement of a postsecular mentality, leading them not to pursue, as fully as they might, the parallel threat of secularists not adopting a postsecular openness and respect toward the religious.

It is a virtue of Habermas's approach in particular that he is cognizant of the limits of philosophy in promoting postsecularism, and I will discuss his understanding of these limits presently. However, what Habermas does not say—but my own analysis aims to show—is that the limitations of philosophies of the postsecular remind us of the need for such philosophies to be complemented by *prophets of the postsecular*, who communicate the propriety of mutual respect for religionists and secularists through their own personal narrative that has led them to this state of consciousness, who exert persuasive force on the basis of their charisma and not only their rational qualities, who testify to the truth of postsecularity rather than logically prove it, and who do not simply call for dispassionate harmony between religionists and secularists but help achieve this harmony by viscerally unsettling the self-assurance of extremists on both sides. On the basis of these qualities, a prophet of the postsecular can more powerfully *inspire* the change of consciousness at the heart of postsecular ethics. Dylan, as I will elaborate, plays this role.

Because the ethics of postsecularism involve two separate movements— overcoming religious fundamentalism and overcoming secularist intolerance of religion—there is, strictly speaking, a role for prophets of the postsecular on both sides. But since religious fundamentalists are already confronted with numerous religiously modulated calls for overcoming their fundamentalism, the type of prophet of the postsecular I will address—which has yet to be adequately conceptualized, let alone examined—operates from the opposite direction: contesting secularist intolerance, indifference, and arrogance toward religion and thus eliciting in the secular an abiding respect for the integrity of religiosity. Such a figure occupies a subtle and unusual prophetic position. Ordinarily, we expect religious prophets to appeal to those who are themselves religious or who, in the prophetic encounter, become religious for the first time. What needs to be appreciated, however, is the possibility of an alternate, rarer form of religious prophecy that addresses itself to the non-religious *as such*— that is, one that takes the non-religious as its primary constituency and whose message to this constituency is not to cancel their non-religiosity but to discipline, refine, and elevate it so as to avoid the ethical and spiritual errors of a secularist mindset. This is no easy task, since the non-religious are far less likely than the religious to be receptive to prophetic speech. To achieve it requires someone who both enjoys charismatic authority vis-à-vis would-be secularists and who employs that authority to bring about not religious conversion but greater appreciation for and heeding of the religiously inspired. Dylan is only one person and his postsecular impact may ultimately be modest, but I know of no one within popular culture who better qualifies as a prophet of the postsecular and has done more to inspire the change in mindset that philosophers of the postsecular dispassionately seek.

In order to clarify Dylan's distinctive contribution, I first attend to Habermas's and Taylor's leading philosophies of the postsecular, the limitations besetting their approaches, and how these limitations suggest the need for the prophetic role Habermas and Taylor disclaim but Dylan adopts.

Habermas and the Postsecular

Habermas's point in invoking the postsecular is to call for a state of consciousness according to which both religious and non-religious citizens respect each other in a deep way—not in the manner of a mere modus vivendi, nor in the form of the non-religious treating the religious as a curiosity, but according to a framework of equal citizenship in which both sides adopt genuine solidaristic relations grounded on mutual respect and a belief that each has something of value to contribute to civic dialogue.[30] Achieving this state of consciousness requires that each side engage in a potentially difficult learning process. With respect to the religious, Habermas argues that they must abide by three strictures definitive of reasonable political communication: that they adopt a self-reflexive attitude toward their own religious traditions and thus acknowledge that the public realm is inhabited by citizens with comprehensive worldviews fundamentally different from their own; that they accept the findings of modern science; and that, on the moral and political level, they accept the "egalitarian individualism" that grounds the commitment to liberal democracy and international human rights.[31] Further, even though Habermas does not think reasonable political communication needs to be stripped of religiosity in all cases—indeed, one of his main proposals is that religious speech should be included, welcomed, and heeded by non-religious citizens within the *informal* public sphere—he is clear that the formal public sphere (the debates and decisions of official leaders as they operate within parliaments, courts, and the administrative bureaucracy) should be free from religious utterances: "Only the ideologically neutral exercise of secular governmental authority within the framework of the constitutional

[30] See Habermas, "Reply to My Critics," in *Habermas and Religion*, ed. Craig Calhoun, Eduardo Mendieta, and Jonathan VanAntwerpen (Cambridge, UK: Polity, 2013), 372.

[31] Habermas, *Between Naturalism and Religion*, 137. With respect to the third of these requirements, Habermas does not intend mere legalistic acceptance of "the constitution of the secular state" but an allegiance to it that is made "for good reasons" (129).

state can ensure different communities of belief can coexist on a basis of equal rights and mutual tolerance."[32]

As far as the learning process required from the non-religious, Habermas calls for secular individuals to recognize the theological origins of secular modernity (the formative impact of religious beliefs on the early modern construction of secular societies) and, even more, to recognize that religious utterances often contain valuable semantic contents that, when translated into a secular vocabulary, can be instructive for even atheistic citizens as they deliberate about a variety of contemporary issues. The value of translated religious speech stems, on the one hand, from the fact that it is especially apt at articulating the suffering and frustration any person, religious or non-religious, is prone to experience in the face of injustice and the failure to achieve full-fledged community. Specifically, Habermas refers to the "possibilities of expression and to sensitivities" religious communities possess "with regard to lives that have gone astray, with regard to societal pathologies, with regard to the failure of individuals' plans for their lives, and with regard to the deformation and disfigurement of the lives that people share with one another."[33] On the other hand, the value of religious speech, when translated, stems from the fact that members of contemporary liberal-democratic societies, including secular citizens, are split over certain political and policy questions—such as abortion, voluntary euthanasia, reproductive medicine, animal protection, and climate change—so that religious communities, regardless of whether the metaphysical commitments underlying their standpoints are convincing, can play the role of " 'communities of interpretation' in the political life of secular society."[34] As part of respecting the value of religious speech, non-religious citizens are called upon by Habermas to participate in, if not lead, such acts of translation.

Habermas thus articulates the need, central to a postsecular mindset, for non-religious citizens to overcome a derogatory attitude toward religion that sees religiosity as vestigial, unnatural, or intellectually inferior to non-religiosity. At the same time, though, Habermas also reveals the limits of a merely philosophical or theoretical defense of postsecularism and in doing so implicitly—though unintentionally—points to the need for *prophets of the postsecular* who help to fulfill the goal of mutual respect between the religious and non-religious.

Habermas is himself aware of some of these limits. At the core of his account of postsecularity is the need for both the religious and non-religious to engage

---

[32] Habermas, 2–3.

[33] Jürgen Habermas, "Pre-political Foundations of the Democratic Constitutional State?," in Jürgen Habermas and Joseph Ratzinger, *The Dialectics of Secularization: On Reason and Religion* (San Francisco: Ignatius Press, 2006), 43–44.

[34] Habermas, *Postmetaphysical Thinking II*, 214.

in learning processes so that they can fulfill the normative expectations of democratic citizenship and productively engage with each other in dialogues shaped by mutual respect. Yet Habermas is clear that these learning processes not only cannot be mandated by law (because citizens retain the right to opt out of democratic participation and because the law is powerless to coerce such learning in any case) but also cannot be accomplished by philosophy alone. Postsecularism is ultimately about a state of consciousness: the attitude that understands one's religiosity or lack of religiosity in a self-reflexive manner—that is, in a manner that acknowledges that one's mindset in this regard is contingent and thus not shared by others with different worldviews, who are no less worthy of respect. Such an attitude is the precondition of engaging in the learning processes Habermas calls for and, at the same time, one of the fruits of them. But even as Habermas stresses the importance of the "cognitive structure underlying the required self-reflexive attitude of tolerance," he admits, "Both the secular and the religious side can only *hope* that a complementary learning process will result in those cognitive attitudes that are necessary for satisfying the demanding obligations on either side. These attitudes cannot just be prescribed by political theory."[35]

Why is political theory—or philosophy—by itself unable to bring about postsecular consciousness? Habermas suggests at least four different answers. First, insofar as political theory resembles law and morality in articulating coercible obligations—insofar as it is the science of these obligations—it cannot fully address the attitudes, habits, and practices of a postsecular morality that are, as has been discussed, not officially obligatory.[36] Second, even if postsecular ethics were mandatory, Habermas suggests that philosophy would not be able by itself to bring about the change in consciousness because, in matters of religion and perhaps other fundamental orientations in behavior, it is ineffectual. There are standpoints about which one must be converted and not simply convinced. Something of the Hegelian admission of philosophy's lack of vitality, its grey on grey, seems to inform Habermas's thinking when he suggests (rightly, I believe) that religious fundamentalists are unlikely to adopt a change in attitude simply through encounter with philosophy and when he invokes a *religious* event—"the model of the post-Reformation change in epistemic attitudes that took place within the Christian churches of the West"—as an early modern example of the kind of "shift from a traditional to a more reflexive form of religious

---

[35] Habermas, "Reply to My Critics," 373.

[36] Habermas seems to put forward this idea when he claims: "Such [postsecular] cognitive presuppositions of an ethics of democratic citizenship show us the limits of a normative political theory that can justify only rights and duties. Learning processes can be fostered, but they cannot be morally or legally stipulated." Habermas, *Postmetaphysical Thinking II*, 222.

consciousness" he hopes will be further achieved within the contemporary context.[37] This example points to a third idea: that philosophy is unable to bring about the learning processes it calls for because what is required for such learning is not generalized political-theoretical statements but specific interventions within a multiplicity of particular domains; for example, theological claims that reject science and political equality in the name of a supposed direct relationship with God should be resisted by theological counterarguments, scientists who argue for the truth of atheism ought to be resisted by scientific counterarguments insisting on the boundaries of what can be scientifically known, and so on. Because "controversies with such opponents must be conducted within the proper disciplinary terrain," there are limits to what can be achieved by philosophy and its trans-disciplinary pretensions.[38] Finally, Habermas suggests that philosophy cannot fully bring about postsecular ethics because philosophy, especially in its liberal form, is already on the side of secular reason and for this reason unable to be the sole device that educates and persuades the religiously minded to participate as democratic citizens in a manner that affords equal respect to the secular and religious alike.[39]

Although Habermas does not make the point explicitly, the four reasons he provides for philosophy's inability to independently bring about postsecular learning processes anticipate, by way of contrast, the valuable function of *prophets of postsecularism*, who, unlike the philosopher Habermas contemplates, would instruct about ethical obligations above and beyond what is legally coercible; seek to convert and not simply convince; appeal to specific theological and other domains rather than to decontextualized, abstracted logic; and, in their charismatic and testimonial intensity, operate in a manner beyond secular reason.

At the same time, it needs to be emphasized that the prophet Habermas prepares the way for is only of the traditional type (a religious person speaking

---

[37] Habermas, 222.

[38] Habermas, *Between Naturalism and Religion*, 146.

[39] While applauding John Rawls's efforts in his later work to articulate a philosophy of liberal-democratic justice that might be acceptable within a context of religious pluralism, Habermas challenges Rawls's claim that this philosophy might be "free-standing" in the sense of being beholden to no specific comprehensive worldview. Although he shares Rawls's ambition to defend liberal democracy without appealing to a specific conception of the good life, Habermas nonetheless operates with "an awareness of the limits of normative arguments in a supposedly 'free-standing' political theory. For whether the liberal response to religious pluralism can be accepted by the citizens themselves depends not least on whether secular and religious citizens, from their respective points of view, are prepared to accept an interpretation of the relationship between faith and knowledge that first makes it possible for them to treat one another in a self-reflexive manner in the political arena" Habermas, 147.

to religious people), whereas the specific kind of postsecular prophet I am invoking here (who would address non-religious citizens) seems to be entirely outside the scope of Habermas's theoretical imagination. That is, in at least three of the four cases, when Habermas recognizes the need for extra-philosophical resources—to convert citizens to self-reflexivity, to operate in a specific theological domain, to get beyond secular reason—he understands the main target of these extra-philosophical appeals to be religious citizens not yet prepared to accept the constraints of a postsecular public sphere.[40] Habermas thus overlooks the possibility that prophetic resources also are needed to shake secularists out of intolerance and to motivate them to respectfully translate religious speech into a secular idiom. Habermas imagines that philosophy's confinement to secular reason is only a weakness in its incapacity to address certain religious communities, forgetting that if secularists are to overcome their hostility or indifference toward religion then they, too, will need to be confronted by religiously inspired speech, not just as something to translate from without, but more fundamentally as something that inspires from within the virtue and value of such acts of translation in the first place. This kind of postsecular prophetic speech would serve to convert the secular—not to religion per se, but to an appreciation of religion's humanity.

In the absence of prophets of the postsecular who principally address the non-religious, there is the danger that secularists will have insufficient motivation to take up the postsecular mentality Habermas recommends. After all, why *should* secular citizens—both aggressive secularists and merely indifferent ones—take

---

[40] With regard to Habermas's appreciation of the need to convert and not just convince citizens to adopt a postsecular mentality, his examples seem to be drawn exclusively from the religious side. In one passage, for instance, upon presenting the problem of political theory's inability to mandate postsecular learning processes, Habermas refers to "many Muslim communities" as the immediate context in which extra-philosophical learning will have to go on (*Postmetaphysical Thinking II*, 222). With regard to his insistence that philosophy is limited in its ability to bring about postsecularity because appeals are required from within specific domains, the specific domains he has in mind seem to be exclusively religious, as when he writes: "Religious citizens and communities must not only superficially adjust to the constitutional order. They are expected to appropriate the secular legitimation of constitutional principles under the very premises of their own faith. It is a well-known fact that the Catholic Church first pinned its colors to the mast of liberalism and democracy with the Second Vaticanum in 1965. And in Germany, the Protestant churches did not act differently" (Habermas, "A Post-Secular Society: What Does That Mean?," Reset Dialogues on Civilizations, September 16, 2008, https://www.resetdoc.org/story/a-post-secular-society-what-does-that-mean/). And with regard to the problem that philosophy transacts in secular reason and thus is not free-standing in the way Rawls claims, the clear implication of Habermas's analysis is that this is a problem only insofar as philosophy cannot hope to be fully persuasive to the standpoint of certain religious citizens. See footnote 39.

heed of religious speech uttered in the public sphere and aim to translate its meanings in secular terms? Why is Habermas, an atheist and defender of secular reason, keen to include religious utterances in the public sphere? One reason he presents is historical: reflection on the religious prehistory that inspired and shaped the contemporary liberal-democratic secular state (e.g., belief in equality before God served in numerous contexts as the foundation for the idea of political equality) is supposed to somehow motivate continued respectful heeding of religious communities today. But it is not clear how or why this historical honesty necessarily would have any contemporary relevance, especially insofar as it is possible to defend liberal democracy without any such religious appeals. Another argument that Habermas puts forward concerns the ethics of democratic inclusion. If secular citizens do not take seriously the utterances of the religious and merely tolerate them in the form of legal rights, this would produce no more than a modus vivendi between the secular and religious and therefore fail to achieve the "mutual recognition which is constitutive for shared citizenship." Here Habermas is sympathetic to the problem that some religious people are "neither willing nor able to divide their moral convictions and their vocabulary into profane and religious strands"—they cannot speak in a way abstracted from their religious faith—and so, for the sake of including such individuals as fellow citizens, it is important that they be able to express themselves in religiously laden speech.[41] But outside of its potential conflation of problem with solution (since the failure to attain mutual recognition is the starting point from which postsecular ethics begins), Habermas's appeal to a kind of democratically inspired benevolence, on the basis of which the non-religious genuinely attend to speech otherwise thought to be groundless, seems unlikely to have much traction.

Habermas's strongest reason for overcoming the secularist standpoint is that there is in fact secular value in religious speech. Religious speech has the capacity to generate solidarity that cannot be produced simply on the basis of secular reason alone.[42] Moreover, religious speech has potential cognitive content even for non-believers: when translated, it can play a productive role in contemporary political debates and, relatedly, it can uniquely articulate the sense of failure and incompleteness that besets any extant regime's efforts to realize free and equal

---

[41] Habermas, *Postmetaphysical Thinking II*, 223.

[42] Consider in this regard Habermas's point: "The decision to engage in action based on solidarity when faced with threats which can be averted only by collective efforts calls for more than insight into good reasons." Habermas, *An Awareness of What Is Missing: Faith and Reason in a Post-Secular Age* (Cambridge, UK: Polity, 2010), 18–19.

citizenship and other promises of modernity.[43] While I am sympathetic to these claims, one can still wonder why a secularist would find religious expression a compelling articulation of or inspiration for solidarity. And even if the content of religious utterances *can* be translated into secular speech and produce fresh insight, the time and mental energy required for this uncertain bounty, while they do not argue against the propriety of Habermas's recommendations, nonetheless remind us of the motivational deficits likely to inhibit secular citizens' willingness to take up such heedful attention of perspectives that, in their religiosity, seem alien.

The purpose of these criticisms of Habermas is not to dismiss his justifications for taking up a postsecular mentality but to suggest that these justifications are, by themselves, insufficient. What is almost altogether missing in Habermas's analysis—and what a prophet of the postsecular such as Dylan speaks to—is an additional motivation for secularists to take religion seriously: namely, that the religious other is not in fact entirely other, that because religiosity and atheism are choices, not truths, each *remains* viable at all times for all people, and, therefore, that in heeding the religious the non-religious can understand themselves to be engaging with not an alien with whom one can at best hope to establish solidaristic reciprocity via acts of translation, but a manifestation of one's *own* spiritual and religious capacities, which, even if they lie dormant, exist and can still function. There is only one instance in Habermas's writing of which I am aware that even gestures toward this idea.[44] But exegetical matters aside, the key point is to see the prophet of the postsecular as someone who brings about in the secular not a conventional religious mentality, but a newfound appreciation for religiosity that stems from the recognition that certain religious thoughts, commitments, concerns, and ideas could also be one's own.

---

[43] See, for example, Habermas, *Postmetaphysical Thinking II*, 223: "The democratic state should not rashly reduce the polyphonic complexity of the diverse public voices, because it cannot know whether to do so would be to cut society off from scarce resources for generating meanings and shaping identities. In particular, with regard to vulnerable social relations, religious traditions have the power to convincingly articulate moral sensitivities and solidaristic intuitions." Also see Habermas, "Pre-political Foundations of the Democratic Constitutional State?," 43–44. Further, whereas for Kant the limits of reason make room for faith, Habermas reinterprets this dynamic so that it instead "explains why enlightened reason unavoidably loses its grip on the images, preserved by religion, of the moral whole—of the Kingdom of God on earth—as collectively binding ideals. . . . Practical reason fails to fulfill its own vocation when it no longer has sufficient strength to awaken, and to keep awake, in the minds of secular subjects, an awareness of the violations of solidarity throughout the world, an awareness of what is missing, of what cries out to heaven." Habermas, *An Awareness of What Is Missing*, 19.

[44] "Citizens may not exclude the possibility that religious utterances contain semantic contents, *and even secret intuitions of their own*, that can be translated and introduced into secular discourse." Habermas, *Postmetaphysical Thinking II*, 223–24 (emphasis added).

Just as self-consciousness is, as Hegel has shown, inseparable from recognition of the other (since to be self-conscious is to consider how others would perceive oneself), the ultimate form of recognition of the other is the realization that this other could be you. This hypothetical recognition of the secular self in the religious other is the deepest and most powerful motivation for taking up postsecular ethics—especially as it pertains to overcoming a secularist mentality—and a chief achievement of prophets of the postsecular such as Dylan.

It is not just philosophy's transmission in the language of secular reason, but its characteristic dispassionate and detached tone, that makes it unable to fully bring about acknowledgment from secularists of their own genuine, if muted, religious possibilities. The confrontational vitriol distinctive of prophetic speech has an important role to play in this context. The process by which a prophet of the postsecular alerts secularists to the potentiality of their own religiosity is not strictly friendly but involves various forms of spiritual provocation and challenge. Even if the goal remains a mutual respect and sympathetic heeding between the religious and non-religious, the means toward this harmonious end cannot themselves always be harmonious.

The need for vitriol stems from the fact that there are inevitable asymmetries between the treatment of religious and non-religious constituencies in even a relatively well-ordered liberal-democratic state. I have discussed some of these asymmetries above—for example, the way in which the political and educational systems of contemporary liberal-democratic secular regimes are governed much more by secular-rational norms, a circumstance that might be appropriate but is nonetheless disproportionately burdensome for certain religious people. Habermas's own theory reflects these asymmetries as well: the formal public sphere is restricted to secular-rational appeals and thus excludes exclusively religious speech; the self-reflexivity he prizes as intrinsic to the learning process both religionists and secularists must undergo seems itself to be a secular value;[45] and the cognitive burdens placed upon the religious arguably are heavier than those placed on the non-religious, since whereas the religious must accept modern science and a non-theological state, the non-religious, even when translating religious utterances into a secular register, never have to overcome their own disbelief in any religious teaching.[46]

---

[45] On this point, see Amy Allen, "Having One's Cake and Eating It Too: Habermas' Genealogy of Postsecular Reason," in *Habermas and Religion*, 150, 152. In making this claim, Allen draws attention to Habermas's own words: "the capacity for decentering one's own perspectives, self-reflection, and a self-critical distancing from one's own tradition" is one of the West's "greatest cultural achievements." Habermas, *Religion and Rationality: Essays on Reason, God, and Modernity* (Cambridge, MA: MIT Press, 2002), 154.

[46] Allen, for example, refers to "a residual asymmetry in Habermas' account of . . . cognitive burdens" ("Having One's Cake and Eating It Too," 149). J. M. Bernstein likewise argues that these

Such considerations have led numerous critics to find fatal weaknesses in Habermas's account and to suggest that his theory fails to be authentically postsecular. In the face of such criticism, Habermas has denied that there are asymmetries within his philosophy of postsecularism.[47] It strikes me that both sides are mistaken: there are indeed asymmetries, but these do not in themselves invalidate Habermas's proposals or, more generally, a liberal-democratic state that seeks accommodation with religionists in the way that Habermas describes. An arrangement can be just—as well as genuinely postsecular—without being symmetrical. What the asymmetries do indicate, however, is the enduring threat of a secularist mentality surviving even in the context of the institutional structures and practices Habermas recommends. In his critique of Habermas, J. M. Bernstein observes that Habermas's postsecular proposals, despite themselves, denature religion but not non-religion: "the burdens on the religious believer are denaturing of faith, while, whatever the burdens on the secular citizen, they do not denature her secular commitments." For this reason, he claims that Habermas's theory is not entitled to describe itself as postsecular.[48] While I do not think this critique disqualifies the postsecular credentials of Habermas's theory, Bernstein's point is helpful in reminding us how the mere institutional and translational practices Habermas recommends are not enough to bring about the postsecular change in consciousness he supports. In order to ensure that the denaturing of religiosity is complemented by the denaturing of non-religiosity, confrontational prophetic voices are needed—not to convert the secular but to force them to face the contingency of their atheism, a contingency that is always in danger of being occluded by the dominance of secular reason within a liberal-democratic society and, of course, within philosophy itself. One of the main functions of a prophet of postsecularism is to accomplish this not

burdens are uneven, with those upon the secularist as "almost negligible." Bernstein, "Forgetting Isaac: Faith and the Philosophical Impossibility of a Postsecular Society," in *Habermas and Religion*, 154. Habermas denies such asymmetry but nonetheless acknowledges that whereas certain kinds of religious citizens (fundamentalists) need to adjust their beliefs, secular citizens within a postsecular framework do not have to overcome their non-religiosity in any way: "Secular citizens can meet this obligation [of postsecularism] without denying their own disbelief in any kind of religious teaching. They are only asked not to exclude the possibility that religious speech might contain traces of a lost or repressed, or otherwise unavailable, normative intuition that is compelling and still awaits a saving translation" (Habermas, "Reply to My Critics," in *Habermas and Religion*, 372).

[47] See, for example, Habermas, *Between Naturalism and Religion*, 143: "Democratic citizenship assumes a mentality on the part of secular citizens that is no less demanding than the corresponding mentality of their religious counterparts." The non-religious, he emphasizes, must carry out "a self-reflexive overcoming of a rigid and exclusive secularist self-understanding of modernity" that is "no less cognitively exacting than the adaptation of religious consciousness to the challenges of an environment that is becoming progressively more secular" (138–39).

[48] Bernstein, "Forgetting Isaac," 159.

by rejecting secular reason but by exposing, through extrarational charismatic authority, how those who wish to transact strictly in secular reason are making a merely existential—as opposed to a "modern," "natural," "intelligent," or otherwise superior—choice.

The prophet of the postsecular thus not only motivates the acts of translation Habermas supports as central to secular citizens' ethical obligations in a postsecular society but also helps ensure that such acts of translation are not allowed to take place via the covert secularistic tendencies numerous critics have found unaddressed in Habermas's theory. The denaturalization of religiosity requires more than Habermas's institutional and translational proposals can accomplish, and it is within this lacuna in Habermas's thinking that the prophet of the postsecular plays an important role. The need to perpetually *combat* the inherent asymmetries within the liberal-democratic state means that the advocacy of postsecular ethics cannot depend on the dispassionate discourse of secular reason alone. It requires as well the adversarial fire of the prophetic conscience.

Charles Taylor and the Postsecular

Charles Taylor is a leading philosopher of the postsecular who, along with Habermas, has profoundly influenced its contours. Although Taylor is more concerned with the trajectory of Western history over the last half millennium than with institutional design, he nonetheless supports political structures roughly equivalent to Habermas's proposals.[49] More deeply, Taylor parallels Habermas in articulating the need, central to a postsecular mindset, for religious and non-religious citizens to find ways to cooperate under conditions of mutual respect. Taylor calls on all citizens—from the extremes of atheistic materialism and religious orthodoxy to those in between—to be able to operate at two different levels: an engaged perspective in which one acts according to one's religious/non-religious position and a disengaged standpoint in which one recognizes the contingency and non-naturalness of one's standpoint and thus the integrity of radically divergent spiritual alternatives.[50] Taylor likewise shares Habermas's view that solidarity is an urgent need of democratic societies and a

---

[49] Charles Taylor, "Why We Need a Radical Redefinition of Secularism," in *The Power of Religion in the Public Sphere*, ed. Eduardo Mendieta and Jonathan VanAntwerpen (New York: Columbia University Press, 2011), 49–53. For instance, Taylor argues that religious language should not be part of "the official language of the state: the language in which legislative, administrative decrees, and court judgments must be couched" (50).

[50] Charles Taylor, *A Secular Age* (Cambridge, MA: Belknap Press of Harvard University Press, 2007), 12.

goal that makes the achievement of postsecular respect between religious and non-religious people especially important.[51]

But also like Habermas, albeit in a different way, Taylor reveals the limits of a purely philosophical approach to postsecular ethics. One element of these limits concerns the circumstance that even though Taylor is a theist, this personal aspect is kept in abeyance; that is, rather than exploit the fact that he is an extremely well-regarded leading practitioner of secular reason who also happens to be a religious believer—and thus in his own person testify to the dignity and coequal integrity of the twin calls of secularism and religiosity—Taylor opts to frame his appeals strictly in the impersonal, argument-driven idiom of contemporary philosophical speech.[52] There is good reason for this reticence, no doubt, as it helps buttress the secular-rational credentials of his arguments, but Taylor nonetheless forgoes an alternate fruitful path, whereby the religious testimony of someone celebrated within secular society for his mastery of secular-rational expression (logic, encyclopedic historical learning, and dispassionate scholarship) would dramatize, in a concrete and immediate way, the endurance of an extrarational religious faith. Instead, Taylor manifests the detachment of philosophy—its restrained non-disclosure of the lived experience of the author—over and against the vitality of a first-person testimonial. The decision is all the more stark because it is nonetheless widely known—and Taylor does not conceal—that he is a theist. But this personal perspective never becomes the grounds of his claims. Thus, even though one of the highest ambitions of Taylor's work on religion is to show that someone committed to modern science, liberal-democratic governance focused on maximizing human welfare, philosophical reason, and social science can still be a believer, his personal truth of embodying just this combination is left unarticulated within his study of religion. This means both that Taylor has no special credibility for atheists (because he can be read as a theist) and that this theism nonetheless plays no role in his arguments for postsecular ethics.

Beyond this absence of an otherwise available prophetic potential, Taylor's philosophy of postsecularism is further attenuated by an imbalance, which itself

---

[51] Taylor, "Why We Need a Radical Redefinition of Secularism," 44.

[52] To be sure, at the conclusion of his *Sources of the Self*, Taylor shares his "hunch . . . that great as the power of naturalist sources might be, the potential of a certain theistic perspective is incomparably greater" and he likewise expresses "a hope that I see implicit in Judeo-Christian theism . . . and in its central promise of a divine affirmation of the human, more total than humans can ever attain unaided." But Taylor's support for theism here is not only exceedingly brief but immediately attenuated by his admission that his reflections lack scholarly and philosophical authority: that his theism is an "unsupported assertion," that he is incapable of demonstrating it, and that he has refrained from expressing his theism through the vast majority of the book "partly out of delicacy, but largely out of lack of arguments." Charles Taylor, *Sources of the Self: The Making of Modern Identity* (Cambridge, MA: Harvard University Press, 1989), 517–18, 520–21.

reminds us of the need for the prophetic standpoint Taylor does not take up. This imbalance emerges out of the particular historical narrative Taylor emphasizes in his account of postsecularism in *A Secular Age*, his most significant contribution to the philosophy of religion. Taylor's central point in *A Secular Age* is to argue for moving beyond two traditional conceptions of secularism (the reduction of religious belief and the neutrality of the state toward religion) so as to also appreciate a third, *postsecular* conception of secularity as a circumstance in which religious people have to practice their religion in newfound cognizance that non-religious ways of life are plausible. Whereas in earlier times of more bounded communities and more pervasive religious cultures, adherents of religion could encounter their religion as something natural, obvious, and uncontested, Taylor argues that today's religious individuals increasingly must practice their faiths in awareness of—and often in periodic participation within—an alternate framework, which Taylor calls "the immanent frame," that dispenses with religion as a basis of explanation or understanding. The immanent frame—a sphere of life conducted entirely in reference to instrumental rationality, humanist values, natural-scientific interpretations of the universe, and forms of governance stripped of any religious grounding or purpose—is a modality of being some fully inhabit and others aim to resist, but Taylor's point is that it is something *all* Westerners have become aware of as a possibility and that even the religious must operate within its parameters for significant portions of their day-to-day lives. I mean neither to dispute the accuracy of Taylor's account of the immanent frame that has arisen in the West over the last five hundred years, nor to deny his central arguments about how the pervasiveness of the frame in contemporary Western culture dramatically conditions the experience of religiosity today. But there is nonetheless an unnecessary imbalance promoted by Taylor's historical account that leads him to emphasize only one half of postsecular ethics (the self-reflexivity the immanent frame generates for the religious, i.e., their unprecedented awareness of a non-religious frame of existence that they *elect* not to occupy), leaving far less explored the parallel postsecular self-awareness of the non-religious (who themselves ought to conceive of their non-religiosity as no less contingent or "chosen" than the religiosity they do not practice).

To get a sense of this imbalance, consider some of Taylor's key statements of his overarching purpose in *A Secular Age*:

> The change I want to define and trace is one which takes us from a society in which it was virtually impossible not to believe in God, to one in which faith, even for the staunchest believer, is one human possibility among others. I may find it inconceivable that I would abandon my faith, but there are others, including possibly some very close to me, whose way of living I cannot in all honesty just dismiss as depraved, or

blind, or unworthy, who have no faith (at least not in God, or the transcendent). Belief in God is no longer axiomatic. There are alternatives.
And this will also likely mean that at least in certain milieux, it may be
hard to sustain one's faith.[53]

We have . . . changed from a condition in which belief was the default
option, not just for the naïve but also for those who knew, considered,
talked about atheism; to a condition in which for more and more people
unbelieving construals seem at first blush the only plausible ones.[54]

One way to put the question that I want to answer here is this: why
was it virtually impossible not to believe in God in, say, 1500 in our
Western society, while in 2000 many of us find this not only easy, but
even inescapable.[55]

What Taylor does not so much address is the opposite movement: namely, non-
religious people's increased attention to the fact that their lack of religion is but a
contingency—a choice and not a truth—and thus that religiosity remains a genuine
alternative. Perhaps this imbalance stems from Taylor's descriptivism: the impact
of postsecularism that he does predominantly address (its effect on the religious) is
something that is already occurring, indeed steadily growing for centuries, whereas
the parallel impact of postsecularism that he largely ignores (its effect on atheists)
is something that *ought* to occur but in fact may not be happening. Of course, this
circumstance further highlights the need for greater attention to the latter dynamic.
Yet Taylor marginalizes this concern, disproportionately emphasizing the meaning
of postsecularism for people of faith, even if its correspondent meaning for the non-
religious is, as a matter of ethics, no less fundamental.

To be sure, Taylor's marginalization is by no means complete. To a meaningful extent, he does, after all, aim to contest aggressive secularist thinking.
Crucially, Taylor insists that the immanent frame that we all share can be *spun* in
two different, equally plausible ways. When it is "closed," those who live within
the immanent frame make its features—secular reason, naturalistic explanation
for all phenomena, disconnection from considerations of the spiritual or divine,
strictly humanistic conceptions of ethics and justice according to which human
flourishing is the only or highest good—the limiting parameters within which
they operate. Taylor argues, however, that there is nothing intrinsic in the immanent frame that makes an "open" standpoint any less plausible. The immanent

[53] Taylor, *A Secular Age*, 3.
[54] Taylor, 12.
[55] Taylor, 25.

frame is a place we all occupy, but our occupying it does not require that we close ourselves off to "transcendence." Those who see the immanent frame as open recognize that its features do not themselves undermine the integrity of religious belief and other aspirations for transcendence, even if the immanent frame will condition how these are experienced and practiced. On the basis of this reasoning, Taylor is led to identify and criticize what he calls "closed world structures" (CWSs)—that is, secularist narratives that interpret the loss of religion as a kind of maturation and thus wrongly understand the closed rendering of the immanent frame as the only possible one. Specifically, Taylor singles out and aims to undermine the plausibility of four such narratives: the idea that science has shown that God does not exist or at least that religion is irrelevant to human life; the idea that secularism means subtraction (i.e., jettisoning speculative, unverifiable religious and metaphysical illusions); the idea that the achievement of "modern political-moral spaces"—in which discrete individuals collectively pursue liberty, power, mutual benefit, and reason—requires a liberation from religious institutions and values; and the idea that rejection of religion is concomitant with becoming an autonomous self who takes personal responsibility for deciding what ultimate values to heed.[56] While the specific details of Taylor's arguments here are varied and complex, the basic point is straightforward: in challenging these four narratives, Taylor means to challenge any sense that the closed spin on the immanent frame is natural or obvious.

Yet Taylor's contestation of these closed-world structures does not lead him to sufficiently address the crucial second prong of postsecularism: not the disciplining of religious communities to accept the contingency and non-superiority of religiosity, but the parallel disciplining of the non-religious to recognize the same regarding their non-religiosity. Rather than directly confront the situation of an atheist having to acknowledge the contingency (i.e., non-naturalness and non-superiority) of his or her view—that is, rather than force the atheist to acknowledge that atheism and theism remain equally plausible choices that any individual at any time might elect to pursue—Taylor rests his case on claims that, even if related to this, still fall short. Specifically, Taylor ends up focusing on two tangential issues, which in effect leave the militant atheist off the hook.

First, as I have explained, Taylor's chief challenge to secularist thinking is to argue that the immanent frame does not in itself preclude the pursuit and attainment of religiosity or other states of spiritual transcendence. But this challenge is not quite equivalent to what would be the postsecularist challenge par excellence: challenging the non-believer to face his or her non-belief as "chosen" in

---

[56] Taylor, 589–90; also see 551–89.

the specific way I am rendering that term. The difference is reflected when Taylor argues that the decision about whether the immanent frame is open or closed (which he thinks we all face) is not the same as the decision between religious faith and unbelief (which he thinks few actually face): "We don't stand there [in the face of this latter question], because . . . the immanent frame [is] itself not usually, or even mainly a set of *beliefs* which we entertain about our predicament, however it may have started out; rather it is the sensed context in which we develop our beliefs."[57] Taylor thus understands the challenge he does lodge against secularists (questioning the necessity of closed readings of the immanent frame) as something distinct from the more fundamental postsecular challenge against secularists he mostly does *not* take up (questioning secularists' sense of their non-belief as natural, true, or otherwise superior). Taylor's tepidness in this regard is reflected when he importantly clarifies the limited ambition of his critique of the so-called closed-world structures: "All CWSs may be illegitimate, and yet there may be nothing beyond the immanent frame. I will not be arguing either for or against an open or closed reading, just trying to dissipate the false aura of the obvious that surrounds one of these."[58] The tepidness is twofold: Taylor is not only contesting a closed reading of the immanent frame (which we have just seen is not the same as directly contesting a secularist's excessive self-confidence about the naturalness or superiority of his or her atheism) but also arguing that doing so does not establish the integrity of a reality beyond the immanent frame. We can admire Taylor's restraint and judiciousness here, but their effect is avoidance of what is, for the prophet of the postsecular, a crucial purpose: a direct combating of secularists' failure to understand religiosity as a potential they themselves possess and which, if they do not actualize it, limits them only for existential reasons, not genuinely cognitive or moral ones. Taylor's key idea that both open and closed readings of the immanent frame are equally plausible is, in the final analysis, a claim about how to understand the meaning of Western history over the last five hundred years—an argument that, properly understood, this history has not made religiosity suspect or inferior to non-religiosity. But this sweeping historical survey is ultimately orthogonal to the matter of compelling secularists to recognize that religiosity remains plausible *for them*.

The second way in which Taylor's challenge to secularist thinking still leaves the militant atheist off the hook is that while it appears to suggest that individuals today, when they honestly reflect upon their situation, are caught between the equally plausible claims of religious and non-religious modes of being—the postsecular situation distilled into its ethical essence—in fact Taylor

[57] Taylor, 549.
[58] Taylor, 551.

almost altogether minimizes this situation to one of cultural insignificance. One of Taylor's recurrent themes in his analysis of contemporary Western society is that individuals today are unprecedently "cross-pressured" between the poles of militant atheism and fundamentalist religious belief. While this idea might seem to refer to postsecular individuals who must wrestle with the competing claims of religion and non-religion as standpoints of coeval, coequal existential integrity, Taylor's most precise rendering of the concept drains it of this very meaning: "Cross pressure doesn't mean that all or even most people in this culture ['Western culture today'] feel torn, but rather that virtually all positions held are drawn to define themselves at least partly in relation to these extremes [the extremes of 'orthodox religion' and 'hard-line materialistic atheism']."[59] Rather than referring to the situation of confronting the rival calls of faith and unbelief simultaneously, the concept of cross pressure is defined to mean only that the self-definition of any community of belief (or non-belief) is based upon distinction vis-à-vis other alternatives.

It is not that Taylor is altogether unaware of the ultimate postsecular standpoint—the circumstance of approaching the opposing claims of religion and non-religion as equally plausible possibilities—but that he treats this standpoint as both extremely rare (few actually do it) and without normative emphasis (there is no sense in Taylor's analysis that this perspective is one we should either try to occupy or at least recognize as emblematic of the authentic truth of our existential situation regarding religion). To be sure, Taylor evinces respect and appreciation for William James, who he thinks did occupy this standpoint and eloquently described it. But James is not treated as exemplary in an ethical way.[60] While Taylor admires James's position, the fact that he does not consider it a kind of ethical lodestar is confirmed when Taylor provides two further examples of the experience of being caught between the twin calls of faith and unbelief— two instances of what it might mean "to stand here . . . [and] be at the mid-point of the cross-pressures that define our culture"[61]—neither of which contains any postsecular disciplining of would-be secularists. One of these examples involves

[59] Taylor, 676.

[60] Part of the reason for this is that Taylor treats James's position as highly exceptional, without any expectation that it be a model for everyone else: "Standing in the Jamesian open space requires that you have gone farther . . . and can actually feel some of the force of each opposing position. But so far apart are belief and unbelief, openness and closure here, that this feat is relatively rare. Most of us are . . . either unable to see how the other view makes sense at all, or else struggling to make sense of it." Taylor, *A Secular Age*, 549. Likewise, in an earlier work, Taylor emphasizes James's "very exceptional qualities" that enabled him to experience and describe being at the cusp between faith and unbelief. Taylor, *Varieties of Religion Today: William James Revisited* (Cambridge, MA: Harvard University Press, 2002), 59.

[61] Taylor, *A Secular Age*, 592.

those who, non-believing, nonetheless find themselves mourning the loss of God, as in Thomas Hardy's poem "God's Funeral" and a broader tradition—especially prominent in the nineteenth century—articulating the loss of God in terms of regret and nostalgia.[62] The second concerns those who, though "haunted by a sense that the universe might after all be as meaningless as the most reductive materialism describes," still are moved "towards at least some search for spiritual meaning, and often towards God." Such individuals—figures like Goethe, Blake, Dostoevsky, and Milosz—"feel that their [religious] vision has to struggle against this flat and empty world; they fear that their strong desire for God, or for eternity, might after all be the self-induced illusion that materialists claim it to be."[63] I have no doubt that these two examples reference situations of cultural importance and that they represent a subtle melding of religious and non-religious standpoints. It is true, after all, that one important meaning of postsecularism is precisely the proliferation of spiritual attitudes that break down easy divisions between the religious and non-religious—and both examples signify precisely this. But postsecularism is not just a description of novel and emergent spiritual perspectives that combine religious and non-religious sensibilities in surprising ways. As an ethical paradigm, postsecularism is a call for both the non-religious and adherents of traditional and familiar religious perspectives to recognize each other as coequal citizens worthy of mutual respect and attention. Taylor occludes this ethical dimension when he treats the experience of being simultaneously open to both belief and unbelief—of recognizing the religious or non-religious other in oneself—as rare and when he interprets it in such a fashion that it no longer challenges the overconfidence of one side over the other.

Taylor thus develops the idea of the postsecular such that it stands much more for the circumstance of religious people having to confront the contingency and embattlement of their faiths than it does for the parallel situation of non-religious individuals having to acknowledge, as a matter of ethical incumbency, that their lack of religion is no more true, sensible, or natural than the theist's position. Even if, strictly speaking, Taylor wants to affirm that *all* citizens need to face the contingency of their perspectives—"all see their options as one among many"[64]—numerous aspects of his work nonetheless render the postsecular as a state of affairs in which the religious are challenged but the non-religious are not. My point is not to suggest that Taylor would be opposed to the mission of a prophet of the postsecular, only that he does not play this role and

---

[62] On this tradition, see A. N. Wilson, *God's Funeral: The Decline of Faith in Western Civilization* (New York: Norton, 1999).

[63] Taylor, *A Secular Age*, 593.

[64] Taylor, 470; also see 11, 21.

that his philosophical intervention, despite its virtues, dramatizes the need for such a figure.

Having demonstrated the shortcomings of the most influential philosophical meditations on the postsecular, I now turn to Dylan as a prophet of the postsecular. Going beyond Habermas and Taylor, Dylan contests secularist overconfidence by challenging secularists to recognize their own latent religiosity as a plausible existential possibility and one that ought to inculcate in them greater respect and appreciation for traditional religious belief. Dylan makes at least four such challenges in this regard. I pursue these in sections II.3–II.6.

II.3. Gotta Serve Somebody: Dylan's Recovery of the Religious Vocation

At the root of Dylan's capacity to be a prophet of the postsecular who challenges secularists is the fact that he has had tremendous credibility among the non-religious. Especially in the period before his conversion, Dylan seemed to exemplify both skepticism toward all dubious sources of authority (including religious ones) and the confident, vital ability to exist and operate as an independent individual unbuttressed by soothing yet false metaphysical illusions. Both the skepticism and the individualism are perhaps most strikingly declared in Dylan's 1964 song "It's Alright, Ma (I'm Only Bleeding)," which might be his most essential creation from the 1960s due to its splendid imagery and the fact that, more than any other work from this period, it seems to articulate his over-arching philosophy at this time in his life.[65] In this song, Dylan presents himself as a strong agent, capable of seeing through the mendacity in contemporary culture and making his way on his own terms. Declaring "Propaganda, all is phony," Dylan lacerates the metaphysical pretension that ultimate reality might be deciphered ("To understand you know too soon / There is no sense in trying") as well as various external would-be authorities that likewise pretend to have answers but in fact are either corrupted by hypocrisy ("Advertising signs they

---

[65] Dylan himself signals its importance when he chose to perform it as his contribution to a 1992 concert and live album celebrating his thirty years as a recording artist, which included covers of his music by more than two dozen highly prominent musicians. See *The 30th Anniversary Concert Celebration*, recorded October 16, 1992, at Madison Square Garden, New York, NY, Columbia, 1992, compact disc. He also highlights its significance in a 2004 interview with Ed Bradley for *60 Minutes*, in which he singles out the song to exemplify the kind of poetry of which he no longer is capable— adding, though, that he can now do "other things." Likewise, consider that in a 1997 interview, in which Dylan reflects, "I've written some songs that I look at, and they just give me a sense of awe," the one concrete example he provides is "It's Alright, Ma." Cott, "Interview with John Pareles, *New York Times*, September 28, 1997," in *Essential Interviews*, 420.

con / You into thinking you're the one / That can do what's never been done";
"Teachers teach that knowledge waits / Can lead to hundred-dollar plates";
those who dare "To push fake morals, insult, and stare"; those who "Tell nothing
except who to idolize") or simply unable to deliver (as in "a trembling distant
voice, unclear / Startles your sleeping ears to hear / That somebody thinks they
really found you").

False assertions of religious piety play an important role in Dylan's diagnosis of phoniness. Dylan excoriates "preachers [who] preach of evil fates." He
lambasts political parties, which are really "social clubs in drag disguise," for
being exclusionary and intolerant yet nonetheless comfortable in saying of their
idols "God bless him." Most pointedly, Dylan identifies and rejects fake claims
about divinity within the culture:

> My eyes collide head-on with stuffed
> Graveyards, false gods, I scuff

And also the cynical commercialization of religion by would-be "human gods":

> Disillusioned words like bullets bark
> As human gods aim for their mark
> Make everything from toy guns that spark
> To flesh-colored Christs that glow in the dark
> It's easy to see without looking too far
> That not much is really sacred

Most brutally, Dylan suggests that an insistent defense of metaphysical notions,
such as religious ones, is as pointlessly earnest and sexless as it is foolhardy and
fanatical:

> While them that defend what they cannot see
> With a killer's pride, security
> It blows the minds most bitterly
> For them that think death's honesty
> Won't fall upon them naturally
> Life sometimes must get lonely

Seen in light of Dylan's later religious conversion, one can detect what in
fact is restrained and measured in his critique of religion here: he takes aim,
for instance, at "false gods," not God; "not much is really sacred" rather than
nothing at all; and so on. But my point in this context is not to take a stand
on the question of how utterly sharp Dylan's later conversion was—whether,

as seems likely, there already were diffuse and unformed religious sensibilities at work within his earlier period—but simply to emphasize how Dylan in the mid-1960s, as he achieved unprecedented fame as a countercultural icon, seemed to stand for the importance of individuals making their own decisions and pursuing their own sense of life's values over and against the various false messages emanating from the broader culture, including from religious sources. Rejecting this falsity, Dylan in "It's Alright, Ma" powerfully exhorts his listeners to live according to their own lights and presents himself as exemplifying just this capacity:

> An' though the rules of the road have been lodged
> It's only people's games that you got to dodge
> And it's alright, Ma, I can make it

And:

> A question in your nerves is lit
> Yet you know there is no answer fit
> To satisfy, insure you not to quit
> To keep it in your mind and not forget
> That it is not he or she or them or it
> That you belong to

And:

> But I mean no harm nor put fault
> On anyone that lives in a vault
> But it's alright, Ma, if I can't please him

Dylan in the mid-60s, then, testifies to what can be described as the *secular vocational ideal*—the ideal of each individual finding his or her purpose and setting out to fulfill that purpose without any sense that one's vocation is universal or even explicable or justifiable to anyone else. In doing so, he offers only a supremely poetic, intelligent, and caustic account of what in fact is a fundamental ideal within liberal-democratic society: the promise that individuals be able to identify and pursue work that is *personally* meaningful, usually rendered in terms of familiar professional careers. I refer to the *secular* conception of the vocational ideal to differentiate it from an older, more originary *religious* conceptualization of the vocation. One of the recurrent features of a secular society is that it divests formerly religious concepts and practices of religious content. Nowhere is this more apparent than with regard to the idea of a vocation—which initially had a primary meaning as service to God, either directly or through work in-tended to realize divine purposes in the world—but today, in common parlance, refers simply to one's work within a profession. If the religious meaning im-plied duty to what lies above and beyond us, the secular one implies individual freedom and choice to live in accordance with one's own proclivities. If the re-ligious meaning, with its appeal to God, points to a unified source of value for all humanity, the secular concept implies diversity and even conflict, since not only might our vocations be different from each other but they also may seek opposed purposes. Socioeconomically, if the religious version of the vocation invokes, in its reference to the divine, something that might transcend sublunary human divisions, the secular version, by contrast, is profoundly connected with educational and economic privilege: only some get to have professions, with the rest confined to mere jobs. Finally, whereas the original, religious conception involves meditation on one's moral duty, the secular conception involves deci-sion about which way of life will be *personally* most fulfilling and meaningful. In "It's Alright, Ma," along with other works and statements, especially from the 1960s and early 1970s, Dylan expresses the intense individualism underlying the secular vocational ideal.[66]

But the contemporary secular conception of the vocation is not just different from its traditional religious rendering; it also has been philosophized, experi-enced, and practiced as being *opposed* to the religious conception—that is, as being intimately connected to a vision of the world that sees religion as ves-tigial, irrational, unnatural, or otherwise inferior to a non-religious sensibility. In other words, there are secular*ist* aspects of the secular vocation. Max Weber not only provides the most philosophically deep articulation of the contempo-rary secular vocational ideal but also presents the logic of this ideal in a manner in which its anti-religious elements are clearly perceptible. For Weber, the eth-ical urgency of finding a vocation arises precisely as belief in religion, and the all-encompassing direction it can provide, wanes. That is to say, Weber argues that in a world in which it no longer is compelling to think that one's ethical behavior might be guided by the comprehensive worldview of a universal reli-gion of salvation, dedication to a vocation becomes the best remaining ethical

---

[66] Many later statements also underline the importance of finding and pursuing individually meaningful work, though in some cases they are now infused with religious elements. In 1997, describing the process of making the album *Time Out of Mind*, Dylan discusses how he repeatedly considered the injunction (which has its source in John 9:4) "Work while the day lasts, because the night of death cometh when no man can work," claiming that "this one phrase was going through my head" (Cott, "Interview with John Pareles," in *Essential Interviews*, 417). In a 2015 interview, Dylan fully endorses the view that "productive work is a kind of salvation." Robert Love, "Bob Dylan Uncut," *AARP: The Magazine*, February/March 2015, 36.

possibility for a meaningful and responsible human life.[67] It is a virtue of Weber's theory of the vocation that it attends to how vocational life is irreducible to self-authorship, usually leading individuals to affiliate themselves, either explicitly or implicitly, with a specific, more or less permanent set of external values—for example, an artist is committed to beauty, a scientist to truth, a bureaucrat to instrumental rationality, a politician to an ethics of responsibility (i.e., a willingness to transgress conventional moral norms when doing so serves the populace), and so forth. But Weber presents this process of allegiance to a higher set of values in a manner clearly at odds with traditional and orthodox monotheistic religious belief. Weber insists on the metaphor of *polytheism* to describe the dynamics of vocational life. Every vocational choice in his view requires that an individual follow a specific "god" (i.e., a particular value system) but in doing so also violate other "gods" (representing not just different but opposing, and equally legitimate, values). A political leader, for example, rejects the value of employing only morally pure means. A pacifist, by contrast, rejects the value of responsibly administering violence within the state. But there is no way to arbitrate between them. Instead, one must accept the struggle between the "gods" as inevitable and permanent. Mature vocational life means, for Weber, identifying which god you serve, which you are destined to offend, and overcoming any naïve belief that your work might uphold a universal, singularly authoritative set of normative commitments. The traditional vocational question—how can I serve a *universal* God?—is thus rejected by Weber in the name of committing oneself to only a partial set of values that cannot claim comprehensiveness or any kind of complete authority. To deny this metaphorical polytheism in the name of a genuinely religious theism—or, more precisely, to invoke the traditional and originary conception of the vocation as service to a monotheistic god (i.e., to a singular and universally authoritative set of values)—is denigrated by Weber as both *unmanly* (for refusing to acknowledge endless struggle against competing, equally valid value systems as definitive of the human condition) and *vestigial* (since it is inconsistent with the "fate of the times," the true meaning of which for Weber is acceptance of the non-existence of God or other universal moral frameworks).[68] This denigration is not incidental to Weber's theory of the vocation but essential to it. For Weber, what had been central to the traditional,

---

[67] See Jeffrey Edward Green, "Two Meanings of Disenchantment: Sociological Condition vs. Philosophical Act—Reassessing Max Weber's Thesis of the Disenchantment of the World," *Philosophy & Theology* 17, no. 1–2 (2007): 63–64.

[68] Consider Weber's claim: "To anyone who is unable to endure the fate of the age like a man we must say that he should return to the welcoming and merciful embrace of the old churches—simply, silently, and without any of the usual public bluster of the renegade. They will surely not make it hard for him." Weber, "Science as a Vocation," 30.

religiously infused conception of vocation—identifying one's particular duty vis-à-vis a transcendent and universal source of value—is rendered antithetical to the allegedly true, modern, secular conception of the vocation, for which the definitive human act is not *identification* of externally imposed duties but existential *decision* about what type of individual one should be. Indeed, the key ethical consequence that Weber derives from his account of vocationalism is the decision itself: to select which god to follow and which to offend, to specialize, and to thereby avoid the false universalism (and endless experimentation) that prevents genuine vocational choice. According to this type of thinking, then, moral universalism is not just an old-fashioned and unconvincing account of one's vocation, but an approach toward vocationalism that interferes with the "genuine" modern variant and that therefore needs to be actively opposed.

This secularist aspect of the contemporary understanding of the vocation is hardly particular to Weber but is reflected in the prevailing tendency to reduce vocationalism to professional choice and, relatedly, in the proliferation of psychological and pedagogical discourses on the vocation that render the religious conception of the vocation a practical impossibility. The secularist rendering of the vocation is reflected, too, in the great degree to which it assumed that the process of figuring out one's vocation is above all a private matter and not one based on the determination of universal ethical obligation.

Dylan's conversion in the late 1970s leads him to challenge precisely these aspects of the secular vocation and in effect recover the integrity of the competing idea of the religious vocation, in which individual fulfillment is understood to involve consideration of what is required to serve God or, by extension, the dictates of universal justice. This challenge is postsecular in character because the effect of Dylan's intervention is less to demand, as a condition of vocational integrity, adherence to divine justice, but rather to demonstrate that the religious rendering of the vocation is not rightly seen as being obviated by contemporary secular culture: to the extent one decides to pursue a vocation at all, the religious rendering is as plausible as the secular one. Given Dylan's prior status as a darling of secular, anti-religious culture, his move here has both authority and force.

How does Dylan resist the secularist reduction of the vocation? Following Habermas and the philosophical approach to postsecularism he represents, one strategy could have been to alert the secularist to the "theological origins of modernity," which in this context would mean emphasizing both the religious history of the contemporary concept of the vocation (its original formulation as an inherently theistic notion) and the fact that Weberian decisionism (and existentialism more generally) has its ultimate roots in the religious idea of revelation, since the phenomenon of a radical, extrarational choice inexplicable to others but still somehow authoritative for the individual is modeled within the existentialist tradition in God's call to Abraham, Moses, and other prophets.[69] But Dylan, as a prophet of postsecularism, goes further than this. In the period of his conversion and afterward, he reintroduces the religious conception to challenge the self-confidence of the secularist variant. That is, for Dylan, it is not just that the idea of the vocation *used to mean* service to God, but that anyone who takes seriously the notion of the vocation today ought to continue to at least consider the God's eye perspective.

To recognize Dylan's postsecular move here, it is important to reiterate that in his first two decades as a public figure, he seems to subscribe to something like the Weberian secular vocational ideal. In key works like "It's Alright, Ma," as we have seen, the call to find direction—to abide by the song's dictum that "he not busy being born is busy dying"—takes as its context an individual finding an authentic path over and against the false claims of organized religion and other bankrupt pretensions of universal authority. Dylan's early career as a recording artist, furthermore, seemed to exemplify the values of the secular vocation, both in the sense that Dylan clearly had committed himself to a profession (singer-songwriter) and in the sense that one of the features of this profession is that it requires continual self-expression and creativity. Other statements about the vocation from Dylan in this period seem to repeat the secularist idea that one of the chief reasons to find work that is personally meaningful is that there is no other source of direction in human life. Consider, for instance, the concluding verse from "Buckets of Rain" (1975), the final song on *Blood on the Tracks*:

> Life is sad
> Life is a bust
> All ya can do is do what you must
> You do what you must do and ya do it well

But beginning in his conversion period, Dylan challenges the very idea of the secular vocation, insisting, contra Weber, that it is not vestigial or unmanly to consider what God (or universal justice) demands of one; if anything, it is noble and vital. One finds this idea most memorably expressed in Dylan's well-known, Grammy-winning song from 1979, "Gotta Serve Somebody." The song might sound Weberian, as Dylan describes over thirty divergent vocational

---

[69] Pascal, considered a pioneer of existentialism, famously distinguishes, upon having a visionary experience in 1654, the "God of the philosophers" (reducible to reason) from the "God of Abraham, the God of Isaac, the God of Jacob" (accessible by revelation and faith), privileging the latter construct and, with it, the proto-existentialist values of radical individualism and choice. See Blaise Pascal, "The Memorial," in *Pensées*, trans. A. J. Krailsheimer (London: Penguin, 1995), 285. Kierkegaard, whose existentialism bridges religious and secular meanings, likewise reminds us of the existentialist tradition's origins in the Judeo-Christian experience of revelation.

choices—including ambassador, gambler, dancer, boxer, socialite, rock and roll musician, businessman, thief, doctor, policeman, TV executive, construction worker, landlord, banker, preacher, local politician, barber, and heir—never suggesting any one is better than another. Further, as the title of the song makes clear, Dylan, like Weber, understands that individual vocational choice is experienced as *service* to a set of values implied by each profession. But Dylan reintroduces what Weber—and the concept of the secular vocation more generally—had excised: namely, the religious idea that a vocation requires not just a personal selection of an individual way of life, but an answer to the question of whether, in pursuing one's individual path, one will be serving God or not. The song's refrain is decidedly un-Weberian:

> But you're gonna have to serve somebody, yes indeed
> You're gonna have to serve somebody
> Well, it may be the devil or it may be the Lord
> But you're gonna have to serve somebody

This choice between God and the devil is precisely what Weber and the prevailing concept of the secular vocation rejects. We can choose among the warring gods, Weber says, and thus have the gods we do not choose become like demons opposed to us, but Weber is both polytheistic and merely metaphorical in his polytheism.[70] What Weber rules out is the idea that an individual might serve "the one thing that is needful,"[71] some overarching comprehensive worldview partaking of universalism and completeness. Dylan, though, in his mode as a prophet of the postsecular, admonishes individuals who have settled upon a profession that they have a further and more crucial choice to make: whether they are serving only themselves or also something universal. In making this challenge, Dylan in effect appeals to the original Christian understanding of the vocation as having a double foundation, whereby both worldly work and service to God are joined simultaneously.[72]

The question, of course, is: How can this be compelling and not hopelessly speculative, metaphysical, and thus meaningless to a skeptical secularist? How

---

[70] Weber declares, "To put it metaphorically, if you choose this particular standpoint, you will be serving this particular god and will *give offense to every other god.*... [As] long as life is left to itself and is understood in its own terms, it knows only that the conflict between these gods is never-ending." Weber, "Science as a Vocation," 26, 27.

[71] Weber, 23, quoting Luke 10:42.

[72] See William C. Placher, ed., *Callings: Twenty Centuries of Christian Wisdom on Vocation* (Grand Rapids, MI: Eerdmans, 2005), 4, passim.

can Dylan's reconceptualization of the vocation survive the critique of being immature, naïve, utterly unconvincing?

For one thing, Dylan's stature shields him from the ad hominem aspects of Weber's critique of the religious conceptualization of the vocation. In arguing that the "sacrifice of the intellect" is a defining feature of religiosity, Weber can be read as not simply naming the value that the religious vocation must transgress (science) but indicting the intelligence of religious belief more generally. Dylan's public persona as a person of genius, however, challenges this construct of cognitive deficiency. Weber's critique of the unmanliness of the religious—their alleged unwillingness to stare a disenchanted world squarely in the face—likewise finds refutation in Dylan, who, in his less explicitly religious periods, confronted no less than Weber a world stripped of transcendental meaning and found vocational purpose without buttress from religion or dubious metaphysical commitments.[73] Dylan's turn to explicit Christian religiosity comes after deep familiarity with individualism of the Weberian sort and, in a sense, emanates as an alternate manifestation of it: for what could be a more existentialist act of deciding one's values without external support than presenting oneself as a Christian—a resolution that, in a context of secular modernity, is without rational justification, evidentiary basis, or social approval?

Even more important, Dylan in his gospel period does not just pronounce his religiosity but insists, in prophetic fashion, that *everyone* who has a vocation needs to decide if they are serving God. Because my point is that Dylan is a prophet of the postsecular, and not a prophet of a more traditional type, it is not relevant whether Dylan effectively or persuasively communicates the reality of God. What is at stake, rather, is whether Dylan effectively and persuasively suggests that the idea of a secular vocation is unstable in the sense that the very notion of a vocation makes consideration of the God's eye perspective as plausible as the secular rendering of vocation that would remove all appeal to a divine perspective. Here, I think, Dylan is on strong ground.

First of all, Dylan calls into question what previously had seemed essential to his message, namely the attractiveness of an individual finding his or her own way in a disenchanted world. This is most strikingly expressed in Dylan's 1979 song "Gonna Change My Way of Thinking":

---

[73] To be sure, some thoughtful interpreters suggest that a psychology of pain and suffering, stemming from such factors as Dylan's 1977 divorce from Sara Dylan, was a key motivation of his conversion to evangelical Christianity. See Paul Williams, *Dylan—What Happened?* (Glen Ellen, CA: Entwhistle Books, 1980), 77–79, passim; Britta Lee Shain, *Seeing the Real You at Last: Life and Love on the Road with Bob Dylan* (London: Jawbone, 2016), 191. Still, Dylan's background as a countercultural icon, entirely familiar with and at times seemingly espousing a non-theistic, skeptical standpoint, makes his later turn to religiosity, in the eyes of the public, resistant to Weber's critique of religiosity as flowing out of a cowardly inability to see the world as it is.

> Well don't know which one is worse
> Doing your own thing or just being cool
> Well don't know which one is worse
> Doing your own thing or just being cool
> You remember only about the brass ring
> You forget all about the golden rule

It is arresting to hear Dylan, of all people—the arch-individualist of the 1960s—pronounce upon the limitations of "doing one's thing" and of pursuing a life of mere self-direction. And it is important to recognize that this passage is not an isolated thought but paralleled by numerous other instances of Dylan in his conversion and postconversion periods challenging the ethics of expressive individualism.[74] In any case, Dylan's claims in this regard challenge the secularized vocational ideal by critiquing its guiding idea of individual fulfillment. This critique contains two different claims. The first is a prediction that a life focused on mere individual self-fulfillment is ultimately unappealing—both to behold from the outside and to live from within. People may disagree here. But perhaps the stronger critique is the second idea: Dylan's calling into question the existence of a coherent individual identity that possesses a singular, autonomous truth to be fulfilled in the first place. Dylan explicitly states this idea in 1985, reflecting on one of his masterpieces from his gospel period, "Every Grain of Sand":

> That lie about everybody having their own truth inside of them has done a lot of damage and made a lot of people crazy.[75]

This second claim seems incisive when juxtaposed to the secularist critique of the religious vocation for its alleged fictiveness. Recall that one of the chief objections to the religious concept of the vocation—which understands vocational work as work in the service of God—is that this divine-orienting entity,

---

[74] Consider these lines from "Slow Train":

> Man's ego's inflated, his laws are outdated, they don't apply no more
> You can't rely no more to be standin' around waitin'
> In the home of the brave
> Jefferson turnin' over in his grave
> Fools glorifying themselves, trying to manipulate Satan
> And there's a slow, slow train comin' up around the bend

And these from "Foot of Pride":

> Did he make it to the top, well he probably did and dropped
> Struck down by the strength of the will

[75] Liner notes to *Biograph* (1985) for "Every Grain of Sand," 32.

this comprehensiveness, simply does not exist. Secularists like Weber thus claim that the traditional religious concept of the vocation does not make sense. But Dylan interrogates this notion of comprehensiveness, in effect asking: If we are suspicious of the comprehensive worldview of universal religions of salvation, why should we not also be skeptical of the idea of a comprehensive individual identity that defines each person's authentic secular self? Why should we see ourselves as having a distinct professional calling to pursue? Is not the very premise of a calling reflective of a mystical element within the secular conception of the vocation, which, if we are being skeptical, is as objectionable as positing God? Or, to frame it in more positive and constructive terms: If we can hypothesize a comprehensive *individuality* (the real, genuine self that finds unique fulfillment when it has located its true vocation), why can we not hypothesize a comprehensive *macro-perspective* that defines when vocational action is also in the service of God or at least the universal social good?

That the secularist denigration of the religious vocation is not free from its own mystical conception of selfhood is reflected by Weber, who, despite his pretensions of disenchanted skepticism, still ends up positing the highly speculative notion of the *daemon*: an underlying identity dictating the content of authentic vocational choice. The idea of the daemon has a long history, dating back to classical antiquity. If for Socrates the daemon was a voice that told him only what behavior he should refrain from, for Weber the daemon is the spiritual core defining that which we are destined to live in light of when we are living authentically. So important is the idea of the daemon to Weber's analysis of vocationalism that it concludes his most important meditation on the secular vocation, "Science as a Vocation": "We must go about our work and meet 'the challenges of the day'—both in our human relations and our vocation. But that moral is simple and straightforward if each person finds and obeys the daemon that holds the threads of *his* life."[76] Weber's invocation of the daemon is not, in fact, a metaphysical excess particular to him, but reminds us of what the secularized notion of the vocation stands for: not any possible choice of career, but a choice that is somehow uniquely consistent with our genuine selfhood. When we refer to our work as our calling, we do not simply mean that it is our favorite thing to do, but rather that we have chosen it because we feel it best defines what we are most able or intended to do. But this premise of a totalizing singular identity exceeds

---

[76] Weber, "Science as a Vocation," 31. As David Owen and Tracy Strong note in their edition of Weber's vocation lectures, the idea of the daemon not only has Socratic roots but was known to Weber and his contemporaries through Goethe's poem "Dämon," which includes the lines: "Even as the sun and planets stood, to salute one another on the day you entered the world—even so you began straightaway to grow and have continued to do so, according to the law that prevailed over your beginning. It is thus that you must be, you cannot escape yourself" (31, n. 33).

empirical verification and therefore alerts us to the mystical quality inherent in even the secular conception of the vocation. Weber, with his idea of the daemon, simply crystallizes what any secular thinking on the vocation stands for: namely, the assumption that there really is some preexisting, comprehensive, definitive identity that our work needs to harmonize with in order for it to constitute a genuine calling. As much as the secularized notion of the vocation denies that there is some external divine voice calling to us, it nonetheless affirms that there is an inner voice—or inner self—that is not simply a chooser but instead is already determined to such an extent that it defines what a proper vocational choice will look like.

Perhaps the daemon is real. Perhaps it is a fantasy. Either way, all of us who consider what our professional calling should be cannot help but wonder about it. Without some notion of who we as individuals really are, the idea of the vocation would collapse and all we would be left with is mere job choices rather than the sense of pursuing an authentic calling. Some people happily live in this more modest and metaphysically chastened state, but the idea of the vocation, and the mystical element it presupposes, is in fact a readily familiar orienting ethic in contemporary secular culture and, within contexts of socioeconomic privilege especially, a guiding consideration as young adults go out into the world.

One response to the mystical aspect of even the secular vocation is to reject the idea of the vocation *tout court*. But another response would be: If we are able to operate on the basis of a hypothetical, not fully verifiable notion of selfhood, why can we not also operate on the basis of a hypothetical, not fully verifiable notion of divinity? If we are willing to ask what the "real me" is meant to do in this world—even though the concept of the "real me" exceeds any actual information I have about myself and uncritically posits the inauthenticity of non-vocational ways of life (such as endless experimentation) as well as the inauthenticity of ongoing reinvention (i.e., a multiplicity of selves, none of which is fully authoritative or determinative of ultimate purpose)—then why can we not also ask what I should do in order to serve God, however I choose to define that notion? To be sure, an honest secularist alternative would be to dispense with all considerations of the vocation and, in the name of radical materialism, no longer ask if work is in accordance with one's daemon but instead pursue a mere job rather than a vocation, or perhaps look to avoid work altogether if that were possible. But insofar as this alternative is unappealing—insofar as we crave meditation on and pursuit of *singular purpose*—then the question needs to be asked why only the inner voice of authentic selfhood, and not also the external voice of God, should ground vocational thinking, decision, and practice. To operate in only half of the vocation—a mystical vision of identity but not a vision of God—is not only imbalanced but consequential in a predictable way: it means employing vocational thinking only for the purpose of individual expressivity and fulfillment and not (directly, at least) in the name of serving some more universal purpose suggested by the idea of service to God.

Defenders of the secular vocation will, of course, say that the inner voice, even if not fully verifiable as a source of an ultimate, authoritative identity, is much more real than an entirely hypothesized God's eye view. But Dylan's prophetic impulse is perhaps at its most piercing when he indicts secularist thinking not for disobeying straightforward divine commands, but for not even *wondering about* how consideration of a divine vantage point might alter our behavior, as in these lines from "When You Gonna Wake Up?":

> Do you ever wonder just what God requires?
> You think He's just an errand boy to satisfy your wandering desires
> When you gonna wake up, when you gonna wake up
> When you gonna wake up and strengthen the things that remain?

Dylan's challenge here and in other similar songs (e.g., "What Can I Do for You?") to stop considering God as an "errand boy" is not merely a critique of an avaricious relationship with the divine, but a recognition that because meditation on God involves considering what one could *do for* God, it is productive of a sense of vocation. The call to wonder about what God wants may not be convincing to radical materialists and skeptics, but for those in the throes of vocational thinking—who believe they have some specific work or purpose to effect in the world (and again, this is a group that includes countless self-described secularists like Weber)—Dylan's postsecular prophetic provocation is to affirm the integrity of the God's eye view as no less relevant and no less convincing (and perhaps more socially beneficial) than the appeal to a purely daemonic inner voice.

Dylan's emphasis on "wondering" reminds us that his specific challenge is not to follow God but to *imagine*—to make the hypothesized divine perspective a relevant, or at least respectable, aspect of meditation on a vocation. It is significant in this regard that a long line of otherwise humanistic philosophy has itself appealed to the meaningfulness and value of a God's eye perspective for effective moral reasoning. In the sentimentalist model advocated by Adam Smith, for example, whereby moral judgment requires taking up the position of an impartial spectator, this spectator often is linked to the God's eye view. Smith refers to one's conscience—that is, the impartial spectator as it acts upon the individual—as God's "vicegerent upon earth,"[77] and likewise describes the

---

[77] Adam Smith, *The Theory of Moral Sentiments* (Indianapolis: Liberty Fund, 1984), 130 [III.2.31]; also see 165 [III.5.6].

impartial spectator as "the substitute of the deity"[78] and "the great demigod within the breast."[79] Whether it is only the idea of a God's eye perspective or its reality—and perhaps both possibilities are suggested by Smith—he nonetheless deems it meaningful, if not necessary, to contemplate a divine viewpoint in order to behave morally. This religiosity is not limited to sentimentalist thought. The utilitarian R. M. Hare, albeit with an air of metaphor, refers to the ideal moral agent as an "archangel"[80]; and Peter Singer, in developing his own account of utilitarianism, likewise invokes the moral necessity of taking up "the view of the universe."[81] Nor is the adopting of this godlike perspective particular to utilitarian theories, as even deontological approaches have to adopt consequentialist elements for which a God's eye perspective could also be relevant.[82] The appeal to God by such philosophies has not been merely perspectival but also motivational; that is, it has been invoked not only to cognize an impartial frame of reference but also sometimes to explain why this impartial perspective ought to be followed over and against one's private interests. Sidgwick's highly influential and otherwise secular utilitarian theory of ethics, for instance, concludes with the observation that, without an appeal to divine providence, there can be no basis for preferring the impartial standpoint to the egoistic one.[83] That such philosophies have made reference to at least the idea of God—to the mental exercise of wondering what God would want—is a reminder that Dylan's own call for precisely this same consideration is not so far outside the boundaries of secular thinking when matters of ethical obligation are at play.

Critics will say that to bring God into the discussion of justice is misleading and mystifying—and that if the point is to inspire individuals to do the right thing (defined in utilitarian terms or otherwise), then this can be achieved much more effectively and persuasively without any dubious appeal to religion. To be sure, the bulk of modern and contemporary moral philosophy is defined precisely by grounding our moral duties in something other than religious faith.

---

[78] Smith, 130 [III.2.31r].

[79] Smith, 245 [VI.iii.18], 247 [VI.iii.25].

[80] R. M. Hare, *Moral Thinking: Its Levels, Method and Point* (Oxford: Oxford University Press, 1981), 44–52, passim.

[81] Peter Singer, *How Are We to Live?* (East Melbourne, Australia: Text Publishing Co., 1993), 219–35.

[82] Deontological theories present themselves as upholding considerations (such as the protection of individual liberties) that will trump the maximization of social welfare (such as aggregate income, wealth, or other forms of material well-being), not obviate these considerations altogether. Thus, even deontologists seek the maximization of the good within the limiting parameters of such trumps.

[83] Henry Sidgwick, *The Methods of Ethics*, 1st ed. (London: Macmillan, 1874), 473. I discuss Sidgwick's view in this respect in section I.4.

My point, though, is not to reduce religiosity to morality, nor to say that one necessarily needs to be religious in order to be moral, but to note that one consequence of the secular vocational ideal is to marginalize moral concerns and that this marginalization is questionable both in its substance (does it make sense to pursue questions of individual fulfillment over those of moral responsibility when considering one's vocation?) and in its illogic (if there is a daemon over us, why is there not one over the whole world? If there is a unity over individual lives, why not over the universe?).

Put differently, it is possible even for thoughtful individuals of uncertain religious belief to ask themselves the question of what is expected from a God's eye perspective. Regardless of whether God exists, this question can always be posed. Choosing to reflect in such a fashion might lead to an understanding of divine obligation, or it might simply produce a newfound willingness, in setting about one's work, to take care to consider not just the meaning of one's pursuits (what they are about) but what they are good for. Wherever the thought of the God's eye perspective leads, the most basic point is that the secular understanding of the vocation—given its metaphysical commitment to a coherent, preexisting inner self—has no resources for denying the religious conception of the vocation a position of complementary, coequal integrity.

Dylan's prophetic speech thus exposes a contemporary secular practice—the commitment to individual self-fulfillment through a vocation—as containing a living and viable religious potential that is no less sensible, sober, or compelling than the godless one. Any vocation, in realizing ourselves, also takes us beyond ourselves: the work that we do, the values that work implies, and the notion of wholeness (whether daemonic or divine) that informs the purpose and authority of the vocation. Once one accepts that any vocation contains this "beyond," there is only the question of how far one wants to go.

II.4. The Existence of a Religious Sense

The usual way the propriety of religiosity is adjudicated by secularists is to begin with the question of whether the external objects of religious belief—God, heaven, hell, the immortal soul, spirits, and the like—exist and then, on the basis of this determination, evaluate whether the internal mindset of religious faith makes sense. Once the likelihood of external religious objects is shown to be negligible, then secularists conclude that the internal standpoint of belief is highly suspect. It is difficult, of course, to achieve postsecular relations of reciprocity and respect if one side (secularists) considers the other side (religionists) caught up in the irrationalism and illusion of false belief. But one way to better establish relations of respectful reciprocity is to reverse this customary framework.

Rather than begin with the external objects of religious belief, it is possible to flip the relation and recognize that for many religious people the first step is the internal one: some intimation of the holy, some sentiment of the transcendent, some enduring insistence that the world and humanity's place within it cannot be explained entirely in terms of materialistic considerations. We can call this internal source of religious perception the "religious sense." Its most customary features include reverential awe, wonder, mystery, and what Rudolf Otto has labeled the "numinous."[84] The religious sense can be considered as the psychology underlying much religious belief and practice, at least when such belief and practice flow from a persistent sentiment of the holy or sacred rather than merely from the dictates of tradition and clerical authority. If the religious sense is what in fact is primary, then the alleged non-existence of the external objects to which that sense is devoted cannot be invoked to reject it, since these objects are only a particular, provisional, and in many cases symbolic manifestation of an underlying sensibility that cannot be cancelled just because any one of these objects is rendered implausible. So conceived, the religious sense is akin to other independent frameworks of evaluation, such as aesthetics and morality, and thus occupies a permanent place in humanity.[85]

Dylan's expression of his religiosity takes numerous forms, including testimony to the experience of divine revelation,[86] quasi-gnostic reflections on the god within ourselves,[87] and assertions about faith itself as the key spiritual

[84] Rudolf Otto, *The Idea of the Holy* (Oxford: Oxford University Press, 1958).

[85] Permanent does not mean innate, just an ever-present possibility. On this point, see Otto, 177.

[86] Dylan's most direct account of divine revelation relates to his alleged conversion experience in a hotel room in Tucson, Arizona, on November 18, 1978: "Jesus did appear to me as King of Kings, and Lord of Lords. . . . There was a presence in the room that couldn't have been anybody but Jesus. . . . Jesus put his hand on me. It was a physical thing. I felt it. I felt it all over me. I felt my whole body tremble. The glory of the Lord knocked me down and picked me up." Quoted in Clinton Heylin, *Bob Dylan: Behind the Shades Revisited* (New York: HarperCollins, 2003), 490, 491. Paul Kirkman contests this chronology but not Dylan's conversion. See Kirkman, "Clinton Heylin's Dylan-Salvation Myth-Hoax of a 1978 Tucson Arizona Hotel-Room Jesus Epiphany: The Wind Blows Where It, Not Heylin, Wills," https://www.scribd.com/document/55777466/Clinton-Hey lin-s-Dylan-Salvation-Myth-Hoax-of-a-1978-Tucson-Arizona-Hotel-Room-Jesus-Epiphany.

[87] See, for example, Dylan's 1980 song "Pressing On," which includes the lines:

> Many try to stop me, shake me up in my mind
> Say, "Prove to me that He's the Lord, show me a sign"
> What kind of sign they need when it all come from within
> When what's lost has been found, what's to come has already been?

Dylan also gestures toward gnosticism in his contemplation of a god prior to and outside of creation—"Well, I'm hanging on to a solid rock / Made before the foundation of the world" ("Solid Rock")—which perhaps can be perceived by human beings only because we ourselves contain something older than creation. Consider God's words from Jeremiah 1:5: "Before I formed you in the womb I knew you, before you were born I set you apart; I appointed you as a prophet to the nations."

experience of religiosity.[88] Statements of these kinds, especially with regard to the first two cases, lead Dylan to some of his most speculative and unverifiable assertions and, thus, to convictions about his religiosity that secularists would be quick to refute or reject. But Dylan also—especially in his postconversion period, though not only then—reflects in a different way upon his religiosity, suggesting that it flows from his religious sense. And it is this kind of statement that is especially relevant to Dylan's status as a prophet of the postsecular whose mission is not to convert secularists to religiosity but to establish the integrity of religious belief in the eyes of non-believers.[89] Indeed, one of Dylan's most striking postsecular gestures occurs when he confesses that his deep exposure to secularist culture has been unable to eradicate his religious sense. What instills this confession with postsecular force is both the personality of the confessor (Dylan's status as someone with clear credentials within secularist culture, as I have discussed) and its modesty and restraint (since the confession of a religious sense is not dogmatic proselytization of religious truth but only testimony to some enduring part of the self that tarries with religious sentiments and refuses to abandon, as Kim Luisi aptly puts it in regard to Dylan, "the desire to understand the nature of humanity beyond the demands and rewards of material existence"[90]).

Dylan testifies to his religious sense in numerous ways, but perhaps the most arresting instance occurs in his 1983 song "Someone's Got a Hold of My Heart," written and recorded soon after the cessation of his gospel period, providing thus an early statement within the long and still ongoing postconversion era of his music, in which Dylan's religious sensibility, even if it no longer contains the vitriol and fervor of the 1979–1981 period, nonetheless has not been refuted or altogether neutralized. The key lines to highlight are these:

[88] Dylan suggests this when, in an interview in 1979, he differentiates Christianity from religion: "Well, Christ is no religion. We're not talking about religion. . . . Jesus Christ is the Way, the Truth, the Life." Cott, "Radio Interview with Bruce Heiman, KMEX (Tucson, Arizona), December 7, 1979," in *Essential Interviews*, 289. And in a 2007 exchange, Dylan is even more pointed: "Religion is something that is mostly outward experience. Faith is a different thing. How many religions are there in the world? Quite a few, actually. . . . Faith doesn't have a name. It doesn't have a category. It's oblique. So it's unspeakable. We degrade faith by talking about religion." Cott, "Interview with Jann Wenner, *Rolling Stone*, May 3–7, 2007," in *Essential Interviews*, 488.

[89] Also relevant to this mission, strictly speaking, is establishing the integrity of *non-belief* in the eyes of believers. If one considers the totality of his oeuvre, Dylan could be seen as doing this too, but, as I have explained, given the context of the secularist attack on religiosity that forms the basis of my analysis here, and given my interest in attending to what makes Dylan *distinct* prophetically speaking, I am focusing primarily on one side of the postsecular mission.

[90] Kim Luisi, "Bob Dylan and the Religious Sense," in *Dylan at Play*, ed. Nick Smart and Nina Gross (Newcastle upon Tyne, UK: Cambridge Scholars Publishing, 2011), 41.

> I been to Babylon
> I gotta confess
> I can still hear that voice crying in the wilderness
> What looks large from a distance, close up is never that big
> Never could learn to drink that blood and call it wine
> Never could learn to look at your face and call it mine
> Someone's got a hold of my heart . . .

With his invocation of Babylon and a voice calling out in the wilderness, Dylan clearly inserts himself within the prophetic tradition. In the Bible, the wilderness is a liminal place where an individual or a people undergoes travails and dislocation, either as punishment for transgression, the context of a new revelation, a spiritual test, or some combination of these.[91] Although John the Baptist claimed to be the voice crying in the wilderness,[92] and Elijah at an earlier biblical moment hears a voice in the wilderness,[93] Dylan's reference appears to be to the biblical passage John the Baptist's prophecy itself references—the opening lines of Second Isaiah, addressed to Jewish exiles in Babylon, following the fall of Jerusalem in 586 BCE:

> The voice of him that cries in the wilderness,
> "Prepare you the way of the Lord,
> Make straight in the desert a highway for our God."[94]

In Isaiah, the voice in the wilderness instructs hope in the very moment of apparent devastation. It exhorts those who heed it to achieve deliverance both in the form of a return to Jerusalem and the Kingdom of Judah and, more deeply, in the form of reconciliation with God, a relationship that will have endured in spite of the destruction of the Temple and the political demise of the Jewish

---

[91] The Israelites' forty years in the wilderness following their escape from bondage in Egypt is a classic example. Other important biblical instances include the experiences of Job, Elijah, Paul, and of course Jesus, who confronts temptation in the wilderness (Mark 1:12–13).

[92] According to John 1:23:

> He [John the Baptist] said, "I am the voice of one crying in the wilderness, 'Make straight the way of the Lord,' as said the prophet Isaiah."

For parallel statements, see Matthew 3:1–3; Mark 1:1–4; Luke 3:2–4.

[93] Elijah claims to hear in the wilderness the words: "Arise and eat, for the journey is too great for you" (1 Kings 19:7). However, the more specific phenomenon, or at least language, of a "voice crying in the wilderness" appears to have its source in Isaiah 40:3.

[94] Isaiah 40:3. An alternate translation makes the wilderness the place of religious practice: "A voice cries: in the wilderness prepare the way of the Lord."

people.[95] Dylan, however, invokes these lines in a postsecular rather than a traditionally religious way, employing them to testify not to faithful obedience to God but to the endurance of a religious sense that will not perish. The key line is the penultimate one of the stanza quoted above—"Never could learn to drink that blood and call it wine"—because it seems to clearly announce a refusal to transmute a religious phenomenon (encountering the blood of Christ) into a secular one (the drinking of wine). Remarkably, Dylan reverses the more familiar doubts of someone practicing the Eucharist. Rather than doubt whether the wine being drunk is in fact the blood of Christ (a doubt that must have been felt by centuries of Christians, let alone those of today), Dylan's reversal communicates his inability to accept that the material world is the extent of everything, that human beings are the sole generators of meaning in a godless, disenchanted, purposeless universe. And in the final line of the stanza—"Never could learn to look at your face and call it mine"—if the "your face" is the depiction of God in religious literature and religious experience, then here, too, Dylan is announcing a similar skeptical refusal of skepticism: he cannot, like Feuerbach, Marx, and centuries of secularist critics have insisted, come to understand, with any permanence or stability, the divine to be a mere projection of his own humanity, any more than he can understand aesthetic beauty, scientific truth, or moral rightness to be.

Part of what imbues this reversal of skepticism—so that its object is atheism, not theism—with special postsecular poignancy is the temporality of the singer's posture. Dylan's inability to take up the standpoint of pure materialism comes after long exposure to and familiarity with those secularist scientific and cultural forces that would "teach" him to abandon his religiosity. That is, it is expressed by someone who has considered the usual sources of secularist skepticism: atheism, naturalistic explanations for everything, the idea of a universe composed entirely of purposeless matter, the idea of human rationality as the sole creative intellectual and moral force in the world, and so on. Dylan does not merely hear a voice in the wilderness, but *still* hears it in spite of what the secularist culture surrounding him has tried to make him learn. This notion of a religiosity that has persisted—though also perhaps has been shaped, reformed, and

---

[95] The voice continues at Isaiah 40:6–8:

> A voice says, "Cry out."
> And I said, "What shall I cry?"
> "All people are like grass,
>   and all their faithfulness is like the flowers of the field.
> The grass withers and the flowers fall, because the breath of the Lord blows
>   on them. Surely the people are grass.
> The grass withers and the flowers fall,
>   but the word of our God endures forever."

altered by exposure to secular humanism—is only further emphasized by the repeated "Never could learn." "Never could learn" means that that which stands against the religious sense presents itself in the mantle of science and learning. It means that Dylan tried in some way to adopt a non-religious mentality but could not. It means that, in his enduring religiosity, he remains cognizant of others who are not religious and who, as the purveyors of learning, condition the experience of his spiritual life. In these respects, Dylan crystallizes the situation of postsecular religious believers. He is aware of a non-theistic, naturalistic explanation of his situation—he is not ignorant on this account—but he cannot fully adopt it. And he presents this resistance as an inability rather than a simple preference[96]—as a testimony to the endurance of a *religious sense*. The hopefulness expressed by Isaiah about a return to religious adherence—namely, that the road back to Jerusalem and God is not as far as it seems (an idea that Dylan seems to reference with the line: "What looks large from a distance, close up is never that big")—is thus transformed by Dylan into a confident confession that, despite the barrage of secularist culture, his religious sense has not been lost. This confession is not to any particular dogma or church but to the enduring presence of the sentiment of the transcendent within his life. What also imbues these lines with special postsecular poignancy is their defensive posture. Dylan is not pronouncing certainty about Judeo-Christianity, only his inability to be entirely divested of his religious beliefs. His words are less a statement of religiosity than a statement of refusal of non-religiosity.

As a testimony to the religious sense rather than to dogmatic religious belief, Dylan's reference to Isaiah is especially apt. There is mystery about the nature of the voice: it does not seem to be the voice of God (since the voice itself says, "Prepare you the way of the Lord"), nor does it seem to be Isaiah's voice (since Isaiah is himself reporting the voice). But since what the religious sense most precisely indicates is not unambiguous communion with the divine but only tarrying with the perception of some transcendent mystery and the intuition of a larger order that this perception instills, a voice in the wilderness of uncertain authorship is in fact a fitting symbol for the expression of this sense.

Dylan's appeal to his religious sense is not limited to his postconversion period but can be found in earlier moments as well. Indeed, when seen in terms of a testimony to his religious sense, Dylan's gospel period was less about a stark

---

[96] In saying this, I am not contradicting one of the basic points of Part II: that both religiosity and non-religiosity ought to be understood as existential choices, rather than as (opposing views on) truth. Dylan *is* choosing to refuse radical materialism, but this choice is experienced not as a simple selection of one among many external options (as if religiosity and non-religiosity were choices on a menu) but as the continued activation—rather than cancellation—of an extant religious sense. In other words, to be religious or not is an existential choice, but the capacity to be religious or not, insofar as we possess a religious sense, is not a choice.

conversion than a more intense and focused channeling of something he always had felt. In 1974, five years before his gospel period, Dylan states: "Religion to me is a fleeting thing. Can't nail it down. It's in me and out of me. It does give me, on the surface, some images, but I don't know to what degree."[97] A song recorded at this time, "Up to Me," likewise refers to the hazy effervescence of religiosity:

> We heard the Sermon on the Mount and I knew it was too complex
> It didn't amount to anything more than what the broken glass reflects

From one perspective, these reflections could be read as Dylan's distance from religious faith in his preconversion period, but with respect to the matter at hand—the idea of a religious sense as a widely held human capacity, shared by the religious and non-religious alike—Dylan's reflections are important for suggesting that he already was aware of this sense prior to his turn to evangelical Christianity. Indeed, Dylan later commented that in becoming a Christian he was in fact crystallizing something he had long felt: "What I learned in Bible school [which he attended in 1979] was just . . . an extension of the same thing I believed in all along, but just couldn't verbalize or articulate."[98] And in fact, the effervescent aspect of Dylan's preconversion religious sense did not entirely dissipate even at the height of his religious fervor. One of the most beautiful lines of one of Dylan's most beautiful religious songs ("Every Grain of Sand") speaks directly to this phenomenon:

> I hear the ancient footsteps like the motion of the sea
> Sometimes I turn, there's someone there, other times it's only me

These words can be read as postsecular testimony to a spiritual life that knows both faith and doubt, but, relatedly, they also testify to a religious sense that is neither permanently activated nor permanently cancelled. And this same

---

[97] Ben Fong-Torres, "Knockin' on Bob Dylan's Door," *Rolling Stone*, February 14, 1974, https://www.rollingstone.com/music/music-news/knockin-on-bob-dylans-door-191025/.

[98] Scott Cohen, "Bob Dylan Revisited," *SPIN*, December 1985, https://www.spin.com/featured/bob-dylan-december-1985-cover-story/. Other of Dylan's statements referring to his preconversion religiosity include his 1984 comment: "I don't think I've ever been an agnostic. I've always thought there's a superior power, that this is not the real world and that there's a world to come. That no soul has died, every soul is alive, either in holiness or in flames. And there's probably a lot of middle ground." Cott, "Interview with Kurt Loder, *Rolling Stone*, June 21, 1984," in *Essential Interviews*, 305. Also relevant is Dylan's reflection from 1980: "I guess He's always been calling me. Of course, how would I have ever known that? That it was Jesus calling me. I always thought it was some voice that would be more identifiable. But Christ is calling everybody; we just turn him off. We just don't want to hear. We think he's gonna make our lives miserable, you know what I mean. We think he's gonna make us do things we don't want to do. Or keep us from doing things we want to do. But God's got his own purpose and time for everything. He knew when I would respond to His call." Cott, "Interview with Karen Hughes, *The Dominion*, May 21, 1980," in *Essential Interviews*, 294.

effervescent quality becomes definitive of Dylan's religious meditations in his postconversion period (the era that begins with the end of his gospel period in 1981 and which Dylan still occupies today). In lines that both recall "Every Grain of Sand" but also suggest a much more frustrated religious sense, Dylan's "Floater (Too Much to Ask)," from 2001, reflects:

> I keep listenin' for footsteps
> But I ain't hearing any

And yet a song from roughly the same period, "Cold Irons Bound" (1997), suggests that Dylan's religious sense still operates:

> I'm beginning to hear voices and there's no one around

Dylan's appeal to a religious sense as something both the religious and non-religious possess makes it fitting that Dylan himself gives voice to this sense in periods both before and after his religious fervor of 1979–1981. Dylan, in his own persona, thus provides ample evidence of the religious sense remaining a permanent possibility regardless of whatever one decides for the time being regarding questions of faith, organized religion, theism, and so forth.

Dylan's personal testimony to his religious sense takes his postsecularism beyond the philosophy of Habermas, whose methodological atheism makes him utterly unable to suggest it as a basic human capacity, and also beyond the philosophy of Taylor, who, even if he wants to establish that sentiments like the religious sense are not ruled by the "immanent frame," does not invoke his own personal experience as evidence. Dylan's reporting of the endurance of his religious sense in the face of the barrage of secularist thinking not only imbues his postsecularism with a distinctly prophetic aspect, but also makes his critique of secularist culture more aggressive, pointed, and impassioned than these philosophical approaches. That Dylan himself has a religious sense, in spite of his deep immersion in atheistic and materialistic worldviews, is not particular to him but elicits in his followers (in a manner wholly lacking for Habermas and Taylor) greater awareness of the possibility that they have one too. If Habermas and Taylor are mostly content to dichotomize between the religious and non-religious, Dylan's testimony to his religious sense raises the possibility that it is a basic human capacity, in principle always available to be accessed at any time. And if this is true, then secularists are not simply abiding by strict standards of evidentiary truth, but electing not to activate a fundamental category of their sensibility. Aesthetic and moral judgments are themselves irreducible to strict evidentiary standards, but we do not say that someone who refuses to transact in such judgments is sober or rational, but rather insensible and unprincipled.

Secularists still might deny the existence of a religious sense or the propriety of acting upon it. They might say with Weber, the great theoretician of contemporary secularist thinking, "It is true that I am absolutely unmusical in matters religious and that I have neither the need nor the ability to erect any religious edifices within me—that is simply impossible for me, and I reject it."[99] But once this becomes the debate—whether one should confidently reject the employment, and perhaps also deny the existence, of one's religious sense—secularists, for three different reasons, are on weaker ground than if the controversy is about the existence of external objects of religious belief.

First of all, when secularists deny the existence of the religious sense, they are denying something extremely widespread and well reported across a broad spectrum of otherwise diverse spiritual standpoints, including numerous atheistic ones. Social-scientific examination of religion often appeals to the religious sense as a foundational reason for treating religion as a permanent category in the study of humanity. William James, for example, in his seminal survey of various forms of religiosity, was led to posit a common underlying human capacity that very much resembles the religious sense: "It is as if there were in the human consciousness a *sense of reality, a feeling of objective presence, a perception* of what we may call 'something there,' more deep and more general than any of the special and particular 'senses' by which the current psychology supposes existent realities to be originally revealed."[100] Inspired in part by James, Otto formalizes the religious sense as the "numinous," which he defines as the *mysterium tremendum et fascinans*—that is, an experience of mystery (of something wholly other to us) that simultaneously elicits both fear and fascination and on the basis of which, due to awe in the face of its overpoweringness, we are likely to feel some sense of dependence.[101] Importantly, Otto defines the numinous as irreducible to reason, ordinary sensory experience, or morality—describing it as a

---

[99] Max Weber, letter to Ferdinand Tönnies, February 19, 1909, quoted in Basit Bilal Koshul, *The Postmodern Significance of Max Weber's Legacy* (New York: Palgrave Macmillan, 2005), 61. The fuller passage, however, suggests a more complicated and elusive meaning and perhaps one that in fact reflects Weber's own enduring religious sense: "It is true that I am absolutely unmusical in matters religious and that I have neither the need nor the ability to erect any religious edifices within me— that is simply impossible for me, and I reject it. *But after examining myself carefully I must say that I am neither anti-religious nor irreligious*" (emphasis added).

[100] William James, *The Varieties of Religious Experience* (London: Longmans, Green, and Co., 1903), 58. James also writes: "Like love, like wrath, like hope, ambition, jealousy, like every other instinctive eagerness and impulse, [religion] adds to life an enchantment which is not rationally or logically deducible from anything else" (47).

[101] See Otto, *The Idea of the Holy*, 140, passim. With regard to this dependence, Otto explains: "I propose to call it 'creature-consciousness' or creature feeling. It is the emotion of a creature, submerged and overwhelmed by its own nothingness in contrast to that which is supreme and above all creatures" (9–10).

"non-rational, non-sensory experience or feeling whose primary and immediate object is outside the self"[102]—thereby indicating its status as an independent sense, that is, "an *a priori category* of mind."[103]

If James and Otto intend their accounts of the religious sense to describe primarily theistic religious experience, the idea of the religious sense also has been invoked by so-called religious atheists who reject notions of God but still find in the contemplation of beauty, the workings of nature, and the behavior of the universe intimations of a higher order that instills them with a sense of awe, wonder, and mystery.[104] To be sure, militant secularists, such as Richard Dawkins, themselves acknowledge that wonderment can be aroused by such contemplation, but they insist on reducing that wonderment to what is surprising and amazing about what we know through natural science: for example, that humans descended from fish after 185 million generations.[105] But this is not the religious sense of the religious atheists I have in mind, who, in their experience of sublime mystery at the border of the knowable, attest to a wonderment at what exceeds the findings of science. Consider, for instance, Einstein's remark: "To know that what is impenetrable to us really exists, manifesting itself as the highest wisdom and the most radiant beauty, which our dull faculties can comprehend only in their most primitive forms—this knowledge, this feeling, is at the center of true religiousness. In this sense, and in this sense only, I belong in the ranks of devoutly religious men." Einstein identifies a sense of the mysterious as both an intrinsically valuable state and as essential to the proper conduct of science: "The most beautiful thing we can experience is the mysterious. It is the source of all true art and science. He to whom this emotion is a stranger, who can no longer pause to wonder and stand rapt in awe, is as good as dead: his eyes are closed."[106] Einstein's awestruck rapture at the beauty of the universe is not at all uncommon and probably the norm among physicists today and, just as important, something that is itself mysterious since it is not at all clear or straightforward wherein the grounds for this wonderment lie.[107] In any

---

[102] Quoted in the synopsis of an alternate edition of *The Idea of the Holy* (New York: Ravenio Books, 1970).

[103] Otto, *The Idea of the Holy*, 58. On the numinous as an a priori category, also see 112, 136, 175.

[104] On the idea of religious atheists, see Dworkin, *Religion Without God*.

[105] Richard Dawkins, *The Magic of Reality: How We Know What's Really True* (New York: Free Press, 2011), 33–54. Dawkins describes his purpose: "I want to show you that the real world, as understood scientifically, has magic of its own—the kind I call poetic magic: an inspiring beauty which is all the more magical because it is real and because we can understand how it works" (31).

[106] Quoted in Henry Goddard Leach, ed., *Living Philosophies: A Series of Intimate Credos* (New York: Simon and Schuster, 1931), 6.

[107] See Dworkin, *Religion Without God*, 50–51. As Dworkin explains, such beauty cannot come from the comprehensibility of a unified theory of physics because that theory has not been found.

case, the religious sense is not just real but widespread: it is reflected both by those one would typically identify as religious and by atheists of a certain type, and it may be the common link that, experientially, unifies both the tradition-ally religious and the so-called spiritual but not religious. Relatedly, the religious sense also can be considered as the underlying ground of modern spiritualistic sensibilities—such as Romanticism or Transcendentalism—that insist upon the persistence of a religious life no longer firmly tethered to organized religious institutions and traditional theological doctrine. And even if the religious sense is not necessarily the way that the religious characterize their religiosity (since they might focus on the alleged existence of the external objects in which they believe, rather than on a religious sense in need of deployment, as the primary driver of their spiritual life), it is still true that many theologians have invoked the religious sense as in fact the originary source of religiosity.[108] In prophetically acknowledging his own religious sense, Dylan thus testifies to an experience likely to be shared or at least recognized by a wide array of both religious and non-religious constituencies, thereby suggesting an experiential bridge between them and raising the possibility that secularists are only *opting* not to express or meditate upon their religious sense—not, as some secularists would maintain, refusing to engage in religious thought merely out of a dedication to truth.

Second, the pervasiveness of the religious sense is linked to the undeniable existence of phenomena that, for most of us, are mysterious, awe-inspiring, gen-erative of wonder, and evocative of what Kant calls "purposiveness without a purpose" (i.e., the experience of the presence of a purpose without any further understanding of its content).[109] That is, there are features of our world that

---

There is a divergence between Einstein's theory of gravity and the so-called standard model (which describes the other three fundamental forces, the strong nuclear force, the weak nuclear force, and electromagnetism). Further, 96 percent of the universe appears to be made up of dark matter and dark energy, and neither Einstein's theory nor the standard model explains this (58-60).

[108] Consider, for instance, Paul Tillich's comment: "The manifestation of this ground and abyss of being and meaning creates what modern theology calls 'the experience of the numi-nous.' . . . The same experience can occur, and occurs for the large majority of men, in connection with the impression some persons, historical or natural events, objects, words, pictures, tunes, dreams, etc. make on the human soul, creating the feeling of the holy, that is, of the presence of the 'numinous.' In such experiences religion lives and tries to maintain the presence of, and com-munity with, this divine depth of our existence. But since it is 'inaccessible' to any objectifying concept it must be expressed in symbols. One of these symbols is Personal God. It is the common opinion of classical theology, practically in all periods of Church history, that the predicate 'per-sonal' can be said of the Divine only symbolically or by analogy or if affirmed and negated at the same time. . . . Without an element of 'atheism' no 'theism' can be maintained." Tillich, "Science and Theology: A Discussion with Einstein," in *Theology of Culture* (New York: Oxford University Press, 1959), 130–31.

[109] Immanuel Kant, *The Critique of Judgment*, 5:220.

elicit the religious sense: phenomena that involve us intimately but also strike us as enigmatically other and thus not fully graspable—generating experiences of fear, humility, and bewilderment, what Burke calls, in his definition of the sublime, "delightful horror."[110] These include death and the passage of time; considerations on the origins of the universe and its spatial and temporal extent; dark matter and energy, which seem to constitute the great majority of matter and energy in the cosmos but about which so little is understood; the origins of life (even if abiogenesis is correct there is still the question, which has not been answered, about how or why life emerged when and where it did); the infinitesimal and the infinite; the divergences between Einstein's theory of general relativity and the standard model in explaining the universe. Perhaps someday some of these mysteries will be solved, but for the foreseeable future it is difficult to imagine facing them without the generation of the numinous in Otto's rendering of the term. These are not simply abstruse technical matters best left for experts to make incremental headway; rather, most are perennial questions most humans have found themselves wondering about at various points in their lives. Those who do confront them are no less sober, no less intelligent, no less responsible than those who do not worry about what they cannot scientifically answer. Something similar might be said, within the bounds of more ordinary human life, about traumatic experiences that overwhelm our sense of understanding.[111] Relatedly, it is well known that "religious intensity and strength of belief" tend to increase as individuals approach the end of their lives.[112] In any case, Dylan's religious sense stems in part from his consideration of these mysteries and experiences,[113] and his testimony to it thus reminds us that it is elicited by fundamental empirical features of the world as we know it—or, what is virtually the same thing in this context, as we do *not* know it. Indeed, our inability to comprehend fundamental elements of ourselves and our world is itself an empirical

---

[110] Edmund Burke, *A Philosophical Enquiry into the Origins of the Sublime and Beautiful: And Other Pre-Revolutionary Writings* (New York: Penguin Classics), 115.

[111] Otto, for example, understands traumas as eliciting the numinous: "Whatever has loomed upon the world of his ordinary concerns as something terrifying and baffling to the intellect; whatever among natural occurrences or events in the human, animal, or vegetable kingdoms has set him astare in wonder and astonishment—such things have ever aroused in man, and become endued with, the 'daemonic dread' and numinous feeling, so as to become 'portents', 'prodigies', and 'marvels'" (*The Idea of the Holy*, 64).

[112] See Vern L. Bengtston et al., "Does Religiousness Increase with Age? Age Changes and Generational Differences Over 35 Years," *Journal for the Scientific Study of Religion* 54, no. 2 (2015): 363–79.

[113] See, for example, Dylan's song, "Whatcha Gonna Do," from the early 1960s, with its invocation of God, which includes: "Tell me what you're gonna do / When the shadow comes under your door / Or Lord, O Lord / What shall you do?" Also see Bob Dylan, *Saved! The Gospel Speeches* (New York: Hanuman Books, 1990), 66–67, 92.

fact—perhaps a universal one—even as it inspires contemplation and concern for what lies beyond empirical measurement. The decision not to participate in meditation upon the inherent mystery of existence is no more plausible than its opposite. Because the universe does not make sense, it makes no sense to insist that speech and practices that give voice to this circumstance have less integrity, as a human matter, than what can be said within the confines of logical or empirical verifiability.

Third, when the debate between secularists and religionists becomes about the religious sense—rather than the existence of external objects of belief the religious sense may posit—secularists are on weaker ground because there is considerable evidence that the activation of the religious sense can be healthy. Some research has suggested that the religious live on average four years longer than the non-religious.[114] Regular worshippers, for instance, are more likely to adopt a healthier lifestyle and, as older adults, maintain stronger social networks.[115] Psychological benefits of religiosity for individuals confronting the final stages of their lives also have been found.[116] These health benefits suggest an evolutionary basis for the religious sense and thus provide further evidence that it is a fundamental human faculty—not, to be sure, an innate quality that all operate on the basis of, but a pervasive capacity that can be employed at any time.[117]

These three features of the religious sense might not persuade secularists to jettison their atheism. But this is not the main issue. The issue at stake in postsecularism is not to convert the non-religious to religiosity, but to instill in them a respect for the dignity and value of religious ideas, practices, and mentalities. The possibility of a universal religious sense—which the religious exercise and the non-religious curtail—strikes me as a more plausible basis for achieving mutual respect than debate about the existence of external objects of religious belief. To consider the religious not as dogmatists but as active and

---

[114] Laura E. Wallace et al., "Does Religion Stave Off the Grave? Religious Affiliation in One's Obituary and Longevity," *Social Psychology and Personality Science* 10, no. 5 (2019): 662–70.

[115] Joey Marshall, "Are Religious People Healthier?," Pew Research Center, January 31, 2019, https://www.pewresearch.org/fact-tank/2019/01/31/are-religious-people-happier-health ier-our-new-global-study-explores-this-question/; Pew Research Center, "Growing Old in America: Expectations vs. Reality," June 29, 2009, 67, https://www.pewresearch.org/wp-content/ uploads/sites/3/2010/10/Getting-Old-in-America.pdf.

[116] See, for example, Kenneth E. Vail et al., "A Terror Management Analysis of the Psychological Functions of Religion," *Personality and Social Psychology Review* 14, no. 1 (2010): 84–94; James W. Fowler, *Stages of Faith: The Psychology of Human Development and the Quest for Meaning* (San Francisco, HarperCollins, 1981); Lars Tornstam, "Gerotranscendence: The Contemplative Dimension of Aging," *Journal of Aging Studies* 11, no. 2 (1997): 143–54.

[117] As Otto writes of the numinous, "*A priori* cognitions are not such as every one does have— such would be *innate* cognitions—but such as every one is *capable* of having" (*The Idea of the Holy*, 177).

provisional channelers of sentiments virtually all of us can feel—sentiments of transcendence, awe, reverence, wonder, and solemnity vis-à-vis the mysterious possibility of an unseen, not fully understood but real larger order—raises the possibility that, in confronting the religious, secularists can in some very real sense understand themselves to be recognizing different versions of themselves.

It is significant in this regard that one of Dylan's most aggressive appeals to the idea of the religious sense in his combating of secularists occurs in 1986, years after his religious fervor of the late '70s and early '80s. Reflecting back on his gospel period, Dylan comments:

> I was doing what I believed that I should be doing. Most artists should do gospel kind of music. If they don't do something gospel, I don't re-ally trust that artist, I don't care who he is. . . . I never considered myself having Christian fans or un-Christian fans. I don't deal with any kind of people on that level.[118]

Dylan not only refuses to divide his audience between religious (Christian) or unreligious (non-Christian) but suggests that what may unite both sides is the presence of a religious sense; at least, this is what is implied when he makes the forceful claim that all people—or "most artists"—have it in them to pursue gospel music, if only for a brief period. That Dylan adds to this diagnosis the crit-ical claim that those who do not experience their own gospel period cannot be trusted only further magnifies the idea that a religious sense is a human capacity—which, Dylan seems to say, ought to be acknowledged if not cultivated—rather than a particular quality shared only by explicitly religious people. Dylan is not always this aggressive—more frequently testifying to his own religious sense than baldly challenging others to pursue theirs—but, in a way, both moves are not so different in their ultimate function, at least insofar as Dylan's leadership elicits not just idealization from his followers, but identification.

A secularist might respond that, fine, we all have dreams and fantasies, but we should not subject each other to these in the public realm. Just because we have a religious sense does not mean that our acting or speaking on the basis of this sense could ever be intelligible to others. There is some truth to this, but it seems to indict not any articulation of the religious sense, just those that are dogmatic, cliché, or devoid of messages that might themselves be of interest to a wide spec-trum of religious and non-religious people alike.

---

[118] "Dylan Press Conference, 1986, Brett Whiteley Studio, Sydney," posted by FilmStretch Australia, video, 18:21, May 23, 2013, https://youtu.be/pDq1jD9nqm4.

The potency of Dylan's "never could learn to drink that blood and call it wine" is that it accentuates the postsecular aspects of the invocation of the religious sense. If Dylan elsewhere articulates a more pronounced and substantive Christian religious faith, his statement here is more modest, bare, ongoing, and exploratory, as it seems to express the idea that even though he does not at this moment possess a solid formulation of his religious sense he nonetheless does have this sense. Stripped of any particular foundation or manifestation, "Never could learn to drink that blood and call it wine" testifies to the religious sense in its pure form: restless and experimental, diffident yet not dead. Dylan does not claim to possess religious truth here, but he compellingly refuses to understand the world or himself in the radically materialistic or naturalistic way urged by secularists. Dylan's confession is thus more limited than the confession of an outright faith, as it is a testimony to the endurance of a religious sense, not to the concretization of that sense in the form of direct access to the holy or reception of stable ethical direction for the ordering of his life. But it is the limited aspect that also makes it so honest and believable.

II.5. Rethinking Religion as a Human Construct

One of the most familiar tropes in secularist thought is to interpret religion as a human construction. Human beings were not created by gods, but gods by human beings. Religion is a human phenomenon, not a divine one. By itself, this idea does not necessarily dictate a secularist denigration of religiosity. Ludwig Feuerbach, for example, whose 1841 book, *The Essence of Christianity*, played a large role in popularizing the notion, argued that human consciousness of the infinite constitutes the genuine ground of religiosity. While he argued that notions of divinity that followed from this consciousness were but outward projections of inner human aspirations—aspirations for morality, wisdom, justice, intelligence, and other benevolent qualities—and while he understood his philosophy as undermining traditional Christian belief and the idea of revealed religion more generally, he did not identify as an atheist, in part because he saw the process of divinity construction as both flowing from the genuine mystery of the infinite and playing a vital role for humanity. Nonetheless, in the hands of Marx and later atheist critics of religion, the notion of religion as but a human construction has been joined to the secularist critique that religion, because it is a construction, is false and illusory; that it stems not from meditation on the infinite, but from surmountable forms of misery, ignorance, and alienation; and that a mature scientific standpoint therefore requires the rejection of religion. Since the nineteenth century, the secularist emphasis on the human construction of religion has been voiced by generations of critics, most recently by secularist scientists claiming to locate the all-too-human and merely contingent neurological, psychological, and evolutionary roots of religious belief.[119]

One of the striking features of Dylan's role as a prophet of the postsecular—that is, as a prophetic figure whose religious messages often serve to bridge the divide between the religious and the anti-religious—is how often he operates within the parameters of religion as a human construct. But unlike secularists who invoke this idea to condemn religiosity, Dylan invokes it to suggest the integrity and enduring plausibility of religious forms of life.

To be sure, there are certainly passages in Dylan's songs and interviews in which he explains his faith in terms of direct experience of God and even a literalist acceptance of particular parts of the Bible. As has been discussed, Dylan claimed to have had a direct experience of Jesus in a hotel room in Arizona in 1978, and certain songs from his gospel period appear to testify unequivocally to the reality of a non-constructed divinity. But upon reflection, what is remarkable is the *absence* of this kind of thinking in the majority of Dylan's religious music. In his still ongoing postconversion period (following the 1981 album *Shot of Love*)—in which faith is sometimes balanced by doubt, the possibility of religious illusion confronted head-on (as in "Jokerman"), and orthodox religious expression almost entirely jettisoned—this absence is a matter of course. But consider even the three albums from Dylan's gospel period. In the first of these, *Slow Train Coming* (1979), only two of the eight songs on the album directly attest to the reality of God, and one of these is still ambiguous in this regard.[120] In the other six, this idea is missing, either because *faith* in God is emphasized as opposed to confident assertions regarding God's actual existence (e.g., "I Believe in You"), political and social critique are privileged rather than direct assertions of God's existence (e.g., "Slow Train"),

[119] See, for example, J. Anderson Thomson and Clare Aukofer, *Why We Believe in God(s): A Concise Guide to the Science of Faith* (Durham, NC: Pitchstone, 2011).

[120] The one definite instance would be "Gonna Change My Way of Thinking," which includes, among other lines:

> There's a kingdom called Heaven
> A place where there is no pain of birth
> There's a kingdom called Heaven
> A place where there is no pain of birth
> Well the Lord created it, mister
> About the same time He made the earth

The second song, which is more ambiguous, is "When You Gonna Wake Up?" On the one hand, the song begins: "God don't make no promises that He don't keep." On the other hand, though, other lyrics—"Do you ever wonder just what God requires?" and "There's a Man up on a cross and He's been crucified / Do you have any idea why or for who He died?"—are expressed in such a manner that the reality of divinity is not in fact presupposed.

or playful biblical fables are retold that do not deal with God as such (e.g., "Man Gave Names to All the Animals"). The next album, *Saved* (1980), is indeed much more theistic, with as many as seven of its nine songs seeming to assert the reality of God. But it is important to stress that one of the two exceptions, "Pressing On," directly considers the question of knowledge of God and makes claims consistent with the idea of God as a human construct:

> Many try to stop me, shake me up in my mind
> Say, "Prove to me that He's the Lord, show me a sign"
> What kind of sign they need when it all come from within
> When what's lost has been found, what's to come has already been?[121]

And in the third album of Dylan's gospel trilogy, *Shot of Love* (1981), nine of the ten songs do not directly testify to the external reality of God, and the one song that can be interpreted as testifying in this fashion ("Every Grain of Sand") does not do so unambiguously.[122] In the album, direct reference to God is muted due to alternate approaches, including songs that, while religious in their sentiment, do not make direct assertions about divinity (e.g., "Shot of Love"), songs that confront the effervescence of religiosity ("In the Summertime"), songs that do not appear to deal with religion at all ("Lenny Bruce"), and, as I will presently examine, songs that focus on the contempt believers endure within a secularist society ("Property of Jesus" and "Watered-Down Love").

If this analysis is correct, then even within Dylan's most religiously fervent period, in which he proclaimed his adherence to Jesus and made his religiosity the central element of his music, there is a pronounced theological hesitance: of the twenty-seven songs on his three Christian albums, seventeen do not assert that God is real and thus do not undermine the idea of religion as a human construction.[123]

---

[121] To be sure, there is a difference between claiming that divinity is a human construction in the sense of human beings inventing religious symbols, ideas, and imagery and claiming that divinity is a human construction in the sense of it flowing out of a quasi-divine human capacity—and this latter, gnostic idea appears to be more what Dylan has in mind here. Nonetheless, Dylan gives voice in this song to the human-generated quality of religiosity.

[122] The ambiguity stems, first, from the fact that the most theistic line from the song ("In the fury of the moment I can see the master's hand") is not included in numerous versions of it (including the version on the album) and, second, from the fact that the song also recognizes that the sense of divine presence is, sometimes at least, in truth a sense of one's own self ("Sometimes I turn, there's someone there, other times it's only me").

[123] There are many other songs from Dylan's gospel period besides those recorded on these three albums. Many of these, it is true, are theistic, but some likewise reflect ideas and sensibilities that do not clearly assert the existence of God or even express religious doubt (see, for example, "Making a Liar Out of Me").

One could interpret this surprising fact as showing that Dylan is somewhat confused in his theology—a circumstance, however, that, far from undermining his prophetic role, only buttresses what makes it distinct and important, reflecting the fact that he is not only a prophet of the postsecular but a *postsecular prophet*: that is, someone who, in transmitting a prophetic message from an absolute source of normative authority, at the same time interrogates and problematizes both the nature of that authority and his relationship to it. Alternatively, one could interpret Dylan's relative reticence about pronouncements regarding the existence of God as evidence that, even in his clearest religious period, he has multiple purposes inspiring his spirituality, which also seems true. Either way, the fact that a majority of Dylan's most religious songs do not insist on the existence of God is yet another key indicator that the significance of Dylan's gospel music, in its substance, is not simply religious but postsecular. Even at his most explicitly religious, Dylan still often communicates his religiosity in terms that might be accepted by non-theists. By itself, this point goes only so far. What needs to be added is that Dylan does not simply write religious songs in a way that frequently leaves unopposed the possibility of the human construction of religion, but that an important and repeated trope within Dylan's contribution to religious thought is his rethinking of the meaning of the human construction of religion. Rather than engage with the human construction of religion in the manner of Feuerbach, Marx, or others who follow in their wake in invoking the notion to challenge numerous, if not all, forms of religious life, Dylan approaches the human construction of religion from a different angle, invoking it to reorient the debate about religion—away from theological questions and toward the sociopolitics of religious belief—with the result of thereby bolstering sympathy for and understanding of the situation religious believers face within a secularist society.

Dylan achieves this rethinking of the human construction of religion in three main ways: testifying to other human beings' prophetic role in his own life; testifying, in particular, to the assistance of other human beings in awakening and guiding his own religiosity; and expressing his vitriol at the condescension with which non-believers sometimes treat the religious. These three dynamics make up a significant and underappreciated element of Dylan's music and public statements. Their importance consists in framing religious life in human terms—and, thus, not simply in metaphysical or theological ones—and thereby shifting Dylan's profession of his religiosity to a terrain upon which the non-religious might also be engaged and productively included.

Dylan's Prophets

One of the ways Dylan employs the human construction of religion in a postsecular, rather than secularist, direction concerns his own testimony to other human beings who have played prophetic roles in providing him with guidance in his life. I am arguing in these pages that Dylan himself is a prophetic figure—and a very influential one at that—but the fact is that he is a prophet who has had prophets of his own. And the main point to stress is that the existence of the prophetic relation—some humans' belief that other humans are especially endowed or otherwise situated to provide profound ethical instruction—is a *human* basis for constituting and appreciating the quasi-religious posture of pious adherence. Regardless of whether or not gods are real, there is an undeniable and enduring tendency, which has existed throughout human history, for some to find in others' prophetic-charismatic authority a crucial vehicle of religiosity, even if that religiosity is ultimately an anthropological or sociological—rather than divine—phenomenon. In testifying to his own prophets, Dylan as a prophet reminds us of the religiosity inherent in sublunary, strictly human affairs.

Throughout his life, Dylan has credited other individuals with prophetic significance. Johnny Cash, Dylan reports, "was more like a religious figure to me."[124] Mike Seeger, the American folk singer and folklorist, is described by Dylan, upon a chance meeting, as someone who "holds up a mirror, unlocks the door" and all of a sudden "you're set free"; Dylan says that his encounter with Seeger made his brain "wide awake," as if "something hit me," leading him to realize "I might have to disorientate myself."[125] Joan Baez, too, is described as having a stunning effect on Dylan when he hears her sing for the first time.[126] But what should most be emphasized is how at crucial moments in his life—especially at periods in which he found himself vocationally adrift—Dylan credits the influence of

---

[124] Interview in *American Masters*, season 19, episode 7, "No Direction Home: Bob Dylan," directed by Martin Scorsese, aired September 27, 2005, on PBS, https://www.imdb.com/title/tt0367555/?ref_=adv_li_tt.

[125] Quoted in Gilmour, *Gospel According to Bob Dylan*, 19.

[126] See, for example, Dylan's "Poem to Joanie," which includes the lines:

> When all at once the silent air
> Split open from her soundin voice
> Without no warnin from her lips
> An by instinct my blood reversed
> An I shook an started reachin for
> That wall that was supposed t fall
> But my restin nerves weren't restless now
> An this time they wouldn't jump

Liner notes to *Joan Baez in Concert Part 2* (1963). As published on the album the poem had no title, but subsequent publications refer to the title I use here.

chance encounters with other individuals who, often unbeknownst to them, inspire and direct him. Perhaps the most dramatic of these were three incidents from the late 1980s, a period in which, as Dylan describes it in his autobiography *Chronicles*, he had lost purpose and direction:

> Always prolific but never exact, too many distractions had turned my musical path into a jungle of vines. I'd been following established customs and they weren't working. The windows had been boarded up for years and covered with cobwebs, and it's not like I didn't know. . . . Many times I'd come near the stage before a show and would catch myself thinking that I wasn't keeping my word with myself. What that word was, I couldn't exactly remember, but I knew it was back there somewhere. . . . It's nice to be known as a legend, and people will pay to see one, but for most people, once is enough. You have to deliver the goods, not waste your time and everybody else's. I hadn't actually disappeared from the scene, but the road had narrowed, almost was shut down and was supposed to be wide open. I hadn't gone away yet. I was lingering on the pavement. There was a missing person inside of myself and I needed to find him.[127]

Dylan, by the beginning of 1987, felt he had become, in his own words, "a '60s troubadour, a folk-rock relic, a wordsmith from bygone days, a fictitious head of state from a place nobody knows . . . in the bottomless pit of cultural oblivion. . . . The previous ten years had left me pretty whitewashed and wasted out professionally."[128] Dylan initially tried to find direction from nature, but nothing came from it:

> I'd find myself on a houseboat, a floating mobile home, hoping to hear a voice—crawling at slow speed—nosed up on a protective beach at night in the wilderness—moose, bear, deer around—the elusive timber wolf not so far off, calm summer evenings listening to the call of the loon. Think things out. But it was no use. I felt done for, an empty burned-out wreck.[129]

Yet, Dylan describes three epiphanies—each aided by prophetic heeding of others—that led him to rediscover "purpose and commitment," overcome excessive focus on the status of his legend, and instead stand by his work no matter what

[127] Bob Dylan, *Chronicles: Volume One* (New York: Simon & Schuster, 2004), 146–47.
[128] Dylan, 146–47.
[129] Dylan, 147.

came from it.[130] The first of these happened in the summer of 1987, when Dylan was playing some shows with the Grateful Dead between tours with Tom Petty and the Heartbreakers. One evening at a rehearsal in San Rafael, California, feeling uncertain about his ability to perform adequately with the Dead, Dylan abruptly left—lying that he had forgotten something in his hotel room—and wandered around the streets, soon finding himself in a tiny jazz bar ("something was calling me to come in and I entered"), where he ordered a gin and tonic and watched the band four feet from the stage. Dylan describes becoming struck by the jazz singer:

> He wasn't very forceful, but he didn't have to be; he was relaxed, but he sang with natural power. Suddenly and without warning, it was like the guy had an open window to my soul. It was like he was saying, "You should do it this way." All of a sudden, I understood something faster than I ever did before. I could feel how he worked at getting his power, what he was doing to get at it. I knew where the power was coming from and it wasn't his voice, though the voice brought me sharply back to myself. I used to do this thing, I'm thinking. It was a long time and it had been automatic. No one had ever taught me. This technique was so elemental, so simple and I'd forgotten. It was like I'd forgotten how to button my own pants. I wondered if I could still do it. I wanted at least a chance to try. If I could in any way get close to handling this technique, I could get off this marathon stunt ride.[131]

Although initially intending not to return to rehearsal, Dylan went back and, upon employing the never fully described technique of the jazz singer, found himself renewed. "It burned, but I was awake. . . . This was revelatory. . . . I had that old jazz singer to thank."[132] As Dylan later reflected in 2001, apparently in reference to the event: "I really had some sort of epiphany then on how to do those songs again, using certain techniques that I had never thought about."[133]

---

[130] In a 2001 interview with Mikal Gilmore, Dylan accepts Gilmore's characterization of his eventual transformation: "You've spoken about some epiphany that changed your purpose and commitment—some recognition that came to you onstage. You've described it as a moment when you realized that what was important was not your legend or how that weighed you down. What was important, you seemed to say, was for you to stand by your work—and that meant playing music on a regular basis, no matter who you were playing it for." Interview with Mikal Gilmore, "Dylan, at 60, Unearths New Revelations," *Rolling Stone*, November 22, 2001. My account of Dylan's epiphanies has been aided by Andrew McCarron, *Light Come Shining: The Transformations of Bob Dylan* (New York: Oxford University Press, 2017), 105–36.

[131] Dylan, *Chronicles*, 150–51.

[132] Dylan, 151.

[133] Gilmore, "New Revelations." Relatedly, in 2004, Dylan told NPR journalist Steve Inskeep more about the San Rafael jazz singer: "A lot happened for me when I went in there and heard them.

The second epiphany occurred later in 1987, in October, when Dylan had returned to touring with Tom Petty and was performing in an outdoor show in Locarno, Switzerland. The new techniques he had absorbed in the summer suddenly failed him as he came on stage.[134] But at this very moment he was struck by another revelation:

> It's almost like I heard it as a voice. It wasn't like it was even me thinking it. *I'm determined to stand, whether God will deliver me or not.* And all of a sudden everything just exploded. It exploded every which way. . . . After that is when I sort of knew: I've got to go out and play these songs. That's just what I must do.[135]

> I was kind of standing on a different foundation at that point and realized, *"I could do this."* I found out I could do it effortlessly—that I could sing night after night after night and never get tired. I could project it out differently.[136]

> That night in Switzerland it all just came to me. All of a sudden I could sing anything. There might've been a time when I was going to quit or retire, but the next day it was like, "I can't really retire now because I really haven't done anything yet," you know? I want to see where this will lead me, because now I can control it all. Before, I wasn't controlling it. I was just being swept by the wind, this way or that way.[137]

Closely connected to this second epiphany is Dylan's recollection, seemingly in the very moment, of words that the musician Lonnie Johnson had told him in the 1960s, describing an almost mystical technique for playing "a mysterious system of triplets."[138] In describing the Locarno evening in a 2001 interview, Dylan stresses the importance of Johnson:

And I felt like I could do something again or I had a fix on something that I hadn't had for many, many years . . . it was the singer who got to me there. I mean, those things happen sometimes, mostly when they do happen, they happen to a person when they're much younger." Quoted in Larry David Smith, *Writing Dylan: The Songs of a Lonesome Traveler*, 2nd ed. (Westport, CT: Praeger, 2018), 481.

[134] See Dylan, *Chronicles*, 152–53.

[135] Gates, "Dylan Revisited" (emphasis added).

[136] Gilmore, "New Revelations."

[137] Gilmore, "New Revelations"; also see Dylan, *Chronicles*, 152–53.

[138] Quoted in McCarron, *Light Come Shining*, 118. For a detailed account of what this musical technique might be, see Eyolf Østrem, "What I Learned from Lonnie Johnson," *Things Twice* (blog), April 13, 2005, https://www.dylanchords.com/content/what-i-learned-lonnie. There is admittedly some

Not only that [the epiphany just described], but Lonnie Johnson, the blues-jazz player, showed me a technique on the guitar in maybe 1964. I hadn't really understood it when he first showed it to me. It had to do with the mathematical order of the scale on a guitar, and how to make things happen, where it gets under somebody's skin and there's really nothing they can do about it, because it's mathematical. He didn't even play that way himself. . . . Anyway, he just told me, "I want to show you something. You might be able to use this someday." It's more kind of an ancient way of playing. I always wanted to use this technique, but I never was really able to do it with my own songs.[139]

Dylan again stresses the importance of Johnson's influence in *Chronicles*, explaining how the advice that Johnson had given him in the 1960s came back to him in a flash in 1987:

[Lonnie Johnson] took me aside one night and showed me a style of playing based on an odd—instead of even—number system. This was just something he knew about, not necessarily something he used because he did so many different kinds of songs. He said, "This might help you," and I had the idea that he was showing me something secretive, though it didn't make any sense to me at that time because I needed to strum the guitar in order to get my ideas across. It's a highly controlled system of playing and relates to the notes of a scale, how they combine numerically, how they form melodies out of triplets and are axiomatic to the rhythm and chord changes. I never used this style, didn't see that there'd be any purpose to it. But now all of a sudden it came back to me, and I realized that this way of playing would revitalize my world. . . . When Lonnie had showed this to me so many years earlier it was as if he was saying something to me in a foreign language. I understood the etymology of it, I just didn't get how it could be applicable in any way. Now it all clicked. Now I could start getting into it. With a new incantation

---

uncertainty about the precise relationship of Johnson's musical method to Dylan's epiphany in Locarno, due to the opaque chronology Dylan employs in Chapter 4 of *Chronicles*, in which he discusses his revitalization in 1987. In understanding Lonnie Johnson's musical techniques as intimately connected to Dylan's Locarno epiphany, I have been guided by numerous passages from *Chronicles* that suggest as much (e.g., *Chronicles*, 146, 157); the fact that Dylan, in a 2001 interview in which he discusses the sources of his 1987 transformation, cites the Locarno evening and the influence of Johnson in almost the same breath (Gilmore, "New Revelations"); and the work of other interpreters, who, on the basis of the evidence, have made this connection (see, e.g., McCarron, *Light Come Shining*, 113).

[139] Gilmore, "New Revelations."

code to infuse my vocals with manifest presence I could ride high, unconsciously drag endless skeletons from the closet. Thematic triplets making everything hypnotic. I could even hypnotize myself. I could do this night after night. No fatigue or weariness.[140]

To the extent, then, that Dylan's epiphany in Locarno in 1987 was inseparable from the influence of Lonnie Johnson, we have a second instance of Dylan receiving a kind of prophetic guidance from another human being.

The third epiphany occurred in 1989, as Dylan was recording *Oh Mercy*, an album widely seen to mark his return to form after three albums from the mid-1980s that were perhaps the most unacclaimed of his career. As Dylan recounts in *Chronicles*, the same doubts from 1987 were not entirely gone yet by 1989—indeed, he treats both the 1987 and 1989 events in the same chapter of *Chronicles*, itself entitled "Oh Mercy." But a crucial moment occurred during a late-night studio session for *Oh Mercy*, parts of which were recorded with the group Rockin' Dopsie and His Cajun Band. Dylan recounts how at 3 AM, once the official recording for the day was done, he and the other musicians started playing numerous songs, traditional numbers as well as a song he had just written, "Where Teardrops Fall." They decided to record the new song and Dylan describes how in the finale the saxophone player from Dopsie's group, someone he had not even noticed up until that point, made a sudden, prophetic impact. The saxophone player:

> played a sobbing solo that nearly took my breath away. I leaned over and caught a glimpse of the musician's face. He'd been sitting there the whole night in the dark and I hadn't noticed him. The man was the spitting image of Blind Gary Davis, the singing reverend that I'd known and followed around years earlier. What was he doing here? Same guy, same cheeks and chin, fedora, dark glasses. Same build, same height, same long black coat—the works. It was eerie. Reverend Gary Davis, one of the wizards of modern music . . . like he'd been raised upright and was watching over things, keeping constant vigilance over what was happening. He peered across the room at me in an odd way, like he had the ability to see beyond the moment, like he'd thrown a rope line out to grip. All of a sudden I know that I'm in the right place doing the right thing at the right time and Lanois [Dylan's producer for the album] is

---

[140] Dylan, *Chronicles*, 157, 161; see 157–62, especially 158, for Dylan's detailed account of the method.

the right cat. *Felt like I had turned a corner and was seeing the sight of a god's face.*[141]

In each of these three instances—Dylan's guidance from a jazz singer in San Rafael, his epiphany in Locarno interwoven with memories of the mysterious musical system of Lonnie Johnson, and his inspiration in 1989 from a saxophonist with "a god's face"—Dylan receives prophetic direction about his vocation from external human sources. As much as he also reports strictly divine revelation—above all, his experience of Jesus—these human-centric revelations are also part of his prophetic consciousness and alert us to how other human beings can play quasi-religious roles within our lives. Who among us has never been affected by other individuals in this way? To the extent that we have, we are reminded not only that human prophets guide us, but that their doing so underlines the credibility of revelational experiences—and thus something resembling religiosity—for even secular people.

Precious Angels

A second way Dylan rethinks the human construction of religion is the high degree of emphasis his religious music places on human intermediaries who have been instrumental to his conversion and spiritual awakening. If we tend to imagine revelation or conversion as solitary experiences that occur in unmediated fashion as direct encounters between the human and divine, in fact very often human mediation assists in inspiring the change of heart. Augustine's seminal account of his conversion in his *Confessions*, as much as it primarily emphasizes his personal spiritual journey as an independent soul, nonetheless makes reference to the role of Ambrose (bishop of Milan); his mother, Monica; and, most memorably, certain unknown children next door whose playful shouts of "*tolle lege* [pick it up, read it]!" immediately precipitate Augustine at last becoming converted to the Christian faith. Dylan's spiritual music places uncommon attention on this kind of human intermediary and, as a result, makes the account of his own Christian conversion more believable and relatable to secular skeptics. Insofar as Dylan sings not about finding God, but about his relationship with individuals who have led him to God, he discusses his Christian awakening in terms that lack the speculative, metaphysical features that often characterize direct testimonies of faith. In doing this, he humanizes his conversion, making it less exclusively about God and instead also about earnestly heeding others who themselves understand themselves as having a relationship with God.

---

[141] Dylan, 190–91 (emphasis added).

This approach allows Dylan to speak simultaneously from *both* secular and religious perspectives: in sometimes placing himself in the role of someone curious though uncertain about another's religiosity, Dylan presents himself—in
the very context of his religious awakening—also as a secular individual, albeit
one who, in good postsecular fashion, respects and listens to the religious. To
be sure, following his conversion, Dylan adopts a more traditionally religious
standpoint. But his attentive relationship to people of faith—a dynamic that
recurs throughout the years leading up to his gospel period—allows him to give
voice to both secular and religious standpoints, and perhaps something in between as well.

It is often observed that Dylan, especially in the 1970s (the period that
precedes and then culminates in his gospel music), oscillates between two
objects of salvation—woman and God—and that the overarching direction in
this period is toward the de-divinization of woman and the focus on God instead.[142] This interpretation seems correct, but what it misses is that even in
Dylan's most explicitly religious period he continues to focus on the human
beings—especially women—who propel, support, and instruct his emergent
faith. His testimony to his religiosity regularly returns to these literal angels (i.e.,
messengers), without whom it seems he would not have achieved his religious
awakening. And beyond this testimony, the biographical record is clear: in addition to the anonymous person who allegedly threw a cross on stage at a show in
San Diego on November 17, 1978, which Dylan reportedly picked up and took
out of his pocket the next night in a Tucson hotel room right before having a
direct experience of Jesus, numerous friends and fellow musicians helped Dylan
along his path toward Christian awakening—above all, perhaps, the female
backup singers with whom he performed during the 1979–1981 period, especially Mary Alice Artes, Regina McCrary, and Helena Springs.[143]

Consider the following examples, which are of interest because they both
demonstrate the significance of "precious angels" (and thus of the human construction of religion, *seen in a religious light*) and figure Dylan in the role not of
religious prophet, but of secular person evincing an incredulity yet fascination
toward others' prayer and spirituality.

First, Helena Springs reports how, in late 1978 or early 1979, she helped
open Dylan to prayer and how he was both extremely curious yet also hesitant
about it:

---

[142] On this, see Michael Gray, *Song and Dance Man III: The Art of Bob Dylan* (New York: Continuum, 2002), 206–48; also see Williams, *Dylan—What Happened?*, 77–79.

[143] Dylan discusses the San Diego experience in *Saved! Gospel Speeches*, 7–8. Heylin clarifies the date of Dylan's reflections in *Dylan: Behind the Shades Revisited*, 491.

I can't really go into too much depth, because that would upset me. I think it had to do with personal things. He was having some problems once and he called me and he asked me questions that no one could possibly help with. And I just said, "Don't you ever pray?" And he said, "*Pray?*" Like that, you know. And I said, "Don't you ever do that?" I said, "When I have trouble, I pray." And he said, "*Really?*" He asked me more questions about it, he started enquiring, he's a very inquisitive person which is one good thing about him—he's always searching for truth, truth in anything he can find. It was like he was exploring Christianity. He didn't give up being a Jewish person, but he learned how to pray, and when he'd learned all he could learn, he went on to something else.[144]

As a second example, consider Mary Alice Artes, Dylan's sometime girlfriend, widely thought to be the "Covenant Woman" and perhaps also "Precious Angel" of whom he sings. Their relationship seemed to produce the same situation of Dylan being deeply interested in another person's faith yet also somewhat incredulous about it. According to Dylan's personal assistant Dave Kelly, the following occurred sometime in late 1978 or early 1979:

As far as I know, they were living together and she had come back to the Lord so she knew it wasn't right for them to be living together without being married. I think it was mind-blowing to him and he had to know why. Why can they no longer live together? He had never had anybody that believed that much that it wasn't the right thing to do. She started witnessing to him about her faith.[145]

Dylan himself seems to confirm what Springs and Kelly describe. In a 1980 interview with Robert Hilburn, which appears to reference his relationship with Artes in late 1970s, Dylan reports:

The funny thing is a lot of people think that Jesus comes into a person's life only when they are either down and out or are miserable or just old and withering away. That's not the way it was for me. . . . I was doing fine.

[144] John Bauldie, ed., "'Don't You Ever Pray?' Helena Springs interviewed by Chris Cooper," in *Wanted Man: In Search of Bob Dylan* (New York: Citadel Press, 1991), 127. A slightly different version of the interview, small elements of which I have included in the cited passage, can be found in Heylin, *Dylan: Behind the Shades Revisited*, 493.

[145] Quoted in Marshall, *Dylan: A Spiritual Life*, 34. This experience appears to have precipitated Dylan's relationship with the Vineyard Christian Fellowship, his conversion, and his months of Bible study.

I had come a long way in just the year we were on the road [1978]. I was relatively content, but a very close friend of mine mentioned a couple of things to me and one of them was Jesus. Well, the whole idea of Jesus was foreign to me. I said to myself, "I can't deal with that. Maybe later." But later it occurred to me that I trusted this person and I had nothing to do for the next couple of days so I called the person back and said I was willing to listen about Jesus.[146]

In this same interview, Dylan further reports that, through a friend, he met two young pastors: "I was kind of skeptical, but I was also open. . . . I certainly wasn't cynical. I asked lots of questions, questions like, 'What's the son of God, what's all that mean?' and, 'What does it mean—dying for my sins?'" Dylan slowly began to accept that "Jesus was real and I wanted that. . . . I knew that He wasn't going to come into my life and make it miserable, so one thing led to another . . . until I had this feeling, this vision and feeling."[147]

These examples—in which Dylan, compared to overtly religious believers, seems skeptical and secular, yet importantly also deeply interested in learning more about the nature of others' faith—are but the most intense instances of a more longstanding tendency he has evinced throughout his life, especially in the period prior to his religious conversion. Dylan's mother recounts how "as a child, Bob attended *all* the churches around Hibbing; he was very interested in religion, and *all* religions, by no means just his own."[148] In 1970, Dylan had an encounter with his friend Scott Ross, a New York DJ, who recently had become a Christian. Ross recalls how, much like in his later encounters with Springs and Artes, Dylan was fascinated by Ross's religiosity:

I started to tell him the story about what happened with the Lord in my life, and he was intrigued, asked a lot of questions. A lot of earlier conversations in my pre-Jesus days were so spacey; we got into some weird, esoteric, you know, ozone-level kind of stuff. Who knew what we were saying? You thought you were intelligent and profound and deep, but it was just a lot of gobbledygook. . . . So I think what he was hearing in me was something pretty clear, that I had come to some realization of truth that he was intrigued by. At that point, I don't think he called that

[146] Cott, "Interview with Robert Hilburn, *The Los Angeles Times*, November 23, 1980," in *Essential Interviews*, 295–96.

[147] Cott, "Interview with Robert Hilburn," in *Essential Interviews*, 296.

[148] Quoted in Toby Thompson, *Positively Main Street: Bob Dylan in Minnesota* (Minneapolis: University of Minnesota Press, 2008), 161.

truth "Jesus," but he was certainly interested. God certainly came into the conversation, and I was clear that my conversion was to Jesus.[149]

Something similar happened, too, when Jonathan Cott shared with Dylan materials from Jewish mysticism.[150] And, to give one more example, in 1974 Dylan requested a meeting with Arthur Blessit, one of the speakers at a religious rally in Miami that Dylan attended. Blessit recounts Dylan's skeptical but earnest questioning:

> [Dylan] asked how did I know Jesus was in my life; how did I know there was a God, and that He really cares; and how did I know Jesus was the right way. Our conversation was all about Jesus, not religion. He was wanting to know if Jesus was really the Way, the Truth, and the Life. I sought to answer the questions he asked as best as I could. The talk was very intense, and he was totally interested in Jesus. . . . [And then] I prayed for him, that he would come to know and follow Jesus. He said he had come to hear me, and see what a real Jesus follower would say to his questions. . . . It was a powerful time. Here was a radical man of music who was talking with a radical follower of Jesus. We understood each other. We did not talk about his music, or my life, just Jesus.[151]

In all of these examples, Dylan is described by others or describes himself as someone not at all fully on board with evangelical Christianity but amazed by and appreciative of those who are. What he models in these cases is the very postsecular mindset his later religious prophecy elicits in those who are secular: not religiosity itself but a willingness to understand it better, see it as a potential we all possess, and, in doing so, respect it more.

Of course, the meaning of precious angels for Dylan is not only that in initially confronting them he manifests a key postsecular mentality, but that they also help propel him to his own conversion. Yet even in this latter context, the idea of precious angels has a postsecular significance. In insisting on the vital role of actual human beings to his own faith, Dylan makes that faith more relatable to those who are not religious. Consider the opening lines from his gospel song "Precious Angel":

> Precious angel, under the sun
> How was I to know you'd be the one

---

[149] Quoted in Marshall, *Dylan: A Spiritual Life*, 17–18.
[150] See Marshall, 26–27.
[151] Quoted in Marshall, 21–22.

> To show me I was blinded, to show me I was gone
> How weak was the foundation I was standing upon?

And the chorus:

> Shine your light, shine your light on me
> Shine your light, shine your light on me
> Shine your light, shine your light on me
> Ya know I just couldn't make it by myself
> I'm a little too blind to see

One of the fixtures of orthodox Christian belief—especially in its Augustinian and later Protestant forms—is the idea that human beings cannot achieve human flourishing on their own but require the help of God to overcome sin and achieve whatever happiness is most possible in the sublunary realm. Dylan clearly references this idea, but not unequivocally. The help he most directly seems to acknowledge is the help of an angel—a human woman instrumental to his finding God. There is ambiguity, then, in regard to the light Dylan wishes for: Is it the light of God or the light of those who will help him believe in God and orient his life in terms of this belief? If the former, Dylan is on familiar theological ground. But if the latter, he has shifted the analysis so that what he actually is praying for is not simply a relationship with God, but human intermediaries who will continue to get him there. In this case, what he would be extolling is not God directly, but the people in his life most responsible for inspiring his connection to the divine. That is to say, there is a double blindness: the singer's alienation from God and his inability to overcome that alienation without human help. By doubling these religious sentiments—so they refer both to God and to the human messengers who help make God believable—Dylan renders his religiosity more tangible, credible, and accessible to skeptics. Secularists can deny that God exists. But they cannot deny that some actual human beings who believe in God can inspire other human beings to do the same. Insofar as Dylan is praising not God but those who, through their belief, have helped to make his own possible, he enunciates a religious hope that ought to be fully understandable—and even acceptable—to secular people who do not themselves believe.

In "Covenant Woman," from 1980, something similar is at play:

> And I just got to tell you
> I do intend
> To stay closer than any friend
> I just got to thank you
> Once again

For making your prayers known
Unto heaven for me
And to you, always, so grateful
I will forever be

I've been broken, shattered like an empty cup
I'm just waiting on the Lord to rebuild and fill me up
And I know He will do it 'cause He's faithful and He's true
He must have loved me so much to send me someone as fine as you

Like the precious angel, the covenant woman is a human intermediary who reminds us that, as a phenomenological matter, religiosity is something empirical, measurable, and thus undeniably real (i.e., how religious one feels, not the truth of the doctrines). Further, insofar as one's religiosity can be elicited by human intermediaries, there is the parallel reminder that religiosity is not fixed, that we have possibilities for transcendent experiences that are always being more or less realized.

Dylan's deep attention to such human intermediaries thus has a twofold postsecular significance: on the one hand, his initial encounters with them leads him to model a postsecular mentality suitable to secular people (a respectful interest in religious others); on the other hand, the crucial role played by such intermediaries in Dylan's own coming to faith makes that faith more human and so more relatable to those who themselves are not religious. To be sure, Dylan's religious praise of the human intermediaries who have enabled his own religiosity could be read by secularists as proof that the objects of religious belief are only human constructions. But it can also be seen as an honest celebration of the real humans who make religion no less real for those who experience it—and from this angle, there is no illusion, just forthrightness, about the dynamics of an authentic and abidingly genuine religiosity.

Vitriol at the Condescension Sometimes Suffered by the Religious

A final dynamic of Dylan's rethinking of religion as a human construct relates to his sociopolitical articulation of the life of faith, exposing and contesting the disparagement believers often are subjected to by contemporary secularists. Indeed, one of Dylan's greatest postsecular moves is to alter the vantage point so that what is at stake is less an internal, purely spiritual account of his finding of God, but a sociological frame of reference in which the condescension toward belief is analyzed and indignantly resisted.

Dylan himself suffered from this kind of condescension. His 1979–1980 tour that debuted his Christian music generated contestation and abuse from onlookers. There are different reports, but most describe how Dylan and his music, initially at least, were widely booed, mocked, and opposed by large numbers of his audiences, a circumstance that of course fits the customary choreography of prophets as they appear in public.[152] A 1979 article from *Rolling Stone* recounts that Dylan's first Christian shows were greeted with much jeering and calls for refunds from disappointed fans.[153] One of Dylan's bandmates, Spooner Oldham, recalls that "half the audience booed, half clapped."[154] Eyewitnesses report an "undercurrent of hostility in the audience" and that "people walked out . . . boiling mad."[155] Even sympathetic onlookers admit how uncomfortable the audience was, with one attendee describing the situation as: "Everybody stunned, absolutely stunned."[156] Initial press coverage only intensified the mix of consternation and mockery Dylan so often received in this period. The *San Francisco Examiner* ran a story with the headline "Dylan Bombs." A much-discussed review in the *San Francisco Chronicle* by Joel Selvin, entitled "Bob Dylan's God-Awful Gospel," took Dylan to task as well, writing that "when social historians look back over these years, Dylan's conversion will serve as a concise metaphor for the vast emptiness of the era. Dylan is no longer asking hard questions. Instead, he turned to the most prosaic source of truth on Earth, so aptly dubbed 'opium of the masses' by Karl Marx." Amazingly, Dylan was sufficiently bothered by this review that he called Selvin's home, telling Selvin's wife that he was trying to figure out what kind of person Selvin was and that Selvin had "lost his license to review."[157]

Part of what made Dylan's gospel tour so controversial is that, in between songs, he routinely delivered evangelical sermons. Tapes of some of these gospel speeches capture the contested aspect of it all, with members of the audience repeatedly engaging in boos and catcalls and pleas for Dylan to stop his

[152] Dylan's gospel speeches, delivered in between songs at his concerts, frequently mention or allude to heckling from the audience. See Dylan, *Saved! The Gospel Speeches*, 24, 33, 37, 38, 41, 47, 78, 99, 107.

[153] "Dylan Tour Off to Shaky Start," *Rolling Stone*, December 14, 1979, https://www.rollingstone.com/music/music-news/dylan-tour-off-to-shaky-start-104216/.

[154] Interview in the documentary *Inside Bob Dylan's Jesus Years: Busy Being Born . . . Again*, directed by Joel Gilbert (Los Angeles: Highway 61 Entertainment, 2008), DVD, https://www.imdb.com/title/tt2165867/?ref_=tt_mv_close.

[155] Joel Selvin, interview in *Inside Bob Dylan's Jesus Years*.

[156] Mitch Glaser, interview in *Inside Bob Dylan's Jesus Years*.

[157] As recounted by Selvin, interview in *Inside Bob Dylan's Jesus Years*. Also see Selvin, "Bob Dylan's God-Awful Gospel," *San Francisco Chronicle*, November 3, 1979.

preaching.[158] Dylan remained undeterred, sometimes lashing back at the audience, as when, in response to cries that he play rock music and desist from sermonizing, he retorted: "If you want rock'n roll, you go down and rock'n roll. You can go and see KISS *and you can rock'n roll all the way down to the pit!*"[159] Stephen Webb suggests—correctly, I think—just how daunting it was for Dylan to perform in the face of such "disparagement and incomprehension."[160] In part because of Dylan's sermons, these shows were the most criticized and controversial of any he had performed. In short, audiences were not at all prepared for what they were getting from Dylan, and many turned on him, with one witness reporting "extremely violent" harangues against him and another describing the reception of Dylan's religious message as "a brawl."[161]

The abuse Dylan received came not only from those who were in actual attendance listening to him sing and preach. Given Dylan's cultural prominence, his public conversion and its music became objects of more general kinds of criticism. The music critic Anthony DeCurtis reports that Dylan's "idea of *serving* really bothered people at the time," offending the individualism they valued and expected Dylan to stand for, and that many were outraged by his embrace of Christianity because it was seen as a betrayal and an insult to their intelligence. Further, DeCurtis observes that Dylan also was castigated because it seemed that the former paragon of cool was now doing something incredibly unhip.[162] As Selvin himself later reflected, Dylan in 1979 was taking the most "antipathetical posture" possible within rock music at that time.[163] Heylin puts it modestly when he says that Dylan "made people feel uncomfortable."[164] It was not just "religiosity" as such that caused such perturbation, but the particular brand of Christianity Dylan was preaching, which, as Webb well summarizes it, included three transgressive elements: theological exclusivity, a lack of a progressive social program, and Dylan's anger.[165]

The disparagement Dylan suffered was intensified by the fact that theists were not necessarily quick to embrace him either. As one of his pastors, Bill Dwyer, recounts: "There was a lot of suspicion from both sides of the fence initially."[166]

---

[158] Consider "Bob Dylan Armageddon Sermon/Solid Rock Tempe Arizona 1979 First Gospel Tour," posted by Start To Continue, video, 9:59, January 24, 2021, https://youtu.be/J11spW0zPlk.

[159] Dylan, *Saved! The Gospel Speeches*, 38 (emphasis added).

[160] Webb, *Dylan Redeemed*, 64.

[161] These comments, made by Dylan biographer Clinton Heylin and music critic Anthony DeCurtis, respectively, are featured in the documentary *Bob Dylan—1978–1989: Both Ends of the Rainbow*, produced by Prism Films (Surrey, UK: Chrome Dreams Media, 2008), DVD.

[162] DeCurtis makes these observations in *Bob Dylan—1978–1989*.

[163] Interview in *Inside Bob Dylan's Jesus Years*.

[164] Interview in *Bob Dylan—1978–1989*.

[165] Webb, *Dylan Redeemed*, 86.

[166] Interview in *Inside Bob Dylan's Jesus Years*.

Many in the Jewish community objected to Dylan's conversion. Nadine Epstein and Rebecca Frankel commented: "Not since Shabbatai Tzvi's 17th century about-face [in converting to Islam] did an exit from Judaism shock the tribe like Dylan's Christian period."[167] The abuse Dylan endured was magnified, too, by the lack of support he received from his friends and formerly sympathetic followers and critics. John Lennon replied to Dylan's "Gotta Serve Somebody" with his own "Serve Yourself." Allen Ginsberg reported his happiness when, with the song "Lenny Bruce" on *Shot of Love* (1981), Dylan seemed to signal the end of his gospel period.[168] Others took aim at Dylan's sincerity, with Keith Richards ridiculing Dylan as a "prophet of profit."[169] As far as erstwhile sympathetic critics, Greil Marcus wrote: "Listening to the new Bob Dylan album [*Slow Train Coming*] is something like being accosted in an airport."[170] Even Paul Williams, in an early and generally positive account of Dylan's conversion (which Dylan himself liked and appreciated), said of Dylan's born-again transformation: "Now he has or seems to have joined up with the forces of sexual repression, mindless nationalism, and religious intolerance."[171] To be sure, there were always many who appreciated Dylan's performances from this period—with some rock critics citing the exceptional musical quality of his shows during 1979–1981[172]—and it seems the responses got somewhat more favorable over time. There were also others, of course, who welcomed Dylan's religious message. But the level of opposition was acute, and it went beyond the negative reaction of ticketholders to become a broader secularist critique from journalists, social critics, and other artists.

Dylan confronted secularist hostility not just by enduring it at his concerts and their aftermath; he also made the very issue of intolerance toward religion central to lyrics he wrote and sang during his gospel period. In his music, he repeatedly identifies and criticizes those who mock religious belief. And this is important because it, too, places his religious message on the human level (addressing the relation between human beings rather than between humans and divinity) and thus goes to the heart of postsecular ethics, which stands for inculcating respect between the religious and non-religious. Sometimes Dylan's perspective is to be concerned about friends and acquaintances who, lacking a proper relationship with

[167] Nadine Epstein and Rebecca Frankel, "Bob Dylan: The Unauthorized Spiritual Biography," *Moment*, July–August 2005, 81.

[168] Webb, *Dylan Redeemed*, 33.

[169] Quoted in Gilmour, *Gospel According to Bob Dylan*, 80.

[170] Greil Marcus, "Amazing Chutzpah," in *The Dylan Companion*, ed. Elizabeth Thomson and David Gutman (Cambridge, MA: Da Capo Press, 2001), 237.

[171] Williams, *Dylan—What Happened?*, 120.

[172] Clinton Heylin describes Dylan's 1979–1980 shows as "his greatest ever … body of concerts." Quoted in *Bob Dylan—1978–1989*.

God and religion, have fallen into spiritually dead materialism and lostness.[173] But the starkest example of this socialized angle of analysis arises in Dylan's prophetic laments about the way followers of God are treated, thereby making the issue less about the truth of religious faith than the unkind and callous disrespect believers face within a secularist society. Perhaps the most significant instance in this regard is Dylan's 1981 song "Property of Jesus":

Go ahead and talk about him because he makes you doubt
Because he has denied himself the things that you can't live without
Laugh at him behind his back just like the others do
Remind him of what he used to be when he comes walkin' through

He's the property of Jesus
Resent him to the bone
You got something better
You've got a heart of stone
[recurring chorus]

Stop your conversation when he passes on the street
Hope he falls upon himself, oh, won't that be sweet
Because he can't be exploited by superstition anymore
Because he can't be bribed or bought by the things that you adore
When the whip that's keeping you in line doesn't make him jump

[173] Dylan often expresses worry about others in his midst who are not realizing their potential. Such a perspective is like proselytizing but is frequently couched in language that falls short of explicit and thus less believable theological musings. Consider the following, from "Precious Angel":

My so-called friends have fallen under a spell
They look me squarely in the eye and they say, "All is well"
Can they imagine the darkness that will fall from on high
When men will beg God to kill them and they won't be able to die?

It is true that this is still theistic and quite speculative, but what most concerns Dylan here is the experience of being surrounded by unbelievers whose greatest error, it seems, is excessive ease and, with it, a misdiagnosis of the world and humanity and a concomitant failure to recognize the need to strengthen what remains. As a second example, consider this from "Slow Train":

Sometimes I feel so low-down and disgusted
Can't help but wonder what's happenin' to my companions
Are they lost or are they found
Have they counted the cost it'll take to bring down
All their earthly principles they're gonna have to abandon?
There's a slow, slow train comin' up around the bend

And, finally, from "When the Night Comes Falling from the Sky":

I saw thousands who could have overcome the darkness
For the love of a lousy buck, I watched them die

Say he's hard-of-hearin', say that he's a chump
Say he's out of step with reality as you try to test his nerve

Because he doesn't pay tribute to the king that you serve
Say that he's a loser 'cause he got no common sense
Because he don't increase his worth at someone else's expense
Because he's not afraid of trying, 'cause he don't look at you and smile
'Cause he doesn't tell you jokes or fairy tales, say he's got no style

You can laugh at salvation, you can play Olympic games
You think that when you rest at last you'll go back from where you came
But you've picked up quite a story and you've changed since the womb
What happened to the real you, you've been captured but by whom?

What is remarkable about "Property of Jesus" is that it pitches the whole conversation about religion in terms that have nothing to do with belief and its truth but rather relate to the interpersonal dynamics between believers and nonbelievers. The choice between callous secularism and religiosity is not presented as a choice about what is true but as about two ways of being in the world: materialism versus self-denial; conformity versus attunement to individual conscience; susceptibility to corruption versus integrity; pursuit of worldly success versus orientation around some other standard; obedience to social/corporate structures versus freedom from this whip; being fully at home in ordinary human relations versus not being entirely comfortable or at ease; being false versus being honest ("he don't look at you and smile"). Maybe most surprising is that Dylan associates the religious with an anti-superstitious mentality, recalling that early Judeo-Christians understood themselves to have rejected pagan superstition. In fact, the precise line—"he can't be exploited by superstition anymore"—suggests that the ultimate issue here is not whether one believes things that are untrue but whether one's beliefs (true or not) are a condition of being taken advantage of economically or otherwise. Perhaps, Dylan could be read to say, religion is a kind of superstition, but one that insulates from other, more dangerous variants.

In any case, there is a twofold postsecular quality to "Property of Jesus." First, Dylan frames the choice between religion and non-religion as being between two concrete ethical ways of being in the world, so that religiosity is irreducible to abstract theological commitments and instead involves a substantive form of life that follows upon belief in God. This makes religiosity incontrovertibly real regardless of the truth of its theological claims. And second, Dylan's focus is not to attest to the truth of Christian theology but to highlight the cruelty and unfairness with which one side treats the other. In pointing to the ridicule believers face from secularists, he is not defending the existence of God but defending those derided for their belief in God. His polemical target is not unbelief itself, but the callousness so often threatened by it. In taking aim at secularists' "heart of stone," Dylan alludes to biblical sources—above all, Ezekiel 36:26.[174] The great scholar of biblical prophecy Abraham Heschel has reminded us that the ultimate objective of the Hebrew prophets was to identify, indict, and overcome callousness in their listeners.[175] But if for the biblical prophets overcoming callousness was inseparable from forging a relationship with God, with Dylan the object is more modest, as it seems to principally refer to desisting from an arrogant mockery of believers.

Dylan's postsecular defense of *believers in God*, in place of God as such, is not limited to "Property of Jesus" but is a repeated trope in his religious music, especially in his final gospel album, *Shot of Love*. Consider the line from "The Groom's Still Waiting at the Altar":

> Try to be pure at heart, they arrest you for robbery,
> Mistake your shyness for aloofness, your silence for snobbery

And in "Watered-Down Love," Dylan attacks non-believers with the chorus:

> You don't want a love that's pure
> You wanna drown love
> You want a watered-down love

While this song could be read in a non-postsecular fashion (as a simple articulation of the superiority of faith to unbelief), its main focus seems to be a reaction to the perceived threat posed by secularist intolerance—and in any case, it is yet another instance of Dylan pitching his religious reflections not simply in terms of the relationship between human and God (which secularists would reject as absurd) but in terms of the relationship between two types of people (believers and non-believers), which even the most ardent materialist has to recognize is a real occurrence with ethical implications.

We are all too aware, of course, of the opposite form of intolerance, in which religious fundamentalists denigrate the non-religious, but Dylan's angle in these songs is from the other side, attending to the ridicule and condescension with which overly confident secularists treat the religious. And if fundamentalists are likely to be overt in their intolerance, a salutary feature of Dylan's approach is that it acutely describes the much more subtle kind of haughtiness that arises in

---

[174] Ezekiel 36:26 reads: "I will give you a new heart and put a new spirit in you; I will remove from you your heart of stone and give you a heart of flesh."

[175] Abraham J. Heschel, *The Prophets* (New York: Harper Perennial, 2001), 20, passim.

the inner mind of secularists. The depiction of unfair abuse from non-believers both places Dylan's prophecy on the fully credible sociological level and aims to redress a moral wrong.

In sum, these three recurring features of Dylan's spiritual life and religious music—his reception of guidance from others' prophetic aura, his fascination with and ultimate religious awakening through others' devout religiosity, and his concern about how people of faith are disparaged by secularists—are all examples of Dylan making what Feuerbach called "the true or anthropological essence of religion"[176] not what it is usually taken to be (a grounds for skepticism toward alleged religious truth) but, on the contrary, a basis for inspiring greater respect for the undeniable reality of religious belief and its integrity.

II.6. Everybody Must Get Stoned

Dylan's song "Rainy Day Women #12 & 35" is one of his weirdest. Interpreters have long mused over how to make sense of its meaning. Given the extent and diversity of the critical attention it has received, it is surprising that few, if any, commentators have treated it in prophetic terms, with the line that concludes each verse (and the de facto title by which the song is widely known)—"Everybody must get stoned"—taken as an imperative pronouncement to take drugs. Why this reticence? For some, the silliness and joviality of the recording on Dylan's 1966 album *Blonde on Blonde*—with Dylan laughing at least twice on the track, wild shouting in the background, a gaudy brass musical accompaniment, and an initial title of "A Long-Haired Mule and a Porcupine Here"—make it too unserious to possess prophetic content. In the eyes of such critics, it might be a "drug song," but this is taken to mean only that it is about drugs or maybe also a polite invitation to take them, not a prophetic summons.[177] Other commentators have focused on various double entendres Dylan employs—a rainy day woman is both slang for a joint and a reference to Proverbs 27:15[178] and, further, getting stoned can itself refer to drugs or a well-known biblical punishment—but do not pursue the implicit suggestion that both sides (the drug allusions and the religious ones) might properly be combined to form elements of a *single message.*

---

[176] This is the title to Part I of Feuerbach's *The Essence of Christianity*, trans. George Eliot (Mineola, NY: Dover, 2008 [1841]).

[177] Hinchey, for instance, reads the song's meaning as: "The world is out to get us, but we're all in this together—and so (whispering) let's smoke a joint and enjoy each other's company." John Hinchey, *Like a Complete Unknown: The Poetry of Bob Dylan's Songs* (New York: Stealing Home, 2002), 187.

[178] Proverbs 27:15 states: "A continual dripping on a rainy day [most likely, as in a leaky house] and a contentious woman are alike."

Still other commentators have downplayed the drug focus, choosing to interpret the song primarily as about paranoia,[179] as concerning a "solidarity in isolation" that applies not just to drug users but to alienated hipsterism more generally,[180] or even as a religious song with no genuine connection to drugs at all.[181] Underlying these and most other interpretations of which I am aware is a preference for reading the *must* in "Everybody must get stoned" in predictive rather than imperative terms: as "most of us are bound to get stoned" (whether high or persecuted), instead of "you, listeners, ought to get stoned" (high).

I have no interest in insisting on the "correct" meaning of "Rainy Day Women #12 & 35," as it is clearly polyvocal. All I mean to emphasize is that the prophetic injunction to seek transcendence via drugs is an obvious reading of "Everybody must get stoned" and one whose lack of attention from critics (which oddly mirrors the bans from radio play the song received when first released) reminds us of what is uncomfortable, provocative, and, by extension, prophetic about the piece. The prophetic aspect is enhanced when one appreciates not only that the line "Everybody must get stoned" is the title by which the song is commonly known, but also that the song became Dylan's biggest hit at the time, giving it a very wide audience despite the censorship. The divergence between "Rainy Day Women" and "Let's Go Get Stoned," the Ray Charles song (written by Nickolas Ashford, Valerie Simpson, and Josephine Armstead) that partially inspired it, further emphasizes the imperative, prophetic aspect: what for Charles is merely an invitation becomes for Dylan (at least potentially) a command.

Most of all, though, Dylan's injunction to get high is not confined to this work but finds parallel in numerous other of his writings and public statements. Dylan sometimes seems to support the use of pot, hash, and opium, among other substances, as an ethical imperative. Consider his comments in a 1966 *Playboy* interview:

> I wouldn't advise anybody to use drugs—certainly not the hard drugs; drugs are medicine. But opium and hash and pot—now, these aren't drugs; they just bend your mind a little. I think *everybody's* mind should be bent once in a while. Not by LSD, though. LSD is medicine—a different kind of medicine. It makes you aware of the universe, so to speak; you realize how foolish *objects* are. But LSD is not for groovy people; it's

---

[179] Hinchey, *Like a Complete Unknown*, 187.

[180] John Gibbens, *The Nightingale's Code: A Poetic Study of Bob Dylan* (London: Touched Press, 2001), 271; also see Mike Marqusee, *Wicked Messenger: Bob Dylan and the 1960s* (New York: Seven Stories Press, 2005), 196–200.

[181] Webb, *Dylan Redeemed*, 50–51.

for mad, hateful people who want revenge. It's for people who usually have heart attacks. They ought to use it at the Geneva Convention.[182]

Note the moralized "should" that Dylan attaches to soft drug use. And if assigning hard drugs to the category of medicine seems to restrict them, it also suggests an appropriate context for their usage as well, as Dylan claims here that LSD is especially well suited to treat a kind of psychological sickness bordering on sin. As a historical aside, LSD was legal in the U.S. at the time of Dylan's comments, only becoming illegal the following year, and had been used in therapeutic contexts for over a decade, including with well-publicized patients such as Cary Grant, Anaïs Nin, Jack Nicholson, Stanley Kubrick, André Previn, James Coburn, and Lord Buckley.[183]

In the original interview with *Playboy*, which did not get published, Dylan was more extreme than in his published remarks, seeming to endorse all forms of drug use:

It's fine if they use pot and LSD and heroin . . . everything. I mean, that's groovy. . . . To know pot—or to know any drug—is fine; and it's not gonna fuck you up. . . . I mean, LSD is a medicine. You take it and you know . . . [that] you don't really have to keep taking it all the time.[184]

In part because of comments such as these, it is common knowledge that Dylan himself is or has been a serious drug user. The facts are well known to his biographers and, key in this context, also part of the public perception of the man. Those of us who treat Dylan prophetically follow someone we know to have experimented heavily with drugs: alcohol, pot, hash, opium, psilocybin, LSD, cocaine, heroin, and methamphetamine. And this circumstance is itself a kind of indirect endorsement of drug use. Dylan does not follow the usual celebrity model of someone who went astray through drug addiction. Despite his serious bouts with heroin, cocaine, and methamphetamines in the 1960s and with alcohol later in life, he is not someone who clearly fell victim to drugs. It is not just that he seems to have mostly kicked his most serious drug habit (heroin) by

[182] Cott, "Interview with Nat Hentoff, *Playboy*, March 1966," in *Essential Interviews*, 115.

[183] Michael Pollan, *How to Change Your Mind: What the New Science of Psychedelics Teaches Us about Consciousness, Dying, Addiction, Depression, and Transcendence* (New York: Penguin Press, 2019), 156–57.

[184] Quoted in Heylin, *Dylan: Behind the Shades Revisited*, 231. For the unedited audio interview, see Josh Jones, "Hear Bob Dylan's Unedited & Bewildering Interview with Nat Hentoff for *Playboy Magazine* (1965)," Open Culture, September 17, 2014, https://www.openculture.com/2014/09/hear-bob-dylans-unedited-bewildering-interview-with-nat-hentoff.html.

the end of the 1960s and that at various times since has had periods—perhaps long ones—where he has abstained from alcohol and cigarettes. The broader point is that he does not sing of or otherwise report any lasting regrets from his drug experiences. Whatever he continues to use has not led him to be perceived primarily or at all as a "drug addict," nor interfered with a long and physically healthy life. It is clear drugs did not ruin his life as they did for some of his compatriots. His exhortation to bend one's mind every once in a while is something he has performed in exemplary fashion. Indeed, he is one of the world's best advertisements—at most times, at least—for the use of drugs.[185] Dylan himself, as late as his recent "Nettie Moore" from 2006, succinctly summarizes it:

> They say whisky'll kill you, but I don't think it will
> I'm ridin' with you to the top of the hill

This is not to say that Dylan glorifies drugs. Not only has he had genuine personal struggles at times, but some of his songs also report the travails of being high. Consider, for instance, these lines from "Stuck Inside of Mobile with the Memphis Blues Again":

> Now the rainman gave me two cures
> Then he said, "Jump right in"
> The one was Texas medicine
> The other was just railroad gin
> An' like a fool I mixed them
> An' it strangled up my mind
> An' now people just get uglier
> An' I have no sense of time

And these from "Just Like Tom Thumb's Blues":

> I started out on burgundy
> But soon hit the harder stuff
> Everybody said they'd stand behind me

---

[185] Michael Gray makes a similar point but confines his evaluation to the 1960s. See *Song and Dance Man III*, 855. It is also worth noting that Dylan has seemed to poke fun at his reputation for drug use, beginning countless shows from 2002 onward with stage manager Al Santos reciting lines from a 2002 story about Dylan by Jeff Miers in the *Buffalo News*: "Ladies and gentlemen, please welcome the poet laureate of rock 'n' roll. The voice of the promise of the '60s counterculture. The guy who forced folk into bed with rock, who donned makeup in the '70s and disappeared into a haze of substance abuse, who emerged to find Jesus, and who suddenly shifted gears, releasing some of the strongest music of his career beginning in the late '90s. Ladies and gentlemen, Bob Dylan!"

> When the game got rough
> But the joke was on me
> There was nobody even there to call my bluff
> I'm going back to New York City
> I do believe I've had enough

Yet even here there is an abiding appreciation for the derangement of drug experiences. One cannot hear in either of these two songs unambiguous condemnation or regret of drug use, even if they make clear the suffering that is so often concomitant with intoxication.

I am less interested in establishing Dylan's success as a drug user, however, than in linking the confidence with which he has used drugs to his prophetic status. This linkage has been surprisingly absent in interpretations otherwise most likely to make it, namely those that read Dylan in prophetic terms. Religious interpreters of Dylan almost universally have ignored or downplayed his drug use and, most relevantly, have imagined a total separation between his drug use and his religiosity. Otherwise excellent accounts of Dylan's spiritual life and religious music, such as those of Scott Marshall and Michael Gilmour, for the most part disregard Dylan's experimentation with and advocacy of drugs.[186] Stephen Webb is aggressive in this regard, not only resisting the seemingly obvious drug references in songs like "Rainy Day Women #12 and 35" but constantly juxtaposing intoxication and religiosity as separate and opposed phenomena.[187]

---

[186] For example, Dylan's drug use is not emphasized in Marshall, *Restless Pilgrim*; Marshall, *Dylan: A Spiritual Life*; or Gilmour, *Gospel According to Bob Dylan*. In a different book on Dylan's religiosity, Gilmour does address the possibility of "Mr. Tambourine Man" being about drugs, but prefers an alternate interpretation that the song is primarily about the relationship between the artist and his muse (*Tangled Up in the Bible*, 47). In a footnote, Gilmour makes the caveat that he is not denying "that drug imagery is likely involved" too, but goes on to cite other interpreters, such as Andy Gill and Anthony Varesi, who themselves favor the artist-muse reading (Gilmour, 54; referring to Gill, *Classic Bob Dylan, 1962–1989: My Back Pages* [London: Carlton, 1998], 74; and Varesi, *The Bob Dylan Albums* [Toronto: Guernica, 2002], 52). With regard to "Rainy Day Women, #12 & 35," after noting the song's multiple biblical allusions (Exodus 21:29, Numbers 15:36, Deuteronomy 13:10, 21:21; Joshua 7:25; John 8:5–7, 59; Acts 7:54–60), Gilmour addresses the song's seemingly overt drug reference only in a highly tentative way: "Perhaps there is a double entendre here, with the obvious reference to drug use on the one hand, and the further idea of being attacked for living and speaking as one sees fit on the other" (Gilmour, 112; 138, n. 17). Seth Rogovoy's treatment of Dylan from a Jewish perspective does acknowledge the possible drug reference of "Rainy Day Women, #12 & 35" but stresses an interpretation of the song as about the "vicissitudes of fame." Rogovoy emphasizes Dylan's occasional denials that "Mr. Tambourine Man" is about drugs and, in general, does not confront the potential connection between drugs and religiosity. Rogovoy, *Bob Dylan: Prophet, Mystic, Poet* (New York: Scribner, 2009), 81–82, 101.

[187] Of "Rainy Day Women #12 & 35," Webb writes: "This is hardly a drug song. At most, it is a parody of a drug song, with Dylan and the musicians having a laugh at trying to sound like what people who have never been high might think it sounds like to be on drugs. Within that parody,

Michael Gray comes closer to the mark, I think, when he finds in drugs a source of Dylan's remarkable visionary capacities. Arguing that Dylan "is not a natural visionary in the sense that Blake is" and that there is "no way that Dylan's mind is intrinsically Eastern," Gray suggests that "Dylan's mysticism must have come through drugs as well as literature," adding "as with most of us, for Dylan 'the mystical experience' was surely sparked off by 'the acid experience.' The West has a million mystics now."[188] But even if this interpretation is correct, it treats drug use only as the partial cause of Dylan's visions and not also as part of the *substance* of his prophetic message.

By contrast, the point I mean to stress—and that the line "Everybody must get stoned" seems on its face to say—is not simply that Dylan is a drug user who has advocated to some degree for its use, but that he interprets the total abstention from drugs as a kind of ethical flaw. This idea comes across starkly in his *Chronicles*, in which Dylan criticizes the cluelessness of Billy James, the head of publicity at Columbia Records in the early 1960s: "He looked like he'd never been stoned a day in his life."[189]

Wherein might the *imperative* to intoxicate lie? The readiest, though far from complete, answer is the idea that the use of intoxicants expands one's mind and thus generates artistic creativity and experience as such. Such a view, which speaks to the overriding value of individual expressivity and self-discovery, has a long lineage. It is well known that the Romantic poets relied heavily on opium;[190] Thomas De Quincey, for instance, found in the drug "the apocalypse of the world inside me." Arthur Rimbaud, a major influence upon Dylan, turned to hashish and absinthe as part of his pursuit of poetic inspiration and made the influential declaration: "I say one must be a seer, make oneself a seer. The Poet makes himself a seer by a long, gigantic and rational derangement of all the senses." For Walter Benjamin, "hashish, opium, or whatever else can give an introductory lesson" to what he calls *"profane illumination . . . a materialistic, anthropological inspiration."*[191] Allen Ginsberg, a friend of Dylan's, hailed cannabis and hallucinogens as devices for "the augmentation of the senses" and "the exploration of modes of consciousness," though he lamented that in the

---

however, is one of the most tragic (and Christian) messages that Dylan ever sung: you try to be good in this world, you get killed." Webb, *Dylan Redeemed*, 50–51. On Webb's juxtaposition of religion and drugs as entirely separate—and his interpretation of other of Dylan's songs as concerning religion, not drugs—see Webb, 78, 133, 135, 145, 182.

[188] Gray, *Song and Dance Man III*, 194.

[189] Dylan, *Chronicles*, 7.

[190] See Alethea Hayter, *Opium and the Romantic Imagination* (London: Faber, 1968).

[191] Walter Benjamin, "Surrealism: the Last Snapshot of the European Intelligentsia," in *Walter Benjamin: Selected Writings, Volume 2: 1927–1934*, trans. Rodney Livingston et al. (Cambridge, MA: Belknap Press of Harvard University Press, 1999), 209.

late-twentieth-century culture in which such drugs had come to proliferate they ended up being more "for party purposes rather than study purposes."[192] Dylan himself seems to follow in this tradition of turning to drugs to foster intellectual and artistic creativity, not just in his parallel exhortation that everyone bend their minds from time to time, but (at least in the '60s) in his use of amphetamine and other drugs to give himself the stamina to stay up for extended periods in order to finish songs in the initial moments of their inspiration.

But it would be a mistake to read "Everybody must get stoned" only as a mantra for aspiring artists and intellectuals and not to appreciate, in addition, the religious—or, more precisely, postsecular—dimension of the idea. That "Everybody must get stoned" is phrased in the imperative and itself contains (along with other lyrics from the song in which it appears) biblical allusions already alerts us to this. That some of the very artists who have embraced drug use have framed the impact of such use as igniting a mystical or visionary quality (recall that Rimbaud insists on deranging the senses so that he could become a *seer* and, on this mystical basis, then become a poet) further emphasizes the point. Most of all, the historical anthropology of drugs reminds us of their close connection—if not equivalence—to religious sacrament. For perhaps 6,500 years, if not longer, various communities have made sacred use of hallucinogens.[193] Soma (thought by some to possess hallucinogenic properties) is mentioned in both the Vedas and the Avesta, texts that are likely more than three thousand years old, where it is described as producing a sense of the divine.[194] The Eleusinian Mysteries, initiations held annually for approximately nine centuries (fifth century BCE to fourth century CE) to celebrate the goddesses Demeter and Persephone, made use of a special mixture, or *kykeon,* at the climax of their ceremonies, widely thought to possess psychoactive properties.[195] In the eighteenth century, European travelers discovered that Koryak tribesmen in Siberia, in a practice now thought to be thousands of years of old, made use of the psychedelic mushroom *amanita muscaria.*[196] Other extremely long-standing

[192] The quotes from De Quincey and Ginsberg come from Marqusee, *Wicked Messenger,* 196. The Rimbaud quote is from his May 15, 1871, letter to Paul Demeny, in Arthur Rimbaud, *Complete Works,* trans. Wallace Fowlie (Chicago: University of Chicago Press, 2005), 377.

[193] See Giorgio Samorini, "The Oldest Archeological Data Evidencing the Relationship of *Homo Sapiens* with Psychoactive Plants: A Worldwide Overview," *Journal of Psychedelic Studies* 3, no. 2 (2019): 63–80.

[194] Consider a passage from the *Rig Veda*: "We have drunk Soma and become immortal; we have attained the light, the Gods discovered." *The Rig Veda,* trans. Ralph T. H. Griffith (London: Global Grey, 2018), 666 [Book 8, Hymn LXVIII]. Also see Richard J. Miller, "Religion as a Byproduct of Psychotropic Drug Use," *Atlantic,* December 27, 2013, https://www.theatlantic.com/health/arch ive/2013/12/religion-as-a-product-of-psychotropic-drug-use/282484/.

[195] Pollan, *How to Change Your Mind,* 194.

[196] Miller, "Religion as a Byproduct of Psychotropic Drug Use."

practices include the ritualistic use of mescaline by indigenous North Americans, psilocybin by Meso-American natives, and ayahuasca by indigenous peoples from throughout Central and South America. Within Aztec culture, the Nahuatl word for the psychedelic mushroom they ingested is "flesh of the gods," pointing to their entheogenic properties.[197] A U.S. Supreme Court decision from 2006 recognized and allowed the religious use of ayahuasca for the New Mexican branch of UDV, a Brazilian church.[198] Because many of the world's most dominant organized religions—Buddhism, Judaism, Christianity, and Islam—mostly have opposed and in some cases even persecuted drug use, it is easy to overlook the fact that certain drugs, like hallucinogens, are clearly conducive of mystical experiences parallel to those described within those very traditions.[199] And it is relevant to add that very often the non-drug-induced ecstasy experienced by believers within these traditions has been *likened* to drug-induced intoxication, further reminding us of the overlap between the two.[200]

The key point is not that already religious communities use drugs as sacraments, but that secular people can have religious-like experiences by taking them and that, with the discovery of LSD in 1943 and rediscovery of psilocybin in the West (or global North) in 1955, such experiences are an increasingly available choice. As James Bakalar and Harvard psychiatry professor Lester Grinspoon reflect: "Psychedelic drugs opened to mass tourism mental territories previously explored only by small parties of particularly intrepid adventurers, mainly religious mystics."[201]

Dylan clearly was one of these new explorers. In addition to cannabis and opium, which might be considered to have some entheogenic aspects, we know that he has experimented with LSD, psilocybin, and mescaline, which are perhaps the quintessential entheogenic substances available within the secular West.[202] To try mushrooms, Dylan traveled to Huautla in Mexico, the same

---

[197] Pollan, *How to Change Your Mind*, 109.

[198] *Gonzales v. O Centro Espirita Beneficente União do Vegetal*, 546 U.S. 418 (2006).

[199] The Catholic Church, during the time of the Inquisition and in conjunction with the Spanish conquest of the Americas, was one of the first religious institutions to police, repress, and oppose drugs like psilocybin and mescaline.

[200] In the Bible, on the day of the Pentecost, onlookers exclaim at the strange behavior of the disciples: "These men are full of new wine" (Acts 2:13). Somewhat analogously, St. Teresa of Ávila claims that she "regards the center of our soul as a cellar, into which God admits us and when it pleases him, so as to intoxicate us with the delicious wine of His Grace." Both examples are mentioned in Aldous Huxley, "Drugs That Shape Men's Minds," in *The Drug User: Documents 1840–1960*, ed. John Strausbaugh and Donald Blaise (New York: Blast, 1991), 221–22.

[201] Lester Grinspoon and James B. Bakalar, *Psychedelic Drugs Reconsidered* (New York: Basic Books, 1979), 86.

[202] For Dylan's use of mescaline, see Lenni Brenner, "How Dylan Found His Voice," *Counterpunch*, May 1, 2003, https://www.counterpunch.org/2003/05/01/how-dylan-found-his-voice/.

location where they were rediscovered by Robert Gordon Wasson in 1955. Dylan reports, and is reported by others to have had, numerous experiences on this drug.[203] His use of mescaline and especially LSD is also well documented.[204] Dylan's song "Mr. Tambourine Man" is often thought to concern the altered and heightened aesthetic sensitivity that can be generated by psychedelics.

However, more important than the biographical facts of Dylan's psychedelic drug use is the broader point, increasingly substantiated by science, that drugs of these kinds can generate quasi-religious states. What are the postsecular implications of "Everybody must get stoned" in light of this circumstance?

From the start of the introduction of such drugs as LSD and psilocybin into secular Western culture, experimenters have emphasized the substances' generation of mystical, religious, and quasi-religious states. Aldous Huxley describes his taking mescaline as "without question the most extraordinary and significant experience this side of the Beatific Vision" and reports how, on the drug, everyday objects radiated with a divinity he called "the Mind at Large."[205] Over the last few decades, and especially recently, research studies have confirmed the religion-inducing effects of such drugs and begun to uncover the biological mechanisms by which they operate. The 1962 Marsh Chapel Experiment, also known as the Good Friday Experiment, conducted by the Harvard Psilocybin Project, was a double-blind study in which divinity students were given psilocybin to test its entheogenic properties. In all eight categories by which mystical experiences were evaluated, those who took psilocybin scored higher than the control group, with the researchers concluding that 80 percent of those taking psilocybin reported a powerful mystical experience (compared to just 10 percent of the control group).[206] Walter Pahnke, the Harvard graduate student who

---

[203] On Dylan's trip to Huautla, see Pollan, *How to Change Your Mind*, 113–14. On a mushroom experience Dylan allegedly had in Ecuador, see Marcos Echeverría Ortiz, "Is It True That Bob Dylan Ate Hallucinogenic Mushrooms in Ecuador?," *Marcos Echeverría Ortiz* (blog), December 7, 2017, https://www.marcosecheverriaortiz.com/blog-1/2017/12/7/is-it-true-that-bob-dylan-ate-hal lucinogenic-mushrooms-in-ecuador. Additionally, Susan Green, who had been brought on Dylan's Rolling Thunder tour as an herbalist, recounts a conversation with Dylan about mushrooms in 1976, in which he allegedly said: "When I was in Mexico making *Pat Garrett and Billy the Kid*, everybody was eating mushrooms. . . . They would all be tripping, but I'd barely get a buzz. Drugs don't do it for me anymore. But herbs, man, they get me high. You know how people on acid see a tree come alive? . . . That's how I see things all the time." Quoted in Heylin, *Dylan: Behind the Shades Revisited*, 437. Heylin points out that Dylan's words here recall something Dylan said to Jules Siegel ten years earlier: "I see things that other people don't see. . . . It's terrible. They laugh" (Heylin, 438).

[204] On LSD, see McCarron, *Light Come Shining*, 68.

[205] Quoted in Pollan, *How to Change Your Mind*, 160–61.

[206] Walter Norman Pahnke, "Drugs and Mysticism: An Analysis of the Relationship between Psychedelic Drugs and the Mystical Consciousness" (thesis presented to the Committee on Higher Degrees in History and Philosophy of Religion, Harvard University, June 1963). Also see Rick Doblin, "Pahnke's 'Good Friday Experiment': A Long-Term Follow-Up and Methodological

led the study, concluded that psilocybin could "induce states of consciousness which are apparently indistinguishable from, if not identical with, those experienced by mystics."[207] The religious scholar Huston Smith, one of the participants in the study, commented: "Until the Good Friday Experiment, I had had no direct personal encounter with God."[208] A follow-up study that interviewed the test subjects a quarter-century later (between 1986 and 1989) found that they "unanimously described their Good Friday psilocybin experience as having had elements of a genuinely mystical nature and characterized it as one of the highpoints of their spiritual life."[209] Subsequent studies testing the mysticism-inducing effects of psychedelics have confirmed these earlier findings on the basis of even more rigorous techniques. Most notably, the landmark 2002 study (published in 2006) conducted by Roland Griffiths at Johns Hopkins University, which tested the effects of psilocybin, found results well summarized by its title: "Psilocybin Can Occasion Mystical-Type Experiences Having Substantial and Sustained Personal Meaning and Spiritual Significance."[210] In a follow-up study fourteen months later, two-thirds of the participants rated the psilocybin session among the five most spiritually significant experiences of their lives, and a similar percentage indicated that it had increased their sense of well-being or life satisfaction either moderately or very much.[211] Related studies at New York University (NYU) have demonstrated, along with the Hopkins trials, the psychological benefits of psilocybin and LSD for patients facing terminal illnesses, depression, and addiction, with the degree of therapeutic benefit correlated with the intensity of mystical experience induced by the drugs.[212]

Critique," *Journal of Transpersonal Psychology* 23, no. 1 (1991): 1–28; Pollan, *The Life You Can Save*, 45.

[207] Quoted in Matthew Oram, *The Trials of Psychedelic Therapy: LSD Psychotherapy in America* (Baltimore: Johns Hopkins University Press, 2018), 139.

[208] Huston Smith, "Empirical Metaphysics," in *The Huston Smith Reader*, ed. Jeffery Paine (Berkeley: University of California Press, 2012), 73.

[209] Doblin, "Pahnke's 'Good Friday Experiment,'" 13.

[210] Roland Griffiths et al., "Psilocybin Can Occasion Mystical-Type Experiences Having Substantial and Sustained Personal Meaning and Spiritual Significance," *Psychopharmacology* 187, no. 3 (2006): 268–83.

[211] Roland Griffiths et al., "Mystical-Type Experiences Occasioned by Psilocybin Mediate the Attribution of Personal Meaning and Spiritual Significance 14 Months Later," *Journal of Psychopharmacology* 22, no. 6 (2008): 621–32. The study also found that no one reported a decrease in well-being or life satisfaction due to the drug experience (630). Also see Katherine MacLean, Matthew Johnson, and Roland Griffiths, "Mystical Experiences Occasioned by the Hallucinogen Psilocybin Lead to Increases in the Personality Domain of Openness," *Journal of Psychopharmacology* 25, no. 11 (2011): 1453–61.

[212] In both the NYU and Hopkins trials, for instance, 80 percent of cancer patients demonstrated clinically significant reductions of anxiety and depression. This effect endured for at least six months

The writer Michael Pollan interviewed participants from the Hopkins and NYU trials and found not only that "for many of them, these were among the two or three most profound experiences of their lives," but that a common result of taking psychedelics was to push back against secularist tendencies: "Many of the people I'd interviewed had started out stone-cold materialists and atheists, no more spiritually developed than I, and yet several had had 'mystical experiences' that left them with the unshakable conviction that there was something more to this world than we know—a 'beyond' of some kind that transcended the material universe I presumed to constitute the whole shebang. I thought of one of the cancer patients I interviewed, an avowed atheist who had nevertheless found herself 'bathed in God's love.' "[213] This is not to say that everyone who takes such drugs will become more religious. Even the woman who felt "bathed in God's love" also reported afterward that she remained a "solid atheist." Pollan himself, who tried the drugs being administered in the Hopkins and NYU trials, reports that his atheism likewise remained intact, as he did not come to hold "any belief in a supernatural reality," even though he did satisfy the clinical definition of a mystical experience while on psilocybin, having experienced "something profoundly sacred and holy," "unity with ultimate reality," and "being at a spiritual height"—all of which are components of the Mystical Experience Questionnaire used in the studies.[214] But even a mysticism divorced from religiosity needs to be recognized as a state that challenges a secularist mentality. For one thing, a key feature of mystical experience is the enhancement of a *noetic* sense (the perception that objective truths about ultimate reality have been revealed, as in Pollan's report of "unity with ultimate reality" and what he also describes as a "novel mode of cognition"[215]) that transgresses the strict empiricism of natural science upheld by secularists. For another, even the mere spirituality of a *mystical but not religious* perspective represents a departure from the increasingly prevalent "neither spiritual nor religious" demographic category, which is disproportionately made up of avowed secularists. At the very least, psychedelics make it easier for atheists to hypothetically identify with a more far-ranging religious perspective. It is not by chance, after all, that one of the concepts by which hallucinogenic drugs have been understood—in addition to psychotomimetic ("psychosis mimicking"), psycholytic ("mind loosening"), and the now more customary psychedelic ("mind manifesting")—is *entheogen*, coined

and its degree corresponded with the intensity of mystical experience stimulated by the psychedelics. Pollan, *How to Change Your Mind*, 349.

[213] Pollan, 222.
[214] Pollan, 284, 345.
[215] Pollan, 253.

in 1979, which means "God within" or "that which causes God to be within an individual."[216]

The postsecular implications of entheogens—and by extension of Dylan's exhortation to attempt experimentation with them—consist of at least three factors. First, such drugs embody the postsecular breakdown of rigid divisions between the religious and non-religious and between the spiritual and material.[217] The effects of these drugs are a function of chemical processes, capable of being analyzed by neuroscience, yet at the same time generate experiences that routinely resist a merely materialistic explanation of the world. Pollan emphasizes the paradox that material substances can ignite for many a deeply felt confidence in the limitations of a strictly materialistic outlook, commenting that while it is possible, of course, to interpret drug experience as simply a chemical intervention in the brain:

> surprisingly, most of the people who have had these experiences don't see the matter that way at all. Even the most secular among them come away from their journeys convinced there exists something that transcends a material understanding of reality: some sort of a 'Beyond.' It's not that they deny a naturalistic basis for this revelation; they just interpret it differently.... So here was a curious paradox. The same phenomenon that pointed to a materialist explanation for spiritual and religious belief gave people an experience so powerful it convinced them of the existence of a nonmaterial reality—the very basis of religious belief.[218]

By existing on the border between science and trans-scientific thinking, the mystical experience induced by psychedelic drugs can be considered as a postsecular object, an *idea* of the postsecular in the Hegelian sense. Whereas secularists like E. O. Wilson have asserted that one must ultimately choose between science and religion (and called for eliminating traditional religious faiths for the sake

---

[216] See Pollan, 154–55.

[217] As discussed in section II.1, the "ideational" rendering of the postsecular refers to precisely this fraying of the boundary between the religious and non-religious, even if the ethical meaning of the idea, central to my analysis, is the call for respect between these groups (and thus the implicit recognition that there is an abiding difference between them). However, these two concerns are not mutually exclusive, as the ethical concern with achieving respect between the religious and non-religious can stem in part from awareness of the instability of the boundary between the two. Indeed, I am myself bringing together these two concerns, arguing that the ultimate path to postsecular respect between the religious and non-religious is recognition that each of us has the capacity for either standpoint.

[218] Pollan, *How to Change Your Mind*, 85.

of "human progress"), the existence of entheogens, as many have suggested, provides yet another piece of evidence that this is a false choice.[219]

Second, such drugs give significant force to the key postsecular assertion that not just religiosity but *non-religiosity too* is a choice (not a truth), with neither perspective able to claim that it is superior. Thus far, in emphasizing the choice underlying religiosity and non-religiosity, I have been most interested to stress that neither side can be grounded in some objectively superior status and that, in particular, it is misguided for the non-religious to conceive of their lack of religiosity as being in accordance with nature, science, or some alleged direction in human history; rather, both religion and non-religion, properly understood, are "subjective" in the sense of stemming from the personal dispositions and proclivities of individuals or from the broader and *contingent* cultural, social, and familial contexts conditioning their upbringing. The existence of entheogens not only buttresses this argument but takes it a step further because these drugs suggest that even individuals' subjective certainty regarding their own personal non-religiosity—their sense of being "religiously unmusical," to quote Max Weber—is likely not as fixed or as solid as it might feel. To those who say, "I'm just not religious or spiritual. . . . It's just not who I am or how I have been raised," the existence of entheogens reminds us of the enduring *acts of will*, and not just acculturation, underlying any alleged indifference toward or incapacity for religious or mystical states of being. The fact that the emergence of psychedelics has enabled the possibility of what Grob has called "applied mysticism" within communities otherwise bereft of religiosity and spirituality dramatizes the postsecular reality that religiosity remains a potential for all people—even the avowedly secularist.[220] This does not mean, of course, that everyone should elect to activate their religious and mystical capacities through the use of drugs, only that their not doing so is a decision. The absence of mystical states is not a sign of sober honesty but unwillingness to experiment. Or, put differently, that drugs can ignite a mystical sense of awe and wonder at the universe is a reminder that the aforementioned religious sense remains a possibility

[219] For Wilson, see Penny Sarchet, "E. O. Wilson: Religious Faith Is Dragging Us Down," *New Scientist*, January 21, 2015, https://www.newscientist.com/article/mg22530050-400-e-o-wilson-religious-faith-is-dragging-us-down/. By contrast, Huston Smith claims: "The Johns Hopkins experiment shows—proves—that under controlled, experimental conditions, psilocybin can occasion genuine mystical experiences. It uses science, which modernity trusts, to undermine modernity's secularism. In so doing, it offers hope of nothing less than a re-sacralization of the natural and social world, a spiritual revival that is our best defense against not only soullessness, but against religious fanaticism. And it does so in the very teeth of the unscientific prejudices built into our current drug laws." Quoted in Pollan, *How to Change Your Mind*, 81.

[220] Charles S. Grob, "Psychiatric Research with Hallucinogens: What Have We Learned?," *Heffter Review of Psychedelic Research* 1 (1998): 8–20.

for all of us—its employment is not even necessarily a matter of disposition or proclivity—and that a this-worldly, matter-of-fact, conventionally empirical orientation is not the only genuine one. As William Richards, one of the lead researchers for the Hopkins trials, has put it: "You go deep enough or far out enough in consciousness and you will bump into the sacred. It's not something we generate; it's something out there waiting to be discovered. And this reliably happens to nonbelievers as well as believers."[221]

Third, it is not just that psychedelics can elicit religious experiences and thus lead otherwise secular people to better identify with religiosity as a potentiality they themselves possess, but one of the surprising findings from recent research is that these drugs promote a long-term personality change that is itself generative of a postsecular mentality. Specifically, while it is quite uncommon for adults to undergo transformations in the so-called big five personality traits (extroversion, neuroticism, conscientiousness, agreeableness, and openness), one of the striking discoveries of recent studies is that psychedelics produce lasting increases in *openness*, a trait that is intimately connected to postsecularism and its call for greater understanding and mutual sympathy between religious and non-religious perspectives.[222] Such openness, as Pollan explains, "encompasses aesthetic appreciation and sensitivity, fantasy and imagination, as well as tolerance of others' viewpoints and values; it also predicts creativity in both the arts and the sciences, as well as, presumably, a willingness to entertain ideas at odds with those of current science. Such pronounced and lasting changes in the personalities of adults are rare."[223] What is more, it is possible that the openness generated by psychedelics is not necessarily limited to test subjects but includes test administrators as well. As Katherine MacLean, who helped lead the trials at Hopkins, reports: "I started out on the atheist side, but I began seeing things every day in my work that were at odds with this belief. My world became more and more mysterious as I sat with people on psilocybin."[224] In any case, even if psychedelics do not lead one to experience religiosity, it can lead one to have greater respect for it. This idea was already presaged by William James who, on the basis of his own experimentation with nitrous oxide, did not understand himself to have become a mystic—writing of mystical states "my own constitution shuts me out from their enjoyment almost entirely, and I can speak of them only at second hand"—but nonetheless was led to reject the "pretension of non-mystical states to be the sole and ultimate dictators of what we may believe."[225]

[221] Quoted in Pollan, *How to Change Your Mind*, 55.
[222] MacLean et al., "Mystical Experiences."
[223] Pollan, *How to Change Your Mind*, 74.
[224] Pollan, 74.
[225] James, *Varieties of Religious Experience*, 379, 427.

I do not mean to present Dylan's injunction "Everybody must get stoned" as a call for habitual drug use, still less as an unambiguous celebration of drugs. In public statements, Dylan sometimes has expressed reservations about the limitations of drugs and distanced himself from movements and communities that have made drugs central. If there is an ethical imperative to "Everybody must get stoned," it is more the imperative to experiment at least a little than the injunction to use a lot. But regardless of this distinction, the clear postsecular implication is that the psychological experience of even brief usage, combined with the knowledge that additional experience is always a possibility ready to be realized, contributes to overcoming a secularist intolerance of religiosity.

To get a sense of the stakes, consider a prominent secularist, the scientist Richard Dawkins, who recently was asked, in the context of his opposition to religion, about whether he had taken or would consider taking psychedelics such as ayahuasca and whether his doing so might lead him to better identify with the religious worldviews he routinely condemns or even "challenge [his] own concept of what is real." Dawkins replied:

> I would be very curious, I must say, to take, perhaps not that drug, but something like LSD or mescaline. . . . I would be prepared to do that under proper medical supervision, if I were absolutely convinced that it would do me no lasting harm. And I would actually like to do it. . . . [However,] I think it very unlikely that, whatever happened to me, I would interpret it as indicating anything supernatural. . . . I would on the contrary interpret it as a manifestation of what a wonderful thing the brain is, and how the brain can see and can experience even more things, under the right kinds of chemical stimulation.[226]

Dawkins here not only violates Dylan's injunction that "Everybody must get stoned" but does so in a fashion the underlines the postsecular implications of the idea. Dawkins, the militant secularist, at an advanced age, has never tried psychedelics. The conditions under which he says he would experiment with them seem at once excessively high (i.e., absolute certainty about lasting effects) and thus likely to prevent him from ever experimenting with them and yet also meaningfully satisfied in the present context in which scientific research increasingly has established the safety of such drugs as well as their beneficial uses. In spite of his never having tried psychedelics, Dawkins nonetheless feels comfortable prejudging what experiencing them would mean for him: that it

[226] Greg Hancock, "Richard Dawkins Would Like to Trip on LSD," *Daily Grail*, August 9, 2012, https://www.dailygrail.com/2012/08/richard-dawkins-would-like-to-trip-on-lsd/.

would be entirely consonant with his anti-religious worldview. Such a prejudgment not only violates the empirical foundation of scientific research but also disregards what studies like the Hopkins and NYU trials have demonstrated about psychedelics: their generation of religious and mystical states, in believers and non-believers alike, that lead them to contemplate the nature of ultimate reality and leave them "convinced there is more to this world than science can explain."[227] Dawkins's overconfidence about what science can know (that it can be used to disprove the integrity of religiosity) is thus joined to an overconfidence about the effects of psychedelic drugs (the belief, without any evidence, that their effects will not challenge either his atheism or his intolerance of religiosity). My claim is not that secularists who use drugs necessarily will overcome their secularist mentality, only that the resistance to drug experimentation by secularists is, in the case of Dawkins and no doubt many others whom he represents, a feature of secularist hubris itself. Even if Dawkins is correct that his atheism would remain unchanged following experimentation with psychedelics (and he certainly would not be alone in this regard), we have reason to suspect that its militancy and aggressiveness—its lack of empathetic understanding for the religious—would be meaningfully abated.

Dylan does not simply testify to the use of drugs for artists and intellectuals, but suggests a more universal ethical imperative. To be sure, he certainly does not wholeheartedly embrace psychedelics; he is critical of the illusions they cause and suggests he stopped using them after a while.[228] But he tried them. He changed his mind. And this change—which is at the heart of drug use—is at the heart of postsecular ethics as well.

II.7. The Impact of Dylan's Postsecularism

The four specific challenges to secularists I have discussed suggest some of the most incisive elements of Dylan's prophetic contestation of secularist thinking and demonstrate how a prophet of the postsecular can meaningfully operate in

---

[227] Pollan, *How to Change Your Mind*, 348.

[228] In 1978, Dylan looked back critically at the spread of psychedelics: "When psychedelics happened, everything became irrelevant. Because that had nothing to do with making music, or writing poems. . . . People were deluded into thinking they were something that they weren't: birds, fire hydrants, whatever." Cott, "Interview with Ron Rosenbaum," in *Essential Interviews*, 223. Likewise, also in 1978, Dylan said in an interview: "The drugs at the end of the '60s were artificial. . . . I was never involved in the acid scene either." Jim Ellison, ed., "Interview with an Icon" (interview with Lynne Allen in *Trouser Press*, December 12, 1978) in *Younger Than That Now: The Collected Interviews with Bob Dylan* (New York: Thunder's Mouth Press, 2004), 167.

a manner that philosophers of the postsecular, such as Habermas and Taylor, cannot. But how we can judge their impact?

We get an example of the postsecular effect of Dylan's Christian prophecy in the person of Joel Selvin, previously mentioned as the author of an especially scathing secularist review of one of Dylan's first gospel concerts ("Bob Dylan's God-Awful Gospel Music"), which affected Dylan enough to lead him to track down Selvin's phone number and call his home. Originally, Selvin had been only alienated and angered by Dylan's Christianity.[229] But over time—as Dylan produced more gospel albums yet also eventually turned away from explicitly religious music—Selvin, with the benefit of historical distance and more opportunity for reflection, came to see things differently, expressing numerous reservations about his initial review and acknowledging a newfound respect for the integrity of Dylan's gospel period. In a 2008 documentary about Dylan's religiosity, Selvin provided a revised assessment:

> As the years go by and I think about what the guy did, and what chances he was taking and what risks, and what his motivations were, there was something brave about it, there was something cracked about it too, something out of step with his audience, but something powerfully artistic. . . . So here we are years later and I'm thinking about this review. I'd probably write it a little bit differently. I'd have a little bit more respect for what he did. I still think he was nuts but being nuts is not a bad thing. It's part of the job description of the artist to be nuts. . . . Now looking back on it and thinking about it, it stands out as a moment of integrity on this guy's part.[230]

This is tepid praise, to be sure, but compared to Selvin's anti-religious condemnation of Dylan in 1979 it marks a meaningful transformation, a newfound respect for Dylan's religiosity and presumably, by extension, for the sincere faith of other religious people too. Dylan's religious message did not bring Selvin to religion, but it brought him to greater appreciation for it. And this function is the core meaning of Dylan's status as a prophet of the postsecular.

Another example is Paul Williams, who attended Dylan's earliest gospel shows and was one of the first to write about them and try to explain the

---

[229] Selvin recounts that his initial reaction to Dylan's gospel music and preaching was that "this has no relevance for me . . . no me in there," that he was "not ready to hear Christian music from Bob Dylan," that he did not "want to hear a Christian message in my rock shows," and that Dylan could "take that Christian message and just take it down the street. . . . I don't care to hear it at all." Interview in *Inside Bob Dylan's Jesus Years*.

[230] Interview in *Inside Bob Dylan's Jesus Years*.

profound change in Dylan's music and public persona. Though more respectful of Dylan's religiosity than Selvin initially was, Williams acknowledged that the Dylan who had been a hero to him—"a poet/hero of stalwart individualism"—seemed to renounce those values in adopting an evangelicalism Williams could not fully share or understand. Yet, confronting Dylan's gospel period became for Williams an occasion for deeper self-reflection. Williams began to ask himself, "If I've identified with Dylan all this time, where have we diverged? Is he wrong, or are we different in some deep way, or does this mean one day I'm going to wake up in love with Jesus too?"[231] In pondering such questions—and further exposing himself to Dylan's religious music and message—Williams did not ultimately turn closer to God, but he came to have a kind of postsecular awakening that gave him, as someone not fully committed to Christianity, more respect and appreciation for religious belief. Part of this awakening involved an explicit rejection of what is diametrically opposed to postsecularism: the prediction that religion is bound to wane in the face of modernity. Williams writes, "So when Dylan plays the harmonica in 'What Can I Do for You?' and sings, 'Whatever pleases you, tell it to my heart,' we are forced at least to realize that the 'Is God dead?' controversy is a sick joke a million miles away from our present awareness." Reflecting on the surprising circumstance that in 1979, through Dylan's conversion, the topic of religiosity had become a major subject of discussion within rock and roll and the broader popular culture, Williams perfectly describes the postsecular impact Dylan's music had on both himself and many others: "I am pleased that this event, Dylan's announcement for Christ, is stimulating people to think about and discuss the religious, moral, spiritual side of our lives; and I like to think that this helps open a channel of communication between born-again Christians and the rest of Dylan's past or present audience."[232] Williams stresses that while there are elements of Dylan's religious message that he strongly rejects, especially aspects that suggest damnation for those unsaved by Christ, the ultimate function of Dylan's gospel music and sermonizing, for him, involved not proselytization but testimony—testimony teaching secular individuals to appreciate and respect religiosity.

As a third instance, consider a case that Dylan himself learned about and related in 1980: a cab driver who, though not a Christian, became more cognizant of the possibility of his becoming one as a result of listening to Dylan's gospel music. Speaking of the woman mentioned in Dylan's "Precious Angel," the driver reflects to his passenger: "If I could meet that person that brought Bob Dylan to the Lord, I think I might become a Christian too."[233] That Dylan

[231] Williams, *Dylan—What Happened?*, 82–83.
[232] Williams, 118.
[233] Dylan, *Saved! The Gospel Speeches*, 10–11.

found this story of sufficient interest to discuss it in a gospel speech at one of his concerts reflects his own appreciation for the capacity of his religious music to produce postsecular effects in his audience.

Selvin, Williams, and the cab driver are but three examples, but they provide concrete evidence of Dylan's impact as a prophet of the postsecular. What explains Dylan's ability to have made such an impact? I already have discussed some of the most important causes. Dylan's tremendous stature and credibility within secularist circles prior to his conversion makes him someone whose subsequent religiosity cannot easily be ignored. And the fact that his gospel music challenges secularists in surprising ways—interrogating their idea of a vocation, emphasizing the existence of a religious sense rather than only the objects of that sense, rehabilitating the human construction of religion as a reason to take religion seriously, and recalling the ever-present possibility for heightened spirituality enabled by drugs—means that secularists who listen closely can find in Dylan's religious fervor less a direct attack on their atheism (against which they could easily defend themselves) than a compelling call to understand their atheism as a personal choice as opposed to a superior way of life grounded in truth.

But beyond these dynamics, Dylan's ability to exert a postsecular impact has been heightened by two additional factors. First, his remarkable self-reflexivity about his faith (his persistent contemplation of it from the perspective of religious skeptics) routinely has led him to acknowledge, care about, and at times even empathize with the secularist standpoint. Even at the height of his religious fervor, in moments of unambiguous evangelical faith, he could imagine how his religiosity might seem in the eyes of the non-religious. As he put it in one of his gospel speeches in 1980: "Some of you might have seen me before and [are now saying], 'What is up with this man? Has he lost his mind.'"[234] In another gospel speech from the same year, Dylan's self-reflexivity was joined to a respect for spiritual autonomy of his audience:

> I know you might look at me and say, "Now he's just lost his mind."
> But I never did lie to you, and I never told you to vote for anybody.
> I never told you what to eat. Never told you what records to buy, what
> girlfriends to go out with. I never could go for any of that stuff. I'm

---

[234] Dylan, 83. Likewise, in an interview from 1985 in which Dylan discusses his understanding of the so-called messianic complex, he replies: "People who believe in the coming of the Messiah live their lives right now, as if He were here. That's my idea of it, anyway. I know people are going to say to themselves, '*What the fuck is this guy talking about?*' But it's all there in black and white, the written and unwritten word. I don't have to defend this. The scriptures back me up." Cohen, "Bob Dylan Revisited."

telling you the truth now, but it's like everything else, you gotta tell yourself what a piece of bread tastes like. So it's just one of them things you gotta do, or not do, by yourself.[235]

In an interview soon after the release of his first gospel album, *Slow Train Coming*, Dylan's consideration of his religiosity from a position of self-distance led him even to partially identify with the secularist audiences who vitriolically rejected him:

> Well, I can understand why they [are] rebellious about [*Slow Train Coming*], because up until the time the Lord came into my life, I'd known nothing about him, *and was just as rebellious, and didn't think much about it either way*. I never did care much for preachers who just ask for donations all the time, and talk about the world to come. I was always growing up with what's right here and now, and until Jesus became real to me in that way, *I couldn't understand*."[236]

In fact, in the immediate aftermath of his conversion, Dylan reports that he kept quiet about it because he knew that so many of the people he associated with would be incredulous:

> I hadn't told anybody about it because I felt they would say, "Aw, come on." Most of the people I know don't believe that Jesus was resurrected, that He is alive. It's like He was just another prophet or something, one of many good people. That's not the way it was any longer for me. I had always read the Bible, but I only looked at it as literature. I was never really instructed in it in a way that was meaningful to me.[237]

Dylan could understand the disconcertion his conversion would cause others because he experienced this disconcertion himself. He admitted to feeling fear in writing the songs of his first evangelical album: "The songs that I wrote for the *Slow Train* album [frightened me]. . . . I didn't like writing them. I didn't want to write them."[238] Dylan therefore was speaking not only about others, but to a

---

[235] Dylan, *Saved! The Gospel Speeches*, 91–92.

[236] Quoted in *Bob Dylan 1975–1981: Rolling Thunder and the Gospel Years*, directed by Joel Gilbert (Pottstown, PA: MVD Entertainment, 2006), DVD, https://www.imdb.com/title/tt1285 159/?ref_=ttfc_fc_tt, transcribed by Gilmour, *Gospel According to Bob Dylan*, 67 (emphasis added).

[237] Cott, "Interview with Robert Hilburn," in *Essential Interviews*, 298.

[238] Interview with Bono (1984) in Kathleen Mackay, ed., *Bob Dylan: Intimate Insights from Friends and Fellow Musicians* (London: Omnibus Press, 2007), 150–51. Dylan's comments are in response to Bono's question about whether the process of writing any of his songs ever had "frightened you in some way."

certain extent about himself, when he observed in 1985: "Make something religious and people don't have to deal with it, they can say it's irrelevant. 'Repent, the kingdom of God is at hand.' That scares the shit out of people."[239] In any case, Dylan's self-reflexive mindset no doubt has been a source of his effectiveness as a prophet of the postsecular and his capacity to demand a parallel self-reflexivity—not conversion—from secularists.

Second, the long and still-ongoing period following Dylan's final gospel album in 1981, what I have been referring to as his postconversion period, has only further enhanced his ability to challenge secularists to respect the integrity of religious belief. As I have mentioned, this respect is achieved most deeply by encouraging an awareness in secularists that religiosity, even if it is not practiced, remains a possibility that they genuinely possess, so that they come to see their respect for the religious as a respect for latent aspects of their own subjectivity as well. A striking feature of Dylan's postconversion is how often he is willing to countenance religious doubt and distance himself from his previous religious fervor.[240] If Dylan's gospel period led him to promote a postsecular consciousness through the indirect means of his religious intensity, in his postconversion period he has approximated the postsecular mentality itself, treating his own fervent past as a kind of other self, different from his current persona but about whom he continues to manifest respect. To be sure, Dylan's postconversion cannot be reduced to a non-religious outlook, as he never has renounced his religiosity, and there are many signs he remains devout.[241] But songs and public statements from his later years often express a hesitance about religion and at times an uncertainty that goes well beyond the typical doubt faced by believers, expressed in Mark 9:24 as: "I believe; help my unbelief!" Dylan's curious posture makes him at once someone with whom a secularist might identify and at the same time someone from whom the secularist might learn.

Consider Dylan's 1997 statement in an interview in *Newsweek*:

[239] Liner notes to *Biograph* for "Every Grain of Sand," 32.

[240] To be sure, as discussed, even some works from *within* Dylan's gospel period might plausibly be understood to include considerations of doubt. See footnote 8.

[241] Regina McCrary, a back-up vocalist on Dylan's gospel albums who sang with him up until 1986, emphatically stated at a talk at Belmont University in 2014: "He [Dylan] is a born-again Christian to this still day. And I take great pride spiritually in saying that because a lot of people don't know that." "Regina McCrary talks Bob Dylan at Belmont University 4/3/14," posted by CurbCollegeBelmontU, video, 35:47, May 21, 2014, https://youtu.be/e7Yqj-QzwZE?t=1163. In a 2009 interview, Dylan himself said, "I am a true believer." Interview with Bill Flanagan, *Street News Service*, November 23, 2009, quoted in Jeff Taylor and Chad Israelson, *The Political World of Bob Dylan: Freedom and Justice, Power and Sin* (London: Palgrave Macmillan, 2015), 140.

Here's the thing with me and the religious thing. This is the flat-out truth: I find the religiosity and philosophy in the music. I don't find it anywhere else. Songs like "Let Me Rest on a Peaceful Mountain" or "I Saw the Light"—that's my religion. I don't adhere to rabbis, preachers, evangelists, all of that. I've learned more from the songs than I've learned from any of this kind of entity. The songs are my lexicon. I believe the songs.[242]

It might seem that Dylan here forswears his Christianity, announcing a redirection of his spiritual energies, away from what is speculative and immaterial (divinity) to what is tangible, worldly, and undeniably real (music). A *New York Times* story about Dylan published soon after the *Newsweek* interview lends support to this narrative, reporting: "Dylan says he now subscribes to no organized religion."[243] Such a transformation would make Dylan's spiritual life more akin to that of a religious skeptic. Upon reflection, however, he is not in fact announcing an abandonment of Christianity. It makes little sense to understand Dylan as moving away from "organized religion," because even at the height of his gospel period he did not affiliate himself closely with any church (outside of a three-month Bible study course at the Vineyard Christian Fellowship in Reseda, California, in 1979) and resisted easy categorization of his religious identification. The narrative of apostasy is also challenged by the fact that the very songs that Dylan invokes as the enduring vehicle of his religiosity are *gospel music*. Rather than a profound alteration in the *content* of his religious thinking, what does seem to be communicated here is Dylan's newfound *religious reticence*: his unwillingness to elaborate the nature of his religiosity, make dogmatic theistic proclamations, or testify with the fervor that previously had animated him. In the actual interview connected to the *New York Times* story, Dylan expresses reluctance to expatiate upon his religious views (again pointing to traditional music as a ready source of his ideas) and even suggests that this hesitance is linked to diminished religious intensity and passion, not an alternate theological (or non-theological) view:

Those old songs are my lexicon and my prayer book.... You can find all my philosophy in those old songs. I believe in a God of time and space, but if people ask me about that, my impulse is to point them back toward those songs. I believe in Hank Williams singing "I Saw the Light." I've seen that light, too.[244]

---

[242] David Gates, "Dylan Revisited," *Newsweek*, October 5, 1997.

[243] Cott, "Interview with John Pareles," in *Essential Interviews*, 420.

[244] Cott, 419–20.

Dylan's reticence is reflected not only in his substitution of other people's music for his own philosophy of religion, but also in the retrospective tenor with which he alludes to his experience of God. If Hank Williams's song describes how his finding Jesus inaugurated a permanent change of heart,[245] one cannot help but note the alternate temporality with which Dylan describes his own divine inspiration: something he *has* experienced in the past, but not necessarily something he continues to experience. Williams's conversion brings the lasting transformation of "no more darkness, no more night," whereas Dylan's simply does not have this function. Instead, Dylan speaks at a spiritual distance from his conversion, suggesting at once its reality and its uncertain legacy and, in this respect, bridging the divide between religionists and secularists. That he can speak about his fervor without being fervent makes him all the more communicable to a nonreligious standpoint.

Dylan's honesty in contemplating the diminished ardor of his postconversion spiritual life pervades his later work. His 2006 song "Thunder on the Mountain," for instance, includes the reflection:

> I've already confessed—no need to confess again

While this could be read simply as a refusal to have his public life defined exclusively by his religiosity, that it also speaks to a loss of religious enthusiasm seems more than likely given the context of other similar statements. Lyrics from other songs recorded or released from this same period describe a faith that is real but also tentative, if not weak. Consider the following from "Huck's Tune":

> My faith is as cold as can be

From "Dreamin' of You":

> I'm hidin' my faith
> In the rain

---

[245] "I Saw the Light," which Williams released as a single in 1948, opens with these lines:

> I wandered so aimless, life filled with sin
> I wouldn't let my dear Savior in
> Then Jesus came like a stranger in the night
> Praise the Lord, I saw the light
> I saw the light, I saw the light
> No more darkness, no more night
> Now I'm so happy, no sorrow in sight
> Praise the Lord, I saw the light

And from "Ain't Talkin'":

> I practice a faith that's been long abandoned
> Ain't no altars on this long and lonesome road

Whereas Dylan's gospel period demanded from secularists that they acknowledge the plausibility of religiosity, in these statements Dylan, as a believer, wrestles with something like the plausibility of a life lived without religious intensity. The two mindsets together strengthen the force of each and lend even greater potency to his status as a prophet of the postsecular.

In 2009, Dylan commented, "Religion isn't meant for everybody."[246] This is a remarkable reflection for someone who devoted three years of his life to proselytizing. Yet, rather than a contradiction of that earlier period of religious fervor, Dylan's comment is better understood as a further reminder that the most distinct and important feature of his Christian prophecy, from a sociological perspective at least, is not religious in the traditional sense but postsecular: not urging people to make a religious choice but urging them to understand religiosity as a choice they could, with integrity, make.

[246] Interview with Bill Flanagan quoted in Taylor and Israelson, *Political World of Bob Dylan*, 140.

Part III

Strengthen the Things
that Remain

My overall claim in this book has been to suggest that Dylan be understood as a prophet without God. Most basically this means appreciating that Dylan lacks the traditional grounding of prophets in a stable or singular source of authority. Specifically, he channels not one single authoritative standard of normative guidance, but three—*selfhood*, *social justice*, and *divinity*—and he testifies to the circumstance that these three foundations of normative guidance are not in harmony with one another but in fact are in conflict. There is thus no easy teaching of salvation—theological or otherwise—in Dylan's prophecy taken as a whole, only a tragic awareness of the normative diremption at the heart of the human world.

But importantly, there are ethical implications that come from each of the three sets of conflicts underlying Dylan's tragic prophetic message. The conflict between selfhood and social justice—that is, Dylan's presentation of himself as someone whose commitment to individual freedom makes him *not* reliably committed to social justice—is a call for others similarly situated to recognize themselves as such, to thereby practice a self-reliance less self-satisfied than the canonical form of self-reliance celebrated by Emerson and Thoreau, to likewise practice a bourgeois progressivism that does not falsely imagine itself as militant, and, further, to acknowledge that the liberal-democratic regime's pretension to harmonize individual freedom and social justice is itself fundamentally untrue. The conflict between selfhood and God—Dylan's wrestling with religion, his inability to achieve a consistent skepticism or a consistent faith, his inability to decide ultimately whether his religiosity stems only from his own mind or from his attunement to realities transcending it—is a call to see both religion and non-religion as equally compelling existential choices and thus to contest atheists when they fail to respect the integrity and dignity of religious life.

Bob Dylan. Jeffrey Edward Green, Oxford University Press. © Oxford University Press 2024.
DOI: 10.1093/oso/9780197651742.003.0004

What remains to be analyzed is the third conflict—between God and social justice—and the ethical implications that follow from it. To insist upon the conflict between God and social justice is to insist that the political world will never become the site of secular salvation, that the human effort to achieve freedom, equality, and peace for all will never succeed. Why is this pessimism about human society best expressed as a conflict between *God* and the political world? For one thing, the idea to which this pessimism is polemically opposed—that humanity can achieve social justice—so often has been infused with theological significance, as in the American regime's pretension to be a "city upon a hill" (a phrase stemming from Matthew 5:14 and, as first articulated by John Winthrop in 1630, one that explicitly links the accomplishment of social justice to the fulfillment of a Puritan covenant with God) or, likewise, Martin Luther King Jr.'s famous assurance that "the universe is on the side of justice," which for him was inseparable from his faith in a "God [who] is interested in the freedom of the whole human race and in the creation of a society where all men can live together as brothers, where every man will respect the dignity and the worth of human personality."[1] The opposite, pessimistic standpoint that Dylan stands for, which insists upon the permanent fallenness of humanity, most commonly has been expressed by adherents of religion—such as adherents of Augustinian and neo-Orthodox Christianity and certain strains of Buddhism—who have juxtaposed divinity to a worldly realm of sin, suffering, and forlornness. It is not by chance, I think, that the most familiar voices in the debate about whether the human world is or is not capable of achieving social justice have been infused with meditations on God, since the very object of the analysis—the world in its totality—is, as I will discuss, a metaphysical notion that exceeds empirical verification and requires for its comprehension, if only metaphorically, a God's eye view.

However, in explicating Dylan's pessimism about the world and the human capacity to achieve social justice, I do not in fact intend to center my analysis on strictly theological considerations. After all, it is certainly possible to articulate a faith (or despair) about the ultimate achievability of social justice in nontheological language, and some of the leading contemporary versions of this faith have been devoid of explicitly religious ideas. Just as important, as I explain in section III.1, Dylan's pessimism—and the ethical implications he derives from it—is not consistently, solely, or even primarily presented as theological claims. To be sure, Dylan remains both spiritually and textually close to Christian doctrines

---

[1] Martin Luther King Jr., "The American Dream," in *A Testament of Hope: The Essential Writings and Speeches*, ed. James M. Washington (New York: HarperCollins, 1986), 215. On King's idea that "the universe is on the side of justice," see his "Facing the Challenge of a New Age," in *Testament of Hope*, 141; also see "If the Negro Wins, Labor Wins," 207, and "A Christmas Sermon on Peace," 257, both in *Testament of Hope.*

regarding original sin, but his prophetic message about the fallenness of humanity is largely bereft of the Christian answer to this problematic: that one seek salvation through God and thereby overcome the world and its failings. It is not just that Dylan's Christianity is too brief and inconsistent in its explicit manifestations for it to stand as his chief ethical response to his pessimistic view of human affairs (a pessimism that, for him, is a far more longstanding and consistently expressed standpoint than his Christian belief). What also matters is that Dylan's approach to the fallenness of the world leads him primarily to focus on this-worldly responses rather than seek transcendence through such familiar religious practices as faith in a world to come, communion with God, or self-abnegation. In prophetically suggesting that the universe is not on the side of justice—that the human realm of politics will not be a site of divine or secular salvation—Dylan explores predominately human responses to the problem of fallen humanity.

For these reasons, in locating what is fresh and important in Dylan's pessimism about the world, I situate Dylan not primarily within a theological tradition of religious thought but within *the tradition of political realism*, which, like Dylan, understands a tragic divergence between morality and politics. Dylan is deeply familiar with numerous exponents of this tradition (Thucydides and Carl von Clausewitz, for example) and, in any case, shares with this tradition a pessimism rooted primarily in human nature rather than theological considerations. However, as much as Dylan shares and supports many of the insights of the tradition of political realism, it is precisely vis-à-vis this tradition that his distinctive prophetic edge is most apparent. Dylan is as much a critic of the tradition of political realism as he is a subscriber to it. Indeed, I argue that Dylan's contribution can be seen as a kind of *realer realism*. Dylan is truer to political realism's own pessimistic premises, avoiding the latent utopianism that paradoxically and persistently resurfaces within influential statements of political realist thought. He directs himself to a real constituency—ordinary, non-specially-empowered individuals—typically overlooked by canonical political realists with their focus on leadership. And Dylan is not guided by grandiose pretensions of mastery (i.e., the mastery of successfully navigating an otherwise fallen political landscape) that so often have accompanied the tradition of political realism and lent it, despite itself, an illusory air.

By way of summarizing what has been said so far and anticipating the argument that lies ahead, I turn to the opening lines of one of Dylan's sharpest statements of his prophetic pessimism about the world, his 1979 song "When You Gonna Wake Up?":

> God don't make promises that He don't keep
> You got some big dreams baby, but in order to dream you gotta
>   still be asleep
> When you gonna wake up, when you gonna wake up

When you gonna wake up and strengthen the things that remain?
Counterfeit philosophies have polluted all of your thoughts
Karl Marx has got ya by the throat, Henry Kissinger's got you tied up
    in knots
When you gonna wake up, when you gonna wake up
When you gonna wake up and strengthen the things that remain?

Unelaborated, these lines are more evocative than definitive, but they nonetheless help clarify all of the main ideas I put forward here in Part III. First of all, there is a clear pessimism in these words, as the call to strengthen the things that remain suggests the impossibility of a more ambitious set of aims and suggests, too, that even within the sphere of what can be achieved, only strengthening and not perfectibility is possible. What Dylan has in mind by this pessimism—his doctrine of a "world gone wrong"—is the topic of section III.1. At the same time, what lends this passage prophetic force is the sense that within fallen conditions vital ethical purposes nonetheless might be pursued. The exhortation to wake up and strengthen the things that remain combines profound pessimism with the equally intense idea that valuable ends might nevertheless be realized if only one could overcome illusion, awaken to the truth of a world gone wrong, and devote oneself to what can be salvaged in the face of its fallenness. Dylan's message is not one of utter despondency, but rather a call to achieve, through the very acceptance of a pessimistic view toward the world, an enlightened mentality and strategy of action. The remainder of Part III attempts to elucidate Dylan's prophecy of pessimism in this regard. Even if his thinking here is close to Christianity—even if these lines themselves suggest a Christian worldview with the appeal to "God" and a refrain that clearly recalls Revelation 3:2 ("Wake up, and strengthen what remains and is about to die, for I have not found your works complete in the sight of my God"[2])—section III.2 elaborates why Dylan's

---

[2] It is worth considering the biblical background of the passage. Jesus instructs John of Patmos to send messages to seven churches. Whereas other churches are given a mixture of commendation and castigation, the church at Sardis is only criticized. It might have a reputation for spiritual vitality, but in fact it has failed: "You have the reputation of being alive, but you are dead" (Revelation 3:1). Jesus's message to the church is: "Wake up, and strengthen what remains and is about to die, for I have not found your works complete in the sight of my God" (Revelation 3:2). Note that there are at least two readings of "about to die." On one reading, the message is to strengthen what remains and otherwise would perish. The darker reading, however, would be to strengthen what remains but will die nonetheless. Whichever reading is privileged, the message is not one of idealism or success. Either way, the idea appears to be: in a world of failure and emergency, wake up from false notions of total rectitude and total repair, and instead focus on what can be salvaged. As I elaborate, Dylan's suggestion is that both Marx/idealism and Kissinger/realism are versions of being asleep that promise something too aspirational and, in doing so, prevent a more honest, direct, and local effort to accomplish what can in fact be achieved.

pessimism is best contextualized within the tradition of political theory rather than Christian theology or other religious worldviews. Indeed, the passage itself gestures in the direction of political theory when it suggests that the meaning of Dylan's prophetic pessimism lies in its contrast to both "Karl Marx" and "Henry Kissinger," metonyms for political idealism and political realism, respectively. Dylan's exhortation not only calls for a third way but also polemically suggests that both idealism and conventional realism are prone to illusion, self-deception, and hence unreality. Why Dylan thinks this is true of idealism, Marxist or otherwise, is not hard to decipher, since the *sine non qua* of idealism is to deny what Dylan takes to be a hard truth—the permanent divergence between morality and politics and, with it, the fallenness of the world—and instead to articulate the conditions through which social justice might finally be achieved. But what is not obvious or straightforward is why the political realism represented by Kissinger, which would seem to share Dylan's pessimism about the world, is accused of its own unreality. How does traditional political realism represent a kind of being asleep akin to, even if different from, the soporific dreaming of excessive idealism, utopianism, and optimism regarding the world? How would avoiding the flaws of conventional political realism lead to a distinct ethic? Answering these questions is the focus of sections III.3–6, in which I elaborate four different ways in which Dylan's realism is related to, yet still distinct from and *realer than*, the political realism most commonly put forward in the tradition of political thought. The distinctive prophetic message of Dylan's pessimism about the world lies precisely here. Section III.7 further summarizes this message by discussing the meaning of Dylan's persistent tendency to refer to his politics as "upwing" as opposed to a location on the more familiar left-right continuum.

III.1. Dylan's Doctrine of a World Gone Wrong

One of the functions of prophetic speech is to pronounce upon the nature of the world. Although it might seem to be the quintessence of what is physical and tangible, in fact the world is a metaphysical and speculative notion. The idea of the world—abstracted from specific, local, measurable situations—exceeds any fully persuasive empirical verification. Accordingly, Kant rightly presents the notion of the world as a "hypothesis of reason," something we presuppose and invoke to guide our study of empirical phenomena (i.e., the presupposition that our individual discoveries in the natural world will harmonize and consolidate into truths applicable for the generalized whole) but that in itself goes beyond what can be scientifically known. Kant intended this as an epistemological premise guiding scientific research, but it can also be seen as having an ethical correlate: the *way of the world*, specifically the question of whether it is a place that ultimately favors, supports, or otherwise welcomes the realization of justice—or, to put the question in the religious terms with which it most commonly has been posed, whether the world is or can be a site of divine salvation or, instead, must remain a realm permanently alienated from God. This notion of the ethical disposition of the world is no less vital to our ethical orientation than Kant's hypotheses of reason are to our epistemological orientation. Our understanding of the ethical disposition of the world informs how we envision what is possible, our conception of moral responsibility, and our judgments about not just whether but *how* to act. Insofar as the world is synonymous with humanity, operating with the idea of the world means operating with a notion of what humanity is like—which, of course, generalizes our empirical knowledge of specific individuals into an extra-empirical abstraction—thereby enabling us to address essential questions: Who are we? What is a human community like? What can we expect from our politics and, relatedly, from our education and future enlightenment? Pure secularism, pure materialism, and pure naturalism each want to dispense with these questions since any answer provided would be, in their view, an uncritical overgeneralization. Nietzsche understood this well, arguing that once we let go of a notion of a "true" other-worldly divine realm, strictly speaking we should lose a sense of the merely temporal world as well: "The true world—we have abolished. What world has remained? The apparent one perhaps? But no! *With the true world we have also abolished the apparent one.*"[3]

Nietzsche's skepticism and relativism here suggest that in fact there is no way of the world and that the notion ought to be dissolved in light of radical contingency and the ever-present possibility of social construction. Perhaps he is right. But for those of us unprepared to let go of the reality and authoritativeness

---

[3] Friedrich Nietzsche, "How the True World Became a Fable," *Twilight of the Idols*, in *The Portable Nietzsche*, ed. and trans. Walter Kaufmann (New York: Penguin, 1976), 486. This passage most commonly is interpreted to say that the loss of a sense of genuine reality also undermines a sense of the merely apparent, but I focus here on the *world* aspect of Nietzsche's reflections: that is, the suggestion that *any* conception of world—whether the so-called empirical world or the way of the world (its ethical disposition)—means adopting a God's eye and, in any case, *metaphysical* perspective. It is thus entirely understandable that Habermas, for instance, credits *religions* with providing the valuable function of enabling a conceptualization of the world as such. Specifically, Habermas praises monotheistic religions, as they emerged in the so-called Axial Age, for cultivating "a divine standpoint outside the world . . . a unifying perspective that allowed the new intellectual elites to transcend occurrences within the world and to distance themselves from and objectify the latter *as a whole.*" As Habermas explains, "Without such a standpoint or principle the human mind cannot develop a picture of the world, or of the ages of the world, as a whole from a theoretical perspective or a universalistically oriented ethics from a practical perspective." Jürgen Habermas, "The Sacred Roots of the Axial Age Traditions," quoted in Amy Allen, "Having One's Cake and Eating It Too: Habermas' Genealogy of Postsecular Reason," in *Habermas and Religion*, ed. Craig Calhoun, Eduardo Mendieta, and Jonathan VanAntwerpen (Cambridge, UK: Polity, 2013), 144-45.

of objective moral standards, there is an irrepressible need to consider how well suited the world is to these moral aspirations. Further, the fact that there already is an answer to this question that dominates within contemporary culture—a regnant progressivism holding that the world ultimately can be brought into accordance with standards of justice, which is voiced both within leading paradigms of political and religious thought (with major exceptions, to be sure) and within informal social norms (the person who pronounces the opposite view that the world is forever mired in injustice is much more likely to be rebuked for saying something counterproductive, if not outright false, than someone who pronounces an optimistic faith in the ultimate redemption of the world)—means that the issue of the moral disposition of the world is already being addressed in a specific way, however much the forces of mere empiricism would prefer to jettison it.

Given this context—the world as a prophetic object, the vitality of the question of the world's moral disposition, and the progressive, optimistic answer to this question that currently prevails—Dylan's profound pessimism about the world ought to interest us. Even for a prophet, Dylan stands out for focusing so ardently and unremittingly on the world as an inescapably fallen domain, characterized by rampant egotism, violence and aggression, unjust suffering, greed, irresponsible power, and chaos.

Dylan's pessimism consists of three overarching elements. First and most foundationally, it involves a deep suspicion of the human being. Believing that "human nature is always the enemy of anything superior," Dylan does not deny that some of us can approximate moral heroism and moral purity, but he understands prideful egotism both as the default human quality and as one that permanently threatens the safety of influential moral leaders.[4] Entire songs, like "Foot of Pride" and "Disease of Conceit," depict humanity in its fallen state of pridefulness.[5] Part of what makes pride so objectionable for Dylan is how misguided it is, since it is based on a grandiose view of the human being's ability to achieve something great and lasting:

> You're gonna die. You're gonna go off the earth. You're gonna be dead. It could be 20 years, it could be tomorrow, anytime. So am I. I mean, we're just going to be gone. *The world's going to go on without us.* All right, now

---

[4] Bob Dylan, *Chronicles: Volume One* (New York: Simon & Schuster, 2004), 37.

[5] Also consider lyrics from other songs: "Well, God is in His heaven / And we all want what's his / But power and greed and corruptible seed / Seem to be all that there is" ("Blind Willie McTell"); "Now he worships at an altar of a stagnant pool / And when he sees his reflection, he's fulfilled / Oh, man is opposed to fair play / He wants it all and he wants it his way" ("License to Kill"); "Man's ego's inflated" ("Slow Train").

you do your job in the face of that, and how seriously you take yourself you decide for yourself.[6]

For Dylan, this circumstance cautions against pride by revealing its foolishness: "I've never been able to understand the seriousness of it all, the seriousness of pride. People talk, act, live as if they're never going to die. And what do they leave behind? Nothing. Nothing but a mask."[7]

In any case, the ethical implications for Dylan are clear: the world is fallen because too many of us are and always will be. In a 1985 interview, he states:

> Most people walking around have this strange conception that they're born good, that they're really good people—but the *world* has just made a mess out of their lives. I have another point of view.[8]

Rare individuals—or each of us in rare moments—can overcome this egotism and achieve a perspective that is more generous, outward, and self-sacrificing, but Dylan expects that there will always be larger and more powerful counterforces undermining the full triumph of such moral action.[9]

Second, pride and egotism ensure that the world always will be shaped by violent conflict. War, in Dylan's view, is a permanent way of the world. As he expressed it in an interview from 1984: "There is not going to *be* any peace. . . .

---

[6] Interview with *TIME* Magazine (1965; emphasis added), featured in the documentary *Don't Look Back*, written and directed by D. A. Pennebaker (New York: Leacock-Pennebaker, Inc., 1967); see a video and transcript at Andreea Diana Tanasescu, " 'Really the Truth Is Just a Plain Picture,' Bob Dylan *Time Magazine* Interview," 10.1, October 5, 2010, https://10point1.blogspot.com/2010/10/really-truth-is-just-plain-picture-bob.html.

[7] Interview with Scott Cohen, "Bob Dylan Revisited," *SPIN* (December 1985), https://www.spin.com/featured/bob-dylan-december-1985-cover-story/

[8] Interview with Bill Flanagan (March 1985), in Flanagan, *Written in My Soul: Conversations with Rock's Great Songwriters* (Chicago: Contemporary Books, 1986), 104.

[9] It is true that at the height of his gospel period Dylan upholds the possibility of human redemption—that is, of overcoming egotism and other forms of sin—through faith. Still, for Dylan's pessimistic view of humanity to hold it is not necessary that all behave pridefully, only a majority (or even fraction) sufficient to disrupt everybody else and thereby shape the world. Even Dylan's most ecstatic gospel music dispenses with the expectation that more than the elect few will overcome their base pridefulness. See, for example, the 1980 song "What Can I Do for You?," which includes the line "You've chosen me to be among the few." Moreover, as I have emphasized, Dylan's messianic religious fervor is short lived. This means that those who treat Dylan prophetically, upon reflection, do not follow someone consistently preaching the ultimate transformation of humanity or the salvation of the world. No one who listens to Dylan in his entirety can really think he is providing a straightforward, unambiguous message that the fallenness of the world is best addressed through expectations of a world to come.

You can reload your rifle, and that moment you're reloading it, that's peace. It may last for a few years."[10] And as he sings in "Union Sundown":

> Democracy don't rule the world
> You'd better get that in your head
> This world is ruled by violence
> But I guess that's better left unsaid

It is not that Dylan is in denial about the possibilities for local improvements that might achieve more democracy and less violence in specific contexts, but he prophetically insists that the world in general—significant portions of the globe, if not all portions to some degree—operates inescapably in conjunction with fighting, bloodshed, and arrogant aggression.

Third, politics—even democratic politics—is debased in Dylan's eyes. Part of the problem is that genuine moral leaders, in Dylan's view, are likely to be assassinated. Recall his statement "If somebody *really* had something to say to help somebody out, just bluntly say the truth, well obviously they're gonna be done away with. They're gonna be *killed.*" And also consider his song "Band of the Hand," from 1986, which includes the lines:

> They kill people here who stand up for their rights
> The system's just too damned corrupt
> It's always the same, the name of the game
> Is who do you know higher up

A related issue is that ordinary individuals are unlikely to be able to make a difference:

> You see, nobody in power has to worry about anybody from the outside, any cat that's very evidently on the outside, criticizing their society, because he's on the outside, he's not in it anyway, and he's not gonna make a dent. You can't go around criticizing something you're not part of and hope to make it better. It ain't gonna work. I'm just not gonna be a part of it. I'm not gonna make a dent or anything, so why be part of it by even trying to criticize it? That's a waste of time. The kids know that. The kids today, by the time they're twenty-one, they realize it's all bullshit. I know it's all bullshit.[11]

[10] Jonathan Cott, ed., "Interview with Kurt Loder, *Rolling Stone,* June 21, 1984," in *Bob Dylan: The Essential Interviews* (New York: Simon & Schuster, 2017), 309.

[11] Quoted in Anthony Scaduto, *Bob Dylan: An Intimate Biography* (New York: Grosset & Dunlap, 1971), 176–77.

The problem for Dylan is not just that ordinary civic action is woefully inadequate to achieve peace and social justice, but that politics itself—politicians and conventional political spaces like courts, parliaments, and so forth—is reflective of the fallen conditions of the world. Dylan's depiction of politicians is uniformly negative, pointing to corruption, selfish power-seeking, and unfair plutocratic relations. Consider the following example from "I Want You":

> The drunken politician leaps
> Upon the street where mothers weep

From "Band of the Hand":

> There are pimps on the make, politicians on the take

These lyrics from "Summer Days":

> Politician got on his jogging shoes
> He must be running for office, got no time to lose
> He been suckin' the blood out of the genius of generosity

From "It's All Good":

> Big politician telling lies

And from "Pay in Blood":

> Another politician pumping out the piss

Dylan continually returns to the connection between politics and the rule of the rich, but with no faith in Marxist solutions.[12] He is fond of the joke that the Golden Rule means those who have the gold make the rules. And he conceives of the marketplace as inhabited by "merchants and thieves, hungry for power" ("Changing of the Guards"). If Dylan at times can at least contemplate the personal transcendence of politics, he leaves no doubt that the world that is transcended is inherently political and for this reason fallen, as in these lines from "Political World":

---

[12] On his impatience with socialism, consider both what I already have cited regarding Marx from "When You Gonna Wake Up?" ("Karl Marx has got ya by the throat") and also a line from "No Time to Think" ("Socialism, hypnotism, patriotism, materialism").

We live in a political world
Love don't have any place
We're living in times where men commit crimes
And crime don't have a face

Politics for Dylan is thus not only incapable of achieving justice or salvation but—as a venue where human egotism, violence, and rapacity are all the more likely to manifest themselves—a leading reason why the human condition is fallen. As he puts it starkly: "I think politics is an instrument of the Devil. Just that clear. I think politics is what kills; it doesn't bring anything alive. Politics is corrupt; I mean, anybody knows that."[13] Without denying that some improvements are possible, he indicts politics regardless of its ideological or institutional form.

For these reasons—the nature of the human being, the persistence of war and violence, and the wickedness of politics—Dylan can take the world to be "this earthly domain, full of disappointment and pain" ("When the Deal Goes Down"). The world, he insists, is not something that we should expect to be fixed: "The struggle against oppression and injustice is always going to be there."[14] Such struggles can make progress within local contexts and help contain disasters and emergencies as they arise, but the world as a whole in Dylan's view will always be shaped by profound moral failure.

III.2. Dylan's Pessimism as *Realer* Political Realism

Although clearly influenced to some degree by Christianity, Dylan's pessimism about the world is more consistently and more fundamentally animated by a political realism that, however much it recalls elements of canonical political realists (many of whom, such as Thucydides and Clausewitz, Dylan knows as a reader), departs in key and critical respects from this tradition, representing instead a kind of "realer realism" more attuned to the lived realities of ordinary life. Notwithstanding the powerful influence of Judeo-Christian ideas and imagery on Dylan's own prophetic music, when it comes to the question of understanding the prophetic impact of his pessimism about the world, conventional

[13] Cott, "Interview with Kurt Loder," in *Essential Interviews*, 309. Likewise, Dylan tells a crowd at a May 1980 concert: "The Devil's behind politics." Bob Dylan, *Saved! The Gospel Speeches* (New York: Hanuman Books, 1990), 95.

[14] Jim Ellison, ed., "The Diamond Voice from Within" (interview with Neil Spencer, *New Musical Express*, August 15, 1981), in *Younger Than That Now: The Collected Interviews with Bob Dylan* (New York: Thunder's Mouth Press, 2004), 182.

religious interpretations are either not appropriate or not nearly as illuminating as situating Dylan's pessimism within the tradition of political realism.

Dylan's pessimism about the world is most obviously distinct from the most dominant prophetic impulse, which is to uphold the ultimate redemption of humanity, or some segment of it, as an appropriate expectation *for this world*. Within the Jewish tradition, for example, biblical prophets typically taught their followers that if the Israelites "returned to [God], their sufferings would end and their political sovereignty would be restored."[15] Within the Christian tradition, numerous prophetic currents—including postmillennial eschatological ideas (positing a humanly wrought millennium of peace and justice prior to the Second Coming of Jesus) and, in a very different way, persistent movements (like Pelagianism, liberal Christianity, and the Social Gospel) that minimize the problem of original sin and link Christianity to the pursuit and achievement of social justice—likewise have presented the world as ultimately harmonizable with both God and justice. This optimism about the world has been influential to the theorization and practice of republican and democratic values in the West, as the idea of a well-ordered democratic republic very often has been treated as an essential element of the human achievement of peace and justice on earth. Dylan powerfully rejects this kind of prophetic thinking. Expressed theologically, Dylan's pessimism about the world leads him to insist upon the inescapable reality of sin (consider his song "Ain't No Man Righteous, No Not One") and to predict not the ultimate redemption of humanity in this world, but its destruction: "I believe that ever since Adam and Eve got thrown out of the garden, that the whole nature of the planet has been heading in one direction—towards apocalypse."[16]

To be sure, even if the dominant trend within the West's prophetic tradition has been optimism regarding the ultimate redemption of the world, there are powerful countercurrents, of long and distinguished pedigree, that themselves suggest that the world is hopelessly fallen. For example, Eastern religions—such as Hinduism, Buddhism, Jainism, and Sikhism—typically present the world (*saṃsāra*) as inherently full of suffering. In Buddhism, for instance, the first of the Four Noble Truths is that worldly existence is inescapably tied to *duḥkha*: a suffering arising from anxiety, distress, frustration, unease, and a general sense of life as unsatisfactory.[17] And within Christianity, perspectives that have insisted upon original sin, the radical separation between God and humanity, and a

---

[15] Alison McQueen, *Political Realism in Apocalyptic Times* (New York: Cambridge University Press, 2018), 25.

[16] Jim Ellison, ed., "Jesus, Who's Got Time to Keep Up with the Times?" (interview with Mick Brown in the *Sunday Times*, July 1, 1984), in *Younger Than That Now*, 190.

[17] Damien Keown, *Oxford Dictionary of Buddhism* (Oxford: Oxford University Press, 2004), 81.

salvation that can only be fully realized via divine grace in a world to come—such as Augustinian, certain Calvinist, and neo-Orthodox Christian theologies, as well as the premillennial eschatological idea that Jesus must return to earth in order to inaugurate the millennium—have insisted upon the permanent fallenness of humanity in this life.

Dylan, however, cannot be reduced to these perspectives because whereas they promise the ultimate transcendence of the world, his pessimism about the world still takes the world as the most important horizon for spiritual and ethical life. That Dylan is distinct from Buddhist and other Eastern religions is a matter of course. It is not just that he never espouses their specific doctrines, but the general idea of spiritually transcending worldly disappointment and suffering is entirely outside of his prophetic purposes.[18] Even if Buddhism insists upon suffering as an intrinsic aspect of the world, the world itself is presented as something that might be overcome. By taming craving and unwise clinging to the impermanent things of the world, a practitioner of Buddhism aims to be released from *duḥkha* and achieve *nirvana*. Other Eastern religions rely on this same notion of *moksha* (liberation from the world).[19] Whether such practices are best understood as the renunciation or redemption of the world, the challenge of living within permanently fallen mundane conditions is not the purpose of these religions, which by contrast want to transcend the mundane for spiritual heights. Dylan, however, lives in the mundane and pitches his prophetic utterances primarily there.

For similar reasons it does not make sense to understand the prophetic implications of Dylan's pessimism about the world as simply falling within a familiar Christian tradition that—in the hands of such theologians as Augustine, Calvin, Jonathan Edwards, Reinhold Niebuhr, and countless others—has presented life in this world as permanently depraved, sinful, and alienated from God. While Dylan shares the pessimism and, at times, many of the theological tropes of this tradition, what he importantly lacks (as any kind of longstanding perspective) is this tradition's animating faith that the world and its problems ultimately can be overcome through divine salvation. For canonical Christian

---

[18] It is not by chance, I think, that the two references to Buddha in Dylan's songs are both to some extent critical: "Rubin sits like Buddha in a ten-foot cell / An innocent man in a living hell" ("Hurricane"), and "Sister, lemme tell you about a vision I saw / You were drawing water for your husband, you were suffering under the law / You were telling him about Buddha, you were telling him about Mohammed in the same breath / You never mentioned one time the Man who came and died a criminal's death" ("Precious Angel"). Dylan also sharply dissociates himself from "Eastern religions" in his gospel speeches: see, for example, *Saved! The Gospel Speeches*, 100.

[19] Liberation from the world figures as an important idea in Hinduism (including in the Upanishads and the Bhagavad Gita), Buddhism, Sikhism, and Jainism. See, for example, Jack Sikora, *Religions of India* (San Jose, CA: Writers Club Press, 2002), 2, 3, 18, 39.

pessimists, pessimism about the world is balanced, indeed superseded, by an awareness of God and faith in divine grace. As Edwards puts it: "The same eye that discerns the transcendent beauty of holiness, necessarily therein sees the exceeding odiousness of sin."[20] But Dylan lacks this balance. He is much readier to accept the Christian diagnosis of the world as fallen than the Christian solution that the world can somehow be transcended through a relationship to God, whether in this life or the next. To be sure, at the height of his gospel period, Dylan does indeed point to the possibility of divine salvation and, with it, the transcendence of the world.[21] But these utterances must be seen as highly exceptional. Dylan's gospel period, after all, is just a relatively brief period in his public life. The Christian theology he voiced during this period thus cannot be invoked to explain a pessimism about the world that both precedes and endures after his gospel period and, indeed, is one of the most consistently communicated ideas throughout his more than sixty years on the public stage. Dylan's Christianity is too brief, inconsistent, and full of doubt for it to explain or answer his conception of a "world gone wrong"—a conception that, in running through the entirety of his public career, is avowed as much by works that veer in a skeptical (if not atheistic) direction as by Christian songs and messages.[22] Moreover, even within Dylan's gospel period the idea of divine salvation plays a relatively small role, at least in comparison to his much more pronounced Christian-inspired critique of the world for its injustice, callousness, false piety, hypocrisy, and unknowing mockery of genuine people of faith.[23] Dylan's contemplation of another

---

[20] Jonathan Edwards, *A Treatise Concerning Religious Affections*, in *The Works of President Edwards* (New York: Leavitt & Allen, 1851), III:131. Edwards continues: "He now sees the dreadful pollution of his heart, and the desperate depravity of his nature, in a new manner; for his soul has now a sense given it to feel the pain of such a disease" (131).

[21] See especially songs from the album *Saved*, including "Solid Rock," "Saved," and "Are You Ready?" See also "When He Returns," from *Slow Train Coming*.

[22] Dylan's 1963 song "With God on Our Side," exposes and challenges the American regime's pretension that its various military exploits have been divinely sanctioned, and, in this sense, gestures in the direction of religious skepticism; yet the same diagnosis of the world—that it is full of illegitimate aggression and violence—repeats in evangelical pieces such as "Slow Train." As these examples suggest, Dylan's pessimism about the world is not intrinsically connected to his periods of pronounced religious faith.

[23] Cartwright is perceptive when he observes that for Dylan the chief religious figure to be contended with is not God but the devil, whom Dylan, following Paul, is fond of referring to as "the god of this world" (2 Corinthians 4:4). As Cartwright puts it: "For Dylan, the Devil is the preeminent spiritual force at work in the world perverting and distorting all existence. There is nothing beyond the Devil's control. In matters of the world, the Devil holds absolute sway.... Upon surveying Dylan's dialogue with the Devil throughout his public life, it appears that, for Dylan, the Devil is a much more lively character than Christ. The god of this world is the Devil who is the primary being with whom one must deal. God in Christ is notably absent from the world and is helpless to transform it. For Dylan, the chief referent in the world is the Devil, not God. It is the Devil with whom one deals on a daily basis. An aloof God has visited the planet in Jesus Christ to strike a telling

world beyond our own is not just brief and vague, but often minimalistic (an intimation of *some* reality beyond our world, not necessarily a Christian reality) as well as sometimes self-consciously invoked in a therapeutic rather than clearly devout way (as something we need to believe in so as not to be entirely demoralized by the world as it is).[24] Finally, and more generally, if one of the central claims of this book is correct—that Dylan is not a prophet of salvation, but a prophet of diremption, because he wrestles with three conflicting sources of normative authority (namely, God, justice, and selfhood)—then it is simply not credible to read him as teaching the path to salvation, whether Christian or otherwise.

For these reasons, Dylan, viewed holistically in light of his more than six decades of music and public statements, communicates the Christian problematic of original sin much more consistently and forcefully than the Christian solution to this problem. In this regard he is close to Niebuhr when Niebuhr observes that original sin is the one thing that has been empirically proven about Christianity.[25] But if Niebuhr puts this forward as a truth about the world that reminds us of the importance of the Christian outlook, Dylan encourages us to see the idea from a different angle—namely, that there is an imbalance in what is most persuasive about Christianity: the pessimistic doctrine seems more credible than the divinity that would lead us out of it. Accordingly, Dylan's pessimism is prophetically distinct from canonical Christianity because, on balance, his chief concern is with how the fallenness of the world might be endured rather than transcended. If Augustine, for instance, presents the Christian as a pilgrim, forced to travel within a fallen world on a path toward ultimate salvation, Dylan's prophetic pessimism largely ceases to be driven by any firm eschatological expectation, as evident in these lines from "Mississippi":

blow against the Devil, but the cosmic effects do not take place till the end of time." Bert Cartwright, "Talkin' Devil with Bob Dylan," *Telegraph* 49 (Summer 1994), https://www.expectingrain.com/dok/who/d/devil.html.

[24] On Dylan's minimalism, consider his reflection from 1984: "I don't think I've ever been an agnostic. I've always thought there's a superior power, that this is not the real world and that there's a world to come. That no soul has died, every soul is alive, either in holiness or in flames. And there's probably a lot of middle ground." Cott, "Interview with Kurt Loder," in *Essential Interviews*, 305. Also relevant is Dylan's invocation of nature as another potential source, besides Christianity, of relating to the divine: "Of course you can look on the desert and wake up to the sun and the sand and the beauty of the stars and know there is a higher being, and worship that creator. But being thrown into the cities you're faced more with man than with God. We're dealing here with man, you know, and in order to know where man's at, you have to know what God would do if he was man." Ellison, "The Diamond Voice from Within," in *Younger Than That Now*, 182.

[25] Reinhold Niebuhr, *Man's Nature and His Communities: Essays on the Dynamics and Enigmas of Man's Personal and Social Existence* (New York: Charles Scribner's Sons, 1965), 24, quoting with approval the idea as it appeared in the *Times Literary Supplement*.

Time is pilin' up, we struggle and we scrape
We're all boxed in, nowhere to escape

Dylan invites his listeners to consider themselves as walking and wandering without an extra-worldly destination, with no direction home, forced to operate in a world gone wrong. Canonical Christian pessimists might agree with the reality of this situation as an account of *this life*, but also look past it due to eschatological and theological commitments Dylan simply does not consistently share.

My insistence that Dylan's pessimism be read in terms of political realism rather than Christianity is not meant to deny the Christian aspects of his thinking but instead to suggest that the distinctive prophetic contribution of his pessimism lies in its critical divergence from the political realist tradition. Even so, some critics will say that my dichotomy between politics and religion is simplistic since politics and theology in fact presuppose each other[26] and that, specifically, there is the school of *Christian realism* that explicitly aims to apply Christian insights to a realist conception of politics. To the general point about the intersection of politics and religion, this may be true in some ultimate sense, but with regard to the matter at hand there nonetheless is a substantial difference whether the sources and implications of pessimism about the world relate primarily to attitudes toward divinity, eschatological notions regarding the final destiny of mankind, or other religious ideas—or, instead, apply above all to this-worldly phenomena likely to be cognizable to individuals from a diversity of religious and atheistic perspectives. The most distinctive aspects of Dylan's pessimism, I will explain, are best understood according to this latter construct. With regard to Christian realism—a tradition of thought associated with numerous figures, such as Augustine and especially Niebuhr[27]—it is indeed true that, much more so than other forms of Christianity that also posit an unbridgeable separation between divinity and the human world, it is focused on the political implications of this condition, specifically the need to take up responsible political action within fallen conditions and to recognize that doing so nonetheless inevitably will fall short of moral norms of goodness and religious norms of piety. What is more, Dylan's brand of realer realism is perhaps closer to Christian realism than any other standpoint, since both Dylan and contemporary Christian realists can be read as providing a corrective to prevailing,

[26] For a statement of this idea, see Eric Nelson, *The Theology of Liberalism: Political Philosophy and the Justice of God* (Cambridge, MA: Belknap Press of Harvard University Press, 2019).

[27] But note the importance of D. C. Macintosh, Walter Marshall, and John C. Bennett, among others, who can be credited as originating the movement of Christian realism prior to Niebuhr. See Robin W. Lovin, *Reinhold Niebuhr and Christian Realism* (Cambridge, UK: Cambridge University Press, 1995), 1.

canonical forms of political realism. When Christian realists like Niebuhr object to the tradition of political realism for being too much concerned with
achieving an impossible mastery, too prideful in its ambition to manage history,
too dismissive of universal norms of morality and justice (even if these cannot
be fully realized in this life), and too unwilling to be humbled and restrained by
an awareness that human machinations take place within a wider, mysterious
cosmic setting, they articulate a standpoint that is indeed close to key aspects of
Dylan's realism.[28] At the same time, however, it does not make sense to classify
Dylan as a Christian realist since there are important discontinuities. Christian
realism mostly has been directed to politicians, statesmen, and the context of
grand politics (e.g., urging the incumbency of fighting global communism and
the rejection of American isolationism) and thus has been much less concerned
with what is the primary focus of Dylan's realism: namely, the conditions of *ordinary* political life.[29] Further, even if Christian realists emphasize divinity as an
ultimate rather than a direct and immediate concern,[30] they are still much more
theological than Dylan is in his realism. And this greater theological bent has
meant that Christian realists are not nearly as pessimistic as Dylan is about the
world. Conceptually, this difference is reflected in the fact that Niebuhr, for instance, has objected to the very idea of tragedy in describing the human separation from the divine (opting instead for irony[31]) and that he actually has taken
aim against too much pessimism as a mentality that is irresponsible and likely to
promote tyranny.[32] Tsoncho Tsonchev goes so far as to say that Christian realism

[28] See Reinhold Niebuhr, *The Irony of American History* (Chicago: University of Chicago Press, 2008), 5, 37, 88.

[29] Niebuhr's focus on grand politics and political leadership can be seen in his emphasis on the "balance of powers" as an essential, realistic, and responsible political goal. On this, see Tsoncho Tsonchev, *The Political Theology of Augustine, Thomas Aquinas, and Reinhold Niebuhr* (Montreal: The Montreal Review, 2018), 16, 119–20. It can also be seen in Niebuhr's continual invocation of *statesmen* as those who already recognize (more than disconnected idealists) the truth of realism and in the fact that statesmen are a clearly intended audience of his reflections. As Niebuhr writes, "There is consequently a remarkable hiatus between the shrewdness of practical men of affairs and the [faulty] speculations of our wise men" (*Irony of American History*, 17–18). And likewise: "We cannot choose between violence and non-violence, but only between violence and a statesmanship which seeks to adjust social forces without violence but cannot guarantee immunity from clashes." Niebuhr, "An Interpretation of Christian Ethics," in *Reinhold Niebuhr on Politics*, ed. Harry R. Davis and Robert C. Good (Eugene, OR: Wipf & Stock, 1960), 137.

[30] Niebuhr argues that "the law of love stands on the edge of history and not in history, that it represents an ultimate and not an immediate possibility.... Sin introduces an element of conflict into the world and ... even the most loving relations are not free of it" (*Niebuhr on Politics*, 145, 147).

[31] See, for example, Niebuhr, *Irony of American History*, 157.

[32] As Niebuhr puts it: "Both moral sentimentality in politics and moral pessimism encourage totalitarian regimes, the one because it encourages the opinion that it is not necessary to check the power of government, and the second because it believes that only absolute political authority can restrain the anarchy, created by conflicting and competitive interests." Niebuhr, *The Children of Light*

"is not in any way pessimism."[33] Substantively, this difference is reflected in the enduring role of faith, hope, forgiveness, and love in Niebuhr's account and the way his Christian realism is more about a limited progressivism than a rejection of historical progress as such.[34] Thus, even though Dylan follows Christian realists in providing a corrective to the tradition of political realism, and even though he sometimes is guided by Christian notions in doing so (though not at all consistently), Dylan is much more willing to countenance a truly pessimistic account of the world and to explore the ethical implications for everyday people that might follow from it.

If Dylan's pessimism about the world is thus not reducible to a familiar theological perspective, neither can it be drained of its prophetic aspect altogether and treated simply as a species of mere philosophical pessimism—that is, as simply rejecting the idea of progress.[35] Dylan does indeed dispense with any expectation of progress on the global scale of the world, but he adds to this a powerful prophetic element that for the most part is lacking in the pessimistic philosophies of such figures as Leopardi, Schopenhauer, Nietzsche, Camus, and Cioran, among others. This prophetic element stems not just from the intense emotionality of Dylan's singing but also from the fact that his pessimism is animated by a sense of moral disappointment and outrage at a world that is unjust. Indeed, as I will discuss, Dylan's indignation frequently leads him to claim, following Paul, that the world is *satanic*, governed by the devil, the so-called god of this world. Dylan, then, does not simply reject progress but does so from a standpoint that understands the baseline—the world that will not be improved upon—as inescapably iniquitous, oppressive, and violent. This differs from pessimists who embrace the world or who, as Joshua Dienstag reminds us,

---

and the Children of Darkness (Chicago: University of Chicago Press, 2011), xxvii. Also see his critique of what he terms a "too consistent pessimism" (44).

[33] Tsonchev, *Political Theology of Augustine, Thomas Aquinas, and Reinhold Niebuhr*, 132.

[34] See, for example, Niebuhr's comment that we do not choose between injustice and perfect equality "but only between injustice and a justice which moves toward equality and incorporates some of its values" (*Niebuhr on Politics*, 137). The progressivism—and, with it, faith in salvation—that figures so centrally in Christian realism, but is largely lacking in Dylan, can also be found in Niebuhr's well-known exhortation: "Nothing that is worth doing can be achieved in our lifetime; therefore we must be saved by hope. Nothing which is true or beautiful or good makes complete sense in any immediate context of history; therefore we must be saved by faith. Nothing we do, however virtuous, can be accomplished alone; therefore we are saved by love. No virtuous act is quite as virtuous from the standpoint of our friend or foe as it is from our standpoint. Therefore we must be saved by the final form of love which is forgiveness." Niebuhr, *Irony of American History*, 63.

[35] On this definition, see Joshua Foa Dienstag, *Pessimism: Philosophy, Spirit, Ethic* (Princeton, NJ: Princeton University Press, 2006), 5, passim.

frequently "deny the existence of natural or permanent moral structures to guide our behavior."[36]

What, then, is the right way to understand the prophetic implications of Dylan's pessimism about the world? Given the irreducibility of his prophetic pessimism to familiar Christian standpoints—and given his focus on confronting rather than transcending or simply accepting a world gone wrong—it is appropriate to place Dylan within a different tradition, which itself posits an inescapable divergence between justice and humanity and likewise concentrates on the worldly implications of this tragic circumstance. This is the tradition of *political realism*—running through such seminal figures as Thucydides, Machiavelli, Hobbes in a certain sense, Clausewitz, Weber, Morgenthau, and various recent statesmen espousing a doctrine of realpolitik in the manner of Kissinger—which accepts war and conflict as endemic, insists on the inevitable clash between politics and morality, and thus puts forward a tragic view of the world as permanently unable to achieve the highest human aspirations for social justice. For canonical political realists, too, the world is fallen. Dylan is close to them but also directs his prophetic ire most distinctly in their direction.

The decision to situate Dylan within political realist thought stems not only from similarities he shares with canonical political realists, but also from the fact that Dylan himself invites this linkage in numerous respects. For one thing, he often refers to the *realism* of his pessimism about the world.[37] More deeply, Dylan is familiar with the writings of key figures within the political realist tradition, accepts the accuracy of their diagnoses in numerous respects, and, just as important, appreciates their prophetic character. In *Chronicles*, describing a period of active reading and study, Dylan reserves singular praise for Thucydides, perhaps the first exponent of political realism in the West. As much as Dylan elsewhere criticizes political theory for "memorizing politics of ancient history"

[36] Dienstag, 149. Dienstag makes this observation in regard to Camus, but it also applies to numerous other pessimistic figures, such as Leopardi, Nietzsche, and, in a different way, Cioran, who claims: "Don't be fair to me: I can do without everything but the tonic of injustice" (250). The difference between the philosophical pessimism studied by Dienstag and the prophetic pessimism voiced by Dylan is that, at its core, the former rejects progressivism by eliminating all expectation—as Dienstag explains, pessimism "does not simply tell us to expect less. It tells us, in fact, to expect nothing" (5)—whereas the prophetic variant rejects progressivism only in the sense of accepting that justice will not be achieved in the world (and thus does not dispense with moral expectations as such). To be sure, Schopenhauer's pessimism, to the extent it is infused with a sense of moral indignation and informed by the alleged existence of permanent moral structures, does resemble Dylan's perspective to a certain degree.

[37] In responding to Dylan's view that the world is inescapably mired in violence, Kurt Loder challenges Dylan: "That's a very fatalistic view, isn't it?" Dylan replies by emphasizing its realism: "I think it's *realistic*." Cott, "Interview with Kurt Loder," in *Essential Interviews*, 310 (emphasis added).

("My Back Pages"), he attests to his fascination with Thucydides's account of the Peloponnesian War. Indeed, Dylan recounts that all the other books he was reading paled in comparison to Thucydides:

> I read some Albertus Magnus book . . . the guy who mixed up scientific theories with theology. It was lightweight compared to Thucydides . . . a lot of books were too big to read, like giant shoes fitted for large-footed people. I read the poetry books, mostly. . . . This stuff pales in comparison to Thucydides, too. The books make the room vibrate in a nauseating and forceful way. The words of "La Vita Solitaria" by Leopardi seemed to come out of the trunk of a tree, hopeless, uncrushable sentiments.[38]

What is it that strikes Dylan about Thucydides's account? Dylan describes it as:

> a narrative which would give you chills. It was written four hundred years before Christ and it talks about *how human nature is always the enemy of anything superior.* Thucydides writes about how words in his time have changed from their ordinary meaning, how actions and opinions can be altered in the blink of an eye. It's like nothing has changed from his time to mine.[39]

Dylan takes Thucydides's own pessimism to denote not the complete absence of moral excellence (of what truly is "superior"), but the problem that humanity, on balance, represents a permanent and powerful counterbalance to its highest aspirations.

Dylan expresses similar fascination with and praise for Clausewitz for the same underlying issue—insight into the tragic divergence between morality and politics:

> Clausewitz's book seemed outdated, but there's a lot in it that's real, and you can understand a lot about conventional life and the pressures of environment by reading it. When he claims that politics has taken the place of morality and politics is brute force, he's not playing. You have to believe it. You do exactly as you're told, whoever you are. Knuckle under or you're dead. Don't give me any of that jazz about hope or nonsense about righteousness. Don't give me that dance that God is with us, or that God supports us. Let's get down to brass tacks. There isn't

[38] Dylan, *Chronicles*, 37.
[39] Dylan, 36 (emphasis added).

any moral order. You can forget that. *Morality has nothing in common with politics.* It's not there to transgress. It's either high ground or low ground. That is the way the world is and nothing's gonna change it. It's a crazy, mixed up world and you have to look it right in the eye. *Clausewitz in some ways is a prophet.* Without realizing it, some of the stuff in his book can shape your ideas. If you think you're a dreamer, you can read this stuff and realize you're not even capable of dreaming. Dreaming is dangerous. Reading Clausewitz makes you take your own thoughts a little less seriously.[40]

When Dylan reflects that "morality has nothing in common with politics," I think he means not that it is wrong to have moral expectations about politics (i.e., not that we should leave behind morality and analyze politics "beyond good and evil"), but that the political as such is incapable of operating according to pure moral means. The pathos of Dylan's reflections, his own life-long interest in questions of social justice, his occasional pursuit of just causes in specific local contexts, and his admiration for moral heroes like Gandhi and King, who, in Dylan's view, were killed precisely because they attempted a more genuine moralization of politics all suggest as much—that is, all suggest that Dylan understands political realism, the irreducibility of politics to morality, as a tragic and not simply amoral descriptive perspective. In any case, the upshot of Clausewitz's analysis for Dylan is that it instills in him a better appreciation for the flawed nature of the world: "It's a crazy, mixed up world and you have to look it right in the eye." Moreover, Dylan attributes to Clausewitz a quasi-prophetic quality, thus recognizing that the tradition of political realism is wrongly reduced to mere sobriety about politics but contains a prophetic potential insofar as it provides an account of the nature of the world (e.g., "That is the way the world is and nothing's gonna change it"), exhorts its adherents to dispense with false dreams and misperceptions, and suggests the ethical incumbency of confronting the world as it really is in its tragic aspect.

On the one hand, what Dylan says about Clausewitz I want to say about Dylan: that he "in some ways is a prophet" and that he, too, shares a tragic conception of the world as a fallen human realm permanently unable to satisfactorily realize norms of morality and justice. On the other hand, though, Dylan is different because he suggests that the tradition of political realism represented by Thucydides and Clausewitz can itself be an obstacle in the way of an honest confrontation with political reality. Recall that Dylan presents his pessimistic

---

[40] Dylan, 45 (emphasis added).

ethic of "strengthening the things that remain" in *contradistinction* to canonical political realism:

> Counterfeit philosophies have polluted all of your thoughts
> Karl Marx has got ya by the throat, Henry Kissinger's got you tied up
>   in knots
> When you gonna wake up, when you gonna wake up
> When you gonna wake up and strengthen the things that remain?

"Karl Marx" and "Henry Kissinger," as I have observed, are metonyms for idealism and realism, respectively. Dylan's call to "wake up and strengthen the things that remain" would seem to stand for a third way: a realism related to, yet still distinct from, the political realism most commonly put forward in the tradition of political thought. But how can this be? How can the conventional tradition of political realism, represented by Kissinger, be accused of failure to attend sufficiently to political reality and in this sense replicate some of the problems of excessive utopianism in politics? To answer this question requires understanding how Dylan's pessimism about the world diverges from the political realists he nonetheless appreciates. It is here that the uniqueness of Dylan's prophetic pessimism most reveals itself.

Dylan's realism, while sharing the same idea of the tragic divergence between morality and politics, differs from the tradition of political realism, most fundamentally by not being shaped by a *spirit of mastery*—that is, a tendency to pitch political realism from the standpoint of powerful leaders, often with high expectations for how such leaders can manage a fallen world—prone to downplay rather than dwell upon the very animating idea that political regimes are irreducible to justice. Whereas the canonical expositors of political realism (Machiavelli, Hobbes in a certain sense, Clausewitz, Morgenthau, Schlesinger, and even Thucydides[41]) operate from a position that holds, seeks, or aims to

---

[41] Thucydides is admittedly a complex case. On the one hand, he unambiguously reflects the tradition of political realism's focus on political leadership. Thucydides was himself an Athenian general in the Peloponnesian War and the world his history discloses is one of power politics conducted by states and those who direct them. On the other hand, there are features of Thucydides's account of the war that make it less shaped by the spirit of mastery informing other canonical political realists. On the personal level, Thucydides was exiled from Athens at a relatively early moment in the war (424 BCE), making his reflections those of a kind of outsider. More deeply, in ways somewhat parallel to Dylan, Thucydides offers few prescriptions to leaders (providing instead a historical account of what happened as an unelaborated lesson in human nature), does not shy away from the tragic implications of his narrative (i.e., does not suggest a clear way out of the impasse arising from the conflict between politics and morality), and does not seem in any way to be at peace with the ways of the world even if he does not express psychological distress at them either. These qualities differentiate Thucydides from later leading exponents of political realism and perhaps can explain how Dylan's

advise the highest echelons of political power, Dylan, by contrast, approaches the fallen political world from the perspective of an ordinary (i.e., not specially empowered) person, does not anticipate the mastery of political problems, and remains troubled by the divergence between politics and morality in ethically consequential ways.

It is important to emphasize just how clearly and often Dylan presents himself as occupying a position of political ordinariness, with no special claim to statesmanship or power. Even when he does make reference to the traditional context of political realism—power politics of global dimension—he does so, warily, from the outside. Consider what Dylan writes of the political situation into which he was born in 1941:

> I was born in the spring of 1941. The Second World War was already raging in Europe, and America would soon be in it. The world was being blown apart and chaos was already driving its fist into the face of all new visitors. . . . Hitler, Churchill, Mussolini, Stalin, Roosevelt— towering figures that the world would never see the likes of again, men who relied on their own resolve, for better or worse, every one of them prepared to act alone, indifferent to approval—indifferent to wealth or love, all presiding over the destiny of mankind and reducing the world to rubble. Coming from a long line of Alexanders and Julius Caesars, Genghis Khans, Charlemagnes, and Napoleons, they carved up the world like a really dainty dinner. Whether they parted their hair in the middle or wore a Viking helmet, they would not be denied and were impossible to reckon with—rude barbarians stampeding across the earth and hammering out their own ideas of geography.[42]

Dylan is thus all too aware of the impact of leaders on the world stage who, acting without moral fastidiousness, have shaped political history. But for him this leadership is not the model to follow or something to praise. He operates from a different perspective and with a different ethical focus. Recalling prophets of old, Dylan positions himself outside of political power, as in these lines from "She's Your Lover Now":

> Ev'rybody that cares
> Is going up the castle stairs
> But I'm not up in the castle, honey

praise of Thucydides is consistent with his critique of "Kissinger" and the broader tradition indicted by that metonym.

[42] Dylan, *Chronicles*, 28–29.

Nowhere perhaps is this positionally more emphasized than in a brief vignette from "Stuck Inside of Mobile with the Memphis Blues Again":

> Now the senator came down here
> Showing ev'ryone his gun
> Handing out free tickets
> To the wedding of his son
> An' me, I nearly got busted
> An' wouldn't it be my luck
> To get caught without a ticket
> And be discovered beneath a truck
> Oh, Mama, can this really be the end
> To be stuck inside of Mobile
> With the Memphis blues again

The nature of the transgression the singer committed (but avoids getting busted for) is obscure. On one reading, the singer is beneath a truck, perhaps intoxicated, and were he to be discovered it would mean, in addition to any other violation, the informal infraction of not having a ticket—showing no interest in the politician's wedding. A different reading—more direct but also more perplexing—is that the singer almost got busted for not having a ticket to the wedding, even though the tickets were free and even though the singer was not at the wedding, but beneath a truck. The song is full of surreal imagery, so it is perhaps naïve to resolve its precise meaning, but if we read Dylan as the singer what comes across clearly is his dissociation of himself from political power. This dissociation is spatial (he is not at the politician's event), socio-logical (the senator has come "down here" where Dylan and others lacking political authority are), and ideological (Dylan indicts the violence and plutocracy of political power, symbolized by a gun-toting senator throwing a large public party for his son). At the same time, as much as this dissociation is self-chosen (as Dylan refuses a free ticket), it is also only very imperfectly achieved: Dylan remains threatened by the law and political power despite his efforts to avoid them. Yet the tale is ultimately one of genuine, if modest, success. The singer has managed to avoid getting busted and thereby operate in a space not entirely determined by the wielders of authority. That this space is cramped and darkened—carved out between the ground and the bottom of a truck—does not prevent it from housing for Dylan a partial independence from the machinations of power. Dylan thus positions himself on the margins of conventional politics, menaced by it, but just as importantly resisting the full reach of its force.

How does this altered positionality affect the meaning of Dylan's realer realism? Dylan reworks and critiques the tradition of political realism in four different ways. He challenges a conventional understanding of politics, one that is obsessively focused on leadership and power within a nation-state, in the name of an emergency model of politics based on alleviating suffering and counteracting the worst effects of oppression and injustice (section III.3). As a result, Dylan exposes and challenges the grandiosity that so often has been part of the realist tradition, upholding instead goals that are more modest but also more achievable by everyday people (section III.4). He likewise addresses the problem of futility, which is an important implication of the irreducibility of politics to morality, but one that has been studiously avoided by canonical political realists (section III.5). And he attends to one of the key features of political realism—its recurrent reflections on the paradox that evil can be used for good (as this, too, is part of the meaning of the irreducibility of politics to morality)—but does so from an alternate direction, addressing the ethical paradoxes afflicting more ordinary and widespread forms of political experience (section III.6). In my elaboration of each of these four dynamics, Dylan's critique of utopianism, progressivism, and other idealistic standpoints also becomes apparent. But it is in his divergences from the tradition of political realism that the ethical implications of his pessimism—the meaning of waking up and strengthening the things that remain—take their sharpest and most distinct form.

III.3. Emergency versus Conventional Politics

Dylan's insistence that "the struggle against oppression and injustice is always going to be there" is pessimistic and yet at the same time imbued with ethical purpose. The idea suggests both the impossibility of progress on the global level and yet the enduring moral relevance of certain forms of political action within such circumstances. The kind of politics it calls for can be described as *emergency politics*, directed at addressing crises rather than fixing the world. So conceived, emergency politics is necessarily local, modest, and largely free from the most familiar forms of political ideology. It is modeled more by the nurse or fireman than the soldier or statesman.

In principle there is nothing that would logically prevent political realists from recognizing emergency politics and making it their core concern. After all, the key idea informing political realism—the tragic divergence between politics and morality—would appear to explain why the world always will be mired in injustice, violent conflict, and other forms of suffering and why, therefore, there is a constant need for forms of emergency relief that, while not preventing new crises, nonetheless aim to alleviate suffering from the world's ongoing disasters.

But this manifestly has not been the case, as canonical realists routinely have failed to treat emergency politics with any kind of urgency or primacy. They have overlooked emergency politics because of their dogged interest in leadership and power, which leads them to take for granted a *conventional* understanding of politics centered on partisan rivalries within nation-states, diplomatic and military relations between them, the selection process of politicians and other high officials, and the conduct of those who hold office. Weber goes so far as to degrade emergency politics as a lower, merely "neighborly" kind of politics.[43] Even Niebuhr—who, more than other recent influential political realists, does sometimes raise the issue of humanitarian relief—does not do this as a principal focus because of his conventional assumptions about what politics ultimately and most truly is.

Political realists are hardly alone in subscribing to this conventional model of politics. Indeed, the assumption that the most genuine substance of politics consists of leadership and power is perhaps no less visible among those who deny the tragic divergence between morality and politics and, instead, posit social justice as a fully realizable goal. The lionization of electoral politics—the passionate support of partisan leaders as meriting our unambiguous support in an election, the celebration of certain statesman from political history in quasi-divine terms (as in the American cult surrounding the Founders), and the conception of voting for leaders as a profound moral duty—is a familiar progressive trope in contemporary politics. And so, too, is the acceptance of the nation-state as the key horizon of politics, since patriotism (which is presupposed in some form by virtually all political realists) is only slightly less common among more idealistic citizens.

Dylan does not deny the reality or potential significance of conventional politics, but he suggests that ordinary people are only vicariously related to much of what goes on within it and, more deeply, that their excessive attachment to it can undermine the awareness of and commitment to an emergency variant of politics in which they might after all directly, if modestly, assist.

For one thing, Dylan inveighs against the left-right continuum, so familiar within the conventional conceptualization of politics, claiming that it lacks reality and is hostile to a more genuine responsibility. Further, not only does he invite us to see leadership from the outside—observing morally transgressive leaders from a position of marginality—but, in doing so, also calls into question

[43] I take this degradation to be implied by Weber's differentiation between those who have a genuine vocation for political leadership and those who, unable to face the ethical challenges of this vocation, would do better to confine themselves to "neighborly contacts with other people." Max Weber, "Politics as a Vocation," *Vocation Lectures* (Indianapolis: Hackett, 2004), 93.

the centrality of leaders and the aura that so often surrounds them. Consider this line from "It's Alright, Ma (I'm Only Bleeding)":

> But even the President of the United States
> Sometimes must have to stand naked

And this, from "Is Your Love in Vain?":

> I have dined with kings, I've been offered wings
> And I've never been too impressed

And, finally, from "Subterranean Homesick Blues":

> Don't follow leaders
> Watch the parkin' meters

These are not just abstract thoughts but principles that Dylan has lived. His encounters with leading politicians reflect his refusal to celebrate or fawn. When invited by President Obama to perform at the White House in 2010, Dylan showed none of the usual fascination with political power, something that Obama himself, a longtime appreciator of Dylan and his music, recalled with admiration.[44] More generally, Dylan mocks and opposes the moralization of conventional partisan electoral politics, always alert to the irreducibility of even liberal-democratic politics to genuinely democratic norms. For Dylan, the conventional political space is debased: it is a poor approximation of democracy, it is caught up in plutocratic corruption, and, most problematically, it blinds us to a more direct and fundamental duty to help those in need. Consider in this regard an interview from 2009, in which Dylan commented, "Politics is entertainment.

---

[44] As Obama described the 2010 encounter: "Here's what I love about Dylan: He was exactly as you'd expect he would be. He wouldn't come to the rehearsal; usually, all these guys are practicing before the set in the evening. He didn't want to take a picture with me; usually all the talent is dying to take a picture with me and Michelle before the show, but he didn't show up to that. He came in and played 'The Times They Are A-Changin.' A beautiful rendition. . . . Finishes the song, steps off the stage—I'm sitting right in the front row—comes up, shakes my hand, sort of tips his head, gives me just a little grin, and then leaves. And that was it—then he left. That was our only interaction with him. And I thought: *That's how you want Bob Dylan, right? You don't want him to be all cheesin' and grinnin' with you. You want him to be a little skeptical about the whole enterprise.*" Jann S. Wenner, "Obama in Command: The Rolling Stone Interview," *Rolling Stone*, October 14, 2010 (emphasis added), https://www.rollingstone.com/politics/politics-news/obama-in-command-the-rolling-stone-interview-188620/. Dylan was later awarded the Presidential Medal of Freedom by Obama in 2012.

It's a sport. It's for the well groomed and well heeled. The impeccably dressed. Party animals. Politicians are interchangeable." When asked if he believed in the democratic process, Dylan replied, "Yeah, but what's that got to do with politics? Politics creates more problems than it solves. . . . The real power is in the hands of small groups of people and I don't think they have titles."[45] Rather than celebrate elections as the pinnacle of democracy, Dylan suggests that they are deeply flawed, that they only imperfectly legitimate the politicians who win them, and that they fail to withstand the substantial undemocratic influence exerted by special interests. As he told an audience in 1979, "Now I don't know who you're gonna vote for, but none of those people is gonna straighten out what's happening in the world today."[46]

Dylan's resistance to conventional electoral politics is perhaps most vividly reflected in the context of the 2008 election. Dylan was playing a show on election night and made remarks that, in retrospect, seem to have been intended to distance himself from the enthusiasm of many of his compatriots surrounding the election of Barack Obama. As the results came in, Dylan repeated his general pessimism toward the world but also concluded with a phrase that appeared to some, however, to be more hopeful: "[Bassist] Tony Garnier, wearin' the Obama button. . . . Tony likes to think it's a brand-new time right now. An age of light. Me, I was born in 1941—that's the year they bombed Pearl Harbor. Well, I been livin' in a world of darkness ever since. But it looks like things are gonna change now." When pressed in a 2012 interview in *Rolling Stone* to clarify what he had meant by his comment "it looks like things are gonna change now"—as this could be read to indicate support for Obama and the capacity of electoral politics to inaugurate fundamental political and social transformation—Dylan frustrated the interviewer by refusing to confirm that he had even voted and by refusing, as well, to imbue electoral politics with the deep significance with which it most commonly is treated:

ROLLING STONE: Did you hope or imagine that the election of President Obama would signal a shift, or that it was in fact a sea change?
DYLAN: I don't have any opinion on that. You have to change your heart if you want to change.
RS: Do you vote?
DYLAN: Uh . . .

---

[45] Interview with Bill Flanagan (March 2009), quoted in Jeff Taylor and Chad Israelson, *The Political World of Bob Dylan: Freedom and Justice, Power and Sin* (London: Palgrave Macmillan, 2015), 197–98, https://beatpatrol.wordpress.com/2009/04/07/bill-flanagan-interview-with-bob-dylan-part-2-2009/.

[46] Dylan, *Saved! The Gospel Speeches*, 12.

RS: Should we do that? Should we vote?

DYLAN: Yeah, why not vote? I respect the voting process. Everybody ought to have the right to vote. We live in a democracy. What do you want me to say? Voting is a good thing.

RS: I was curious if you vote.

DYLAN: [Smiling] Huh?

RS: What's your estimation of President Obama been when you've met him?

DYLAN: What do I think of him? I like him. But you're asking the wrong person. You know who you should be asking that to? You should be asking his wife what she thinks of him. She's the only one that matters. Look, I only met him a few times. I mean, what do you want me to say? He loves music. He's person-able. He dresses good. What the fuck do you want me to say?

RS: It was Election Night 2008. Onstage at the University of Minnesota, introducing your band's members, you indicated your bassist and said, "Tony Garnier, wearing the Obama button. Tony likes to think it's a brand-new time right now. An age of light. Me, I was born in 1941—that's the year they bombed Pearl Harbor. Well, I been living in a world of darkness ever since. But it looks like things are gonna change now."

DYLAN: I don't know what I said or didn't say. As far as Tony goes, yeah, maybe he was wearing an Obama button and maybe I said some stuff because right there in the moment it all made sense. Maybe I said things looked like they could change. And maybe they did change. I don't think I could have predicted how they would change, but whatever was said, it was said for people in that hall for that night. You know what I'm saying? It wasn't said to be played on a record forever. Or did I go down to the middle of town and give a speech?

RS: It was onstage.

DYLAN: It was on the streets?

RS: Stage. Stage.

DYLAN: OK. It was on the stage. I don't know what I could have meant by that. You say things sometimes, you don't know what the hell you mean. But you're sincere when you say it. I would hope that things have changed. That's all I can say, for whatever it is that I said. I'm not going to deny what I said, but I would have hoped that things would've changed. I certainly hope they have.

RS: I get the impression when we talk that you're reluctant to say much about the president or how he's been criticized.

DYLAN: Well, you know, I told you what I could.[47]

[47] Mikal Gilmore, "Bob Dylan Unleashed," *Rolling Stone*, September 27, 2012, https://www.rolli ngstone.com/music/music-news/bob-dylan-unleashed-189723/.

Dylan's doubts about the transformative possibilities of the 2008 election are reflected in the strange temporality of his hope, which is not for the future but the immediate past: "I would have hoped that things would have changed." In any case, Dylan's refusal to make conventional electoral politics the central political concern—his suggestion that there is always another kind of political reality being occluded by a false and excessive fixation on elections and the leaders they empower—is a recurrent feature of his commentary on politics. In declining to say whether he supported Obama or even voted at all, Dylan in 2012 was only repeating a more longstanding perspective. With regard to the seemingly momentous 2000 presidential election between George W. Bush and Al Gore, for example, Dylan refused to be taken in by the apparent magnitude of it, reporting of himself: "Did I follow the election? Yeah, I followed to see who would win. But in the larger scheme of things, the government is irrelevant. Everybody, everything can be bought and sold."[48] More generally, Dylan has insisted: "All these political and religious labels are irrelevant."[49] It is not surprising, then, that Dylan routinely has refused to endorse political candidates, taking pride in never having told his fans to vote a certain way.[50]

Of course this type of thinking, by itself, can only go so far. It seems wrong to say that the government is "irrelevant" and to deny wholesale the political, economic, and social significance, in numerous elections at least, of selecting one set of leaders over another. Even if we often exaggerate the impact of voting, it is hard to deny the pivotal meaning of certain elections and, more fundamentally, the essential difference between regimes that do and do not allow elections to occur. Dylan himself acknowledges, as discussed in Part I, that there are in fact worthy political causes that can be pursued through government—such as the civil rights movement—and that if he fails to commit himself dependably in these cases it is because of his personal preference not to sacrifice time and energy, not any presumption about the ineffectuality of elections and law-making.

For these reasons, I think it is a mistake to understand Dylan's skepticism toward conventional electoral politics ultimately as a statement about its irrelevance. His broader and far more persuasive critique is that conventional electoral politics can be *illusory* in numerous respects, most of all perhaps because it can distract from a more modest, but effective and honest, emergency form of politics. Dylan continually compares a debased conventional politics to a more positive, if limited, effort to directly help those suffering and in need. Consider,

[48] Robert Hilburn, "How Does It Feel? Don't Ask," *Los Angeles Times*, September 16, 2001, quoted in Taylor and Israelson, *Political World of Bob Dylan*, 196.

[49] Interview with Robert Hilburn, "Bob Dylan at 42: Rolling Down Highway 61 Again," *Los Angeles Times*, October 30, 1983, quoted in Taylor and Israelson, *Political World of Bob Dylan*, 137.

[50] See Dylan, *Saved! The Gospel Speeches*, 43, 65, 91, 92.

for example, a statement from 1983 in which he criticizes conventional politics precisely for failing to accomplish, in any kind of immediate or consistent way, the amelioration of humanitarian emergencies:

> I don't write political songs. Political songs are slogans. I don't even know the definition of politics. At one time it could have been a good thing, but right now it's all part of that so-called corruptible crown. Like you know, the law is a good thing until it's used against the innocent. Politics could be useful if it was used for good purposes. *For instance, like feeding the hungry and taking care of orphans.* But it's not. It's like the snake with the tail in its mouth. A merry-go-round of sin. All you hear about are US interests in Latin America. But what are those interests? You can't find out. Show me an honest politician and I'll show you a sanctified whore. You know that old story about the murderer who kills the judge and puts on his robe. But he's still a murderer.[51]

The "good purposes" to which Dylan refers are not idealistic and progressive be-cause they are about abating the direst effects of emergency, rather than achieving an unprecedented state of social justice.

Dylan, throughout his life, repeats this juxtaposition between conventional pol-itics and efforts that bypass them to directly help the destitute. It is reflected in his singing of the plight of orphans and widows and the hungry. It is reflected in the fact that the leaders he *does* celebrate—Jesus, Gandhi, and Martin Luther King—are not politicians but moral advocates transcending conventional political institutions and concerns. And, more concretely, it is reflected in Dylan's explanation of his decision to donate the royalties of his 2009 *Christmas in the Heart* album to three charities focusing on hunger: Feeding America, the United Nations World Food Programme, and Crisis, an organization in the United Kingdom dedicated to home-lessness. When asked why he picked these charities, Dylan answered, "Because they get food straight to the people. No military organization, no bureaucracy, no governments to deal with."[52] As he elaborates:

> It's a tragedy that more than 35 million people in this country alone—
> 12 million of those children—often go to bed hungry and wake up
> each morning unsure of where their next meal is coming from. I join

---

[51] Quoted in Taylor and Israelson, *Political World of Bob Dylan*, 195 (emphasis added).

[52] Interview with Bill Flanagan, *Street News Service*, November 23, 2009, quoted in Taylor and Israelson, *Political World of Bob Dylan*, 198.

the good people of Feeding America in the hope that our efforts can bring some food security to people in need during this holiday season.[53]

And:

That the problem of hunger is ultimately solvable means we must each do what we can to help feed those who are suffering and support efforts to find long-term solutions. I'm honored to partner with the World Food Programme and Crisis in their fight against hunger and homelessness.[54]

Dylan thus juxtaposes direct assistance to those who are vulnerable to conventional politics, which, at best, is only indirectly connected to the alleviation of misery. This focus on the emergencies that surround us—in regard to which we can always take some action, however small, if we wish—crystallizes a realism that is more real than canonical political realism in the sense of being applicable to so many more people. Because even ordinary people can help alleviate suffering, emergency alleviation is a realist politics suitable to the condition of everyday political life. The canonical tradition of political realism, by contrast, typically is pitched to a level of power possession out of most people's reach. Further, because emergency alleviation does not require the state—and in some ways is occluded by immoderate focus on elections and leadership selection—it is an example of how excessive attention to conventional politics centered on the state can promote a kind of irresponsible dreaming and a failure to attend to the suffering in our midst.[55]

Closely connected to Dylan's critique of electoral politics is his challenge to the idea of patriotism as an unambiguous good. While he has reflected pride in America from time to time—and while he continues to meditate on the meaning and transformations of American history and culture—his most considered and mature view would seem to be that patriotism is another form of being asleep. Dylan quotes Samuel Johnson's line about patriotism being "the last refuge of the scoundrel" in his 1983 song "Sweetheart Like You." In 1986, he differentiated

---

[53] Quoted in "Dylan to Release Christmas Album," *BBC News*, August 27, 2009, http://news.bbc.co.uk/2/hi/8223851.stm.

[54] "Bob Dylan Partners with International Charities to Help Feed Hundreds-of-Thousands During Holiday Season" (press release), September 24, 2009, https://www.bobdylan.com/news/bob-dylan-partners-international-charities-help-feed-hundreds-thousands-during-holiday-season/.

[55] To be sure, Dylan also sometimes criticizes state-centric policies for their own failure to provide aid. Consider what he sings in his 1979 "Slow Train," which seems to refer to the United States grain reserve program from the late 1970s: "People starving and thirsting, grain elevators are bursting / Oh, you know it costs more to store the food than it do to give it."

himself from other singers—Bruce Springsteen and John Cougar—who he felt were more concerned with America as an organizing idea of their messages:

> To me, an audience is an audience, no matter where they are. I'm not particularly into this *American* thing, this Bruce Springsteen–John Cougar–"American first" thing. I feel just as strongly about the American principles as those guys do, but I personally feel that what's important is more eternal things. This American pride thing, that don't mean nothing to me. I'm more locked into what's real forever.

Dylan adds:

> To me, America means the Indians. They were here and this is their country, and *all* the white men are just trespassing. We've devastated the natural resources of this country, for no particular reason except to make money and buy houses and send our lads to college and shit like that. To me, America is the Indians, period. I just don't go for nothing more. Unions, movies, Greta Garbo, Wall Street, Tin Pan Alley or Dodgers baseball games. . . . It don't mean shit. What we did to the Indians is disgraceful. I think America, to get right, has got to start there first.[56]

Dylan's challenge to patriotism is perhaps at its most strident during his gospel period. As he puts it in his "Ain't No Man Righteous, No Not One":

> You can't get to glory by the raising and the lowering of no flag
> Put your goodness next to God's and it comes out like a filthy rag
> In a city of darkness there's no need of the sun
> And there ain't no man righteous, no not one.

Even as Dylan continues to ponder the vagaries of the American tradition in such recent pieces as "Murder Most Foul," the angle of analysis is far more critical than celebratory.[57] And even apparently patriotic gestures seem to contain a suspicious underside, as in Dylan's 2014 Super Bowl commercial for Chrysler, in which his question—"Is there anything more American than America?"—at once appears to support American culture yet at the same time also hints at its

---

[56] Cott, "Interview with Mikal Gilmore, *Rolling Stone*, July 17, 1986," in *Essential Interviews*, 365. In this interview, the principles Dylan most supports are "Biblical principles."

[57] In "Murder Most Foul," which concerns the assassination of President Kennedy, there are such lines as "I said the soul of a nation been torn away / And it's beginning to go into a slow decay."

emptiness. As with Dylan's critique of electoral politics, his attitude toward patriotism is less a wholesale rejection than an accusation of unreality—of an illusoriness that blinds us to worthier and more tangible social goals.

Within the conventional conception, politics is most readily associated with the vicarious matter of whom to support (i.e., which leader or party), voting in elections is thus taken as the central political act and treated as the ethically most important civic obligation a citizen can perform, and the nation-state within which such processes go on is treated as the horizon of political life. Dylan challenges the centrality of this kind of politics as well as the assumptions and pieties on which it rests. For him, each component of this conventional view—partisanship, elections, leadership selection, patriotism—is undeserving of the excessive attention and celebration it receives, especially from ordinary citizens, who can only relate to conventional politics at a profound distance from power. Each element potentially distracts from a more direct and fundamental ethical duty to help those in need. Dylan does not reject outright the components of the conventional view of politics, but he refuses to treat them with the sanctity or primacy with which they are commonly approached. To focus on them too much is one way of being in a soporific dream state that prevents one from strengthening the things that remain.

III.4. Modesty versus Grandiosity

Dylan's realer realism—his appeal to the same underlying dynamic foundational to canonical political realists, the tragic divergence between morality and politics, but from an ordinary person's perspective rather than from a position of power—also leads him to depart from the grandiosity that so often has accompanied political philosophy in both its utopian and traditionally realist formulations. One of the key meanings of Dylan's pessimism regarding the world, his insistence that "nobody's gonna help out the world any,"[58] is that only modest political achievement is possible. This modesty means that oppression, injustice, and misery can be reduced in a local context but not an overarching global one; and it means that one can expect only the alleviation of the worst effects of oppression, injustice, and misery rather than a solution to the root causes of these pathologies. Dylan may be wrong in these ideas, but his reasoning—based on human history (which constantly has been mired in violence, war, and tyranny) and human nature (the ineradicable human temptation

---

[58] "Bob Dylan | Nat Hentoff *Playboy* Interview," posted by Route TV, video, 2:01:55, March 14, 2017, https://www.youtube.com/watch?v=4_WOtx9be0I, minute 20.

for unfair self-preferment and domination)—seems as plausible as the bases on which the much more familiar optimism about the world has been grounded. In any case, in Dylan's view, the world cannot be fixed, and failure to appreciate this can lead not only to illusion and mystification, but irresponsibility as well.

Political philosophy often has resisted the pretension to epistemological mastery (recognizing, instead, limits to what can be known), but rarely has it adopted a parallel hesitance with regard to political mastery, customarily treating its ideas as the blueprint by which the world might be managed and ordered, if not entirely saved. Dylan, by contrast, is more radically and uniformly opposed to mastery in all of its forms.[59] When he sings "Although the masters make the rules / For the wise men and the fools / I got nothing, Ma, to live up to" ("It's Alright, Ma"), he simultaneously recalls philosophy in its classical form (which, as Socrates develops it, stands against both foolish ignorance and the pretension of being wise) yet also departs from classical philosophy and numerous more recent variants in linking the critique of false wisdom to the critique of mastery itself. Dylan, then, not only speaks from a fount of charismatic authority largely lacking in political philosophy but also directs his prophetic intensity against the grandiose pretensions to mastery that so often have shaped political philosophy in its most familiar, canonical forms.

The prophetic edge of Dylan's attack on grandiosity is most readily visible vis-à-vis idealists, utopians, and progressives who imagine that the world can in fact be the site of human salvation. The sacralization of the political—not in any conventional theological sense, but in the sense of deploying religious cravings for perfection and the transcendence of hate and conflict onto the promise of a well-ordered political regime—is a deep and long-standing commitment in political culture. As many have observed, the most profound and ambitious aspiration of democracy—the idea of popular self-rule—is the aspiration for a popular sovereignty that might fully compensate for a world no longer unified around or convinced by conceptions of divine sovereignty.[60] Hobbes's idea of the state as a "mortal god" captures perfectly the overarching ambition of liberal (and later, democratic) political theory to make the world of politics a substitute for an otherwise unavailable divine perfection. Successive generations of thinkers within the liberal-democratic tradition of political thought—Locke, Rousseau, Rawls, Habermas—have upheld the possibility of a properly reformed political community that might achieve justice and thereby be a unique site for the achievement of human equality and freedom. Marx's critique of this tradition nonetheless

---

[59] Dylan indicts the pretension to mastery in such songs as "Masters of War" and "Slow Train" (with its castigation of "masters of the bluff and masters of the proposition").

[60] For but one example, see Joseph Schumpeter, *Capitalism, Socialism, and Democracy* (New York: Harper Perennial, 2008), 265.

repeats the same messianic aspiration of turning to a well-ordered society to realize secularized religious ambitions for perfect justice. The "withering away of
the state"—Engels's famous expression for Marx's elemental idea—is still a utopian vision of public life and one oriented around the underlying values of egal-
itarianism and freedom; it is not anti-political but an account of the perfection
of politics. The conception of the state as *not* inescapably a regime of hierarchy
and power, but potentially one of justice and harmony, is perhaps the most dominant ideology and ambition of political theory over the last five hundred years.
Recent innovations that extend or revise the hegemonic social-contractarian,
liberal-democratic project—whether theories of communitarianism, identity
recognition, global justice and considerations of a world state, socialism, or even
anarchism—all share the underlying structure of outlining a path to political salvation through privileged political reforms that, if followed, would at last allow
individuals to live happily, freely, equally, and fairly, without domination, corruption, or violent conflict. There are important exceptions, to be sure, but just
as the most familiar prophetic trope is to affirm the redemption of the world
and the ultimate reconciliation between God and humanity, so is the most familiar trope in political philosophy the articulation of a set of conditions under
which justice would obtain or, more modestly, the description of an unjust situation of oppression and how it might be overcome. Dylan does not see the eventual achievement of social justice as a credible expectation because, as has been
discussed, he expects too many of us to be mired in egotism, posits war and violence as permanent ways of the world, and understands politics as intrinsically
incapable of withstanding powerful elements of plutocratic corruption.

Yet, in keeping with Dylan's suggestion that "Marx" and "Kissinger" share
something in common that he rejects, it is important to realize that grandiosity
is not limited to idealistic, utopian, and progressive discourses within political
thought, but appears in a parallel way within the tradition of political realism
as well. The most influential realists, those who have done the most within political philosophy to explain the tragic separation of politics and morality, have
themselves routinely subscribed to goals that must be seen as excessively ambitious, because they either violate the underlying premises of realism itself (as
when, surprisingly, goals like universal peace come to be articulated by realists)
or reflect a pretension to mastery (the pretension to successfully manage an otherwise fallen political landscape) that sidesteps the tragic truth that injustice
and oppression are endemic to the world. Dylan, in linking Marx and Kissinger,
invites us to see the persistence of grandiosity even within the would-be sobriety
of realist thought.

With Machiavelli, for instance, beneath his larger point about the tragic divergence between morality and the ethics of political responsibility lie numerous
counterclaims that would seem to moderate this tragic teaching. *The Prince*,

which is rightly hailed as the most important expression of the irreducibility of politics to morality within the West, nonetheless concludes with an untragic encomium to the figure of a "redeemer prince," who, should he or she arise, would possess, as Alison McQueen aptly puts it, "not only God's favor but also unparalleled political power, buttressed by unconditional love and obedience."[61] In the words of Machiavelli: "I cannot express with what love he would be received in all those provinces that have suffered from these floods from outside; with what thirst for revenge, with what obstinate faith, with what piety, with what tears. What doors would be closed to him? What peoples would deny him obedience? What envy would oppose him? What Italian would deny him homage?"[62] The surprising idealism regarding Machiavelli's conceptualization of a prince who might somehow bring political harmony is paralleled by the equally surprising suggestion from Machiavelli that the achievement of such a redemptive figure is not a distant or unlikely wish, but something "not very difficult."[63] Machiavelli's idealism about a redemptive leader is paralleled by his contemplation in his *Discourses on Livy* of the situation in which a republic, under wise leadership, would be able to permanently last: "If a republic were so happy that it often had one who with his example might renew the laws, and not only restrain it from running to ruin but pull it back, it might be perpetual."[64] More generally, while Machiavelli posits the force of fortune as inescapably imposing itself on human affairs, he argues that it controls but half of the world, and he pitches his philosophy as what will enable intelligent, virtuosic leaders to wrestle with fortune effectively (though hardly perfectly). Thus, whether the goal is national unity for Italy, an everlasting republic, or the successful engagement with fortune, Machiavelli's realism is infused with a grandiose spirit of mastery that has the

---

[61] McQueen, *Political Realism in Apocalyptic Times*, 87; Niccolò Machiavelli, *The Prince*, trans. Harvey C. Mansfield (Chicago: University of Chicago Press, 1998), 105.

[62] Machiavelli, 105.

[63] Machiavelli, 103.

[64] Niccolò Machiavelli, *Discourses on Livy*, trans. Harvey C. Mansfield and Nathan Tarcov (Chicago: University of Chicago Press, 1996), 266 [III.22]. Even if Machiavelli wavers on this point—for example, five chapters earlier, he claims: "it follows that it is impossible to order a perpetual republic, because its ruin is caused through a thousand unexpected ways" (Machiavelli, 257, [III.17])—he still is led to consider the conditions that would lead to "the true political way of life and the true quiet of a city" (23 [I.6]). To be sure, even here Machiavelli suggests that such a goal is impossible, observing "since all things of men are in motion and cannot stay steady, they must either rise or fall" (23 [I.6]). The point, then, is not that Machiavelli's idealistic and utopian elements are primary (which of course they are not), but that they are undeniably present and that they seem to center on his expectations for redemptive leadership. I think McQueen is correct, then, in observing that Machiavelli's work is "haunted by the lingering vision of an everlasting republic." McQueen, *Political Realism in Apocalyptic Times*, 103.

result of making more modest and more achievable political goals (such as the reduction of injustice in Italy or the alleviation of pain and suffering stemming from political crises) appear inconsequential and unmanly.

Hobbes admittedly is not obviously a realist, especially with regard to domestic political affairs, as he upholds the possibility of a political community abiding by natural law, whose chief instruction is to overcome strife and violence and seek peace. Further, that Hobbes thinks that many elements of justice are rightly constructed by the state, and thus do not hold the state accountable from without, is another reason that the tragic conflict between morality and politics—the essential thought of political realism—is largely occluded within his philosophy on the domestic level. Thus, even if Hobbes evinces a pessimistic account of the human being, mired in ceaseless egoism and conflict so long as there is no state to create order, he is highly idealistic, if not utopian, about the capacity of a state to subdue and overcome what is fallen in the human being by creating a commonwealth that might generate peace, stability, and prosperity on a permanent basis.[65] Indeed, Hobbes presents himself as someone who has discovered the true principles of politics on the basis of which an everlasting republic and an everlasting peace might be secured.[66] And yet, in international relations, Hobbes typically has been treated—rightly, I think—as a father of contemporary political realism. Even if his conception of domestic politics does not lead him to insist upon the tragic division between morality and politics, his depiction of international politics would seem to be one in which this tragic

[65] Tuck is right to emphasize the strong utopian element in Hobbes, arguing that "*Leviathan* is as much of a utopian work as *The Social Contract*, and may indeed be the greatest piece of utopian writing to come out of the English Revolution." Richard Tuck, "The Utopianism of *Leviathan*," in *Leviathan after 350 Years*, ed. Tom Sorell and Luc Foisneau (Oxford: Oxford University Press, 2004), 125.

[66] On Hobbes's belief that he has discovered nothing less than a scientific solution to politics, consider what he writes in his 1640 Epistle Dedicatory to *The Elements of Law*, in which he describes the work as "the true and only foundation" of a "science" of "justice and policy," elaborating: "The conclusions thereof . . . are of such nature, as for want of them, government and peace have been nothing else, to this day, but mutual fear. And it would be an incomparable benefit to commonwealth, that every man held the opinions concerning law and policy, here delivered." Hobbes goes on to make clear in *The Elements* that he intends to devise principles that will enable an everlasting republic: "Forasmuch as we speak here of a body politic, instituted for the perpetual benefit and defence of them that make it; which therefore men desire should last for ever, I will omit to speak of those that be temporary, and consider those that be for ever." Thomas Hobbes, *The Elements of Law, Natural and Politic* (Scotts Valley, CA: CreateSpace, 2017 [1640]), 3, 66. Hobbes's focus on an everlasting commonwealth continues in *Leviathan*, in which he enunciates his hope that "there may Principles of Reason be found out, by industrious meditation, to make [a commonwealth's] constitution (excepting by external violence) everlasting. And such are those which I have in this discourse set forth." Hobbes, *Leviathan*, ed. Richard Tuck (Cambridge, UK: Cambridge University Press, 1996 [1651]), 232.

circumstance is bound to persist, since in Hobbes's account there are no external political powers (such as a world state) that might quell ever-present interstate conflict and thereby achieve peace and also no universal moral standards that might effectively limit states as they face each other in their foreign policies. That is to say, there would appear to be no escape, in his account, from conflict-ridden anarchy in international relations. Yet, as much as the international realm might seem to be a place where Hobbes's pessimism about the human being is repeated in a pessimism about the political world (i.e., an expectation of persistent violent struggle), in fact this is not the case. Hobbes uncritically and grandiosely suggests that his solution for domestic politics might be a solution for international conflict too. That is, his pretension that he has discovered the principles by which a domestic state might live perpetually and in peace extends, unjustifiably, to a pretension that international conflict might be largely foreclosed as well. Believing that the problems of politics might be solved in the same manner as geometry, Hobbes puts forward the claim that something resembling world peace might be achieved if only states' domestic politics could be ordered according to his philosophical principles:

> If the moral Philosophers had done their job with equal success, I do not know what greater contribution human industry could have made to human happiness. For if the patterns of human action were known with the same certainty as the relations of magnitude in figures, ambition and greed, whose power rests on the false opinions of the common people about right and wrong [*jus et iniuria*], would be disarmed, and the human race would enjoy such secure peace that (apart from conflicts over space as the population grew) it seems unlikely that it would ever have to fight again.[67]

As Richard Tuck points out, the one kind of violent conflict Hobbes anticipates— conflict over space—is something that he "in all his works . . . treated as a rather remote possibility."[68] Thus, even if Hobbes's philosophy of international politics is most commonly taken as a prediction of anarchic, conflict-ridden relations between states, the above passage indicates a different mood and hope: that proper political organization within the domestic sphere might transform, if not human nature itself, then at least the social and political consequences stemming from it. Hobbes's deification of the state and his parallel confidence about political

---

[67] Thomas Hobbes, *De Cive*, ed. Richard Tuck and Michael Silverthorne (Cambridge, UK: Cambridge University Press, 1997 [1642]), 5.

[68] Tuck, "The Utopianism of *Leviathan*," 126. For an instance in which Hobbes downplays the likelihood of territorial conflict, see *Leviathan*, chapter 30.

philosophy's ability to solve the problems of politics thus cancel his otherwise highly pessimistic depiction of individuals and the international scene. Yet, rather than see his thinking here as a violation of his realism about international relations, in fact it is illustrative of a broader trend whereby canonical realists routinely shrink from the consequences of their realism and articulate impossibly grandiose ends out of keeping with their own premises.

More recent political realists also reflect this tendency of remaining inconsistently committed to their tragic vision, allowing the resurfacing of an otherwise rejected idealism, and thereby imbuing their thought with an excessively ambitious, illusory quality. Weber, it is true, usually is quite clear about the tragic conflict between politics and morality. He insists on the "satanic" aspect of politics, insofar as political leaders necessarily transact in violence (which is always ethically ambiguous according to Weber), sometimes sacrifice truth and transparency for the public good, maintain a political machine in a manner that is not always fair to opposing parties, operate within a world of ceaseless political and ethical conflict, and thus accept the inescapable divergence in politics between means and ends. But even Weber, in the conclusion of his most famous and influential statement of this tragic realism, is led to backtrack. Having asserted that one cannot be both purely moral and politically efficacious—that "all . . . action can be guided by either of two *fundamentally different, irredeemably incompatible* maxims . . . an 'ethics of conviction' or an 'ethics of responsibility' "—he concludes his "Politics as a Vocation" address with the invocation of Martin Luther as a model of authentic political leadership who, in pronouncing "Here I stand, I can do no other" and committing himself to a genuine cause, demonstrates that "an ethics of conviction and an ethics of responsibility are *not absolute antitheses but are mutually complementary,* and only when taken together do they constitute the authentic human being who is capable of having a 'vocation for politics.'"[69] We can read this as an innocent mistake or oversight, but the tendency within realist thought to give voice to a resurgent idealism—and, with it, a grandiosity of purposes—is too common for one not to suspect that Weber here is actually reflective of a systematic lack of systematicity within canonical realist thought.

Hans Morgenthau, another so-called father of contemporary political realism, does something similarly inconsistent. His most familiar doctrine is to insist upon, like Weber, the permanence of political conflict and the irreducibility of politics to morality as basic postulates of mature political thinking. Morgenthau appeals, in tragic terms, to "the awareness of unresolvable discord, contradictions, and conflicts which are inherent in the nature of things and which

[69] Weber, "Politics as a Vocation," 83 (emphasis altered), 92.

human reason is powerless to solve."[70] This tragic circumstance inheres in what Morgenthau takes to be three main features of human beings: we are caught between higher and lower drives, with the lower likely to dominate; we cannot control the worldly manifestation of our deeds; and sometimes, if not often, we are forced to choose between equally legitimate conflicting ends.[71] As a result, Morgenthau concludes: "There is no progress toward the good, noticeable from year to year, but undecided conflict which sees today good, tomorrow evil, prevail; and only at the end of time, immeasurably removed from the here and now of our earthly life, the ultimate triumph of the forces of goodness and light will be assured."[72] But in his later work, in the 1960s, Morgenthau diverges from a consistently tragic outlook and finds, in the very context of the new nuclear age, a reason to be hopeful about the possibilities for world government and something approximating world peace. Treating the threat of nuclear apocalypse not only as an existential danger but as a new opportunity for transformations that could enable a world community and give shape to a previously formless "awareness of the unity of mankind," Morgenthau looks forward to the construction of unprecedented global institutions underwritten "by the desire, innate in all men, for self-preservation."[73] He posits that the collective interest in avoiding nuclear annihilation makes it credible to contemplate the elimination of "international relations itself through the merger of all national sovereignties into one world state which would have a monopoly of the most destructive instruments of violence."[74] Thus, much like Hobbes, Morgenthau—late in his life, at least—contemplates the possibility of channeling an allegedly universal human will for self-preservation into institutions that would produce the unity of humanity. Some have seen Morgenthau's transformation as evidence that he is a "fallen realist," but, given the history of canonical political realism, it is better described as emblematic of an inconsistency that percolates throughout realist thought.[75]

---

[70] Hans Morgenthau, *Scientific Man vs. Power Politics* (Chicago: University of Chicago Press, 1967), 206.

[71] Morgenthau, 189, 190, 221–22. In summarizing Morgenthau's views in this regard, I follow McQueen, *Political Realism in Apocalyptic Times*, 176–77.

[72] Morgenthau, *Scientific Man vs. Power Politics*, 205–6.

[73] Hans Morgenthau, "International Relations," in *The Restoration of American Politics* (Chicago: University of Chicago Press, 1962), 174–75. Also see McQueen, *Political Realism in Apocalyptic Times*, 188.

[74] Morgenthau, 174.

[75] For Morgenthau as a fallen realist, see N. A. J. Taylor, "On the Possibility of an Arendtian Nuclear Theory," *Amor Mundi*, January 31, 2016, https://hac.bard.edu/amor-mundi/on-the-poss ibility-of-an-arendtian-nuclear-theory-2016-01-31. Even if Morgenthau understood himself to be reacting to the specific historical situation of the rise of nuclear weapons—"[i]t is obvious that the nuclear age has radically changed man's relation to nature and to his fellow men" (Morgenthau, "Death in the Nuclear Age," *Commentary* 32, no. 3 (1961): 321)—this is how canonical realists

Even Niebuhr, who more than other realists indicts false pretensions of mastery, still centers his analysis on a grandiose conception of statesmanship, according to which the key objective for liberal-democratic leaders is to achieve a balance of powers (a modus vivendi rather than genuine justice on the global level) with non-liberal-democratic states and also to defend the world from the worst forms of evil (Nazism, Stalinism, etc.). Such ideas have been paramount in the work of more recent realists influenced by Niebuhr, like George Kenan, Arthur Schlesinger, and Kissinger, among many others who have followed in their wake. Besides the problem that any invocation of the statesman as the intended audience of political realism either overlooks ordinary citizens or invites them to vicariously identify with a decision-making authority that they lack, the illusory element of this way of thinking also inheres in the fact that what is intended as a modest and realizable aim—the pursuit of a mere modus vivendi over and against international agreement about principles of justice—is itself utopian in its belief that a proper balance of powers might achieve "equilibrium" and avoid war and violent conflict. Given the central role the commitment to a modus vivendi plays within contemporary political realist thought, this is no small issue.[76] And there is at least the potential for a parallel kind of illusoriness when statesmen remain undisturbed by their nations' moral transgressions because they see these as justified in order to defend the world against a so-called worse evil. Dylan's critique of anti-communism operates in this context, with Dylan diagnosing and rejecting the American pretension of having God on its side and mocking, as well, the excesses of anti-communism within American domestic politics and culture.[77] To be sure, there may indeed be a place for the kind of statesmanship Niebuhr extols, but a subtle grandiosity persists within his theory of politics and, with it, a resistance to an open-eyed assessment of political reality. At the very least, when the figure of the statesman monopolizes the meaning of political realism, other political realities are obscured.

Political realism thus has tended to be associated with the articulation of ambitious "dreams"—a redeemer prince (Machiavelli), world peace (Hobbes, Morgenthau), the unification of an ethics of responsibility and an ethics of conviction (Weber), a modus vivendi and the defeat of a worse evil (Niebuhr and

---

typically have operated, pointing to some specific external circumstance (e.g., the possibility of a reunited Italy, the discovery of true philosophical principles) that might enable the transcendence of mere conflict, injustice, oppression and thus cultivate a spirit of mastery that successfully navigates and, to a meaningful extent, cancels the tragic aspects of the world.

[76] See John Horton, "Realism, Liberal Moralism, and a Political Theory of Modus Vivendi," *European Journal of Political Theory* 9, no. 4 (2010): 431–48.

[77] See, for example, Dylan's songs "With God on Our Side"; "Talkin' World War III Blues"; and "Talkin' John Birch Paranoid Blues."

his followers)—that not only violate some of the animating premises of realism but also lead to an overlooking of the goal of strengthening what remains, especially as this goal might be considered by an ordinary person with no special power. There is a latent utopianism in realism that looks past what is small-scale and much more obviously and directly achievable. Dylan alerts us to this dynamic when he suggests that the political realism represented by Kissinger is another form of being asleep.

III.5. Edgy Resignation: Futility and Fatalism Revisited

Closely related to the grandiosity of canonical political realism is another dynamic. One might expect that the tradition of political realism—with its recognition of the irreducibility of politics to morality—would contain within it a powerful meditation on the problem of *futility* (i.e., the ineffectiveness of many forms of action, above all action that would remake the world according to norms of justice) and thus be infused with an element of *fatalism* (the belief that certain bad events in the future cannot be avoided). But, in fact, a sense of futility and fatalism has been completely absent from canonical realist thought. The most typical criticism realists level against what they take to be excessive moral ambition in politics is not that such ambition is inconsequential but that it is dangerous. As Kissinger puts it, "The most fundamental problem of politics ... is not the control of wickedness but the limitation of righteousness," a view that presupposes just how impactful, if misguided, excessive moralization can be.[78] The chief conclusion canonical realists have drawn from the irreducibility of politics to morality is not the limits of what politics can achieve but the autonomy of politics vis-à-vis morality and other domains of human activity. It is not surprising that canonical realists would have little to say about futility or fatalism, since the context guiding their reflections—the situation of leading statesmen in possession of great power—hardly lends itself to such meditations. Political rulers have a much wider sphere of action compared to ordinary people and, in any case, are in no position to throw up their hands but must exert whatever impact their action allows. Accordingly, the most influential purveyors of realist thought, who have assumed this perspective of power within their philosophies, have found no use for any contemplation of human impotence in the face of the ineliminable tragic dimension to politics. Machiavelli, for instance, even as he

---

[78] Henry Kissinger, *A World Restored: Metternich, Castlereagh and the Problems of Peace, 1812–1822* (Boston: Houghton Mifflin, 1957), 206.

posits that fortune controls half of all that occurs, not only makes it his purpose to demonstrate how princely virtù might effectively wrestle with fortune but rejects the attitude of resignation and insists, as a matter of ethical and political duty, on the need to find hope in the capacities for human action. Machiavelli writes that people should "never give up for, since they do not know [fortune's] end and it proceeds by oblique and unknown ways, they have always to hope and, since they hope, not to give up in whatever fortune and in whatever travail they may find themselves."[79] Weber, too, argues that it is essential for political actors to look past the inevitable disappointments of the world, calling on political leaders to be nothing less than "heroes" who seek the impossible so that they might achieve the possible, and insisting that even those who are not leaders "must arm themselves with that staunchness of heart that refuses to be daunted by the collapse of all their hopes, for otherwise they will not even be capable of achieving what is possible today."[80]

In this regard, therefore, canonical political realism is not very different from idealistic, utopian, and progressive accounts of politics, according to which faith in a better future is underwritten either by history (the premise that the present is morally superior to the past), metaphysics (the alleged truth that the universe is on the side of justice), or considerations of practical necessity (the view that the maintenance of our moral motivation requires a belief in the moral progress of humanity). As much as they might object to such explanations, the thing being explained—the rejection of any attitude of resignation toward a fallen world—is something canonical political realists are hardly less prepared to endorse.

The question is whether this feature of realist thought renders it less real, at least as a framework for ordinary individuals who do not possess great power, who do not directly make policies, who do not in any way lead. Among such individuals—who constitute the vast majority of humanity—who has not contemplated the futility of action? Who has not at times concluded, given that the world always has been mired in injustice, violence, war, oppression, and suffering, that there are profound limits to what can be accomplished? Who has not despaired of their ability to change whatever problems lie before them? Who has not looked at the disasters threatening the world in the twenty-first century— whether environmental, financial, nuclear, or biologic—and questioned the capacity of humanity to survive, let alone thrive, in the future? The sources of optimism—the progressive view of history and the moral disposition of the cosmos—are too speculative to permanently foreclose such doubts. At the same time, anyone who breaks from the regnant optimism and publicly proclaims a

---

[79] Machiavelli, *Discourses on Livy*, 199 [II.29].
[80] Weber, "Politics as a Vocation," 93.

sense of futility and fatalism is likely to be met with a variety of ready-made rhetorical devices by which such resignation is immediately castigated—above all
the notion that, true or not, we have no choice but to believe in the future because the alternative, resignation, is a dead end.

Dylan is different, as another distinguishing feature of his pessimism is his
willingness to countenance futility and fatalism, if not as wholesale condemnation of human action as such, at least as a limit to what can be expected and
accomplished in numerous significant domains of political and social life.
Consider the anecdote about Dylan related by Joan Baez: "I asked him what
made us different, and he said it was simple, that I thought I could change things,
and he knew that no one could."[81] This is a bleak depiction of the human situation but one that cannot simply be dismissed as dishonest or necessarily untrue, nor as limited to Dylan's gospel period (even if it does receive especially
sharp articulation during this time). If the biblical idiom by which it has been
expressed has waxed and waned, Dylan's underlying sense of futility and fatalism
has persisted. In a 2020 *New York Times* interview in which he commented on
the global coronavirus pandemic and the political uprising following the killing
of George Floyd, he was asked if he considered the pandemic in biblical terms.
Dylan demurred but nonetheless observed:

> I think it's a forerunner of something else to come. It's an invasion for
> sure, and it's widespread, but biblical? You mean like some kind of
> warning sign for people to repent of their wrongdoings? That would
> imply that the world is in line for some sort of divine punishment.
> Extreme arrogance can have some disastrous penalties. Maybe we
> are on the eve of destruction. There are numerous ways you can think
> about this virus. I think you just have to let it run its course.

Yet, if Dylan questions the relevance of the Bible, he is clear in this interview
in confessing his sense of impending disaster: "I think about the death of the
human race. The long strange trip of the naked ape."[82]

In his futility and fatalism Dylan knows himself to be expressing thoughts
that are widely shared, even if there is little outlet for them in contemporary culture. One of his earliest songs, "Train A-Travelin'" from 1962, contains the lines:

> I'm a-wonderin' if the leaders of the nations understand
> This murder-minded world that they're leavin' in my hands

---

[81] Joan Baez, *And a Voice to Sing With: A Memoir* (New York: Summit, 1987), 95.

[82] Douglas Brinkley, "Bob Dylan Has a Lot on His Mind," *New York Times*, June 12, 2020, https://
www.nytimes.com/2020/06/12/arts/music/bob-dylan-rough-and-rowdy-ways.html.

Have you ever laid awake at night and wondered 'bout the same?
Then you've heard my voice a-singin' and you know my name

Beyond this issue of honest expression of suppressed, almost illicit thoughts, Dylan's pessimistic meditation on futility and fatalism has a more direct, and directly prophetic, function. Dylan exposes the limitations of any simplistic invocation of the practical necessity of hope. It is not just that the appeal to practical necessity bypasses the question of truth—whether the ways of the world in fact are capable of being reformed by human hands—but that castigating the impracticality of resignation forgets that resignation need not be a mere throwing up of one's hands. Resignation is also, at least potentially, a standpoint that can crystallize one's ethical purposes. Dylan realizes this ethical potential latent within resignation. For him, the insistence on futility and fatalism is never just giving up, but a mindset connected to the exposure of illusion and dishonesty and, with it, the clarification—rather than abandonment—of ethical direction. As Dylan puts it, drawing on Henry Miller, his mission has involved trying "to inoculate the world with disillusionment."[83]

Dylan's recurring insistence on the ineffectiveness of various forms of action is continually linked to overcoming deception and, with it, a misguided sense of responsibility. For instance, his insistence on the futility of global justice, peace, and progress as political goals does not equate to a despair of all human action, but rather highlights the value of more modest and achievable ends such as emergency politics. Consider, in this regard, Dylan's reply in a 1966 interview to the question "Do you think it's pointless to dedicate yourself to the cause of peace and racial equality?":

Not pointless to dedicate yourself to peace and racial equality, but rather it's pointless to dedicate yourself to the *cause*: that's *really* pointless. That's very unknowing. To say "cause of peace" is just like saying "hunk of butter." I mean, how can you listen to anybody who wants you to believe he's dedicated to the hunk and not to the butter? People who

---

[83] Cott, "Interview with Ron Rosenbaum, *Playboy*, March 1978," in *Essential Interviews*, 238. The precise quote from Miller that Dylan has in mind is: "A man writes to throw off the poison which he has accumulated because of his false way of life. He is trying to recapture his innocence, yet all he succeeds in doing (by writing) is to inoculate the world with a virus of his disillusionment." Henry Miller, *Sexus* (New York: Grove Press, 1965 [1949]), 24. A similar idea is expressed by W. H. Auden: "The primary function of poetry, as of all the arts, is to make us more aware of ourselves and the world around us. I do not know if such increased awareness makes us more moral or more efficient. I hope not. I think it makes us more human, and I am quite certain it makes us more difficult to deceive." Auden, *Prose and Travel Books in Prose and Verse, 1926–1938* (Princeton, NJ: Princeton University Press, 1996), 470.

can't conceive of how others hurt, they're trying to change the world. They're all afraid to admit that they don't really know each other. They'll all probably be here long after we've gone, and we'll give birth to new ones. But they themselves—I don't think *they'll* give birth to *anything*.[84]

The precise thinking here is difficult to penetrate, but Dylan seems to be making a distinction between seeking peace and racial equality in some direct, unmediated, local fashion (of which he approves) and seeking them self-consciously as a more generalized cause (of which he is deeply critical because, so conceived, they are too abstract or ambitious to become credible objects of political activity).

But it is not just illusory ends that Dylan thinks are futile. His meditation on futility also leads him to raise the possibility that certain means, even for worthy and achievable ends, are not effective. He challenges the celebration of social action as such and the assumption that any well-intentioned action, however slight, is politically meaningful. While not denying the human capacity to effectively intervene in specific contexts, to alleviate emergencies and thereby help particular poor and downtrodden people, Dylan is suspicious about the generalized elevation of social action as intrinsically and categorically beneficial. As discussed, he sometimes reflects on his own impotence to take meaningful action within certain contexts. And he also takes issue with the excessive self-confidence of other activists. Dylan's relationship to protests against the Vietnam War is one example. His refusal to participate in those protests, or even identify as being against the war, dismayed anti-war contemporaries, who had assumed that they could rely on his support given his outspoken opposition to militarism in earlier works like "With God on Our Side" and "Masters of War." While there is little to suggest that Dylan actually supported the war in Vietnam, what his impatience with aspects of the anti-war movement does reveal is his awareness that not all acts of protest are equally worthy and that, specifically, some would-be advocates of the anti-war movement were compromised by elements of artificiality, virtue signaling, and thus detachment from the actual matter at hand. Some of Dylan's *anti-anti-war* comments suggest this critical perspective: "Burning draft cards isn't going to end any war. It's not even going to save any lives. If someone can feel more honest with himself by burning his draft card, then that's great; but if he's just going to feel more important because he does it, then that's a drag."[85] In a similar vein, Dylan frustrated the questions of self-described anti-war musicians John Cohen and Happy Traum, who sought to clarify his position on Vietnam. To their central and repeated question of

[84] Cott, "Interview with Nat Hentoff, *Playboy*, March 1966," in *Essential Interviews*, 112.
[85] Cott, 112.

whether he was "for or against the war" or could be friends with someone supportive of the war, Dylan challenged the underlying construct of being "for or against the war," claiming: "That really doesn't exist."[86] I take Dylan to mean that there are situations in which being for or against war—that is, being committed to peace—has little reality or significance beyond the self-complementary self-identification of the speaker and that he has no interest in voicing perspectives so disconnected from more consequential worldly action.

Another example of Dylan's refusal to treat all action as automatically effective and important is his surprising hesitance about affiliating himself with "Negroes' rights" in the mid-1960s, not because he was against the civil rights movement but because he was uncomfortable about falsely affiliating himself with a cause that was not fully his own and that perhaps he did not fully understand: "It's not that I'm pessimistic about Negroes' rights, but the word Negro sounds foolish coming from my mouth."[87]

Dylan's provocations in this regard are distinct, even as they resemble to some degree interventions occasionally made within recent social theory. Dylan's calling into question the fetishization of social action recalls, for example, Theodor Adorno, who, in his own essay "Resignation," identifies and calls into question "the distrust of whoever distrusts praxis." Adorno diagnoses and *rejects* the widespread view that "the person who at this hour doubts the possibility of radical change in society and who therefore neither participates in spectacular, violent actions nor recommends them has resigned." Labeling the unjustified, hyperbolic celebration of social action "actionism," Adorno criticizes it for leading to illusory rather than real events, for being concerned with its own publicity and self-promotion, and for substituting satisfaction with itself over and against the concern with using action as an instrument of change. Most of all, actionism is denigrated by Adorno for being blind to what he takes to be a crucial pessimistic truth: "At this time no higher form of society is concretely visible: for that reason whatever acts as though it were in easy reach has something regressive about it."[88] Adorno is no idle case, as the suspicion that a good deal of so-called social action is futile because it has more to do with the self-aggrandizement of the actors than the causes they serve is a known problem on the Left. Tom Wolfe critiqued "radical chic" in 1970.[89] Murray Bookchin, in the

---

[86] Jeff Burger, ed., "Conversations with Bob Dylan" (interview by John Cohen and Happy Traum, *Sing Out!*, October/November 1968), in *Dylan on Dylan: Interviews and Encounters* (Chicago: Chicago Review Press, 2018), 185.

[87] Quoted in David Hajdu, *Positively 4th Street: The Lives and Times of Joan Baez, Bob Dylan, Mimi Baez Fariña, and Richard Fariña* (New York: Farrar, Straus and Giroux, 2001), 201.

[88] Theodor Adorno, "Resignation," in *Critical Models: Interventions and Catchwords* (New York: Columbia University Press, 2005), 289, 290, 292, passim.

[89] Tom Wolfe, "Radical Chic: That Party at Lenny's," *New York*, June 8, 1970, 27–56.

mid-1990s, did something similar with his disparagement of mere "lifestyle an-archism" masquerading as a more genuine "social anarchism."[90] And the idea of virtue signaling, coined in 2015, perhaps even more succinctly conceptualizes the problem.[91] Yet, despite Dylan's proximity to these standpoints, his perspec-tive is distinct. It is not just that his reputation as the poetic voice of the civil rights movement makes his critique of indiscriminate social action all the more potent and striking. Most importantly, if critics of false or ineffective action very often have aligned themselves with an alternate, more genuine form of action—as in Bookchin's support of "social anarchism" over "lifestyle anarchism" or Adorno's affirmation, within his very critique of actionism, of the thinking pro-cess itself as "a form of praxis" and as "actually the force of resistance"[92]—Dylan provides a starker and more forceful meditation on futility and fatalism as such.

To be sure, in a world where action in itself is celebrated—where people can credibly describe themselves as "activists"—these considerations can seem unsettling, if not irresponsible. But unless one is prepared to treat all action as equally important, there ought to be a constructive role for challenges, like those of Dylan, to force those who would take action to consider what it is they are ac-tually accomplishing, the degree to which their activism fulfills personal rather than public needs, and how much their fastidiousness about action stems from a refusal to acknowledge even the possibility that some problems are in fact un-solvable. Dylan does not, of course, reject all social action—and, as discussed in Part I, he acknowledges that his lack of political engagement often stems from simple self-preference, not the unworthiness of the cause in question—but he nonetheless insists on the need to discriminate between productive and ineffec-tual forms of advocacy.

However, perhaps the greatest manifestation of Dylan's edgy resignation—his meditation on futility and fatalism that clarifies and redirects, rather than abandons, ethical purpose—can be seen not in his discrimination among means and ends in light of their feasibility, but in his use of resignation to challenge power. Belief in excessive hopes and aspirations is rarely a neutral or trivial affair, but frequently connected to adherence to authorities professing to fulfill such promises. By contrast, resignation contests power when it overpromises and, in overpromising, exerts control and demands obedience. A sense of futility and fatalism, Dylan suggests, can inoculate ordinary people against the machinations of the powerful insofar as they employ false optimism to manipulate or exploit

[90] Murray Bookchin, *Social Anarchism or Lifestyle Anarchism: An Unbridgeable Chasm* (Chico, CA: AK Press, 1995).

[91] See James Bartholomew, "Easy Virtue," *The Spectator*, April 2015.

[92] Adorno, "Resignation," 293.

the public.[93] The germ of the idea is well expressed in Dylan's critique of the advertising industry in "It's Alright, Ma":

> Advertising signs they con
> You into thinking you're the one
> That can do what's never been done
> That can win what's never been won
> Meantime life outside goes on
> All around you

Dylan does not spell out just what false promises are being rejected here, but the underlying point is that pessimistic recognition of the impossibility of certain objectives can be concomitant with liberation from externally driven attempts at influence and control and a parallel awakening to less grand and exultant, but more real, possibilities.

It is not just the advertising industry, however, that promises the impossible. The state, too, can deceive in this fashion.[94] Indeed, the best example of Dylan's edgy resignation exposing and contesting the deceit of the powerful is his approach toward nuclear weapons. In a sense, nuclear weapons are the perfect embodiment of Dylan's pessimism about the world: they threaten the annihilation of humanity by human means (thus pointing to human fallenness), their emergence in the twentieth century problematizes any simplistic account of historical progress, and the secret and intensely hierarchical elements of their management underline the persistence of undemocratic and non-consensual forms of authority, thereby reinforcing in the ordinary person a sense of being profoundly alienated from power.

Dylan departs from both idealistic and realist discourses in political thought when he makes his principal concern not the regulation of nuclear weapons (how they might be strategically deployed or, instead, abolished), but a resignation toward the possibility of nuclear detonation and, with it, the internal

---

[93] This idea is close to the perspective of Lauren Berlant, *Cruel Optimism* (Durham, NC: Duke University Press, 2011).

[94] Consider, in this context, these lines from Dylan's "Masters of War":

> Like Judas of old
> You lie and deceive
> A world war can be won
> You want me to believe
> But I see through your eyes
> And I see through your brain
> Like I see through the water
> That runs down my drain

regulation of the fear such a threat generates. Dylan's sense of futility regarding public policy (his sense of being unable to withstand or prevent nuclear war) is accompanied by his almost opposite insistence that public policy makers not be able to monopolize his and other private individuals' sense of what is to be feared or how to operate in the face of fear.

Consider "Let Me Die in My Footsteps," recorded in 1962, in which Dylan confronts both the fallout shelter movement of the early 1960s and the nuclear age more generally. The resignation of the song could not be clearer. It is a meditation on how the singer would like to die—above ground, outside of a fallout shelter, not obsessively focused on his own protection—rather than a call for political responses that would reduce the nuclear threat itself (whether through successful military strategy, diplomacy, or disarmament):

> I will not go down under the ground
> 'Cause somebody tells me that death's comin' 'round
> An' I will not carry myself down to die
> When I go to my grave my head will be high
> Let me die in my footsteps
> Before I go down under the ground

That this resignation is outside of the usual focus of progressive, aspirational political movements is straightforward. Dylan's central message is his resolution to be buried only once—namely, upon his death and not also prior in the form of cowering in a fallout shelter. To be sure, Dylan imagines the peace he would inaugurate if he had political power, but this part of the song is explicitly hypothetical:

> If I had rubies and riches and crowns
> I'd buy the whole world and change things around
> I'd throw all the guns and the tanks in the sea
> For they are mistakes of a past history
> Let me die in my footsteps
> Before I go down under the ground

Such musings are manifestly *not* the matter at hand: the experience of an existential threat from nuclear weapons.

With idealistic pacifism acknowledged but also marginalized, we are left with two things: the actual threat of nuclear annihilation and the fear that this threat is causing. For Dylan, these two components of the nuclear age are interrelated yet not at all the same. From his earliest memories, he experienced both the threat of nuclear war and a fear of it that was never reducible to the threat itself. As he reflected on his childhood in the 1940s and '50s: "Our reality was fear. Any moment this black cloud would explode where everybody would be dead. They would show you at school how to dive for cover under your desk. We grew up with all of that so it created a sense of paranoia that was . . . probably unforeseen."[95] The paranoia is not an extraneous detail for Dylan but part of the phenomenon of the nuclear age itself. In *Chronicles*, he recounts how kids in his hometown of Hibbing, Minnesota, were told that Russians could parachute over the town at any moment. And he describes his childhood experience of being forced to contemplate and impossibly prepare for nuclear war: "Living under a cloud of fear like this robs a child of his spirit. It's one thing to be afraid when someone's holding a shotgun on you, but it's another thing to be afraid of *something that's just not quite real.*"[96] It is this twofold nature of Dylan's consternation—the actual threat of nuclear violence and the threat of an excessive fear that lacks reality—that distinguishes the psychological challenges posed by nuclear weapons.

Dylan's pronouncement, his imperative to himself to "let me die in my footsteps," works within these two registers. On the one hand, it is an ethic for how the real threat of nuclear annihilation should be met: in the words of Yeats, "proud, open-eyed and laughing to the tomb."[97] This is not courage in the face of a military or political battle, in which one contributes to the outcome and hopes for victory, but courage in the face of a geopolitical disaster entirely outside of one's control. Whereas the usual focus is on how nuclear weapons might be strategically employed or abolished (and it is worth noting that Kissinger has defended both approaches[98]), Dylan's realism here has an altogether different focus: how ordinary citizens, without special claims to power, ought to confront (not *prevent*) their destruction. And the central issue Dylan raises in this context is the admonition not to go down under the ground: not to build or make use of fallout shelters and, perhaps also, not to cower under desks in nuclear drills as he had been forced to do as a child, but, if necessary, to face nuclear annihilation above ground. Why does Dylan reject fallout shelters? Part of the reason is that he considers them morbid, sacrificing too much life in the very effort to protect it:

> Let me drink from the waters where the mountain streams flood
> Let the smell of wildflowers flow free through my blood

---

[95] Interview in *American Masters*, season 19, episode 7, "No Direction Home: Bob Dylan," directed by Martin Scorsese, aired September 27, 2005, on PBS, https://www.imdb.com/title/tt0367555/?ref_=adv_li_tt.

[96] Dylan, *Chronicles*, 29 (emphasis added).

[97] William Butler Yeats, "Vacillation," in *The Collected Poems of W. B. Yeats*, ed. Richard J. Finneran (New York: Scribner, 1996), 250.

[98] For their strategic employment, see Kissinger, *Nuclear Weapons and Foreign Policy* (New York: Harper and Brothers, 1957); for their abolition, see Kissinger's co-authored article "A World Free of Nuclear Weapons," *Wall Street Journal*, January 4, 2007.

Let me sleep in your meadows with the green grassy leaves
Let me walk down the highway with my brother in peace
Let me die in my footsteps
Before I go down under the ground

In a sense, then, Dylan's meditation on death is paradoxically a call not to meditate on death:

There's been rumors of war and wars that have been
The meaning of life has been lost in the wind
And some people thinkin' that the end is close by
'Stead of learnin' to live they are learnin' to die
Let me die in my footsteps
Before I go down under the ground

As Dylan explains elsewhere, the problem with fallout shelters is also that they are "immoral" because, if adopted, they would unravel neighborly relations and pit individuals and families against each other. His thinking in this regard was inspired in part by the behavior of his fellow Northern Minnesotans. Dylan recounts in *Chronicles* that, among his neighbors while he was growing up, "fallout shelters didn't catch on, had no effect whatsoever on the Iron Range."[99] Part of their logic for not having them, he relates, was the concern that building shelters would divide the community between those who did and did not possess them: "It could turn neighbor against neighbor and friend against friend." He concludes: "There wasn't any honorable way out. Bomb shelters divided families and could create mutiny. Not that people weren't concerned about the mushroom cloud—they were. But salesmen hawking the bomb shelters were met with expressionless faces."[100]

Both elements that make fallout shelters undesirable in Dylan's view—their morbidity and their immorality—are reflected in his account from 1963 about how "Let Me Die in My Footsteps" came to him:

I was going through some town and they were making this bomb shelter right outside of town, one of these sort of Coliseum-type things and there were construction workers and everything. I was there for about an hour, just looking at them build, and I just wrote the song in my head

---

[99] Dylan, *Chronicles*, 271. The passage continues: "As far as communists went, there wasn't any paranoia about them. People weren't scared of them, seemed to be a big to-do over nothing. . . . Mine owners were more to be feared, more of an enemy, anyway."

[100] Dylan, 271.

back then, but I carried it with me for two years until I finally wrote it down. As I watched them building, it struck me sort of funny that they would concentrate so much on digging a hole underground when there were so many other things they should do in life. If nothing else, they could look at the sky, and walk around and live a little bit, instead of doing this immoral thing.[101]

Dylan was not uninterested in his protection from nuclear radiation, explaining in *Chronicles* that he kept a Geiger counter in the early 1960s,[102] but one of the clear messages of "Let Me Die in My Footsteps" is the resolution not to make the elongation of his life his singular or overriding concern. Implicit in this resolution is the call to accept that the matter of nuclear annihilation is outside of one's control—and that the only thing to decide is how one will confront the risk of nuclear war on a personal ethical level, which means deciding, at least in the abstract, how one would prefer to be killed.

On the other hand, though, Dylan's song operates in the second register: confronting the element of fear that is rarely neatly correlated with the nuclear threat itself. The decision to die in one's footsteps is both a decision about how one would prefer to meet one's demise *and* a provocative suggestion that the possibility of this demise has been overblown and exaggerated. Consider:

> I don't know if I'm smart but I think I can see
> When someone is pullin' the wool over me
> And if this war comes and death's all around
> Let me die on this land 'fore I die underground
> Let me die in my footsteps
> Before I go down under the ground

And:

> There's always been people that have to cause fear
> They've been talking of the war now for many long years
> I have read all their statements and I've not said a word
> But now Lawd God, let my poor voice be heard
> Let me die in my footsteps
> Before I go down under the ground

---

[101] Original liner notes to *The Freewheelin' Bob Dylan* (1963), referenced in John Bauldie's liner notes for *The Bootleg Series Volumes 1–3* (1991). This commentary was deleted from the liner notes of *The Freewheelin' Bob Dylan* when "Let Me Die in My Footsteps" was removed from the album.

[102] Dylan, *Chronicles*, 271–72.

Dylan here (in real time, no less) has his finger on what now has been historically documented: that the fallout shelter movement had little to do with protecting Americans within a context of actual nuclear attack, but rather was intended to signal to the Soviets the Americans' preparedness to engage in nuclear war. When President Kennedy authored the foreword to the September 1961 *Life* magazine issue devoted to fallout shelters, whose headline read, "Survive Fallout: 97 out of 100 People Can Be Saved. Detailed Plans for Building Shelters"—in which he wrote, "My fellow Americans, nuclear weapons and the possibility of nuclear war are facts of life we cannot ignore today. . . . I urge you to read and consider seriously the contents of this issue of *Life*"—he was telling lies.[103] Even if such lies were intended for the ultimate safety of Americans, ordinary citizens were still being used as pawns. The deception was twofold: first, encouraging Americans to build fallout shelters led them to believe that the threat of Soviet nuclear attack was greater than it perhaps was; and second, there was the falsity that fallout shelters could protect Americans from nuclear attack. Such deception is not incidental to a realist nuclear strategy, but essential to it, since, as Kissinger himself argued in an influential book from the late 1950s, it is incumbent on a nuclear power to project its readiness to use its weapons or else their deterrent effect would be neutralized.[104] The problem with projecting preparedness, though, is that it involves lying to ordinary people and instrumentalizing them.

Dylan's refusal to "go down under the ground" was in effect a calling of the government's bluff. It was an indictment of the political realism of the Kennedy administration—its commitment to permanent geopolitical struggle, its willingness to use weapons of mass destruction, it readiness for war—as being *unreal* because it was based on the generation of fear (the alleged imminence of a nuclear attack that would make Americans want to build fallout shelters) and a proposed solution to that fear (the effectiveness of fallout shelters as a defense against nuclear attack), both of which were to a meaningful extent illusory.[105] Dylan can thus be read as the polar opposite of Kennedy and political realist strategizing. Whereas Kennedy encourages Americans to fear nuclear attack but holds out

---

[103] See George E. Lowe, *Stalking the Antichrists, Volume I, 1940–1965* (Bloomington, IN: Xlibris, 2013), 294–95.

[104] Kissinger, *Nuclear Weapons and Foreign Policy*, 114.

[105] Of course, it is likely that the generation of fear and its reduction were seen by architects of Kennedy's nuclear policy to be one and the same: that is, in order to effectively withstand the Soviet Union and avoid the net fear and destruction that would have been caused by unsuccessfully contesting that regime, it was necessary (at least in the short term) to project readiness for nuclear engagement and thus temporarily heighten Americans' fears. Yet, for reasons I discuss, this calculus— which appeals to the so-called economy of fear—does not function properly in the nuclear age.

the possibility that such an attack might adequately be protected against, Dylan makes no such claim that nuclear war can be survived but expresses this resignation in a spirit of skepticism about just how serious the threat of such a war really is. More generally, Dylan also can be read as opposing, from the position of an ordinary citizen, a central tenet of political realism: that leaders often need to engage in deception as a matter of political necessity.[106] Dylan does not expect to overcome the mendacity of politicians in some ultimate sense, but his prophetic force is directed, at least in the limited sphere in which he operates, to uncovering deception. And it is his resignation toward nuclear annihilation that helps enable him to do so. Whereas deception is an inherent part of canonical political realism, Dylan's realism is realer precisely in aiming to expose, rather than propagate, lies and manipulation—and, in doing so, not allow his own sense of fear, threat, and security to be determined by the state's manipulative regulation of his mind.

Dylan's song is not just an account of how to address the threat of nuclear annihilation in a manner distinct from the leadership-centric, strategy-focused approach of conventional political realists, but a reminder that the nuclear threat itself undermines the categories and perspectives of political realism as it typically has been conceived. Here a comparison with Hobbes is useful. Both Hobbes and Dylan testify to being born in a condition of fear. When Hobbes reflected, "fear and I were born twins together," he meant that his birth year, 1588, was the year of the Spanish Armada and also that it so terrified England that it may have induced his mother into premature delivery.[107] Dylan's birth year, 1941, was the year of Pearl Harbor and the entry of the United States into World War II, the most destructive war in human history, a connection, as discussed, that Dylan himself makes: "Me, I was born in 1941— that's the year they bombed Pearl Harbor. Well, I been livin' in a world of darkness ever since." But as much as Dylan's reflections recall Hobbes and the tradition of political realism, Dylan also points in an entirely different direction. For one thing, he testifies to the first-person experience of a conflict-ridden world irreducible to justice; that is, he does *not* treat this "world of darkness" as a mere fact that wise philosophy or prudent political leadership might successfully navigate or master. Whereas

---

[106] Examples of political realists condoning, if not actively supporting, deception include Machiavelli (*The Prince*, 68–71) and Weber ("Politics as a Vocation," 83). The alleged need for politically responsible leaders to lie is a key reason political realists understand politics as irreducible to morality.

[107] Thomas Hobbes, *The Life of Mr. Thomas Hobbes of Malmsebury*, in *Leviathan*, ed. Edwin Curley (Indianapolis: Hackett, 1994), liv (translation from the Latin slightly altered).

the Hobbesian sovereign, conceived as the Leviathan, does not feel fear[108]—nor, for that matter, do other iconic realist figures, such as the Machiavellian prince or the Weberian statesmen, who likewise aim to handle politics beyond any trepidation—this is not Dylan's reality, nor can it belong to anyone else who is a passive recipient of powerful individuals' decisions and refuses to be in denial about nuclear and other threats or entertain overly optimistic predictions about how such threats might be handled.[109] Further, whereas Hobbes and other realists defend an *economy of fear*—an imposing of the threat of force to reduce overall danger—Dylan testifies both to the fearfulness of ordinary civic life (and thus, to a certain extent, to the contemporary failure of this economy) and, more than this, to the way the nuclear bomb undermines the strategy of using fear to achieve its ultimate reduction.[110] The Hobbesian calculus is that fear of an immediate danger (such as civil war and social chaos) can motivate submission to a sovereign that, though itself something to fear, secures peace, order, safety, and thus the diminishment of overall fear. For Dylan, by contrast, the fear of nuclear annihilation is not immediate but hypothetical; the state to which we submit is the primary exerciser and maximizer of that threat, not its source of containment; and the net result of the nuclear age is not therefore the reduction of fear but the redoubling of it. If Hobbes's overall mission is to turn to the state in order to rescue us from fear, the emergence of nuclear weapons as the ultimate weapon of the state has made this rescuing impossible. Dylan thus offers a different message: not the economy of fear (with the promise of an eventual approximation of fearlessness) but courage in the face of fear (reflected in figuring out how you want to die) mixed with intrepidity (caution about falling into panic over something that might not be real). He rejects the aspiration of being rescued from

[108] In the Bible the Leviathan is described thus: "Upon earth there is not his like, who is made without fear" (Job 41:33). As Tuck explains, "The fact that the Leviathan is 'without fear' is critical, for that corresponds to what Hobbes . . . says repeatedly, that his commonwealth would rescue men from fear. By incorporating themselves into this artificial man who feels no fear, the citizens are themselves able to live a life freed from it." Tuck, "The Utopianism of *Leviathan*," 138.

[109] As an example of an overly optimistic prediction, consider Herman Kahn, who predicted that survivors following a nuclear war could be able to enjoy "relatively normal and happy lives" and that, within a few years, living standards in the United States would be higher than in the early twentieth century. Kahn, *Thinking About the Unthinkable* (New York: Horizon Press, 1962), 87. Also see McQueen, *Political Realism in Apocalyptic Times*, 161.

[110] On this latter point, see Hans Morgenthau, "The Intellectual and Moral Dilemma of Politics," in *The Decline of Democratic Politics* (Chicago: University of Chicago Press, 1962), 12: "[The] rational relationship between the means of violence and the ends of foreign policy has been destroyed by the availability of nuclear power as a means to achieve those ends. For the possibility of universal destruction obliterates the means-end relationship itself by threatening the nations and their ends with total destruction. No such radical qualitative transformation of the structure of international relations has ever occurred in history."

nuclear fear and thus also rejects the politics of preparedness for nuclear disaster. He advises not the implementation of fear to achieve its overall reduction, but caution that this implementation would only be an exacerbation.

Dylan's edgy resignation toward nuclear war, while most directly targeted against the pretensions of conventional political realism, is no less outside the terrain of familiar idealistic approaches to nuclear policy. Perceptive idealists, advocating the abolition of nuclear weapons, recognize that nuclear weapons generate a sense of futility and fatalism in ordinary citizens, but they insist that these sentiments can and must be overcome through political movements seeking disarmament. Elaine Scarry, for instance, explains how nuclear weapons bypass democratic consent and thus cultivate a sense of disempowerment:

> One's own arms are empty of feeling. But that is exactly what it feels like to lose the capacity for consent or dissent: because the weapons are utterly independent of our consent, our consent is irrelevant; and because it is irrelevant, it is unexercised; and because it is unexercised, it atrophies. Once we internalize our own irrelevance, the idea of nuclear weapons incites neither applause nor indignation; we can set aside the thought of savage world-ruining weapons with a shrug or a brief lament, then turn to other thoughts.[111]

Scarry urges that this mindset needs to be resisted because it stands in the way of efforts to achieve nuclear disarmament. Nonetheless, she acknowledges that the nuclear age encourages precisely this mentality by severely weakening traditional avenues of popular consent. Dylan is not against the call for disarmament and if anything supports it as an abstract wish.[112] But his intervention does not take place on this plane and, instead, indicts the unreality that afflicts such a perspective. Though unsettling, Dylan's focus on how he would meet death is true to the situation that Scarry diagnoses but refuses to ethically accept: *that nuclear weapons are outside of popular control.* Her futural focus looks past the circumstance ordinary people face in the here and now: the circumstance of being threatened by nuclear apocalypse with little that might be done to avoid it. Relatedly, Scarry's call for mass mobilization also becomes unreal insofar as it, too, exaggerates the role of ordinary citizens. The examples of activism she applauds in fact come from elites, including Kissinger himself, who, in 2007,

---

[111] Elaine Scarry, *Thermonuclear Monarchy: Choosing Between Democracy and Doom* (New York: Norton, 2014), 149–50.

[112] See, for example, his 1983 song "License to Kill," as well as lyrics from "Let Me Die in My Footsteps," cited in the main text, that express an abstract longing for, but no genuine expectation of, a weaponless future.

joined with former senator Sam Nunn, former secretary of state George Shultz, and former secretary of defense William Perry to publicly "endorse setting the goal of a world free of nuclear weapons and working energetically on the actions required to achieve that goal."[113] The elite quality of the disarmament activists celebrated by Scarry is further revealed when she writes: "Among the few people who actively dissent to nuclear weapons are retired missile officers, retired generals, retired secretaries of state, and retired secretaries of defense. Because their consent was needed in the chain of command, their power to consent or dissent has not wholly atrophied and they can occasionally appear in public and voice their dissent to a population they helped to disenfranchise, many of whom can now not even recognize what they are talking about."[114] Scarry thus calls for a grassroots movement that both is not happening to the degree she would like and, as she seems to acknowledge, will be led by elites. Dylan's resignation, however, operates in the real place of ordinariness and immediacy. He engages with the fear we feel today, not with the institutional changes that might alleviate this fear in a hypothetical future. He reminds us that there are alternate domains of consent still left—in how much we agree to demonize enemies (e.g., communists) and how far we are willing to go for war preparedness. And most pointedly, Dylan suggests that "a shrug or a brief lament" is a meaningful way to respond and not politically inconsequential, at least in times when the state calls for greater fear and imposes a dubious politics of security.

As the example of Dylan's approach to the nuclear age demonstrates, his resignation is no mere mood but an element of his call to strengthen the things that remain—to honestly confront the impossibility of certain objectives and pursuits so as to heighten attunement to what in fact can be achieved—and, in so doing, transcend the usual proclivities and concerns of both idealists and conventional political realists alike. Resignation for Dylan is thus part of his insistence on being real: true to the tragic divergence between politics and morality, as perceived from the ordinary person's perspective. At times he has been explicit about this linkage. Consider this exchange from a 1984 interview, for example, during which Dylan is accused of being fatalistic in considering war and violent conflict to be permanent ways of the world:

DYLAN: Well, you can't be for peace and be global. . . . If you believe in *this* world, you're stuck; you really don't have a chance.
KURT LODER: That's a very fatalistic view, isn't it?

[113] George P. Shultz, William J. Perry, Henry A. Kissinger, and Sam Nunn, "A World Free of Nuclear Weapons," *Wall Street Journal*, January 4, 2007.
[114] Scarry, *Thermonuclear Monarchy*, 464.

DYLAN: I think it's *realistic*. If it is fatalistic, it's only fatalistic on this level, and this level dies anyway, so what's the difference? So you're fatalistic, so what?[115]

Here futility and fatalism are presented as part and parcel of realism itself. Yet, as I have tried to show, in Dylan's hands they are not without ethical effect.

III.6. The Satanic Aspect of Politics

Another element of Dylan's pessimism about the world concerns his insistence upon the paradoxes of political and moral action: specifically, the problem that very often there is a disharmony between means and ends. This problem is entirely outside of the purview of various idealistic-progressive discourses that uphold some allegedly pure means (civic participation, science, human rationality, the interests of the poor) as a device for achieving the equally pure ends of peace, freedom, equality, prosperity, and so on. Belief in the harmony of means and ends does not necessarily mean belief in the current justice of the world, but it is a reason to be optimistic about the eventual achievement of justice. Likewise, belief in the disharmony of means and ends is a key reason why pessimists remain dark about the world's prospects.

Perhaps the most foundational thought of canonical political realism is the calling into question of the harmony of means and ends. This is not the doctrine that the ends justify the means (which wrongly has been attributed to many realists) but the doctrine that political ends require means that are not fully justifiable (e.g., deception, usurpation, killing), thereby making the realm of politics ambiguous, shadowy, and sinister. Appreciation for the disharmony between means and ends within the tradition of political realism usually has been expressed with regard to the perspective of responsible leaders who allegedly must violate moral norms as a condition of achieving political success, not just for themselves but for the broader communities they lead. Consider Machiavelli, who endorses the idea that "it is evil to say evil of evil" and declares in the fifteenth chapter of *The Prince* that it is because we are surrounded by evil doers that moral purity is politically inefficacious and thus irresponsible: "A man who wants to

---

[115] Cott, "Interview with Kurt Loder," in *Essential Interviews*, 310 (emphasis added). Dylan provides a somewhat different response to the accusation of fatalism in a 1978 interview. When told "you sound a bit fatalistic," Dylan rejoins: "I'm not fatalistic. Bank tellers are fatalistic; clerks are fatalistic. I'm a farmer. Who ever heard of a fatalistic farmer? I'm not fatalistic. I smoke a lot of cigarettes, but that doesn't make me fatalistic." Cott, "Interview with Nat Hentoff," in *Essential Interviews*, 112.

make a profession of good in all regards must come to ruin among so many who are not good. Hence it is necessary to a prince, if he wants to maintain himself, to learn to be able not to be good, and to use this and not use it according to necessity."[116] This teaching of learning now *not* to be good—not in the name of cruelty and evil themselves but in the name of political responsibility—finds support throughout the political realist tradition. In recent times, part of what the realist metonym "Kissinger" represents, as one of Kissinger's biographers puts it, is that there is "no way to avoid doing evil in the conduct of foreign policy."[117] This dictum follows directly from Morgenthau, who deeply influenced Kissinger and himself taught that "the political act is inevitably evil," explaining: "The very act of acting destroys our moral integrity. Whoever wants to retain his moral innocence must forsake action altogether."[118] Such reflections are not a call for indiscriminate wrongdoing but rather speak to the tragic awareness that, sometimes at least, good means will produce evil results and evil means good ones.

Both Kissinger and Morgenthau were guided by the seminal thought of Max Weber, who, of all the political realists, is most explicit in understanding that the disharmony between means and ends suggests something of wider significance: not only does the responsible leader have to engage in morally ambiguous action, but the fact that this is a requirement indicates that the political world itself is necessarily caught up in ethical paradoxes that Weber goes so far as to call *satanic*. Like other political realists, Weber destabilizes the opposition between good and evil: "It follows that as far as a person's actions are concerned, it is *not* true that nothing but good comes from good and nothing but evil from evil, but rather quite frequently the opposite is the case. Anyone who does not realize this is in fact a mere child in political matters."[119] Weber provides numerous reasons for this circumstance, but the most fundamental is that politics is inescapably connected to violence (all political actors to some degree engage in it, authorize it, or aim to impact its use) and violence—the imposition of suffering and death—can never be fully justified.[120] This situation

---

[116] Machiavelli, *Discourses on Livy*, 212 [III.1]; *The Prince*, 61. On Machiavelli's admiration of the notion that it is evil to say evil of evil, see Harvey C. Mansfield and Nathan Tarcov, "Introduction," in Machiavelli, *Discourses on Livy*, xxxv.

[117] Barry Gewen, *The Inevitability of Tragedy: Henry Kissinger and His World* (New York: Norton, 2020), 393.

[118] Hans Morgenthau, "The Evil of Politics and the Ethics of Evil," *Ethics* 56, no. 1 (1945): 11, 18.

[119] Weber, "Politics as a Vocation," 86.

[120] Other reasons Weber provides for the inevitable moral ambiguity of politics include leaders' need to serve their apparatus or machine in terms that are not equivalent to public benefit (e.g., indulging the machine's animosity and vengefulness toward rivals and its desire for personal rewards); their need sometimes not to reveal the full truth of certain matters of state; and their "spiritual proletarianization" of the popular bases they mobilize. See Weber, "Politics as a Vocation," 83, 89, 90.

means that political leaders must give up on the expectation of their guiltless-
ness or full moral rectitude. To say this does not mean that all political actors
are equally compromised, since it is possible to employ violence and other
morally ambiguous means for some worthy cause or broader benefit, but for
Weber and the larger tradition of political realism he speaks for, there can be no
question of thereby sanctioning the transgressiveness of political action on utilitarian grounds—that is, on the grounds that the ends justify the means. The
whole point is that the ends do not fully justify the means, with the result that
politically responsible leaders must forgo their sense of being fully good and
instead recognize that they are "entering into relations with the satanic powers
that lurk in every act of violence." Weber thus pronounces: "Whoever becomes
involved with politics, that is to say, with power and violence as a means, has
made a pact with satanic powers."[121]

Dylan shares this appreciation for the disharmony between means and ends
and, with it, a sense of the world being mired in ethical ambiguity. Consider, for
example, these lines from "Jokerman":

> It's a shadowy world
> Skies are slippery grey

And, like Weber, Dylan invokes the concept of the satanic to describe not just
the fallenness of the world, but a fallenness that relates in part to the tragic divergence between means and ends. In public sermons from his gospel period, Dylan
routinely recites Paul's idea of the devil as "the god of this world" (2 Corinthians
4:3)—a designation that indicts not simply human beings who, while confined
to this life, are caught up in sin, but also the broader *world* whose chief goods
(peace, prosperity, comfort, joy) cannot be accepted as unambiguously moral.[122]
Indeed, of all Dylan's many uses of the devil, his most thought-provoking and intellectually challenging are precisely those that point to the paradoxical disharmony between means and ends. Consider his 1983 song "Man of Peace," which
has the refrain:

> Sometimes Satan comes as a man of peace

One could dispense with the paradox of this idea by interpreting Dylan to
mean simply that Satan is a deceiver (he pretends to support what is good for
us when in fact he intends our destruction) and that, more generally, people

[121] Weber, 86, 90.
[122] See Dylan, *Saved! The Gospel Speeches*, 23, 24, 44, 54, 63, 64, 90, 98, 102.

are in the throes of the satanic when they falsely pretend to support good aims that they really oppose. This conception of the satanic as the false appearance of goodness finds support in the biblical passage that likely influenced "Man of Peace": "Satan himself masquerades as an angel of light. It is not surprising, then, if his servants also masquerade as servants of righteousness."[123] And Dylan at times does indict people for falsely supporting certain ostensibly moral ends, including the end of peace. When he observes, for instance, "You can just about *know* that anybody who comes out for peace is not for peace,"[124] he is questioning the motives of many who seemingly—but falsely—seek peace, whether "masters of war" (who cynically pursue war in the name of peace) or would-be peace activists whose activism is more about their own self-promotion than serious and effective work to reduce the incidence of violence in the world.

But it would be a mistake to interpret Dylan here in such a straightforward, non-paradoxical fashion, since there is a second, and indeed more intellectually and ethically vexing, way in which Dylan takes aim at the satanic aspect of peace activism: suggesting that the problem is not simply the false commitment to peace and other related goods but sometimes *the authentic commitment to such goals.* Consider the most challenging lines from "Man of Peace":

> Good intentions can be evil
> Both hands can be full of grease
> You know that sometimes Satan comes as a man of peace

The idea that not the false commitment to apparent goods but the *actual commitment* to them might have a satanic aspect is no isolated thought for Dylan but one he repeats elsewhere: "Sometimes the devil likes to drive you from the neighborhood / He'll even work his ways through those whose intentions are good" ("Ain't No Man Righteous, No Not One"). It also seems reflected when Dylan sings: "Well, the devil's shining light, it can be most blinding," ("Saving Grace"), reminding us of Lucifer's etymological connection to "lux" or "light," and in any case attributing to Satan a genuine quality of luminosity as opposed to a more customary darkness. In these cases, Dylan's thinking takes him beyond what he had castigated in "Slow Train"—"But the enemy I see wears a *cloak* of decency"—as he is led to the far more paradoxical problem that a *real* commitment to apparent goods, such as peace, can potentially turn out to have a sinister quality.

---

[123] 2 Corinthians 11:14–15.
[124] Cott, "Interview with Kurt Loder," in *Essential Interviews*, 310.

What is the prophetic meaning of this strange and paradoxical stance? Dylan is close here to the tradition of political realism, which itself recognizes the satanic ambiguity of political action, but he ultimately reworks, rather than simply repeats, the ostensibly similar pronouncements of Machiavelli, Weber, Morgenthau, and others. Three critical departures are most central.

First, Dylan reverses the traditional focus of canonical political realists, who, in analyzing the ethical paradoxes shadowing political action, concentrate much more on one form of paradox (that evil can produce good) than the other (that good can produce evil). This reversal of focus is especially apparent in Dylan's interrogation of world peace, a goal that would seem to be morally pure and unambiguous, but that Dylan recognizes as possessing a dark and dangerous potentiality. He expresses this view not just in "Man of Peace," but in later statements that reference the song. Consider this exchange with Kurt Loder from 1984:

LODER: Isn't it [peace] worth fighting for?

DYLAN: Nah, none of that matters. I heard somebody on the radio talkin' about what's happenin' in Haiti, you know? "We must be concerned about what's happening in Haiti. We're *global people* now." And they're gettin' everybody in that frame of mind—like we're not just the United States anymore, we're *global.* . . .

LODER: But what if someone genuinely is for peace?

DYLAN: Well, you can't be for peace and be *global.* It's just like that song "Man of Peace."[125]

Although the valorization of peace as a universal ideal is a dominant trope in both the history of political thought and contemporary political culture more generally, Dylan's critical reflections about the satanic aspect of peace place him within a broader minority tradition of peace skeptics. In an important recent contribution to this tradition, Murad Idris states, "The belief in peace as a basic desire and universal aspiration occludes how readily its invocations dehumanize enemies, sanitize violence, and silence dissent."[126] Idris attends in particular to the problematic conception of a "war for the sake of peace"—itself inadvertently referenced by Loder's challenging Dylan with the question "Isn't [peace] worth *fighting* for?"—which Idris claims "has been central to the history of political thought across place, time, and language,

---

[125] Cott, "Interview with Kurt Loder," in *Essential Interviews*, 309–10.

[126] Murad Idris, *War for Peace: Genealogies of a Violent Ideal in Western and Islamic Thought* (New York: Oxford University Press, 2018), xiii.

and . . . remains central to official and public discourses."[127] The ambiguity of a war for peace—not just its logical instability but also its connection to imperialism, militarism, and aggressive violence—finds ample reflection in recent times. President George W. Bush, for instance, declared America's terrorist enemies as enemies of peace and justified wars in Afghanistan and Iraq as wars for peace, stating: "Our aim is a democratic peace."[128] President Obama used the occasion of his being awarded the 2009 Nobel Peace Prize to defend the idea of pursuing peace through the conduct of "just war" and, as Idris points out, "shortly thereafter, Obama engaged in over seven high-intensity military interventions, and authorized regular drone strikes."[129] For these American presidents, then, peace is invoked in the commitment to, rather than immediate suspension of, hostilities, exemplifying Michael Oakeshott's perceptive observation that war and peace "stand almost perfectly for both themselves and their opposites" and Heidegger's insistence on reading peace and war together as what he calls "war-peace."[130] Idris's critical attention to the problematic trope of a war for peace builds upon other theoretical refusals to understand peace as a straightforwardly noble objective, including those that have provocatively suggested not only a reversal of Clausewitz's dictum that war is politics by other means—that is, that politics is war by other means— but, in a further inversion of the idea, that "peace is the continuation of war by other means" (Arendt) and a "form of war" (Foucault), in part because, from at least the twentieth century, the experience of peace has been shaped by cold war, the military industrial complex, and, in Arendt's terms, the constant "development in the techniques of warfare."[131] Frantz Fanon addresses how ambitions for "peaceful coexistence" have been part of colonial oppression, and Carl Schmitt claims that they have served to justify unlimited and total war against enemies.[132] Idris himself argues that peace has been invoked to "delegitimize protests against political oppression, economic inequality, and

---

[127] Idris, 314.

[128] Quoted in Idris, xiv. As Bush put it in the immediate aftermath of the September 11 attacks: "Islam is peace. These terrorists don't represent peace. They represent evil and war. . . . Our war on terror will not end until every terrorist group of global reach has been found, stopped and defeated" (quoted in Idris, xiv).

[129] Idris, War for Peace, xiv.

[130] Michael Oakeshott, The Politics of Faith and the Politics of Skepticism (New Haven, CT: Yale University Press, 2009), 13; Martin Heidegger, What Is Called Thinking? (New York: Harper & Row, 1968), 83; also see Idris, War for Peace, xviii–xix.

[131] Hannah Arendt, On Violence (New York: Houghton Mifflin Harcourt, 1970), 9; Michel Foucault, Power/Knowledge (New York: Vintage, 1980), 123; also see 90.

[132] See Idris, War for Peace, xvii–xviii.

racial injustice."[133] When Dylan indicts not any concern with peace, but peace as a global goal, as a way to fix the world and an overarching ethical purpose, he follows in this tradition of peace skeptics by suggesting the impossibility of peace and thus the power-laden aspect of peace rhetoric—that is, its connection to imperialism, to enduring socioeconomic and other hierarchies, to militarism itself.

Admittedly, this first difference between Dylan and canonical political realists is a subtle one, based more on emphasis than the substance of underlying ideas. After all, canonical political realists are hardly altogether blind to the dynamic of good producing evil, since the very premise of the need for politically responsible moral wrongdoing is based on the threat of the opposite circumstance of politically irresponsible moral purity. Thus, Machiavelli indicts Christian morality ("the weakness into which the present religion has led the world") and Weber takes aim at the sacrosanctity of peace and honesty as political objectives.[134]

But if Dylan's reversal of the usual frame of realist analysis is still quite close to the tradition of political realism, a second and more substantial departure relates to his widening of the scope of people likely to have to endure the world's ethical paradoxes. For Machiavelli, Weber, Morgenthau, Kissinger, and the tradition of political realism they represent, reflection on the paradoxes of good and evil is presented within a narrow context of elite powerholding: the need for *political leaders* sometimes to act with impure means and in this sense be evil. But Dylan not only makes primary the opposite movement (how good can lead to evil); he also understands it as applying to a much more extensive swathe of humanity than the narrow field of statesmen in possession of great power.

In other words, if Machiavelli, Weber, and other canonical political realists present ordinary life as not partaking of the satanic qualities of political leadership—and thus as providing a refuge in which those unable or unwilling to face the ethical paradoxes of politics might take shelter—Dylan suggests that the possibilities for such shelter are in truth not so easy to find. Accordingly, "Man of Peace" takes aim not only at peace itself but at various other goods,

---

[133] Idris, xv. Idris provides, as examples, the Egyptian revolution of 2011, the Occupy movement, protests in Ferguson and Baltimore after incidents of police violence, and the treatment of counter-protesters in Charlottesville, Virginia, in the 2017 "Unite the Right" rally.

[134] Machiavelli, *Discourses on Livy*, 6 [Preface to Book I]. Weber's view that peace ought not be considered an absolute value in politics is reflected when he argues that German pacifists were in part responsible for Germany's failures in World War I: "Now, once the period of exhaustion is over, *it is peace that will be discredited, not war*" ("Politics as a Vocation," 82). As an example of Weber's parallel assertion that honesty ought not be treated as an absolute commitment in politics, consider his claim that, in the context of the immediate aftermath of the war, Germany's publication of all its misdeeds during the conflict would be politically irresponsible (83).

much more connected to ordinary life, that themselves can take on a satanic quality. For example, religion—which represents a sphere of moral purity (however dubious in its political effects) for Machiavelli and Weber—is itself susceptible to satanic evil for Dylan:

> Look out your window, baby, there's a scene you'd like to catch
> The band is playing "Dixie," a man got his hand outstretched
> Could be the Führer
> Could be the local priest
> You know sometimes Satan comes as a man of peace

Maybe the idea is that religion, by itself, is too general a category to ensure moral goodness and that it is wrong to treat it as identical to morality. In any case, the destabilization of any automatic moral quality inhering in religion reaches a crescendo in the final verse when Dylan makes a similar point about the star of Bethlehem and perhaps, by extension, certain followers of Jesus, if not, most perplexingly, Jesus himself:

> Somewhere Mama's weeping for her blue-eyed boy
> She's holding them little white shoes and that little broken toy
> And he's following a star
> The same one them three men followed from the East
> I hear that sometimes Satan comes as a man of peace

This challenge to the sacrosanctity of even divinity—and the parallel call for each of us to overcome any unthinking acceptance of apparent moral authority and employ our own powers of observation and judgment in making moral determinations—recalls Dylan's earlier puzzle about the relationship between Judas and God in his 1963 song "With God on Our Side":

> Through many dark hour
> I've been thinkin' about this
> That Jesus Christ
> Was betrayed by a kiss
> But I can't think for you
> You'll have to decide
> Whether Judas Iscariot
> Had God on his side

These theological puzzles may be insuperable, but I mention them because they are part of Dylan's expansion of the terrain of moral paradox, beyond the leader-centric focus of Machiavelli, Weber, and other canonical political realists to include a much wider area of ordinary human experience.

This expansion is also reflected in what Dylan sings about a talented poet-singer such as himself:

> He got a sweet gift of gab, he got a harmonious tongue
> He knows every song of love that ever has been sung
> Good intentions can be evil
> Both hands can be full of grease
> You know that sometimes Satan comes as a man of peace

This is both a warning to interpreters and followers of Dylan about his own satanic potential as well as a more general warning, similar to Rousseau's reflections in his *Letter to D'Alembert*, about the moral dangers of the passive appreciation of aesthetic beauty. Dylan here seems close to Rousseau when Rousseau indicts the theater for providing onlookers with a false accomplishment.

Likewise, in parallel with recent scholarship on "critical philanthropy," Dylan raises the possibility of a satanic potential inhering in philanthropy, especially the kind that leads to the aggrandizement of those who provide it and achieves for them an inappropriate comfort in a world intrinsically shaped by moral emergency:

> He's a great humanitarian, he's a great philanthropist
> He knows just where to touch you, honey, and how you like to be kissed
> He'll put both his arms around you
> You can feel the tender touch of the beast
> You know that sometimes Satan comes as a man of peace

Indeed, potentially anyone is susceptible to the satanic on Dylan's account. Consider:

> Well, he catch you when you're hoping for a glimpse of the sun
> Catch you when your troubles feel like they weigh a ton
> He could be standing next to you
> The person that you notice least
> I hear that sometimes Satan comes as a man of peace

And:

> Well, he can be fascinating, he can be dull
> He can ride down Niagara Falls in the barrels of your skull

> I can smell something cooking
> I can tell there's going to be a feast
> You know that sometimes Satan comes as a man of peace

It is not just political leaders, then, who have to face the satanic ambiguity of good and evil translating into each other, but a much broader group of persons: for example, priests, philanthropists, humanitarians, artists, romantic partners, comforters. This situation connects to Dylan's critique of the bourgeois discussed in Part I. As Dylan suggests, we who are bourgeois live on protected islands surrounded by a sea of suffering: most of us are egoists insufficiently attentive to ameliorating the correctible hardships and injustices endured by others and, relatedly, our political systems instantiate oligarchy, if not corruption. Whereas canonical political realists often look past just these features of the world (note, for instance, Machiavelli and Weber's ultimate indifference to matters of poverty, inequality, excessive militarism, cronyism, and rampant egoism), Dylan makes them central and in doing so focuses on the ethical ambiguity such circumstances radiate upon more ordinary modes of life.

A third way in which Dylan's concept of the satanic reworks the tradition of political realism is that, while acknowledging the satanic aspect of politics and the world more generally, Dylan's point is to *resist*, not accept, it. This contrasts with political realists who traditionally have urged political leaders to embrace the satanic aspect of politics and learn how not to be good. Weber, for instance, concludes his "Politics as a Vocation" (as well as its companion piece, "Science as a Vocation") with the strange exhortation from Goethe: "The devil is old; grow old to understand him!"[135] Weber is by no means an outlier here. In the hands of canonical political realists, the insight that politics is irreducible to morality does not lead, as one might think it should, to suspicion of the political, but on the contrary becomes the setting for defending the morally transgressive leader who heroically endures this tragic circumstance and makes fateful political decisions without an underlying assurance of their full legitimacy. Consider Morgenthau's encomium to the leader who must operate without a sense of moral rectitude:

> To know with despair that the political act is inevitably evil, and to act nevertheless, is moral courage. To choose among several expedient actions the least evil one is moral judgment. In the combination of political wisdom, moral courage, and moral judgment, man reconciles his political nature with his moral destiny. That this conciliation is nothing

---

[135] Weber, "Politics as a Vocation," 91; "Science as a Vocation," in *Vocation Lectures*, 27 (translation slightly altered).

more than a *modus vivendi*, uneasy, precarious, and even paradoxical, can disappoint only those who prefer to gloss over and to distort the tragic contradictions of human existence with the soothing logic of specious concord.[136]

Morgenthau understands politics to be caught up in evil, yet he somehow also understands the ability to operate within this fallen terrain as reflecting "moral courage." This seemingly schizophrenic attitude is hardly particular to Morgenthau but in fact is the typical position of political realists when they recognize the irreducibility of human affairs to morality. As is often observed, Machiavelli, who praises the moral transgressiveness of political leaders, is guilty of a lack of guilt.[137] Weber likewise celebrates the authentic political leader who sacrifices moral purity for political responsibility as someone who, to him, is "immeasurably moving," "mature," "authentically human," and a model of "the root of the idea of 'vocation' in its highest form"—and someone who, he thinks, ought to move us as well "if we are not inwardly dead."[138] When taken alongside Weber's repeated disparagement of religiously motivated withdrawal from the world as an unmanly inability to face the fate of the times, Weber's remarks about the authentic politician, who sacrifices morality for a genuinely felt cause, leaves us with a sense that Weber understands the sacrifice of moral purity more as an ethical *achievement* than an ethical failing or an insoluble ethical dilemma. There are many other examples of this trend one could point to, including from Thucydides, Clausewitz, Schlesinger, and Niebuhr. But the point I wish to stress is simply that this kind of thinking verges on unreality when it dissolves the moral uneasiness that ought to be concomitant with any account of the irreducibility of politics to morality. If there is a tragic separation between morality and politics, then we should not simply be led to celebrate politics and those who sacrifice their moral integrity for political responsibility, but instead remain disturbed by this circumstance.

Dylan reflects this countermovement. When he presents politics as having a satanic aspect—making such claims as "politics is an instrument of the Devil" and "the Devil's behind politics"[139]—his clear point is not to endorse the kind of

---

[136] Morgenthau, "The Evil of Politics and the Ethics of Evil," 18.

[137] As Michael Walzer puts it, "What the penalties are for not being good, Machiavelli doesn't say, and it is probably for this reason above all that his moral sensitivity has so often been questioned. He is suspect not because he tells political actors they must get their hands dirty, but because he does not specify the state of mind appropriate to a man with dirty hands. A Machiavellian hero has no inwardness." Walzer, "Political Action: The Problem of Dirty Hands," *Philosophy & Public Affairs* 2, no. 2 (1973): 176.

[138] Weber, "Politics as a Vocation," 34–35, 92.

[139] Cott, "Interview with Kurt Loder," in *Essential Interviews*, 309; Dylan, *Saved! The Gospel Speeches*, 95.

leadership celebrated by canonical political realists, but to resist it. Or, as he puts it in a different context, "If there's evil behind good, it doesn't make the good good."[140] Metaphorically, this resistance can be seen in Dylan's repeated invocation of youthfulness, over and against the political realists' call for maturity.[141] Further, Dylan associates the satanic with a deadening of one's conscience vis-à-vis the evils of the world, thus presupposing the capacity to withstand this deadening. Part of what Dylan indicts in his account of the satanic in "Man of Peace," after all, is the false comfort—and, with it, indifference—one might feel in the face of injustice and suffering. Dylan emphasizes this rendering of the satanic in his 1979 song "Trouble in Mind":

> Here comes Satan, prince of the power of the air
> He's gonna make you a law unto yourself, gonna build a bird's nest
>   in your hair
> He's gonna deaden your conscience 'til you worship the work of
>   your own hands
> You'll be serving strangers in a strange, forsaken land

Here, in addition to references to Ephesians 2:2 and Jeremiah 1:16, Dylan alludes to Luther's notion that though we cannot prevent the birds of sin from flying over us, we can refrain from building a bird's nest to attract them.[142] "Trouble in Mind" thus links the satanic to moral insensitivity—pleading, paradoxically, in its conclusion, "Lord, keep my blind side covered and see that I don't bleed"— which has the function of making the satanic something to fight back against rather than, in canonical realist fashion, something with which to compromise and collaborate.

Dylan's resistance to the satanic takes numerous specific forms. Within the realm of political leadership—the realm that, of course, most directly concerns political realists—Dylan emphasizes *exceptions* to the alleged realist truth that

---

[140] Interview with Scott Cohen, "Bob Dylan Revisited."

[141] See, for example, Dylan's song "Abandoned Love," which contains the lines: "Everybody's wearing a disguise / To hide what they've got left behind their eyes / But me, I can't cover what I am / Wherever the children go I'll follow them." Also see "Forever Young" and "My Back Pages."

[142] See Martin Luther, "The Lord's Prayer Explained," in *Luther's Catechetic Writings: God's Call to Repentance, Faith and Prayer*, ed. John Nicholas Lenker (Minneapolis: The Luther Press, 1907 [1519]), 305. Dylan repeats the allusion in his 1981 song "Dead Man, Dead Man":

> Satan got you by the heel, there's a bird's nest in your hair
> Do you have any faith at all? Do you have any love to share?
> The way that you hold your head, cursin' God with every move
> Ooh, I can't stand it, I can't stand it
> What are you tryin' to prove?

effective leaders must act with dirty hands, pointing to rare figures who raise the possibility of non-satanic pure moral leadership. In the song "They Killed Him," written by Kris Kristofferson but recorded by Dylan on his 1986 album *Knocked Out Loaded*, Dylan celebrates Jesus, Gandhi, and Martin Luther King, leaders who arguably used pure means in the pursuit of equally pure ends. That all were assassinated reflects the fallenness of the world, and specifically Dylan's pessimism that activists genuinely committed to positive social change within their communities will have to risk their lives, but the fact that such leaders exist at all, and sometimes have been as successful as more typical political leaders, challenges the would-be universalism of the teachings of Machiavelli, Weber, and other canonical realists. Indeed, neither Machiavelli nor Weber knows how to handle such exceptions to their teachings about leadership. In insisting that the wise prince will need, above all, to be an expert at maintaining and using military arms, Machiavelli is led to the false dictum that "all unarmed prophets have failed," thereby forgetting Jesus, among others.[143] Weber likewise inveighs against what he calls "conviction politicians," who adopt and defend moral purity in politics and, on his telling, in effect say, "The world is stupid and nasty, not I. The responsibility for the consequences cannot be laid at my door but must rest with those who employ me and whose stupidity or nastiness I shall do away with." In opposing these moralistic politicians, Weber's most targeted criticism is that *most of the time* such figures are hypocrites: "I suspect I should come to the conclusion that in nine cases out of ten I was dealing with windbags who do not genuinely feel what they are taking on themselves but who are making themselves drunk on romantic sensations."[144] Dylan would agree with Weber's diagnosis here, except to point out that Weber has forgotten about the one out of ten, the exceptional leader who overcomes the satanic elements of politics and joins pure means to pure ends. If rare moral leaders, willing to sacrifice themselves, can transcend the ethical paradoxes political realists insist upon, then the moral transgressiveness of typical politicians working within these paradoxes is all the more problematic and unworthy of being extolled as it has been within the realist tradition.

Another way that Dylan resists rather than accepts the satanic aspect of politics concerns his refusal to lionize states and their record of moral transgression. Instead, he continually exposes the injustices at the heart of political history. This diverges from Machiavelli and Weber, both of whom would prefer to cover up, rather than publicly acknowledge, the darkness within politics. For Weber, recall that the ultimate meaning of his designation of politics as "satanic" is that

[143] See Machiavelli, *The Prince*, 24.
[144] Weber, "Politics as a Vocation," 92.

324 B O B   D Y L A N :   P R O P H E T   W I T H O U T   G O D

there is an inescapable element of ethical ambiguity within the discharge of political responsibility: no responsible leader can expect to feel fully justified, since
the responsibilities of political office, when effectively carried out, often require
breaking moral norms. But from this circumstance Weber derives no interest in
a state's leaders perpetually acknowledging their violations of morality. Instead,
one of the very transgressions leaders need to commit is shielding the public
from too much revelation of their moral guilt; that is, for Weber, excessive attention to the state's injustices is a paradigmatic instance of irresponsible moral purity.[145] Machiavelli is even more extreme, teaching that the morally transgressive
leader ought to maintain a false reputation for moral purity even when violating
morality for politically necessary purposes.[146] But Dylan speaks as a prophet, not
a politician. And in his prophetic role, he is a witness testifying to the history of
injustice in his country and political history more generally. He is offended by,
rather than accepting of, American political history. One of the best examples
of how Dylan proclaims the kind of information about which Machiavelli and
Weber would prefer leaders to remain silent is his song "With God on Our
Side." In nine short verses, the song dissects major historical events since the
time of the American founding and in each case challenges a narrative of triumphalism and moral self-approval—the justification of the conquering of Native
Americans as a prerequisite for the American experiment; the depiction of the
North as heroes in the Civil War; the interpretation of World War I as a necessary and victorious war; the idea that America's alliance with post–World War
II Germany is morally blameless and its Cold War struggle against the Soviet
Union no less morally pure; and the notion that the American use of nuclear
weapons has been and will continue to be for morally justifiable ends—thereby
rejecting pretensions of America being fully in the right, that is, of having God
on its side. The point is less to oppose each of these moments outright than
to recognize, in good realist fashion, that they are satanic (i.e., ambiguous and
therefore not fully justifiable). Dylan's realism is thus a call for us to be realists
not just as politicians, but also as historians and recipients of a national heritage.
There is no place for dishonesty and deception in his uncovering of the satanic
aspect of the world.

Perhaps the most basic way that Dylan resists the satanic in politics is to subscribe to a different kind of political ethic that operates outside of the grand
nation-state politics envisioned by canonical realists and thus also avoids the
ethical paradoxes leaders within such states arguably have to endure. Dylan's
support of emergency politics instead of conventional politics not only

---

[145] See Weber, "Politics as a Vocation," 83.
[146] Machiavelli, *The Prince*, 70.

promises to bypass the state but—when characterized by modest, small-scale interventions for human welfare that do not redound to the benefit or publicity of the doer—can also escape the paradoxes of the "great humanitarian," "great philanthropist," "local priest," and other socially recognizable leaders who are empowered by their ostensible altruism. Political realists have tended to denigrate this alternate kind of politics, when not overlooking it altogether. Weber, for example, recognizes something similar to it, but only as a consolation for individuals without the manly fortitude for what he takes to be the authentic form of politics, centered on national leadership and geopolitical struggle. To those who do not have the stomach for the satanic ambiguity of political life, Weber urges that they would do "better to cultivate neighborly contacts with other people, individually, in a simple and straightforward way, and apart from that, to go about their daily work without any fuss."[147] Dylan suggests this same alternative, but instills it with dignity rather than weakness, and, in the various ways I have outlined, attacks the haughtiness and moral illogic by which grand politics has been unduly celebrated, *on ethical grounds*, by the very individuals most aware of its paradoxes.

An implication of Dylan's attention to the satanic is that he is led to challenge the propriety of comfort, whether in the form of the self-importance of certain idealists who falsely understand themselves to be unambiguously on the side of the good or in the form of the teachings of realists embracing the capacity to do evil as a prerequisite of political responsibility. Indeed, Dylan raises inappropriate comfort as a key ethical concern, a central aspect of the satanic seduction to which we are susceptible. As he explains, the devil for him ultimately is a spiritual disposition, not a demon or external spirit.[148] And the devil's most usual spiritual function is to tell you that the world and your role within it are fine when in fact they are not. The devil is less what motivates sin than what blinds us to our sins, deadens our conscience, and leads us to overlook our responsibility.

It is in this context that the biblical lineage of the idea of Satan as a "man of peace" becomes most relevant. In the Bible, "man of peace" designates someone giving safe shelter to the disciples.[149] At the same time, the most literal meaning of "Satan" is an opposer, obstructer, or blocker. There is thus something profoundly paradoxical about Dylan's suggestion that sometimes the blocker (Satan) is the one who gives you safe passage (man of peace). But what makes the paradox comprehensible is Dylan's suggestion that a great many of us are not supposed to feel at peace in the world—an idea that challenges peace not just as a geopolitical goal but as a state of mind, and furthermore challenges the two

---

[147] Weber, "Politics as a Vocation," 93.
[148] See Dylan, *Saved! The Gospel Speeches*, 58, 63, 65, 85.
[149] See, for example, Luke 10:5–6.

together (indicting those who, in understanding themselves as seeking world peace, afford themselves the pretension of a clear conscience). Dylan's mockery of the "it's all good" mentality in his song "It's All Good" is but further evidence of his stance in this regard. In a world shaped by emergency, in which injustice abounds and so many of us forgo what we ought to do to alleviate suffering, comfort—and the goods that provide it—itself takes on ethical ambiguity. If theodicy explains how God can permit evil, Dylan explains how Satan sometimes can be on the side of good.

III.7. Upwing

Dylan's self-description as someone striving to be "upwing" as opposed to more familiar positions on the left-right continuum helps to summarize the meaning of his pessimism about the world and its connection to his call to strengthen the things that remain. In a variety of overlapping ways, Dylan repeatedly makes reference to the concept of upwing in classifying his approach to politics.

One central aspect of upwing is that it points to the aspiration to transcend, however occasionally and imperfectly, the political—an aspiration that follows from a pessimistic conceptualization of the world as irredeemably fallen. Idealists with faith in the ultimate achievement of social justice, or traditional realists oriented around the promise of mastery, are less likely to crave such transcendence, but for those like Dylan, who insist upon the inevitability of living in a world gone wrong and whose vantage point is that of the ordinary person rather than powerful leader, the need to transcend—that is, to avoid becoming demoralized and disheartened in the face of ever-present injustice, violence, and egotism—becomes crucial. One of Dylan's earliest statements of the upwing idea—discussed in Part I—stresses just this quest for transcendence:

> There's no black and white, left and right to me anymore; there's only up and down and down is very close to the ground. And I'm trying to go up without thinking about anything trivial such as politics. They has got nothing to do with it. I'm thinking about the general people and when they get hurt.[150]

In castigating politics for being trivial, Dylan almost seems to suggest a desire to overcome it altogether. How he has sought such transcendence has varied, but

---

[150] Quoted in Corliss Lamont, "Transcript of Bob Dylan's Remarks at the Bill of Rights Dinner at the Americana Hotel on 12/13/63," https://www.corliss-lamont.org/dylan.htm.

chief among his approaches have been religion (especially occasional statements about the need to believe in another world so as not to be altogether disheartened in the face of this one);[151] communion with nature;[152] romantic love, particularly insofar as it provides "shelter from the storm";[153] and, as discussed in Part I, a habitual rejection of political responsibility in the name of a free employment of his individuality. That he does frequently achieve transcendence—that his resignation about the world does not usually translate into defeatism and demoralization—is one of the remarkable features of his pessimism.[154] At the

[151] In a 1984 interview, for instance, Dylan suggests religiosity ("believ[ing] in another world") as a way to cope with the fallenness of the world: "If you believe in *this* world, you're stuck; you really don't have a chance. You'll go *mad*, 'cause you won't see the end of it." Cott, "Interview with Kurt Loder," in *Essential Interviews*, 310.

[152] See, for example, Dylan's works "Lay Down Your Weary Tune"; "Watching the River Flow"; and "Last Thoughts on Woody Guthrie," which concludes with the claim that God (as well as Guthrie) can be found "In the Grand Canyon / At Sundown." Also relevant is Dylan's statement in a 1981 interview that whereas for him Jesus is indispensable to his effort to connect with God (or "the creator"), there is a nature-laden path to the same goal. See footnote 24.

[153] See, for example, Dylan's 1975 song "Shelter from the Storm."

[154] Songs of despondence about the world routinely also include a testament to Dylan's persistence, good cheer, joy, and other positive emotions. Consider "Mississippi," which begins:

> Every step of the way we walk the line
> Your days are numbered, so are mine
> Time is pilin' up, we struggle and we scrape
> We're all boxed in, nowhere to escape
> City's just a jungle, more games to play
> Trapped in the heart of it, trying to get away
> I was raised in the country, I been workin' in the town
> I been in trouble ever since I set my suitcase down
> Got nothing for you, I had nothing before
> Don't even have anything for myself anymore
> Sky full of fire, pain pourin' down
> Nothing you can sell me, I'll see you around

But then ends with:

> But my heart is not weary, it's light and it's free
> I've got nothin' but affection for all those who've sailed with me

Also consider this from "Most of the Time" (emphasis added):

> Most of the time
> My head is on straight
> Most of the time
> I'm strong enough not to hate
> I don't build up illusion 'til it makes me sick
> I ain't afraid of confusion no matter how thick
> *I can smile in the face of mankind*
> Don't even remember what her lips felt like on mine
> Most of the time

same time, it would be a mistake to reduce Dylan's conception of upwing to a desire to leave behind the political. Even the above passage contains an abiding political interest in "the general people and when they get hurt," and elsewhere Dylan suggests that a full transcendence of politics is impossible.[155] It is also the case, on the biographical level, that he does not consistently seek, let alone achieve, an overcoming of politics. Above all, as I have tried to show, Dylan's pessimism is prophetically most distinct not when it leads him to imagine escaping the world and its fallenness, but when it suggests approaches for operating within the world, open-eyed, and without either the mystification of false hopes or the equally illusory vicariousness of identification with the statesman.

Other, more politicized renderings of the upwing idea involve just this call for honesty and, with it, the accusation that more typical political standpoints (represented by the "right" and "left") are mired in hypocrisy and bad faith. Consider:

> Well, for me, there is no right and there is no left. There's truth and untruth, y'know? There's honesty and there's hypocrisy.[156]

As an appeal for a more honest engagement with politics, rather than the mere transcendence of it, upwing recalls the central ideas of Dylan's realer realism: his focus on alleviating emergencies rather than engaging in ideological, partisan disputes; his implicit opposition to the grandiosity of canonical political realists; his resistance to deceptive state nuclear policy and its imposition of fear; and his reconsideration of the paradoxical interplay of good and evil from the everyday person's perspective. In each of these cases, Dylan penetrates the mendacity and false complacency of more familiar political standpoints in the name of an honest depiction of a world gone wrong and an individual's ethical situation in the face of it.

To a meaningful degree, both sides of the upwing idea—transcendence of the fallen political world and honest confrontation within it—operate simultaneously for Dylan. Despondency about conventional partisan politics illuminates a competing concern for alleviating emergencies that enables an overcoming of traditional political labels and categories. The fact that canonical political realism has been mired in its own utopianism and grandiosity is a reason not to take it as gospel. Acceptance of futility and fatalism in the face of nuclear weapons sets the stage for a courageous reclamation of when and how to be afraid. The fact that even many purveyors of apparent goods—humanitarians, priests, singers,

---

[155] See Dylan's song "Political World."
[156] Cott, "Interview with Mikal Gilmore, *Rolling Stone* (July 17, 1986)," in *Essential Interviews*, 367.

comforters—are not unambiguously good or free of satanic paradoxes is a call for self-analysis and ultimately thinking and judging for oneself. This mixture of political transcendence and political responsibility would seem to be the deepest meaning of the exhortation to wake up and strengthen the things that remain— a summons that, in Dylan's hands at least, has the effect of crystallizing ethical purposes through acceptance that the world forever will be mired in moral crisis. In the final analysis, there is little to recommend pessimism about the world other than its potential truthfulness. Against a culture disposed to ignore or re-press the possibility of a world gone wrong, Dylan stands out for exemplifying how one might live self-consciously within it.

Afterword

In conclusion, I return to the perspective of the skeptical reader whom I mentioned at the beginning, a reader who doubts the very enterprise of treating Bob Dylan in prophetic terms. I hope the preceding pages have allayed these doubts, but to the extent they persist a few final observations are in order.

It should be emphasized that one does not have to believe in prophecy to take it seriously and that we in a democratic society ought to be especially interested in those who manage to garner large prophetic followings. There always have been and will continue to be some individuals who are followed because of the perceived specialness of who they are. A prophet is not just a pure case of such charismatic authority but someone who most channels charisma into concrete messages that might be wondered at and heeded. Now why should those who doubt the genuineness of the prophet's claim to specialness still want to concern themselves with the prophet's message? Beyond a historical interest in human culture and an edificational interest in seeking out words of wisdom—relating to the overarching moral disposition of the world or ethical instruction about what constitutes time not misspent—which typically cannot be uttered within the skeptical and sober parameters of contemporary, disenchanted social science and philosophy, I believe that there is a further, *democratic* interest in taking seriously prophets like Dylan, even among those who do not believe in him. There is an inescapable popular element in prophecy, since, sociologically speaking, there can be no prophet without a popular following. To be sure, this popular element does not take the form of election. The self-understanding of followers is not that they constitute the prophet's specialness, only that they recognize it. Yet this recognition nonetheless signifies a proto-democratic relation. I submit that we in a democratic society ought to listen to the People—not just in the usual sense of heeding its preferences about laws and policies, but heeding the figures it itself heeds. Of course, most individuals popular within a democratic society do not aim to communicate about fundamental ethical, political, moral, and religious themes and thus cannot be considered in prophetic terms. Yet, with someone

Bob Dylan. Jeffrey Edward Green, Oxford University Press. © Oxford University Press 2024.
DOI: 10.1093/oso/9780197651742.003.0005

such as Dylan, whose fame within popular culture is matched by no less tremendous literary, philosophical, and spiritual depth—and whose prophetic claims are, by virtue of their tentativeness and variability, not beholden to any particular camp but rather open to a more universal audience—questions arise that ought to be of interest to any democrat: Who is this man? Why has he garnered such a following? What is it about his messages that have been perceived by so many to be uniquely riveting? And what might these messages contribute to the understanding of the sociopolitical situation we occupy? Traditionally, the role of the democratic theorist has been to instruct the People or empower it. But there is also the underappreciated but vital role of listening to the People: clarifying its own implicit and inchoate thoughts and concerns by taking seriously the prophetic figures who have fascinated it.

To a reader still skeptical about whether Dylan qualifies as a prophet—who insists that there is a profound gulf separating him from classical representations of the prophetic conscience in such sources as the Bible—I offer two contrasting replies. On the one hand, the gulf is not as wide as it may seem. The intrinsic overlap between poetry and prophecy, the circumstance that the biblical prophets were themselves to a meaningful extent performers and singers, the fact that their own prophetic status was often mocked and rejected, the obvious quasi-religiosity that infuses modern devotion to certain musical artists, and Dylan's especially intense employment of religious ideas and biblical reference throughout his more than sixty years on the public stage are some of the reasons that suggest the continuity, rather than discontinuity, between Dylan and the biblical prophets. On the other hand, however, I readily admit that Dylan does indeed depart in key respects from the biblical representation of the prophetic conscience, but I nonetheless reject the implication that this departure is itself necessarily a mar against Dylan's prophetic status. It is undeniable, after all, that Dylan diverges in important ways from the usual understanding of what it means to be a prophet. The book has emphasized the key substantive difference that Dylan is a prophet of diremption—that is, a prophet without God—rather than a prophet of salvation. To this should be added the fact that if Dylan is a prophet, he is not so in a pure or unambiguous sense. He adopts many roles, including poet, entertainer, businessman, singer, songwriter, pop-cultural icon. And if some of these roles—above all, that of poet—do overlap in important respects with the prophetic one, it nonetheless is clear that Dylan does not present himself (nor is he received, even by his most passionate followers) as a prophetic figure *tout court*. But this circumstance, rather than attenuate the premise of this book, actually recommends it. For one thing, the biblical tradition ought not be allowed entirely to define what a prophet is. There is a danger that in making Jeremiah or Elijah the standard-bearer of genuine prophecy, one makes prophecy something legendary, if not fictitious. Dylan, by contrast, is an undeniably real person, and it is at least possible that his partial, incomplete prophetic posture is the genuine manner in which all actual prophets in fact have appeared. That is to say, it is at least possible that the uncertainty and debate about Dylan's prophetic status is part of the way the earthy, pulpy balm of actual prophecy always has been absorbed. If so, then the still, small voices of real prophets should be recognized even if they are untouched by the burning coal of the Bible—and yet, at the same time, Dylan has more claim to this burning coal than almost anyone else alive today. Moreover, Dylan's partial, subtle, impure prophetic consciousness is actually what enables it to function in a contemporary context of skepticism, postmetaphysical thinking, large pockets of irreligion, and materialist frames of thought. Dylan is an ideal prophet for those otherwise skeptical of prophecy. Because he can be interpreted in non-prophetic terms—indeed, because he himself often calls into question his own prophetic status—Dylan is a prophet who demands the most minimal "sacrifice of the intellect." Since his prophetic element is enveloped and constrained by something else, it is always possible to see it as this something else. From one perspective this might be a weakness, but it is also a strength when it prevents Dylan's prophetic status from being reduced to a religious devotion many would reject as a cult or to an impossible grandiosity in which few, if any, would actually believe. Dylan transforms prophecy by surrounding it in song, in business enterprise, and in a life not always concerned with prophetic matters, but these envelopments protect a genuine, if impure, prophetic consciousness as much as they diminish it.

In any case, regardless of the prophetic form of their dissemination, Dylan's ideas concern problems—the potential conflict between individuality and social justice, the challenge of achieving mutual respect between the religious and non-religious, and the question of how ordinary people might maneuver within a political landscape permanently shaped by violence and injustice—that are vital matters of widespread concern. Furthermore, Dylan's specific perspectives within these topics are very often strikingly distinct. Accordingly, one of the main purposes of the book has been not simply to disclose Dylan's abstracted views on these matters, but to demonstrate how he alters and develops broader traditions of thought. Dylan is both a standard-bearer and a critic of the tradition of self-reliance represented by Emerson and Thoreau. He personally embodies and performs a postsecular consciousness only impersonally described by the tradition of postsecular philosophy represented by Habermas and Taylor. And he democratizes the tradition of political realism represented by Thucydides, Machiavelli, Weber, Morgenthau, Kissinger, and others. Bringing Dylan into conversation with these bodies of thought not only establishes what is philosophically fresh about his views but also enables even those skeptical of Dylan's prophetic status to understand his cultural and intellectual importance.

There are caveats, of course, to Dylan's appeal, and I do not mean to suggest that anyone, no matter how situated, will find his ideas engaging or instructive.

Those who already have figured out how to live—who have selected which commitment to make primary (individual freedom, social justice, or divinity) or who believe that all three commitments are in harmony with one another—likely will consider Dylan's message less resonant or illuminating. So, too, will those who take organized religion to be either completely false or completely compelling, or those who believe that a properly reformed liberal democracy or some other form of political regime might satisfactorily solve the problems of violence, oppression, and injustice. But if you remain diffident in any of these respects, Dylan is your voice, your model, your prophet—someone who reflects back to you what it is like to be a freethinking, self-conscious, eloquent, and courageous being in a world that does not make full sense, intent on searching for and sometimes finding ethical direction in the face of the normative chaos.

There occasionally have been other figures who have played a role like this. Emerson, for instance, is often treated in such a fashion. Indeed, there is probably no one to whom Dylan bears a greater resemblance. Both, with their uncommonly free and nimble minds, prophesize with capaciousness and perspicacity the contours of their general cultures. It is tempting even to read Dylan as an Emersonian. Dylan, after all, self-consciously inherits the Emersonian ideal of self-reliance and at some points over the last sixty-plus years has been its greatest contemporary practitioner and thinker. Like Emerson before him, Dylan resists easy categorization, impersonating an almost unmanageable variation of characters, standpoints, and ideas. Accordingly, it is impossible to assign to either man a simple or straightforward ideology. Dylan, better than anyone since Emerson, has led a life reflective of Emerson's dictum that "creeds [are] a disease of the intellect."[1] This variability has made it possible for both men not only to win huge followings of diverse adherents, so many of whom have found something deeply personal and singular in their reception of the prophetic refulgence, but also to appeal to all sides of the conventional political spectrum, with Emersonian self-reliance informing both the democratic philosophy of John Dewey and the proto-Trumpian nationalism of Henry Ford, and Dylan today hailed as a hero not just by progressives and liberals but, not without plausibility, by social and religious conservatives as well.[2] And, as with Emerson, the linguistic root of Dylan's potency lies in an uncanny command of the English language and, specifically, the injection of poetic brilliance into a domain previously lacking in it; for Emerson this was the essay, for Dylan the pop song.

[1] Emerson, "Self-Reliance," in *Essays and Lectures*, ed. Joel Porte (New York: Library of America, 1971), 263.

[2] This point about Emerson, as well as the idea that Emerson (like, I argue, Dylan) allows us "to see what already is there," comes from Harold Bloom, "The Sage of Concord," *Guardian*, May 23, 2003, https://www.theguardian.com/books/2003/may/24/philosophy.

But the differences between the two are stark and get to the heart of the Dylan phenomenon this book has aimed to uncover. On the aesthetic level, of course, the differences are obvious, with Dylan's meditations most typically sung, not merely written or spoken, and joined to musical accompaniment, realizing what other modern poets like Ezra Pound and Allen Ginsberg could envision but not achieve: the marriage of poetry and music. Indeed, Dylan is better than anyone in taking to heart Pound's warning: "Poetry atrophies when it gets too far from music."[3] But the differences between Emerson and Dylan are no less profound on the level of the content of their ideas. Emerson is ultimately a prophet of salvation who teaches that self-reliance is equivalent to God-reliance and prophesizes the eventual achievement of justice in the world, whereas Dylan doubts just this coalescence and this optimism in the future. Emerson, in the final analysis, imagines a harmony between self-reliance and social justice, whereas Dylan— perhaps due to the changed historical circumstance of a globalized world in which the prosperous and comfortable face unprecedented, almost infinite moral demands to abate distant suffering—speaks to the bourgeois problematic repressed by Emerson: the tragic tradeoff between duty to self and duty to other. And if Emerson could persistently speak to a divine reality—whether in the idiom of Christianity or the gnosticism of Transcendentalism—Dylan's religious voice is at its most distinct as a postsecular vehicle, teaching not the presence of God within but the existence of a religious sense that all of us possess and have the ability to exercise or not exercise, yet whose presumed objects and intuitions are uncertain. Finally, if Emerson is frequently seen as the mind of America—an explorer, who, according to Walt Whitman, discovered the shores of "that new moral American continent"[4]—Dylan, though sometimes treated in parallel fashion, is in fact a pioneer of a post-American world, a world in which America will not have fulfilled its role as a beacon, a city on a hill, and in which so-called liberal democracy comes to be seen, even if preferable, as inherently flawed and mired in unfairness. If Emerson heralds the autonomous philosophy of the New World and the nascent American democratic republic that most embodied it, Dylan is a prophet who tells us that there has been only one world all along; who, to be sure, speaks to the animating ideals of liberal democracy— individuality, justice, freedom of religious faith—but without the pretension that these can solve the puzzles and problems of how to live.

If there is an abiding similarity between Emerson and Dylan, it is that both are prophets even for those who never have heard of them. Emerson, as a prophet of salvation, articulates the ideal of self-reliance, which so powerfully has informed

---

[3] Ezra Pound, *ABC of Reading* (New York: New Directions, 2010), 61. Dylan in large measure also heeds Pound's parallel warning: "Music rots when it gets *too far* from dance" (61).

[4] Walt Whitman, *Leaves of Grass*, 2nd ed. (New York: Fowler & Wells, 1856), 357–58.

American and democratic ethics in their confident, assured, millenarian mode. As a prophet of diremption, a prophet without God, Dylan speaks to those of us who, whether we are aware of it or not, cannot quite believe the good news of the Emersonian gospel. For those who understand themselves as living within a globalized, post-American, postsecular world, shaped by the chaos of competing normative criteria and no special optimism in the future—but who still believe that a uniquely free mind can instruct us—Dylan is the prophet. He allows us to see what already is there.

ACKNOWLEDGMENTS

Quotations of Bob Dylan's song lyrics are taken from the anthology *Bob Dylan: The Lyrics, 1961–2012* (New York: Simon and Schuster, 2016) and Dylan's official website, *BobDylan.com*, though in a few cases differ slightly from these sources, as, when in doubt, I have treated Dylan's recordings as the definitive source. I thank Universal Music for permission to include these lyrics. Part I of the book draws on two of my previously published essays: "Bob Dylan at the March on Washington: Prophet of the Bourgeoisie," *Rock Music Studies* 6, no. 2 (2019): 116–37; and "Self-Reliance Without Self-Satisfaction: Emerson, Thoreau, Dylan and the Problem of Inaction," *Philosophy & Social Criticism* 47, no. 2 (2021): 196–224. I thank both journals for permission to reprint parts of these pieces. I am indebted to Nancy Ameen for her outstanding research assistance during the many years of the book's development, Josh Stanfield for expert copyediting, and numerous colleagues and friends for their feedback— including Carina Åhren, Ibrahim Bakri, Osman Balkan, Loukas Barton, Brendhain Diamond, Natalie Dohrmann, Roxanne Euben, Alex Glass, Loren Goldman, Ashley Gorham, Lorna Grenfell, Murad Idris, Priya Joshi, Archana Kaku, Ian Lustick, Adam Mohr, Eric Orts, Jennifer Rubenstein, Matthew Shafer, Pamela and Eliot Smith, Rogers Smith, Peter Struck, Jonny Thakkar, Richard Thomas, and Stephen White. Portions of the book were presented at workshops at Washington University in St. Louis (2017), ITAM in Mexico City (2018), Georgetown (2018), UCLA (2019), and the University of Virginia (2021). I am grateful to the students and faculty at these venues for their helpful suggestions. I thank David McBride at Oxford University Press for his continuing support. My wife, Amy, and my children—to whom I dedicate this book—have not always shared my passion for Dylan but helped me understand it better.

INDEX

For the benefit of digital users, indexed terms that span two pages (e.g., 52–53) may, on occasion, appear on only one of those pages.

Reece, Florence, 140
"Reforms" (Emerson), 84
religiosity. *See* gospel period of Dylan; postsecularism
religious vocation, 177–91
Remnick, David, 6
Renaldo and Clara (film), 19
"Resignation" (Adorno), 299–300
"Restless Farewell" (1964), 38, 53–54
rethinking religion as a human construct, 205–28
Richards, Keith, 9, 224
Richards, William, 241
Ricks, Christopher, 29
Rimbaud, Arthur, 21–22n.56, 233, 234
Ross, Scott, 218–19
Rousseau, Jean-Jacques, 286, 319
Rubin, Jerry, 53

Saliers, Don, 17
salvation, vii, x, xvi, 32–36, 50, 144n.1, 216,
    253–55, 259n.9, 262, 264–67, 269n.34,
    286–87, 331–32, 334–35
satanic aspect of politics, 311–26
Saved (1980), 207
"Saving Grace" (1980), 314
Scarry, Elaine, 309–10
scriptural references. *See also* Biblical prophetic
    model
  Amos 7:14, 12
  Ephesians
    2:2, 322
    5:19, 25
  Ezekiel
    7:23, 12n.36
    36:26, 227
  Isaiah
    40:3, 12n.36, 194
    40:6–8, 195n.95
  Jeremiah
    1:5, 192n.87
    1:16, 322
  John 1:23, 194n.92
  1 Kings 19:7, 194n.93
  Mark 9:24, 248
  Matthew 5:14, 253
  Proverbs 27:15, 228
  Psalm 106:38, 12n.36
  Revelation
    3:1, 255n.2
    3:2, 36, 255
Secular Age, A (Taylor), 171–72
secularism. *See* postsecularism
Seeger, Mike, 209
Seeger, Pete, 138–39, 140
selfhood and God conflict. *See* postsecularism
self-reliance. *See* Emerson, Ralph Waldo; rebel
    rebelling against rebellion; Thoreau,
    Henry David

"Self-Reliance" (Emerson), 85, 88
Selvin, Joel, 222–23, 244, 246
"Serve Yourself" (Lennon), 23, 224
Shelley, Percy Bysshe, 26–27
Shepard, Sam, 7
"She's Your Lover Now" (1991), xii, 274
Shot of Love (1981), viii–ix, 148, 206, 207, 224, 227
Shultz, George, 309–10
Sidgwick, Henry, 61–62, 79–81, 190
Silber, Irwin, 52n.19, 52–53, 55–56
Singer, M. G., 69–70
Singer, Peter, 67, 101, 190
skepticism toward Dylan's prophetic status, 9–10,
    20–21, 330–32
Slote, Michael, 72
"Slow Train" (1979), 186n.74, 225n.173, 258n.5,
    265n.22, 283n.55, 286n.59, 314
Slow Train Coming (1979), 206–7, 224, 247
Smith, Adam, 189–90
Smith, Huston, 237, 240n.219
social justice. *See* civil rights movement;
    pessimism; rebel rebelling against
    rebellion
Socrates, 48, 187, 286
"Someone's Got a Hold of My Heart" (1983),
    12n.36, 193–94
"Song for Bob Dylan" (Bowie), 23
"Song of Myself" (Whitman), 98–99
"Song to Woody" (1962), 139
Spargo, R. Clifton, 28–29
Springs, Helena, 216–17, 218
Springsteen, Bruce, 15, 22, 283–84
Stanley, Paul, 16
Starr, Ringo, 22
Stevens, Cat, 31
Stevens, Wallace, 27
Sting, 16
Stookey, Paul, 114–15, 121
"Stuck Inside of Mobile with the Memphis Blues
    Again" (1966), 231, 275
"Subterranean Homesick Blues" (1965), 139, 278
"Summer Days" (2001), 261
"Sweetheart Like You" (1983), 283
Sylvan, Robin, 17

"Tangled Up in Blue" (1975), 103–4
Tarantula (Dylan), 19
Taylor, Charles
    closed world structures and, 173–74
    imbalance in thought of, 170–77
    immanent frame and, 171–74
    limits of philosophy and, 170
    moving beyond, 158–60, 198
    postsecularism and, 169–77
    solidarity and, 169–70
    ultimate postsecular standpoint and, 175–76
Taylor, Jeff, 56